THE ART OF NAMEOLOGY

THE ART OF NAMEOLOGY

Uncovering the Meaning Behind a Name

Norma J. Watts

PERMISSIONS

The excerpts from Wizard of Oz used at the beginning of select chapters are used with permission,
Granted courtesy of Turner Entertainment Co.,
An AOL Time Warner Company. All Rights Reserved, © 1939

The Art of Nameology
CHAMPION PRESS, LTD.
BELGIUM, WISCONSIN
Copyright © 2006 Norma J. Watts

All rights reserved. No part of this book shall be reproduced, stored, or transmitted by any means without written permission from the publisher. Although every precaution has been taken in the preparation of this book, the publisher and author assume no responsibility for errors or omissions. Neither is any liability assumed for damages resulting from the use of the information contained herein.

For more information contact:
Champion Press, Ltd.
765 Main Street
Belgium, Wisconsin 53004
http://www.championpress.com
(877) 250-3354

Reasonable care has been taken in the preparation of the text to insure its clarity and accuracy. The book is sold with the understanding that the author and publisher are not engaged in rendering professional service. The author and publisher specifically disclaim any liability, loss, or risk, personal or otherwise, which is incurred as a consequence, directly or indirectly, of the use and application of any of the contents of this book.

ISBN: 1932783539
LCCN: 2005937782

Manufactured in the United States of America
10 9 8 7 6 5 4 3 2

Dedication

To all the Dorothys, Totos, Scarecrows,
Tinmen, Lions, Wizards and Witches.

Acknowledgements

If after reading this book we understand the people in our lives, than it makes the world a better place. What could be more rewarding than having others understand and accept us the way we are? It's twofold—my contribution to the world, and a personal victory.

I'd like to give my deepest thanks and gratitude to the ones who helped me the most—God and the spirits who guided me through the process. God was at my side when I was first given the divine inspiration to write this book. God and my wonderful teachers and guides in the spirit world have helped me say the right thing, at the right time, to the right person, to get my book to the right destination. God was with me every step of the way, through every hurdle, wave of excitement, defeat and final victory. Thank you God!

I would also like to thank my friend Elizabeth for some wonderful names to put in my book. Liz was so supportive with her Aries positive enthusiasm. She was probably one of the only people on earth that seemed to know what I was really trying to accomplish.

4 years ago my daughter Kelly mentioned a baby name book to me. I couldn't get the idea of name book out of my head. A few days later I was struck with divine inspiration on how to write this name book. Thanks Kelly for planting the seed.

My daughter Kim gave me the motivation to reach this goal, as with the accomplishment of getting this book published, I would finally be able to afford the airline tickets to see my two beautiful grandchildren. Thanks for the motivation Hon!

My daughter Mecauley helped me prove the theory that this book was easy enough for a 12 year old to understand. Shortly after her 12th birthday she read the first 3 chapters for me and understood it perfectly. It also helped her understand one of her friends better.

Just before the deadline of getting the final draft to the publisher, my son George never said a word about the Christmas tree still being up in February. He didn't complain once about the dust mites either or my lack of housekeeping, bless his heart.

My younger sister Nita generously helped me as she has in the past with suggestions, thoughts, ideas and all her positive energy. She's a force of nature.

Although my Dad doesn't really understand my passion with this project, he loves me anyway and calls me every Friday to see how I'm doing. Thanks Dad!

Last, but not least, my Mom was always there for me morally, financially, emotionally and otherwise. She never stopped believing in me, not once. Thanks Mom!

Contents

Introduction...11
Numbers...14
Converting a Name to a Number.......................21
Naming Baby..25
Name Compatibility......................................29

Names by Letter
- A...33
- B...43
- C...55
- D...71
- E...84
- F...97
- G...105
- H...117
- I..127
- J..135
- K...149
- L...161
- M..177
- N...197
- O...205
- P..212
- Q...222
- R...226
- S..242
- T..258
- U...270
- V...274
- W..281
- X..289
- Y..292
- Z..297

About the Author...303

THE ART OF NAMEOLOGY X

Introduction

✦

NAMEOLOGY IS THE STUDY of names through the use of numerology. Numbers exist everywhere and to the numerologist, they mean something. This book was written for the person who wants to better understand their fellow co-workers, friends, neighbors, children, boss, in-laws a spouse, or other loved ones through the use of name science. It's fast, easy to read and some will be amazed at the accuracy of the names. This is not a new study. This is an old study brought to light for us to better understand each other. Anyone can become a Nameologist.

The letters in our names can be used to determine aspects of our personalities. Each and every letter in our name says something about who we are, what we most like to do, the people we get along with best, the skills we exceed in and more.

The chapters on "Numbers" and "Converting a Name to a Number" may be used as a study guide for the serious student who wants to learn more about the art of interpretation.

Whether the reader is a serious student, reading for fun, shopping for a baby name or hiring a new employee, this book lends a new and unique way of understanding others through the science of numbers.

How to use this book

The easiest way to use this book is to look up the name in the quick reference. Looking up a person's name will give a brief description of various aspects of their personality; sometimes this is all we need. The number after the name in the quick reference section is called the "power number." Information about the power number can be found in the "Converting a Name to a Number" chapter of this book. The definitions found in that chapter are brief and found in the "P.N.'s in a Nutshell" section of that chapter. For a more thorough interpretation look in the "Numbers" chapter. The power number is the sum total of all the numbers in a person's name; it shows the strength of their name, their overall capabilities.

At the beginning of each chapter, there is a quote from "The Wizard of Oz," a classic movie that almost everyone has seen. The quotes from the familiar characters of the film, help us gain insight into the personality of the particular letters. Just as the characters were searching for something to make them complete, you have chosen to read this book to gain more knowledge about yourself and others.

Another way to use this book is to look up each letter's meaning at the beginning of each quick reference section. The first letter is called the "cornerstone." This letter describes a person's basic personality. It's similar to a rising sign or Ascendant. It shows how a person approaches opportunities and obstacles. (How they are on the outside.) Next, look up the first vowel in the name. This is their "heart's desire" letter. It is the way this person will always feel, this reveals part of a person's deeper nature. A part of their self they may or may not want others to see. (How they are on the inside.) The last letter of a person's name is called the "capstone." This reveals a person's ability and attitude toward finishing what they've started. Each letter of a person's name reveals an aspect of their personality. The quick reference is a short summary; looking up each letter gives a better understanding of that person all together. It explains different aspects of their personality. Looking up the power number after the name gives a brief summary as well.

If a person has several letters ruled by one number, this is called the "intensity" number. For example: Anne= A-1, N-5, N-5, E-5 Anne's first letter is ruled by the number "1". 3 out of 4 letters of her name are ruled by the number "5." So Anne would have a 5 intensity number. This number strongly influences her personality. Therefore, to better understand Anne, look up number 5 under "intensity numbers" in the "Names to a Number" chapter. This number is intensely inside her. It heavily influences her. Even two letters ruled by the same number are worth looking up, because that number is influencing them more than the rest.

If interested in learning how to add up names, or convert names to numbers for names not mentioned in this book; read the "Converting a Name to a Number" chapter. This chapter teaches simplified basic knowledge about the numerology of names.

Another way to analyze a person through their name is to take the first letter of the name, add the second letter to it and see what it adds up to. This is called a "hidden number;" it's an underlying influence in this person's personality. For example: John- J is 1, O is 6, add the first two letters, this equals 7, so John has a "hidden 7." Look up number 7 in the numbers section. John may be spiritual, if he doesn't have a strong spiritual base, then he might be egotistical or prone to escapist tendencies. At any rate, there is some 7 in his personality. This slow way of adding a person's name gives us a deeper understanding of John. The 7 is a part of John even though it is not obvious. Sometimes we are surprised at how accurate the "hidden numbers" are. Then to his 7 add his H-8 = 15 which condenses to a 6 since 1 + 5 = 6. His first vowel is a 6 <u>and</u> he has a hidden 6. John is a nurturer, but may not want everyone to see this aspect of his personality since it's his "heart's desire" and "hidden" number. He may seek the damsel in distress. If John was not taught good moral values at an early age, he may take what does not belong to him; or if brought up with good moral values, he may have strong religious convictions, such as John the Baptist. The 6's in his name make him want to be his own boss, and gives him magnetism. He doesn't like others looking over his shoulder. He may need a garden, children or a pet to love. Last we add 15 to the letter N-5. (Using a calculator will insure accuracy in the power number.) That would equal 20. 2 rules partnership, 0 rules assistance from God. His name sums up to having partnership or social situations being all or nothing at times. John's 1 ruled J and 8 ruled H make half his name independent and of somewhat strong character, yet he has a soft loving, nurturing side he doesn't readily let others see. His feelings could be easily hurt with a power number 20. In fact with the Scorpio-like H and freedom loving N at the end of his name, he may go out of his way to be sure others don't know this about him. Most of the numbers in his name are fixed or stubborn, so he's most likely stubborn as well. John's no softy by any means with a 1 and 8 in his name, but remember the hidden 6 and 7 when interpreting his name. The hidden numbers makes the picture complete. It fills in the whole name and helps us to understand the whole person. When painting a picture, we need to fill in the details. The "art" part of interpreting a name takes a little practice. A successful Nameologist will blend the numbers one by one filling in the whole personality. Personalities are not cut and dried, nor black and white. We are multifaceted; showing many aspects of ourselves. "Blending" the different numbers gives us depth and color. The "Numbers" chapter may serve as a study guide to improve the beginning Nameologist's ability to interpret names.

It's important to use a calculator when adding up the numbers in a name. As we added John's name, although we figured the 15 to be a 6 because 1+5= 6, showing a hidden 6 in his name, we need to continue with the 15 till all the letters are added in his name. If we decreased the 15 to a 6 then added 6 to his last letter 5 it would equal 11, which is a master number. In reality his name equaled 20, not 11. The master number 11 never condenses down to a 2. Although 20 can be condensed down to a 2, take into consideration the "0" means assistance from God. When a zero is in a name anywhere, God is close by to offer assistance.

Numbers

THE NUMBER AFTER the name is the sum total of all the letters added up together in their first name. Numerologists call this the "power number." The power number shows the strength of a name. It gives more information about that person. This number should be read lightly as it is only their first name. Adding all the letters of their entire name would be a more accurate description of their personality. Still, it can be pretty accurate.

The following number descriptions should also be read if a name has several letters (or even two) ruled by that number. Several letters ruled by the same number is called the "intensity number." For example, Jason would have a 1 intensity number, since 3 out of 5 letters are ruled by 1. (J-1, A-1, S-1, O-6, N-5) It's called an intensity number because it's intensely inside that person. Please refer to the conversion chart in the "Converting a Name to a Number" chapter to find out the intensity number of the name, if any. Rock stars and strippers often have a 5 intensity number. Not all with a 5 intensity number will be as wild, but may have "shocking" moments as did 5 intensity number Jennifer Lopez with her famous Oscar dress. E's and N's are ruled by 5 so half of Jennifer's name has a letter ruled by the number 5.

The most important number to study, however, is the number that rules the first vowel of the name. The first vowel represents the "heart's desire." A person's heart's desire number reveals a person's deeper self, something they're going to always feel. It's a small window into their heart that they may or may not want others to see. If Patricia goes by Trish, then she may not want others to see her "A" heart's desire influence. Although she has two "I" letters in her name, giving others the feeling of being safe around her humanitarian personality, she may not want others to see the true leader she really is for some reason. Also the "T" in Trish is partnership oriented. B and T prefer to stand behind their partner instead of enjoying the direct limelight. It's best to read both names to remove any doubt as to which name describes them best. Most likely both names will fit the personality.

Also it might help to get acquainted with the first letter of their name. The first letter is referred to as the "cornerstone.". This is similar to an astrological "rising sign" or "ascendant." It's the beginning of a person's personality or what they wear up front, for the world to see. It's very much what they are and can't help being. The first letter shows how they approach new situations.

Hidden numbers can also influence the personality of the name. Adding the first letter to the second letter of a name will give a "hidden number." Then add the third letter, this tells more about that person. And so on and so forth … each addition of a letter gives another hidden number. Hidden means "not obvious;" a little facet of ourselves similar to a diamond. Some angles are hidden from view, unintentionally and only noticed when turned to a certain angle. Not secretive, just hidden from view, but bright as the rest of our assets.

1

"The leader" Rules letters A, J and S: This person is independent and self-motivated. 1's are critical of themselves and others. They have the tools to become original with a creative approach to problem solving. 1's have a competitive spirit and like to win. They have a bully in their head that's continually pushing them to do better. Soon as they're finished with one task they are on to the next. 1's should try to rely on their wit and intelligence to avoid arguments and resentfulness. This number most closely resembles the Aries personality. A lot of 1 letters in a name can make the bearer a little harsh. Names with many 1 letters have an abundance of energy. This energy needs to be directed or they could become volatile. This number needs validation or approval now and then. They need to keep their ego in check. 1's have the ability to influence the opinions of others. A healthy 1 is independent, self-motivated, a hard worker, very intelligent, and superman-like. 1's living on the right side of their vibration will have their ego in tact. An unhealthy 1 has issues with self-esteem and not being good enough or shows a rebellious nature. They can also suffer egotism and false pride. 1's living on the wrong side of their vibration will have a tendency to be dependent. All 1's need to stand on their own two feet and learn not to depend or lean on others, even when the opportunity presents itself. 1's are happiest when they are independent.

2

"The mediator" Rules letters B, K and T: This person wants peace and harmony. They are excellent mediators because they don't like conflict. This is one of the numbers that does well in business. The 2 vibration makes them dependent upon others. They are social by nature, and the sweetheart of numbers. 2 rules partnership, this is the most supportive number for partners. They are affectionate and need lots of hugs. 2's like music. They have refined tastes in food, music, art, and clothes. 2's come in two personalities, Libra and Taurus. Both are affectionate, the Libra type is more intelligent, but temperamental; the Taurus type is more practical but stubborn. It's best for this number to learn not to take things personally, even if it was meant to be, as they can be overly sensitive. Some with many 2 letters in their name can be overly emotional. They can be as temperamental as a two year old child, when they feel threatened or pushed up against a wall. A healthy 2 is a true diplomat and peacemaker; loving and harmonious. They've got built in radar. Some are very interested in the scientific art studies such as Numerology, Astrology, the tarot, etc. They can be psychic. They don't get bored easily. 2's are compassionate and really care about others. They can be friends with their children. An unhealthy 2 may experience nervous tension or emotional extremes including depression. Some can cling to ideas long after they have outlived their usefulness. Similar to Libra, the scales, this number can be thrown off balance by an unkind word or look. Some 2's are easily offended.

3

"The communicator" Rules letters C, L and U: This person possesses creative skills, mostly in the areas of writing, speaking, acting, or theater. They are warm and friendly and make good conversationalists. 3's are animated and have a great sense of humor. This number most closely resembles the Gemini personality. They are as youthful and flirtatious as a teenager. An intensity number 3 can make for a non-stop talker. 3's are generally slow to make decisions. They are natural comedians. Typically the 3 has above-average ability in some art form. They manage to cope with life's many setbacks and bounce back for more. They are well mannered and conscious of other people's feelings. They make excellent salespeople, if they believe in the product; they'll have no problem selling it. 3's are fiercely loyal—they don't get over others easily. After a break up 3's will be upset if they check their answering machine and there's no message. They have many ups and downs financially and tend to be lucky! 3's are physically and mentally well adjusted. They are the salt of the earth and bring flavor to a bland world. A healthy 3 is cheerful, enthusiastic, optimistic, romantic and upbeat. They're creative, happy and inspired. An unhealthy 3 can be an outright liar, that enjoys making things up as they go along. They may be so delighted with living that life becomes frivolous and superficial.

They may lack discipline and order in their life. The unhealthy 3 can be overly dramatic if they have no outlet for their creativity.

4

"The teacher" Rules letters D, M and V: This person is a natural teacher and is extremely logical. They don't like to look naïve so when they learn a skill they tend to become an expert, that's why they make excellent teachers. They are similar to the astrological sign of Cancer, the 4th sign of the Zodiac; and need to feel financially secure. They're not gold diggers; it's just that the sound of rustling currency calms their nerves. This is a very domestic number, work and family is what they're about. Most people with some 4 letters in their name are excellent cooks. They are honest and direct by nature and don't like flashy or flamboyant people. 4's are very much down-to-earth and practical. They are the most faithful of all the numbers. Most are task oriented and don't mind hard work like gardening, cleaning or paying bills. They are "the terminator" of numbers. They'll go in, access the situation, then get to work on what needs to be done; methodically, systematically, and in an organized manner. Many 4 letters in a name could make the bearer a little cold, maybe harsh especially if they had a difficult childhood. This number also has a bully in their head. Sometimes they consume alcohol to escape the bully in their head. People with 4's in their name will typically say they don't want to argue, then an hour later they are still arguing. A healthy 4 wants to teach others. They're domestic and family oriented. They are hard working and faithful. Also they're logical and work methodically and systematically until finished. An unhealthy 4 might be so interested in preparing for their future that they forget about enjoying today. They can start too many tasks and barely finish anything. An unhealthy 4 will be overly stubborn and rigid.

5

"The free spirit" Rules letters E, N, and W: This person is truly a free spirit. 5's love meeting new people. They love change, excitement and adventure. Freedom is the nucleus around which their life evolves. All of life is a playground for their senses. 5's are capable of doing almost anything. Some enjoy going around shocking people. Rock stars and strippers usually have some 5 letters in their name. They're extremely adaptable; in fact, change is a blessing for them—5's could die of boredom in a humdrum routine. Any sort of boundary could blind them to their natural limits. This may cause overindulgence in food, sweets, sex, alcohol or drugs. They want to try everything at least once. 5's can be gamblers and often play for high stakes. They fall in and out of love, especially early in life. They have a strong sex drive and need to guard against shallow feelings in relationships. This number most resembles the sign of Leo. They usually have a flair for decorating. This number is very opinionated! 5's can liven a dull party. The drawback to a 5's overindulgence is that often they will get "burned out." Sometimes they will get burned out on driving, or throwing parties, or relationships, a demanding job, or sex. If they are over doing it, there is a danger of the burn-out syndrome. A healthy 5 celebrates life and has a sparkling emotional outlook. They manage to attain a sense of freedom and responsibility. They are a social delight and mix well with all types of people, high, low and in the middle. An unhealthy 5's life will be unorganized and scattered. They can be shallow and superficial. Overindulgence and escapism are 5's worst enemies.

6

"The nurturer" Rules letters F, O, and X: This person puts the needs of others before him or herself. That's why they are the natural parent. If they can't have children, they will treat their employees like children. Or they will dress up their pets like children. It's not uncommon for gays and lesbians to have a lot of this number in their make-up. Their lessons have much to do with love. This number is similar to the sign Virgo. A person with 6 anywhere in their name will have a well stocked medicine cabinet. This number likes to shop at warehouse stores to get more for their money. They aren't spendthrifts. A man with this number will attract women who are damsels in distress. A woman with this number who can't have children will often attract men who are little boys. They have to have someone to love and take care of—to nurture. 6's have a natural gift with flowers, gardens, and animals. Why, the very shape of 6 looks pregnant with love. Although they are the natural counselor and healer, they need to be careful not to interfere with the freedom of others. They can be meddlesome, insisting on having their own way in family quarrels. 6's are magnetic. When they walk into a room, people can't help but notice. Sure, they can be attractive, but it's more than that. They have a way about them that just can't be ignored. 6's can't work for others; they need to run their own company. They are all about duty. They make good managers; they don't like to take advantage of others. A healthy 6 has good moral standards, is loving, nurturing and responsible. An unhealthy 6 has a problem letting their children grow up. They can be meddlesome and jealous. Their mood can affect everyone around them.

7

"The faith seeker" Rules letters G, P, and Y: 7's lesson is to learn to have faith. They can't really be happy unless they have faith. If a 7 has faith, they tend to be very spiritual and we can learn from them. If not, they can be exhausting to be around. The 7's with little faith tend to have an overly inflated opinion of themselves. They have a brilliant mind and are driven by the desire for knowledge and truth. 7's are very direct. They tell the truth. If they don't like someone, it's obvious. Their tongue can cut like a sword. 7's operate on a rather different wavelength. Many of their friends may not really know them very well. This number has a Pisces personality. Those with a heavy abundance of 7 in their name look like they are swimming when they walk across a room. Often they end up in the movie industry or on Television. They can be psychic; they can also be overly secretive. They are pretty much loners. The typical 7 neither shows nor understands emotions very well. It's almost is if they're from another planet. They seem to like the technical field, computers, science, and modern technology. 7's like to discover things. It's been said "Genius is 1 percent inspiration and 99 percent perspiration." Our 7 friends receive more spiritual inspiration than any other number. Yet, if they don't take the idea and run with it, it just sits in their head and dies. A healthy 7 has a strong faith base, untiringly seeks the truth, and follows their inspiration. An unhealthy 7 is highly introverted, self-centered, egotistical, overly critical and intolerant, or prone to escapism through drugs or alcohol.

8

"The executive" Rules letters H, Q, and Z: The 8 is well-equipped in a managerial sense. They have outstanding organizational and administrative capabilities. 8's have the power and potential to achieve great things. They make great leaders and are outstanding judges of character. This number most resembles the personality of Scorpio. 8's can read people like a book, don't try to pull anything over on them, they'll know. And they like to control the relationship; it's over when they say it's over, not before. 8's can be very stubborn. They can be demanding of those who work for them, often putting things in no uncertain terms: Do it my way or don't do it at all! They won't hesitate, however, to reward the faithful and hardworking employee. 8's go after their goals with courage and tenacity. They enjoy rivalry and challenge. They understand the larger picture, see the broader challenges. 8's are here to learn that obstacles are merely opportunities to learn how to use their power and authority. Most 8 types have to learn things the hard way. Often 8's adopt the saying, "He who dies with the most toys wins!" They are most eager to get all they can out of the material world. If they use their power for selfish means, however, it could backfire disastrously. Negative 8's are too preoccupied with other people's possessions. This is a highly karmic number. It's crucial for 8's success that they balance the material and the spiritual, give and take, reward and punishment, action and reaction. It's a good luck bad luck number that gives out exactly what the bearer karmically deserves. Despite the obstacles, they are true survivors. A healthy 8 manages to use their power in a positive way, only giving out what they want to get back. An unhealthy 8 uses their power for selfish means. They can be overly materialistic.

9

"The humanitarian" Rules letters I, and R: This number usually produces persons that are very trustworthy and honorable and unlikely to harbor any sort of prejudice. It's a pretty tall order, but, 9's feel very deeply for individuals less fortunate than themselves. 9 is the highest of the single digit numbers and holds certain responsibilities. Judges, spiritual leaders, educators and healers often have a 9 somewhere in their name. 9's tend to do their jobs and everyone else's too, with little or no thanks from those they help. Although material gains are not overly important to the typical 9, they are blessed in some ways. This number is similar to the astrological sign Sagittarius. The 9 has three 3's in it so balance is a major lesson for them. They are often born into money, inherit it, marry it, or win it. People tend to assume 9's know everything. Some people will walk up to a 9 in a supermarket and ask if they know where an item is, assuming they are the manager. If they are in a classroom, children will approach them thinking they are the teacher. They just look as if they have all the answers. An abundance of this number (or if it rules the first vowel or consonant), can make the person very artistic. In a spiritual sense, they are quite evolved. Angels on earth it seems. They can be naughty though. People tend to follow them whether they are right or wrong. Bill Clinton, Michael Jackson, and Britney Spears, all have first vowels ruled by 9. Despite all the bad publicity, people still follow them. 9's typically have old family pain that haunts them. Many have "father issues." They can achieve happiness if they forgive and forget those that hurt them in the past. A healthy 9 personality is compassionate, generous, a humanitarian. An unhealthy 9 needs to speak up when they want something, we can't read their minds. They need to get over their past hurts. Some can be intimidating bullies, using their power the wrong way.

11

"The Lightning Rod" Rules the letter K: Number 11 is one of two master numbers. This number is the most highly charged of all. Whoever bears this number in their name can be a little high-strung. They can be too exacting. They are a lightning rod, attracting powerful intuitions, ideas, even psychic information like unpredictable bolts of lightning. They are a channel for higher vibrations. In order to be emotionally and psychologically at peace, they must learn to control that flow of energy. This double 1 energy gives them ambition and the need to succeed. They will achieve excellence. This number has Aquarian qualities. Aquarius is the 11th sign of the Zodiac. Others can learn from them, that's why it's a master number. With double 1's they can really beat themselves up, thinking they are never good enough. They work well with others because they know how to use persuasion rather than force. 11 has all the aspects of the number 2, enhanced and charged with charisma, leadership, and inspiration. They have good analytical minds, but may not be comfortable in the business world. 11's are definitely creative. A healthy 11 manages to ground their energies and use them for the benefit of mankind. They also make wonderful teachers. An unhealthy 11 can be thrown about by emotional turmoil and nervous tensions. They can be more dreamers than doers—beating themselves up all the while for not doing something with their special talents.

22

"The Master Builder" Rules the letter V: Number 22 is one of two master numbers. Those born with master number 22 in their name tend to be intuitive and psychic. They are natural teachers with lots of knowledge. They could never be like everyone else. They are here to make an impact in a positive way. If they don't use their power, they can end up in torment and depression. 22's dream big, all their goals are enormous in scope. They want to change history, make their mark on human civilization, and create something that will last for centuries. There is no limit to what they are capable of doing. Of all the numbers, 22 possesses the greatest potential for accomplishment. They refuse to back down in the face of a challenge. They like to work in large enterprises on an international scale. They see themselves as a world citizen, playing on this planet, and refuse to be limited by other people's boundaries. 22's should marry someone who does not depend on them for entertainment. Instead, they need a partner who is willing to work with them toward their goals. In choosing a career, there are no real limitations. The field is wide open to them. A healthy 22 strives to make their mark on the world, making it a better place and uses their gift to help humanity. An unhealthy 22, well, the worst they can do is to just be an ordinary 4, it's their choice, whether they use their gift or not.

Converting a Name to a Number

THIS PART OF THE BOOK shows how to convert the letters of a name into numbers by slowly adding them up. This calculation helps us to understand the basic personality traits of each letter or number that rules it. Memorizing these meanings helps us interpret the personality of each name more easily.

Each letter of a name from beginning to end has a number assigned to it. For easy calculations, refer to the "Conversion Chart" below. It's important to use a calculator so not to overlook *hidden numbers, master numbers* and *numbers ending with zero*.

General meaning of numbers:

1- Beginnings	4- Work/Family	7- Spiritual/Religion	0- Assistance
2- Partnership	5- Change	8- Reward	from God
3- Balance	6- Love	9- Completions	

Creative: 3, 6 and 9	Business: 2, 4 and 8	Intelligent: 1, 5 and 7	Master: 11 and 22
3-socially	2-partner	1-personally	11-Intuitive
6-service	4-family	5-groups	22-Global
9-humanity	8-corporate	7-spiritually	

Conversion Chart
Pythagorean Method

1	2	3	4	5	6	7	8	9
A	B	C	D	E	F	G	H	I
J	K	L	M	N	O	P	Q	R
S	T	U	V	W	X	Y	Z	

Example: B R I A N
         2 + 9 + 9 + 1 + 5 = 26 (2 + 6) = 8

Using a calculator:
Add 2 + 9, (B + R) = 11, then add 9, (I) = 20, then add 1, (A) = 21, then add 5, (N) = 26, (2+6) = 8.

Each letter of Brian's name means something. Each letter paints another stroke on the portrait of Brian. The B, ruled by the number 2 at the beginning of his name, or the front of his name is similar to a rising sign. This first letter shows us how Brian first appears. Because the B is ruled by the sensitive number 2, Brian's first impression is that he is understanding and insightful.

Then add the 9th ruled letter, R and we have the number 11. The R is a bit of a bully in the family of alphabets. Although Brian is a sensitive fellow, he does have an ability to intimidate. R is ruled by the number 9 which is ruled by Jupiter, the largest planet. A person with an R in their name anywhere is big in some way. They are prone to making sweeping jesters and accidentally knocking over the salt shaker. Since the B is a consonant and conjuncts another consonant, the second consonant colors or flavors the first. So we have someone who is sensitive and shy, but not afraid. 2 + 9 = 11, that's a master number. His first two letters add up to a master number. This master number paints its portrait as either a dreamer or a doer. 11's are often visionaries and dramatic. They are "the lighting bolt," and often rank as genius, if stubborn enough to see their ideas through. Sometimes they are overwhelmed or a bit high strung. The 9 and 11 influence could make for an absent-minded professor type. In fact, R's in a name often make a person forgetful, misplacing or losing items.

Then we add another 9 ruled letter I, which sums up to the number 20. 20 is partnership; assistance from God. At some point in Brian's life, probably in the middle of his life, he will be involved with partnership and the social aspects of life. It will be all or nothing as the 0 in the 20 lends weight. The third letter of his name is a vowel. This would be called his "heart's desire" letter. Since the I is artistic, philosophical and creative, he most likely is too. Two 9 ruled letters in a row means he will need to learn balance. People will tend to follow him right or wrong with an I first vowel. He may have old family pain that haunts him.

To his 20 we add 1 because A is ruled by the number 1. 2+1=3, so again balance is something he must learn. The hidden 3 in his name makes him a little bit lucky. He is cheerful and easy to get along with. But first vowel I conjuncts another vowel, A, so he could be a bit hard on himself, or a bit of a perfectionist. He's more ambitious than the typical first vowel I usually is.

Last but not least, to his 21 we add the last letter N, which is ruled by 5. That would add up to 26 or 2+6=8. As the 26 he is learning partnership/love. Then after he learns about partnership love, then his name totals the number 8. This sum total of his name gives him Scorpio-like tendencies. He learns lessons having to do with joint finances and other people's money. The material lessons of life are the main theme for him in this lifetime. Sometimes lessons are learned the hard way as this is a karmic-debt number. This may also be a lifetime of rich rewards.

Although the name Brian only has 5 letters in it, many numerological factors exist. The portrait of this person becomes clear only after many brush strokes and much consideration.

Power Numbers

The number after each name is called the "power number." It is the sum total of letters converted to numbers; condensed down to a single digit. What gives the power number its power is that it shows the strength of our name, it shows us who we are. *Note*: the numbers 11 and 22 never condense down as they are Master Numbers. Names with master-number power numbers are here to accomplish something worthwhile. Also listed are power numbers ending in zero. Names with power numbers ending in 10, 20 or 30 have the ability to motivate, uplift and inspire others through the number before it.

The following are brief definitions of the number behind each name. If interested in knowing more about numbers, read the "Numbers" chapter.

P. N.'s in a nutshell...

1 - Self-sufficient, dominant, a leader, stubborn.   Rules letters: A, J & S
2 - Understanding, insightful, often shy or hesitant.   Rules letters: B, K & T
3 – Versatile, playful; a communicator or storyteller.   Rules letters: C, L & U
4 – Productive, domestic, traditional, limited thinking.   Rules letters: D, M & V
5 – Influential, progressive, entertaining, self-indulgent. Rules letters: E, N & W
6 – Responsible, care-giving, anxious and guilt-ridden.   Rules letters: F, O & X
7 – Seeks truth and knowledge, distant, narrow-minded.   Rules letters: G, P & Y
8 – Successful, materialistic, sexy, sometimes ruthless.   Rules letters: H, Q & Z
9 – Philosophical, intuitive, has a tendency to drift.   Rules letters: I & R

11- Visionary, dramatic, nervous, overwhelmed.   Rules letter K-
                                                            (co-ruled by 2)
22- Attuned to higher realms, global, fears limitations.   Rules letter V-
                                                            (co-ruled by 4)

10- Beginning, assistance from God   Rules letter J- (co-ruled by 1)
20- Partnership, assistance from God   Rules letter T-(co-ruled by 2)
30- Balance, assistance from God   Co-ruled by the number 3

Those with 11 power numbers are here to achieve excellence. They are the lightening bolt. They need exercise to keep their fine minds in tune with the universe.

Those with 22 power numbers are intuitive and psychic. They are the master builders. This number is a natural teacher and extremely knowledgeable.

Those with 10, 20 or 30 power numbers after their names have the ability to motivate, uplift and inspire others.

The 10 power number helps others through personal encouragement and mentoring.

The 20 power number helps others through love, support and encouragement.
The 30 power number helps others through communicating, counseling and advice.

Intensity Numbers

When a name has 2 or more letters in it ruled by the same number, that number is "intensely" inside this person. The intensity number shows a leaning toward certain personality characteristics. The following shows how each number influences a name if there is an abundance of the same number.

Examples: JASON, J-1, A-1, S-1, O-6, N-5   Jason has three letters ruled by number 1. Jason has an "intensity number 1" in his name.

BETTY, B-2, E-5, T-2, T-2, Y-7   Betty has three letters ruled by the number 2. Betty has an "intensity number 2" in her name.

The following are brief definitions of the intensity number (if any) of a name. To learn more about each number, re-read the chapter "Numbers" (starting on page 10).

I. N.'s in a nutshell...

1 – (A, J and S): Independent, natural leader, risk taker, pride and ego is only downfall.

2 – (B, K and T): Socially refined, excellent mediator, intuitive, a bit overly sensitive.

3 – (C, L and U): Cheerful, positive, lucky and charming, undisciplined, talkative, lies.

4 – (D, M and V): Methodical, disciplined, reliable, responsible; can be narrow-minded.

5 – (E, N and W): A free spirit, likes sex, needs change and variety, overindulgent.

6 – (F, O and X): Natural healer, service oriented, self-sacrificing, can be meddlesome.

7 – (G, P and Y): Spiritual, scientific, seeks the truth, egotistical, sometimes cruel.

8 – (H, Q and Z): Enjoys rivalry and delegating authority, successful, a bit ruthless.

9 – (I and R): Idealistic, compassionate, hard worker, lacks concern for money.

Also:

The 1 intensity has a strong will, competitive spirit and desire to succeed.
The 2 intensity has a need for partnership, psychic abilities, and need for love.

The 3 intensity makes for an excellent talker, sense of humor and socially adept.
The 4 intensity is a natural teacher. They seek truth and are opinionated.
The 5 intensity is passionate and enjoys sex. They're romantic and love adventure.
The 6 intensity is magnetic, service and task oriented, nurturing and loving.
The 7 intensity is secretive and mysterious. They need their sleep and solitude.
The 8 intensity is successful and business minded. They can be workaholics.
The 9 intensity is a humanitarian. They work hard for the good of the whole.

Naming Baby

✦

DECIDING UPON THE right name for a baby can be a little scary. The name we choose will stay with the child for the rest of his or her life. So much pressure! Many new parents wait until after their baby is born before making the final decision. It could be the hair color, temperament, or overall appearance that helps make the final decision. A suggestion from a family member or being born on a special event or day could help us with the difficult task.

As the child gets older, they may adopt a nickname that seems to fit his or her personality better. When a child is named after someone, such as a Jr., movie star or friend; the child often exhibits aspects of the personality of their namesake. It's not because they were named after that person, it's that they share the same letters in their name, so they will have a similar personality.

With that in mind, when choosing a name for baby, if we like a person with a certain name, we most likely will approve of the child's personality if named the same. If we don't want baby to turn out to be just like daddy, then we shouldn't name the child the same exact name; or most assuredly their personalities will be similar. If the child named after daddy is not the same in personality, the child will most likely adopt a name that more fits their personality. Someone, most likely a family member, will start calling the child a name that "sticks." This is the name that most fits the child.

The birth name is a "destiny" name. It is similar to a natal chart that astrologers read to interpret a person's personality. The nickname or name that the child ends up going by most of the time is a "solar" name. Solar, means Sun and Sun means personality that shines through. It's similar to a solar chart astrologers read to help understand others. Both charts are accurate, but sometimes the natal chart is more accurate and sometimes the solar is more accurate. Many will want to argue this point, but both give information about the person. The destiny name or birth name is accurate. The solar name or nickname is also accurate. Each gives us more information about the person. When in doubt, read both. It is my feeling to give the most weight to the name a person goes by most often. A friend of mine has the first name of William, his close friends call him Bill. When first meeting someone he prefers the new acquaintance to call him William. W's like to meet new people. Sometimes they can be superficial. B's are more sensitive and personal, more easily hurt. B's can be shy at first. My friend Bill has a Cancer rising so the sensitive and shy B name does fit his personality better. The fact that he protects his identity by having new acquaintances call him William also gives me reason to believe his solar name or nick name fits him better.

When choosing a name, it's best to consider using some of the letters in the parent's first names for compatibility. Besides, we know the child will inherit certain qualities anyway. Why not choose the qualities we like best about ourselves? If the child is adopted, then it's even more important to share similar letters or compatible letters. It is in our power to choose a name that has the qualities we most desire. We seem to be more compatible with those who share letters ruled by the same number. For example; Father's name is David, Son's name is Matthew. The letters D, M and V, (Dept of Motor Vehicles) are all ruled by the number 4 vibration. Father and Son will be similar in personality with the first letter of their names ruled by the number 4. They are both systematic and organized; both are ambitious and desire financial security. Both may have excellent teaching skills. Both have the letter A as the first vowel in their names. They have a bully in their head driving them to do better. With these similarities, Father and Son will most likely have a lot in common. Ideally, when Father has a similar personality, Father can help Son through some of the weaknesses. Son can forgive Father some of his faults as he's a chip off the ol' block, heh? They may share the same goals, or at least share a basic understanding of each other.

Having some different letters from each other will allow one another their own personality and individuality. Letters that share the same qualities such as the letters of business ruled by the numbers 2, 4 and 8 can compliment one another. Letters ruled by the numbers 3 and 5 tend to compliment one another also. As a rule odd numbers tend to go well together and even numbers tend to be compatible with each other. As in astrology; the fire signs tend to be more compatible with the air and other fire signs. The earth signs tend to be more compatible with the water and other earth signs. The even numbers are similar to water and earth signs; the odd numbers are similar to fire and air signs.

Letters C, L and U, (CLUE) are ruled by the number 3 and are cheerful, bright and happiest of all the letters. Lucille O'ball had an intensity 3 in her name. She was a natural comedian and performed well on stage. Letters N, E, and W, (NEW) are ruled by the number 5 and love meeting new people, they are the entertainers and party people. The letters ruled by 3 and 5 tend to be sharp dressers and do well out in the public and on stage. The letters ruled by 1, 5 and 7 are complimentary to each other as these numbers in a name show a degree of intelligence. The letters ruled by the number 7 are G, P, and Y, (GYPSY). These letters like their solitude. Similar to gypsies, the 7 ruled letters are more psychic. Although these letters are compatible with letters ruled by the numbers 3 and 5 on the level of intelligence, 3 and 5 letters like to party and 7 ruled letters prefer to be alone more often than not.

7 ruled letters tend to be more compatible with letters ruled by 1 and 9. A, J and S are all ruled by the number 1. Number 1 ruled letters tend to be very independent. Only two letters are ruled by the number 9, they are letters I and R. Letters ruled by the number 9 tend to be similar to the 7 ruled in that they are both more spiritual and closer to God than the rest of the letters. Letters ruled by the number 1 tend to be compatible with 7 for intellectual reasons.

B, K and T, (BUCKET), are the more emotional letters. They can produce a bucket of tears. These letters need and give lots of hugs. If affection and sensitivity are desirable, name the child with a B, K or T in the beginning of their name. K is ruled by the master number 11, and although can be overly emotional, the K tends to be a bit high strung and can either be a dreamer or will be very successful in life. Even if the K doesn't exercise its full potential, it will be emotional and sensitive at times. Again, heredity is a factor as in all the letters.

Our names have a beginning, middle and end. The letters in our names bring us through a complete cycle of each experience again and again. For example, Joan will be independent at the beginning of each new situation. She will then tend to be nurturing in that situation. With "O" she's the boss type. Then she will want to be independent and exhibit her leadership skills. Then she will opt for change and want freedom. This cycle will repeat itself for Joan in every new situation with every person she meets and every job she takes on. Each letter is responsible in providing a lesson for her. Her name is her evolution through life. She travels the way the letters take her. Take into consideration the hidden numbers as they also figure into our travel through each situation.

That in mind, when a child is named with double letters in their name, they will have to repeat certain lessons. They will spend more time learning about the lessons brought about by these letters. If we name a child Kelly, he or she will begin every new situation in a sensitive yet ambitious way. The K makes them friendly, and socially adept at first; yet this letter has a strong desire to succeed. Then they will learn the lessons of the E which are change, variety, excitement, new situations, meeting new people. Then they will learn lessons in communication and transportation. They may drive a lot or talk a lot in this point of their situation. Then they will have more of the lesson of the letter L because of the other L, more driving, more talking. People with 2 L's in their name have many ups and downs financially as well. They tend to make many short trips and have to communicate a lot, twice as much in fact. 2 L's give the bearer of the name a youthful personality and they tend to recuperate from illness faster, but do they really need to repeat certain lessons? The child could learn just as easily with one letter, then move on to the next lesson or begin their new situation. Most numerologists will agree that whenever possible, it's best not have double letters in a name for the simple reason of not making the person have to repeat their lessons. That being said, those with double letters in their names have a certain character about them that most don't have. The intensity of the number that vibrates through their double letters indeed creates their unique personality.

The amount of letters in a name also influences the personality. It's seldom that we find a name with just one letter. However if such a name existed, the letter of the single-lettered name would give much weight in the over all personality. The fact that it would only be one letter makes the child independent, a leader, ambitious, and bolder than the rest. Two letters in a name, such as Al or Ed would make the child more partnership oriented. Three letters in a name, such as Gil or Kim give the child more than an average ability to communicate and get along with others. Four letters in a name, such as Doug or Beth make the child more down-to-earth and practical. Five letters in a name, such as Tracy or Steve gives the child more of a desire for freedom. This child will adapt to change easier. Six letters in a name, such as Ronald or Janice make for a more nurturing personality. This child will make a good boss. Seven letters in a name, such as Melissa or Gilbert can give the child spiritual leanings. They will have lessons in faith. Eight letters in a name, such as Penelope or Clifford give the child a more than average ability to master the material world. Nine letters in a name, such as Gabrielle or Alexander give the child a more blessed life. This child will have humanitarian leanings; they may be artistic as well.

Names Most Likely...

to be successful: names with letters A, D, H, J, K, M, S and V.
to fall in and out of love: names with letters E, N and W.
to nurture children, pets or plants: names with letters F, O and X.
to commit a violent crime: names with letters H, A, J, S, D and M.
to support their partner: names with letters B, K and T in them.
to make a great boss: O first vowels, F first letters.
to be young and sexy: names that have CH or QU in them.
to be a flirt: names with first vowels E and U or letters C, L, and N.
to be affectionate: names with letters B, K and T.
to be artistic: names with I first vowels, R or the letter X in them.
to entertain well: names with letters C, L, U, E, N and W.
to be religious leaders: names with O first vowels and R first letters.
to overindulge: names with E first vowels and letters N, W and X.
to be scientific and philosophical: names with G, P and Y in them.
to be hard workers: names that have I, R, D or M in them.
to lie or make things up: names with letters C, L, U, or number 3 in them.
to teach: names with letters D, M or V or 4 power number.

to beat themselves up: names with A, J, S, and also D and M in them.

to be egotistical: names with letters G, P, Y and number 7 in them.

to be domestic and duty bound: D, M, F and first vowel O.

to cheat on their partner: E first vowels, N, W, and number 5 in their name.

to be faithful partners: names with D, M, V or number 4 in them.

to get good grades: names with vowels A, E and Y, letters J and S.

to be competitive: names that have the letters A, J, S, H, Q and Z in them.

to own their own business: names with first vowel A or O or numbers 1 or 6 in them.

to be lucky: names with the letters C, L, U or number 3 in them.

to get depressed: names with D, M, V, or number 4 in them.

to be musically inclined: names with letters F, O, B, K and T in them.

to be talkative: names with U first vowels or letters C and L in them.

to be gay: names with first vowel E, letter N or power number 6.

to be tight with money: names with letters H, D, M and O first vowel.

to be selfish: names with first vowel U, or number 3 in them.

to keep a list: names with first vowel A, letters D, M, V and number 4 in them.

to have financial ups and downs: letters ruled by numbers 3, 5 and 8 mostly.

to be a stripper or Rock Star: Intensity Number 5's, letters N, E and W.

Name Compatibility

✦

IN THE WORLD OF Nameology, like attracts like. Names that share the same numbers also seem to be attracted to each other. For example, of the rock group Kiss, Gene Simmons and his lovely girlfriend Shannon Tweed of almost 20 years. Let's take the first names alone. G=7, E=5, N=5, E=5, adds up to 22, a master number. S=1, H=8, A=1, N=5, N=5, O=6, N=5, adds up to 13. Both of their numbers add up to the number 4, Gene's 22, 2+2=4, and Shannon's 1+3=4. Normally we don't condense master numbers down; however, 22 is co-ruled by the number 4, so it has many similar personality traits. Both of them have 3-5's in their name. So both Gene and Shannon like variety, romance, freedom and adventure with a 5 intensity number. 5's are physical and passionate. The 4 prevails in their down to earth approach to work and raising their family. The 4 shows itself in the stability of their long term relationship. The 5's show themselves in the fact they are still not married. There's a touch of free spirit in both of them. 5 does rule "change," so don't be surprised if they eventually marry! After 20 plus years of being single together, maybe they will want to make the "change" for better or worse. Gene's first letter G is ruled by 7, Shannon's first letter S is ruled by 1, 1's, 5's and 7's are the most intelligent. So they match up in the cerebral department.

Another fine example is Bill and Hillary Clinton. B=2, I=9, L=3, L=3, adds up to 17, and 1+7=8. So Bill adds up to an 8 numerologically. Hillary adds up to a 4. Bill's 8 influence makes him the corporate type. It's similar to a Scorpio personality. The first letter in Hillary's name is ruled by the number 8, which also has the Scorpio influence. In fact Hillary's birthday is October 26, placing her Sun in Scorpio at birth. Even her birth day 2+6=8. So her name suits her for the Scorpio affect if nothing else. 4 rules work and family, Hillary was the First Lady of Arkansas, (the governor's wife) for 12 years, while raising their daughter, Chelsea and practicing law. They also have the I, L, and L in both their names in common. The numbers 4, 6 and 8 are the business numbers. This brings them together in the business world, they seem highly compatible. The double L's in their names show many financial ups and downs. Also many short trips, a lot of communication, and they are lucky. L is ruled by the number 3 which rules writing. It's to no surprise they've both written books. Both have "I" as their first vowel. The "I" makes them blessed in some ways. They are artistic and creative. With an I first vowel, people tend to follow them, right or wrong. In Hillary's book, she mentioned one of the things that kept her and Bill together through all the turmoil was that they could talk. That's because of the double L's in their names. They are extremely compatible in the area of communication.

Ben Affleck and Jennifer Garner are similar to Bill and Hillary having the beginning of their names with same letters. Ben and Jen like variety, change and adventure. That's great because with both of them being actors, they can count on never knowing what's around the next corner for them. Life should be romantic and exciting and full of surprise and adventure for those two. Ben adds up to a power number 3, Jennifer adds up to a power number 9, so they are both easy going, go-with-the-flow type people. With those power numbers; Ben probably likes to talk and Jennifer probably likes to listen. It's great when people aren't fighting over air space. The numbers 3, 6 and 9 are the creative numbers. So it's to no surprise they've created a child together.

B name men are so supportive of their wives. Bill is supportive of Hillary, Bob Dole supports his wife Elizabeth Dole, no doubt Ben is supportive of Jennifer too. It must be difficult for successful women to find a man who can handle their success. B men don't mind standing in the shadow of their prominent partner. It doesn't bother them to the least. It's not that they lack ego, it's that they are natural partners. They are sensitive and understanding of their partner's needs. It takes a strong man to stand in the background while giving support.

Speaking of high profile men and their wives, how about George W. and Laura Bush? What do their names tell us about them? The name George adds up to a 3, but he insists on using the W, which is a 5 letter. 3+5=8. Laura's first name adds up to an 8. (She's a Scorpio, by the way.) Their last name adds up to a 5, which rules "change." 8+5=13. They both have the karmic debt number 13 which equals 4 for their power numbers. They both must work hard and persevere in order to reach their goals. They must maintain order and focus on the task at hand. That is the 13 lesson. The 4 and 8 are both karmic. They fit perfectly into these troubled times. Their term in office won't be easy; they face a lot of opposition and turmoil from everywhere. In the very beginning they had such a fiasco with the "hanging-chad" ordeal on the voting ballets. The 9-11 twin towers disaster shortly followed. Then the war on terrorism. However long George W. Bush and Laura Bush stay in office, it won't be easy for them. If anyone can handle it, they can. 100 years from now history will speak highly of this President's accomplishments.

So what makes Arnold and Maria so compatible? First let's look at the similarities that make them so similar; the A in their names makes them both critical, they strive for excellence. With the R, they are both very hard workers, they work for the good of the whole. Both of them are idealistic and humanitarian. Maria's name adds up to a 6 power number and Arnold has an O in his name which is ruled by the number 6. Both are nurturing and have much love to give out. They need to have children, pets or a garden to love. Also this number is service oriented and duty bound. Marie's M and Arnold's D are both ruled by number 4; which rules work and family. My, my, they are both such hard working individuals! The 4 is also faithful, down to earth, systematic and practical—the "terminator" of numbers. 4's have the ability to go in and access the situation better than any other number. This couple is certainly not frivolous, wasteful, flaky or phony in any way. This couple will accomplish much at the end of each day or feel guilty about it!

Tom Cruise and Katie Holmes first names show compatibility with his power number 3 and Katie has a hidden 3 in the beginning of her name. This means they are able to communicate easily. Ability to have the gift of gab with the one you love is wonderful. Not only does Katie have a compatible T in her name, but the K is co-ruled by the same number that rules T. This means she has twice the need for companionship than Tom does. She is twice as affectionate, twice as social, twice as cuddly, and twice as emotional. Since his name starts with a T, he should be able to relate to her well. He'll be able to understand her needs.

These are just a few examples of how to match up names. Remember to look for the similarities first. Like attracts like. The more letters that are ruled by the same number show the most compatibility.

The most compatible relationships by far have the first letter of one's name match up to the last letter in another's name. If they have both the beginning and ending letters match up, then this relationship is somewhat karmic. For example: Maria and Arnold; Arnold starts with the same letter that Maria's name ends with. Also her name starts with a letter that is ruled by the number 4, and Arnold's name ends with a letter ruled by the number 4 as well. Even when just the beginning of one name (cornerstone), and ending of another (capstone) are the same it proves to be a more compatible couple. If both the beginning and ending letters are ruled by the same number, as Arnold and Maria have, the couple seems as if they are soul-mates. No doubt this couple has been together many lifetimes. This type of connection does not necessarily mean that those who have it should get married. It simply means the two people have a meaningful connection like no other. It's usually a very comfortable connection and can mean a lifetime friendship or a lifetime partnership. It means we've probably known each other in another life. That's why we feel so comfortable.

Names that have the same letter in the beginning or end or both as Charles and Camilla as both starting with a 3 ruled letter C and both ending with a letter that is ruled by 1, as A and S are both ruled by the number 1 vibration; also prove to be extremely compatible. Even if only the beginning or the ending letter share the same number vibration, it shows a meaningful connection. In that case couples tend to look comfortable with each other, as if they've known each other all their lives. Charles and Camilla are indeed a couple of bookends. Their cornerstone and capstone letters match perfectly.

On same power numbers; this does not guarantee compatibility, but as observed in some of the couples above, it can help. Same power numbers are okay as long as the couple has other letters that are compatible. Sometimes, however, having the same power number is a bit like putting two positives or two negatives together in a battery connection. Sometimes they repel each other. Power numbers alone do not determine compatibility. For same power numbers to be compatible, they need other letters ruled by the same number, or cornerstone or capstone compatibility. It is interesting to note that when in the presence of someone with the same power number, we might be attracted to that person, but something keeps us from getting together with that person. Somehow we are pushed away from each other by some invisible force. So like attracts like, except in power numbers.

Names that have the same letters or letters ruled by the same numbers are most compatible. Names that begin with the letter or letter ruled by the same number of the person with the last letter in a name, as Mary and Tim, or Bill and Linda, tend to be long lasting mates; even soul mates. Same power numbers can repel one another. So when seeking a compatible mate; it's always best to look for someone with similar letters in their name, especially the beginning of one and the ending of another.

Its fun to watch dating shows on television prove this name compatibility theory. While watching, write down the names of the people trying to get the date and check for compatibility; then pick which one is most compatible according to nameology. Usually 9 out of 10 picked are compatible in their names. People are drawn to those with similar letters in their names. If it's difficult to choose between two people, it's because both have compatible letters in their names. The key is to pick the one with the most compatible letters or letters ruled by the same numbers.

A friend of mine who is now divorced was married to someone who had only 1 letter in common with him. He had a C in his name and she had a L in hers. None of the other letters shared any of the same numbers, no cornerstone or capstone compatibility either. So I mentioned that with the C and L, they could talk, but that was all they really had in common. He looked surprised that their names could forecast their compatibility so well. In all other areas of their relationship they were not compatible, and this too he agreed was correct; which goes to show you man cannot live by conversation alone.

I have another friend named Sue that works for a lady nick named "Gus." Sue has worked for this same healthcare facility for over 6 years without a raise. Although the work is very demanding with little reward, she remains loyal and true to her office manager. Nameology would suggest they're compatible because Sue's first letter is the same letter as that of Gus's last letter. Also they share the same middle, "heart's desire" letter U. It's difficult to find dedicated employees. Employers waste money and time training employees only to have them leave shortly after they've been trained. Maybe one day employers will take a look at their name first to see if it's compatible. This not only would save time and money, but would make for happier employer-employee relationships.

Remember, in fairy tales people live happily ever after. Just because our name is compatible with another's does not suggest we will live happily ever after with that person, forever and ever. In reality, there is no such thing as "happily ever after;" however, we can be as compatible as possible. That is the best we could ever hope for. Life being what it is, unpredictable, we can use all the help we can get. For whatever reason we have to begin anew, remember, like attracts like. Nameology can be a tool to help us understand and accept one another.

Not just romantic partners, but friends, co-workers, parents, children, neighbors, animals, cities, and even company's names can be compatible or not. Anything with a name could be compatible or not with our own name. It's to no surprise that Simon Cowell seems to fair well on shows that start with the name American. American Idol and American Inventor are both compatible with Simon's name as "American" starts and ends with the same number-ruled letters that Simon's name starts and ends with. They have the same Cornerstone and Capstone ruled letters. S and A are both ruled by the number 1 and both names end with a number 5 ruled N. So they are a comfortable, if not perfect match. Also Simon's I matches up with the American's I and R, both ruled by the number 9; and both names have an M in them. The more letters that match up, the better and stronger the relationship.

Finding our compatibility and understanding our strengths can build stronger bonds with others. To appreciate and accept one another through name science is empowering; it's an easy tool for any relationship.

> "Oh, but he doesn't do it every day—just once or twice a week. And he can't catch her old cat, anyway. And now she says she's gonna get the sheriff, and—"
> ~*Excerpted from "The Wizard of Oz"*
> *Used with permission*

IF A NAME BEGINS with A, A is the first vowel, has more than one A, or ends with an A, this person is ambitious, independent, energetic and self-motivated.

"A" people are critical of themselves and others. They complain a lot. We can recognize an "A" person by the amount of complaining they do. They make excellent teachers, critics, engineers and entrepreneurs. "A" named people are confident and successful business people. They are great at independently managing or owning a business. Inventors, activists, and politicians also come from "A" type personalities. Race car drivers and daredevils alike have a touch of that 1 vibration somewhere. Since A is the first letter of the alphabet, A is ruled by number 1. They're here to brave the new frontier. A's are natural leaders who want to lead the way. It all comes from that number 1 vibration. It's a "me first" letter. A's are the "Supermen" of letters and are almost perfect. Like Superman, they're hard on themselves for not being perfect. It's as if a bully was inside their head driving them to succeed. They beat themselves up all the time. A's are harder on themselves than anyone else could ever be, except another "A" type that is. Like the song goes, "One is the loneliest number," the vibration of the first letter of the alphabet is to stand alone, independent – or the lessons to be learned from the 1'st vibration will not be learned. In other words, a person with several A's in their name (or 1 letters) needs to not lean on others. Although the opportunity and temptation will be there, it is imperative they learn to stand on their own two feet. "A" types will usually admit to being happiest when they are independent or not depending on others.

They can be stubborn and willful, but stubbornly adhering to their path is what makes the "A" personality successful. They were born achievers. They won't let others talk them out of doing what they know will work. Strength, perseverance and willpower are paramount to their accomplishments. If they walk through life with blinders on, however, their stubbornness could lead to complications. The really stubborn "A" types need to work on seeing all sides more often. They should strive to keep an open mind, so they don't trip or fall over the perfect idea or solution to a problem.

"A" types make good partners, as long as they can be independent within the relationship. They need to follow their own drummer. If their partner understands this and doesn't smother them too much, they can be very happy in a relationship. Support their dreams and goals and you'll have a happy "A." They actually don't *need* your support to reach their goals. They have enough energy and drive on their own; however, giving validation periodically will enhance a relationship with the "A" type. This is also true of the letters J and S, since they are also ruled by the number 1 vibration.

Remember Sally Field's famous speech upon accepting her second Oscar? With tears in her eyes, she said, "You like me, you really like me!" Sally has two 1 vibration letters at the beginning of her name. A's or 1's are hard on themselves and try to be perfect. Sally has 2 letters ruled by 1 in the beginning of her name.

People with 2 or 3 "1" ruled letters are good; they just don't *know* how good they are. Sally's reaction that night showed everyone she didn't know how good she was. Jason, Sarah, Sam, and Janice can be awfully critical of themselves. It's best to give a little word of support or encouragement from time to time. A complement can go a long way; laugh at their jokes, but be sincere. They are very intelligent and can usually detect insincerity right away. In fact, "A" names need to find the humor in situations a little more and get angry a little less. An A personality that can laugh at him or herself is a relief. Some are almost as intense as R names. Sometimes it's hard for them to lighten up.

"A" or 1 types need to get out of their heads from time to time. They enjoy watching people win at football, baseball, soccer, drag racing, boxing, wrestling, rodeo, or game shows. Anything that involves competition helps get our critical friends out of their heads. This provides much needed relief to those with A's in their names from beating themselves up. If they don't have a healthy form of escapism, they sometimes turn to other alternatives, such as alcohol or drugs. Awareness of this tendency could help to make better decisions for our 1 ruled friends.

What do Arnold and Ronald have in common? These names have the same letters in them; just arranged differently. Interestingly enough, both Ronald Reagan and Arnold Schwarzenegger had successful careers in Hollywood before running for Governor of California. The R in their names gives them both the ability to somehow intimidate their opponents. The A in their names makes them leaders in whatever field they choose. Since Arnold wears his heart's desire letter, (first vowel) up front, he is not afraid to let the world see his true heart's desires. Any man whose name starts with an A and has an R right next to it is no "girly man." Ronald's R up front is a humanitarian letter, next to his nurturing O first vowel, made him strong in a different way. The D in their names gives them the ability to assess any situation in a systematic, almost "terminator" fashion. It also helps them to maintain a disciplined effort toward goals. The O gives them the ability to counsel and a tendency to take on the responsibility of others. The L is great for communication, as both men had and have no problem getting their message across. The N makes them original, unconventional and romantic. Since both have D at the end, they clean up in the end. They do the job no one else can. The difference is the first letter. Arnold comes across immediately as a leader because his A is up front. Ronald came across as gentle, kind and hard working. Also no one wanted to test him, he was intimidating, with his R up front. Arnold's R conjuncts or flavors his first letter, so he's also a little intimidating. Because their letters are arranged differently they have different hidden numbers, however, they still have many of the same personality traits because of the same letters and power number. The wild card in their names is the letter N. All that strength in their letters plus the intelligent, yet unpredictable N is what keeps their opponents at bay. They like to keep everyone guessing.

A or 1 types are similar in personality to the astrological sign of Aries the ram, which coincidently also begins with "A." Aries is ruled by Mars which rules the head. This type of personality is known to jump into things head first. A or 1 rule beginnings. A is the baby of the letters. When a baby cries or yells they usually get taken care of right away. A or 1 type personalities operate in a similar manner.

Some other famous A names: Abraham Lincoln, Andy Richter, Aaron Carter, Ashley Olsen, Andy Rooney, Audrey Hepburn, Albert Schweitzer, Aristotle Onasis, Anton Chekhov, Adlai Stevenson, Al Capone, Alan Alda, Amy Irving, Antonio Bandaras, Aretha Franklin, Adam Sandler, Alfred Hitchcock, Andy Griffith, Ashley Judd, Alec Baldwin, Arsenio Hall, Alicia Silverstone, Anita Baker, Art Linkletter, Avril Lavigne, Alanis Morissette, Alexis Bledel, Andy Milonakis, Ashton Kutcher, Ashanti, Anthony Perkins, Anthony Hopkins and Al Pacino.

Quick reference of "A" Names

Aaron, 22- Ambitious leader, great vision. Resolute and purposeful. Gentle, kind, hard worker. Natural counselor and healer. Intuitive and creative.

Abbott, 6- Reads people easily. Friendly, but shy. Affectionate and social. Natural counselor and healer. Dynamic, busy lifestyle. Sensitive and easily hurt.

Abel, 11- Ambitious leader, great vision. Good business partner. Keenly perceptive. Strong verbal skills.

Abigail, 5- Bold, courageous, adventuresome. Sparkling emotional outlook. Blessed in some ways. Scientific and philosophical. Not easily influenced. Artistic, having good taste. Frequent traveler.

Abimael, 7- Not easily influenced. Friendly, but shy. Idealistic and humanitarian. Domestic, hard working. Bold, courageous, a bit stubborn. A free spirit, very adaptable. Strong verbal skills.

Abraham, 8- Resolute and purposeful. An excellent mediator. Gentle, kind, a hard worker. Bold, courageous, a bit stubborn. Great judge of character. Pioneer and risk taker. Systematic and organized.

Abby, 3- Expresses thoughts readily. Loyal and understanding. Emotional and sensitive. Needs a lot of freedom.

Abu, 6- Pioneer and risk taker. Creative in a practical way. Attractive and charming.

Ace, 9- Hard working and helpful. Self-expressive, cheerful. A free spirit, very adaptable.

Adam, 10- Independent, critical of self and others. Reliable, responsible. Bold, courageous, a bit stubborn. Domestic, hard working.

Adel, 4- Natural teaching ability. Down-to-earth, faithful. Loves adventure and excitement. Strong verbal skills.

Adele, 9- Hard working and helpful. Reliable and responsible. Likes to entertain. Communicates skillfully. Physical and passionate.

Adrian, 11- Ambitious leader, great vision. Natural authority. Strives to improve humanity. Blessed in some ways. Bold, courageous, a bit stubborn. Original and unconventional.

Adriana, 30- Expresses thought readily. Reliable, responsible. Optimistic and very kind. Blessed in some ways. Bold, courageous, a bit stubborn. Romantic, sensual. Pioneer and risk taker.

Adrienne, 7- Not easily influenced. Problem solver. Gentle, kind, a hard worker. Blessed in some ways. A free spirit, very adaptable. Original and unconventional. Creative, opinionated. Physical, passionate.

Aeolabi, 9- Hard working and helpful. Loves adventure and excitement. Natural counselor and healer. Strong verbal skills. Bold, courageous, a bit stubborn. Loyal, understanding. Blessed in some ways.

Aeyoung, 7- Not easily influenced. Likes change and variety. Needs a lot of freedom. Natural counselor and healer. Attractive and charming. Original and unconventional. Scientific and philosophical.

Agatha, 11- Ambitious leader, great vision. Scientific, philosophical. Bold, courageous, a bit stubborn. Dynamic, busy lifestyle. Great judge of character. Pioneer and risk taker.

Agnes, 10- Independent, critical of self and others. Extremely intelligent. Creative and opinionated. A free spirit, very adaptable. Charming and devoted.

Agustin, 10- Independent, critical of self and others. An opportunist. Very lucky. Charming and devoted. Dynamic, busy lifestyle. Blessed in some ways. Original and unconventional.

Ahmed, 22- Ambitious leader, great vision. Self-reliant, successful. Domestic, hard working. Likes change and variety. A natural authority.

Akai, 4- Natural teaching ability. Strong desire to succeed. Resolute and purposeful. Blessed in some ways.

Aki, 3- Expresses thoughts readily. Enthusiastic, quick witted. Communicates understanding.

Al, 4- Natural teaching ability. Intellectually sound. Domestic, down to earth.

Alan, 10- Independent, critical of self and others. Frequent traveler. Bold, courageous, a bit stubborn. Original and unconventional.

Alanis, 20- Reads people easily, perceptive. Communicates skillfully. Independent, critical of self and others. Opinionated, romantic. Blessed in some ways. Charming and devoted.

Alann, 6- Pioneer, risk taker. Easy going attitude. Bold, courageous, a bit stubborn. Original and opinionated. Romantic, sensual.

Alannah, 6- Pioneer, risk taker. Strong verbal skills. Independent, critical of self and others. Original and opinionated. Romantic, sensual. Not easily influenced. Enjoys competition.

Albert, 4- Natural teaching ability. Frequent traveler. Friendly, but shy. A free spirit, very adaptable. Gentle, kind, a hard worker. Dynamic, very busy lifestyle.

Aleisha, 10- Independent, critical of self and others. Strong verbal skills. Physical and passionate. Blessed in some ways. Charming and devoted. Enjoys competition. Bold, courageous, a bit stubborn.

Alejandro, 8- Resolute and purposeful. Recuperates quickly. Physical and passionate. Clever and talented. Bold, courageous, a bit stubborn. Original and unconventional. Reliable, responsible. Gentle, kind, a hard worker. Natural counselor and healer.

Alessandra, 4- Natural teaching ability. Strong verbal skills. A free spirit, very adaptable. Charming and devoted. Many mood swings. Bold, courageous, a bit stubborn. Original and unconventional. Reliable, responsible. Gentle, kind, a hard worker. Independent, critical of self and others.

Alex, 6- Pioneer and risk taker. Frequent traveler. Creative in service. Artistic, sensual, very perceptive.

Alexa, 7- Not easily influenced. Strong verbal skills. Likes change and variety. Artistic, sensual, very perceptive. Bold, courageous, a bit stubborn.

Alexander, 3- Expresses thoughts readily. Slow to make decisions. A free spirit, very adaptable. Artistic, sensual, very perceptive. Bold, courageous, a bit stubborn. Original, unconventional. Reliable, responsible. Loves adventure and excitement. Gentle, kind, hard worker.

Alexei, 11- Ambitious leader, great vision. Travels frequently. A free spirit, very adaptable. Artistic, sensual, perceptive. Physical and passionate. Blessed in some ways.

Alexia, 7- Not easily influenced. Intellectually sound. Likes change and variety. Artistic, sensual, perceptive. Blessed in some ways. Independent, critical of self and others..

Alexis, 7- Not easily influenced. Communicates skillfully. Loves adventure and excitement. Artistic, sensual, perceptive. Blessed in some ways. Charming and devoted.

Alfred, 10- Independent, critical of self and others. Strong verbal skills. Nurturing, loving. Gentle, kind, hard worker. A free spirit, very adaptable. Down to earth, faithful.

Ali, 4- Natural teaching ability. Strong verbal skills. Idealistic and humanitarian.

Alia, 5- Bold, courageous, a bit stubborn. Frequent traveler. Idealistic and humanitarian. Independent, critical of self and others.

Alice, 3- Expresses thoughts readily. Slow to make decisions. Artistic, having good taste. Great sense of humor. A free spirit, very adaptable.

Alicia, 8- Resolute and purposeful. Recuperates quickly. Idealistic and humanitarian. Optimistic and outspoken. Blessed in some ways. Not easily influenced.

Alife, 6- Pioneer and risk taker. Frequent traveler. Artistic, having good taste. Self-sacrificing, loving. A free spirit, very adaptable.

Alison, 7- Not easily influenced. Strong verbal skills. Blessed in some ways. Charming and devoted. Natural counselor and healer. Original and unconventional.

Allan, 4- Natural teaching ability. Ups and downs financially. Frequent traveler. Independent, critical of self and others. Original and unconventional.

Allen, 8- Resolute and purposeful. Ups and downs financially. Recuperates quickly. Physical and passionate. Creative and opinionated.

Allison, 10- Independent, critical of self and others. Strong verbal skills. Frequent traveler. Blessed in some ways. Charming and devoted. Natural counselor and healer. Original and unconventional.

Aloha, 10- Independent, critical of self and others. Strong verbal skills. Natural counselor and healer. Self-reliant, successful. Bold, courageous, a bit stubborn.

Alton, 8- Resolute and purposeful. Ups and downs financially. Dynamic, busy lifestyle. Natural counselor and healer. Romantic, sensual.

Alvin, 4- Natural teaching ability. Strong verbal skills. Intuitive and inspired. Blessed in some ways. Original and unconventional.

Alyce, 10- Independent, critical of self and others. Frequent traveler. Dislikes limitations. Effective speaker. A free spirit, adaptable to change.

Alysha, 3- Expresses thoughts readily. Slow to make decisions. Needs a lot of freedom. Charming and devoted. Great judge of character. Bold, courageous, a bit stubborn.

Amanda, 7- Not easily influenced. Desires financial security. Bold, courageous, a bit stubborn. Original and unconventional. Workaholic, shrewd and determined. Independent, critical of self and others.

Amando, 3- Expresses thoughts readily. Family communicator. Bold, courageous, a bit stubborn. Original and unconventional. Serious, yet fun-loving. Natural counselor and healer.

Amber, 3- Expresses thoughts readily. Systematic, organized. Affectionate, social. Loves adventure and excitement. Gentle, kind, a hard worker.

Amelia, 5- Bold, courageous, adventuresome. Domestic, hard working. Physical and passionate. Slow to make decisions. Blessed in some ways. Pioneer and risk taker.

Amir, 5- Bold, courageous, adventuresome. Systematic, organized. Blessed in some ways. Gentle, kind, a hard worker.

Amos, 3- Expresses thoughts readily. Domestic, hardworking. A natural counselor and healer. Charming and devoted.

Amy, 3- Expresses thoughts readily. Family communicator. Needs a lot of freedom.

Ana, 7- Not easily influenced. Creative and opinionated. Bold, courageous, extremely intelligent.

Anabelle, 7- Not easily influenced. Creative and opinionated. Bold, courageous, a bit stubborn. Anticipates next move. Physical, passionate. Strong verbal skills. Ups and downs financially. Loves adventure and excitement.

Anastasia, 4- Natural teaching ability. Original, unconventional. Bold, courageous, a bit stubborn. Charming and devoted. Dynamic, busy lifestyle. Pioneer and risk taker. Impulsive and extreme. Blessed in some ways. Independent, critical of self and others.

Andora, 8- Resolute and purposeful. Original and unconventional. Reliable and responsible. Natural counselor and healer. Intense inner power. Bold, courageous, a bit stubborn.

Andre, 6- Pioneer and risk taker. Creative, opinionated. Domestic, hardworking. Gentle, kind, diligent. Physical and passionate.

Andrea, 7- Not easily influenced. Original and unconventional. Reliable and responsible. Gentle, kind, hard worker. Physical and passionate. Independent, critical of self and others.

Andrew, 11- Ambitious leader, great vision. Creates group harmony. Natural authority. Gentle, kind and hard worker. Physical and passionate. Likes to meet new people.

Andris, 11- Ambitious leader, great vision. Original and unconventional. Natural authority. Gentle, kind, a hard worker. Blessed in some ways. Charming and devoted.

Andy, 8- Resolute and purposeful. Romantic, opinionated. Creative problem solver. Needs a lot of freedom.

Anette, 20- Reads people easily, perceptive. Socially exciting. Physical and passionate. Dynamic, very busy lifestyle. Sensitive and easily hurt. Loves adventure and excitement.

Angel, 3- Expresses thoughts readily. Creative, opinionated. Scientific and philosophical. A free spirit, very adaptable. Slow to make decisions.

Angela, 22- Ambitious leader, great vision. Original and unconventional. Has willpower, determined. A free spirit, very adaptable. Strong verbal skills. Bold, courageous, a bit stubborn.

Angelica, 7- Not easily influenced. Enjoys the mysteries of life. Extremely intelligent. A free spirit, very adaptable. Communicates skillfully. Blessed in some ways. Optimistic, outspoken. Independent, critical of self and others.

Angelina, 9- Hard working and helpful. Sometimes naive. Scientific and philosophical. Physical and passionate. Strong verbal skills. Blessed in some ways. Creative, opinionated. Bold, courageous, a bit stubborn.

Angelo, 9- Hard working and helpful. Creative, opinionated. An opportunist. Physical and passionate. Strong verbal skills. Natural counselor and healer.

Angie, 9- Hard working and helpful. Original and unconventional. Scientific and philosophical. Artistic, having good taste. Physical and passionate.

Angus, 8- Resolute and purposeful. Creative, opinionated. Extremely intelligent. Attractive and charming. Impulsive and extreme.

Anita, 9- Hard working and helpful. Original and romantic. Blessed in some ways. Dynamic, busy lifestyle. Independent, critical of self and others.

Ann, 11- Ambitious leader, great vision. Intuitive and creative. Romantic and sensual.

Anna, 3- Expresses thoughts readily. Creative, opinionated. Romantic and sensual. Pioneer and risk taker.

Annalicia, 10- Independent, critical of self and others. Original, opinionated. Romantic and sensual. Bold, courageous, a bit stubborn. Strong verbal skills. Idealistic and humanitarian. Great sense of humor. Blessed in some ways. Pioneer and risk taker.

Anne, 7- Not easily influenced. Original and unconventional. Original and unconventional. Physical and passionate.

Annette, 7- Not easily influenced. Enjoys the mysteries of life. Creative, opinionated. A free spirit, very adaptable. Dynamic, very busy lifestyle. Sensitive and easily hurt. Physical and passionate.

Ansel, 6- Pioneer and risk taker. Creative and opinionated. Charming and devoted. Physical and passionate. Strong verbal skills.

Anthony, 7- Not easily influenced. Original and unconventional. Dynamic, very busy lifestyle. Self-reliant, successful. Natural counselor and healer. Romantic and sensual. Needs a lot of freedom.

Antoine, 6- Pioneer and risk taker. Puts needs of others first. An excellent mediator. Natural counselor and healer. Artistic, having good taste. Original, creative. Physical and passionate.

Antoinette, 6- Pioneer and risk taker. Creative, opinionated. Dynamic, busy lifestyle. Natural counselor and healer. Artistic, having good taste. Original, unconventional. Physical and passionate. Very protective. Sensitive and easily hurt. Loves adventure and excitement.

Anton, 10- Independent, critical of self and others. Original and unconventional. Dynamic, very busy lifestyle. Natural counselor and healer. Romantic and sensual.

Antony, 8- Resolute and purposeful. Original and unconventional. An excellent mediator. Natural counselor and healer. Romantic and sensual. Needs a lot of freedom.

Anya, 5- Bold, courageous, adventuresome. Opinionated and unconventional. Needs a lot of freedom. Independent, critical of self and others.

Apple, 5- Bold, courageous, adventuresome. Intelligent and knowledgeable. Maintains a high dream. Strong verbal skills. Likes change, very adaptable.

Apolonio, 7- Not easily influenced. Intelligent and knowledgeable. Natural counselor and healer. Frequent traveler. Sometimes meddling. Creative, perceptive. Blessed in some ways. Open to opportunities.

April, 11- Ambitious leader, great vision. Intelligent and knowledgeable. Gentle, kind, a hard worker. Blessed in some ways. Strong verbal skills.

Araceli, 4- Natural teaching ability. Strong and healthy. Independent, critical of self and others. Self-expressive, cheerful. A free spirit, very adaptable. Strong verbal skills. Blessed in some ways.

Aracely, 11- Ambitious leader, great vision. Diligent, helpful. Independent, critical of self and others. Inspiring and highly creative. A free spirit, very adaptable. Strong verbal skills. Needs a lot of freedom.

Archer, 8- Resolute and purposeful. Gentle, kind, a hard worker. Optimistic, outspoken. A great judge of character. Physical and passionate. Intense inner power.

Archibald, 22- Ambitious leader, great vision. Strives to improve humanity. Inspiring, highly creative. Self reliant, successful. Blessed in some ways. Friendly, but shy. Bold, courageous, a bit stubborn. Strong verbal skills. Down-to-earth, faithful.

Archie, 8- Resolute and purposeful. Intense inner power. Optimistic, outspoken. A great judge of character. Blessed in some ways. Physical and passionate.

Ardasher, 11- Ambitious leader, great vision. Strives to improve humanity. Reliable, responsible. Independent, critical of self and others. Charming and devoted. Great judge of character. A free spirit, very adaptable. Tendency to lose items.

Ariel, 9- Hard working and helpful. Sometimes naive. Artistic, may have good taste. A free spirit, very adaptable. Strong verbal skills.

Arjana, 9- Hard working and helpful. Intense inner power. Clever and talented. Resolute and purposeful. Original and unconventional. Bold, courageous, a bit stubborn.

Arjane, 22- Ambitious leader, great vision. Strives to improve humanity. Clever and talented. Resolute and purposeful. Original and unconventional. A free spirit, very adaptable.

Arleen, 10- Independent, critical of self and others. Gentle, kind, a hard worker. Strong verbal skills. A free spirit, very adaptable. Tendency to overindulge. Romantic, sensual.

Arlene, 10- (Same as Arleen)

Arlie, 9- Hard working and helpful. Intense inner power. Strong verbal skills. Blessed in some ways. A free spirit, very adaptable.

Arlo, 10- Independent, critical of self and others. Intense inner power. Frequent traveler. Natural counselor and healer.

Armand, 6- Pioneer and risk taker. Diligent, helpful. Systematic, organized. Bold, courageous, a bit stubborn. Original and unconventional. Reliable and responsible.

Armando, 30- Expresses thoughts readily. Optimistic, very kind. Systematic, organized. Bold, courageous, a bit stubborn. Original and unconventional. Reliable and responsible. Natural counselor and healer.

Armani, 11- Ambitious leader, great vision. Intense inner power. Systematic, organized. Pioneer and risk taker. Original and unconventional. Artistic, having good taste.

Armen, 6- Pioneer and risk taker. Diligent, helpful. Systematic, organized. Physical and passionate. Original and creative.

Arnie, 11- Ambitious leader, great vision. Intense inner power. Original and unconventional. Blessed in some ways. A free spirit, adaptable to change.

Arnold, 10- Independent, critical of self and others. Gentle, kind, a hard worker. Original and unconventional. Natural counselor and healer. Strong verbal skills. Down-to-earth, faithful.

Arsenio, 9- Hard working and helpful. Gentle, kind, and diligent. Charming and devoted. A free spirit, very adaptable. Original and unconventional. Blessed in some ways. A natural counselor and healer.

Art, 3- Expresses thoughts readily. Optimistic, very kind. Dynamic, busy lifestyle.

Arthur, 5- Bold, courageous, adventuresome. Intense inner power. Dynamic, busy lifestyle. Self-reliant, successful. Attractive and lucky. Could be forgetful.

Artie, 8- Resolute and purposeful. Intense inner power. Dynamic, busy lifestyle. Blessed in some ways. Physical and passionate.

Arturo, 30- Expresses thoughts readily. Optimistic, very kind. Dynamic, busy lifestyle. Attractive and charming. Intense inner power. Natural counselor and healer.

Aryana, 6- Pioneer and risk taker. Gentle, kind, a hard worker. Needs a lot of freedom. Bold, courageous, a bit stubborn. Original and unconventional. Independent, critical of self and others.

Aryeh, 30- Expresses thoughts readily. Optimistic, very kind. Needs a lot of freedom. Loves adventure and excitement. Great judge of character.

Ash, 10- Independent, critical of self and others. Very charismatic. Self-reliant, successful.

Ashanti, 9- Hard working and helpful. Intense and extreme. Self-reliant, successful. Independent, critical of self and others. Original, romantic. Dynamic, busy lifestyle. Blessed in some ways.

Ashby, 10- Independent, critical of self and others. Very charismatic.. Self-reliant, successful. Friendly, but shy. Needs a lot of freedom.

Ashley, 7- Not easily influenced. Charming and devoted. Self-reliant, successful. Strong verbal skills. A free spirit, very adaptable. Highly perceptive.

Ashok, 9- Hard working and helpful. Intense and extreme. Great judge of character. Natural counselor and healer. Strong desire to succeed.

Asia, 3- Expresses thoughts readily. Charming and devoted. Blessed in some ways. Bold, courageous, a bit stubborn.

Athena, 4- Natural teaching ability. Dynamic, very busy lifestyle. Great judge of character. A free spirit, very adaptable. Creative and opinionated. Bold, courageous, a bit stubborn.

Aubrey, 9- Hard working and helpful. Attractive and charming. Friendly, but shy. Gentle, kind, hard worker. A free spirit, very adaptable. Dislikes limitations.

Audrey, 11- Ambitious leader, great vision. Creative and inspiring. Reliable and responsible. Gentle, kind, a hard worker. A free spirit, very adaptable. Dislikes limitations.

Augustine, 9- Hard working and helpful. Go with the flow attitude. Scientific and philosophical. Difficulty making decisions. Charming and devoted. Dynamic, busy lifestyle. Blessed in some ways. Original and unconventional. A free spirit, very adaptable.

Aurelia, 4- Natural teaching ability. Slow to make decisions. Gentle, kind, a hard worker. Likes to entertain. Communicates skillfully. Artistic, having good taste. Not easily influenced.

Aureliano, 6- Pioneer and risk taker. Attractive and charming. Diligent, helpful. Likes to entertain. Frequent traveler. Artistic, having good taste. Not easily influenced. Creative, opinionated. Natural counselor and healer.

Aurielle, 11- Ambitious leader, great vision. Very charismatic. Strives to improve humanity. Blessed in some ways. A free spirit, very adaptable. Strong verbal skills. Ups and downs financially. Loves adventure and excitement.

Aurora, 11- Ambitious leader, great vision. Creative and inspiring. Gentle, kind, a hard worker. Natural counselor and healer. Intense inner power. Bold, courageous, a bit stubborn.

Austin, 3- Expresses thoughts readily. Attractive and charming. Impulsive and extreme. Dynamic, busy lifestyle. Blessed in some ways. Original and unconventional.

Ava, 6- Pioneer and risk taker. Intuitive and inspired. Strong leadership qualities.

Avi, 5- Bold, courageous, adventuresome. Intuitive and inspired. Blessed in some ways.

Avril, 8- Resolute and purposeful. Strong imagination. Intense inner power. Blessed in some ways. Slow to make decisions.

Axel, 6- Pioneer and risk taker. Artistic, sensual, perceptive. A free spirit, very adaptable. Strong verbal skills.

A-young, 11- Ambitious leader, great vision. Needs a lot of freedom. Natural counselor and healer. Very charismatic. Original and unconventional. Scientific and philosophical.

Azura, 4- Natural teaching ability. Great mediator, successful. Attractive and charming. Gentle, kind, hard worker. Bold, courageous, a bit stubborn.

> "Please, Aunt Em, Toto didn't mean to. He didn't know he was doing anything wrong. I'm the one that ought to be punished. I let him go in her garden. You can send me to bed without supper —"
> ~*Excerpted from "The Wizard of Oz"*
> *Used with permission*

B

IF THE FIRST LETTER of a name begins with B, or the name has more than one B, or the name ends with a B, then this person is partnership oriented, sensitive and emotional.

"B" people are friendly and social, but shy. They can be timid. They can also get themselves in trouble by jumping in to help others out. Then both are stuck down there. B types are so caring that sometimes they don't think first before jumping in. They are intelligent, but their concern for others sometimes blinds their best judgment. Their emotions are what make them most vulnerable.

B is the 2nd letter of the alphabet and therefore ruled by the number 2 vibration. In numerology, 2 rules partnership. B is almost the opposite of A. Where A needs to be independent, B is more partnership oriented. They look to others for answers, support, decisions; well someone has to do it. Where A's are leaders, B's are followers. They often prefer to be the power behind the throne.

We have some independent B names, for example: Barbara, with all those "A's" in her name, she will be sensitive and partnership oriented. At times she will need to be independent and will naturally be more competitive. Three famous Barbara's; Barbara Streisand, Barbara Walters and Barbara Stanwyck are sensitive to the needs of others but at the same time, feel a need to stand alone, by themselves. Although the B is a social letter, Barbara sums up to a 7 power number, so most likely all Barbara's need their solitude. The average B, however, is very social and dependent by nature.

Employers with names that begin with "B" as Betty or Bob, usually want to provide music for their workers. They are moved by music and will be impelled to provide a harmonic environment. B's can get very upset if conflict arises among their employees, family, or friends. They usually get more upset than those actually having the conflict. That's how sensitive they are. B's or 2's are happiest when everyone is getting along. That's why they are dubbed "the mediator." The 2nd letter serves best in a situation where they can bring two or more parties together in agreement. They're naturals at it.

B's are often musically talented and have a great sense of rhythm. Peace and harmony are essential to their happiness. They are known to quickly snap off the volume of music that is too loud or obnoxious. B names are tactful and refined. Because they are so sensitive to the needs of others, B names make excellent counselors. B's often use their keen intuition to guide them through their sessions.

Young children whose names begin with B are often cry babies. These children get their feelings hurt ever so easily on the playground. They will need lots of hugs for healthy emotional development. These children love to give hugs as well. The B named children are among the most sympathetic and kindest of all. They tend to be more intuitive and interested in psychic studies.

Grown up people with names that begin with B may be naturals at being partners, but can find parenthood a little difficult. They are better as a parent if they have a partner to help them with the children. They often later become friends with their children.

Remember the 1998 movie, "Armageddon" which starred Bruce Willis and Ben Affleck? At the end of the movie both B named actors broke down and cried as one of them was going to sacrifice his life to save the others. The emotional side of the B came out beautifully on screen. This part may have been difficult for most men, however not so for two men named with a B first name!

B names are open-minded, and offer great support with little or no recognition for their efforts. Sometimes they cling to ideas long after they have outlived their usefulness. Some B names must learn to change more with the times. Most B names provide insight and valuable perspective to those in leadership positions. They make great "behind the scenes" helpers. Usually they are too shy to be in the direct limelight. B names willingly accept their position as a valuable helper you couldn't do without.

A "B" person will yearn for a partner if single; and if married will be the better half. They are attentive to their partner's needs. This 2 ruled B letter is similar to the astrological signs Taurus and Libra. Venus rules Taurus and Libra and the number 2. The influence of this social vibration brings good taste in the finer things of life. These individuals enjoy good food, company, art and music. Consequently it seems as if we have two types of this 2 ruled letter. One is the down-to-earth "Taurean" type. The other is the more intellectual "Libra" type. Both have a good head for business. Along with the numbers 4 and 8, 2 ruled letters tend to make excellent business men and women. Don't hesitate to put them in charge of the books.

Bob Dole is a wonderful example of how a "B" named person makes a great partner. Just look at the way Bob supports his wife, Elizabeth Dole. Bob was willing to be the "First Man" of the White House. Senator Elizabeth Dole was candidate for President of the United States in 1999. She also was former President of Red Cross Which goes to show that behind every successful woman is a B named man.

Bill Clinton is another B named man who supports his partner. Just like Bob, he too is willing to take a back seat to his wife's Senator Hillary Clinton's, ambitions. Remember the famous sensitive remark Bill Clinton was quoted to say, "I feel your pain." This is true of a B personality. They are that sensitive.

You can recognize a B personality by the frequent use of the words "we" "let's" "us" and "we're." They talk as if there were a mouse in their pocket. When a breakup occurs, a B could pine away for weeks, months, or even years. As soon as the healing takes place, they are out in the sunshine, looking for another mate. The yearning for a partner calls out to them so strongly. B names need people and social contact more than most other names. Those of us who are looking for a good partner should turn to a B named person. They'll not only be a wonderful partner, they'll be your best friend.

Some other famous B names: Benjamin Franklin, Billy Graham, Bob Newhart, Ben Stiller, Britney Spears, Beyonce Knowles, Bo Derek, Barry Manilow, Brad Pitt, Bernadette Peters, Bobby Darin, Brooke Shields, Bette Midler, Burt Lancaster, Betty Grable, Buddy Ebsen, Bob Dylan, Bob Marley, Barbara Eden, Barry White, Billy Joel, Benjamin Bratt, Bonnie Raite, Bono, Burt Reynolds, Babe Ruth, Buddy Hackett, and Bob Hope.

Quick Reference of "B" Names

Babe, 10- Anticipates next move. Independent, critical of self and others. Sensitive and emotional. Loves adventure and excitement.

Babette, 10- Anticipates next move. Independent, critical of self and others. Emotional and sensitive. A free spirit, very adaptable. Dynamic, very busy lifestyle. Needs to slow down. Loves adventure and excitement.

Babs, 6- Creative in a practical way. Pioneer and risk taker. Emotional and sensitive. Charming and devoted.

Baby, 3- Loyal and understanding. Aims to please. Emotional and sensitive. Dislikes limitations.

Bahram, 7- Quietly supportive. Not easily influenced. Great judge of character. Gentle, kind, a hard worker. Independent, critical of self and others. Systematic, organized.

Bailey, 9- Generous and caring. Hardworking, sincere. Blessed in some ways. Strong verbal skills. A free spirit, very adaptable. Dislikes limitations.

Balazs, 7- Quietly supportive. Not easily influenced. Strong verbal skills. Independent, self-motivated. Great mediator. Charming and devoted.

Baldwin, 11- Good business partner. Intuitive, perceptive. Communicates skillfully. Reliable, responsible. Likes to meet new people. Blessed in some ways. Romantic and sensual.

Barbara, 7- Quietly supportive. Not easily influenced. Gentle, kind, a hard worker. Affectionate and social. Bold, courageous, a bit stubborn. A tendency to lose items. Independent, critical of self and others.

Barclay, 8- Enjoys luxury items. Resolute and purposeful. Diligent, helpful. Self-expressive, cheerful. Strong verbal skills. Bold, courageous, a bit stubborn. Needs a lot of freedom.

Barbie, 10- Anticipates next move. Independent, critical of self and others. Gentle, kind, a hard worker. Loyal and understanding. Artistic, having good taste. Loves adventure and excitement.

Barnabas, 4- Natural business aptitude. Natural teaching ability. Strong and healthy. Creative, opinionated. Bold, courageous, a bit stubborn. Affectionate and social. Resolute and purposeful. Charming and devoted.

Barnaby, 9- Generous and caring. Hardworking, sincere. Gentle, kind, diligent. Creative, opinionated. Bold, courageous, a bit stubborn. Affectionate and social. Needs a lot of freedom.

Barnard, 4- Natural business aptitude. Natural teaching ability. Intense inner power. Creative, opinionated. Bold, courageous, a bit stubborn. Tendency to lose items. Down-to-earth, faithful.

Barney, 11- Good business partner. Resolute, purposeful. Strives to improve humanity. Original and unconventional. Loves adventure and excitement. Needs a lot of freedom.

Baron, 5- Sparkling emotional outlook. Pioneer and risk taker. Diligent, helpful. Natural counselor and healer. Original and unconventional.

Barry, 10- Anticipates next move. Independent, critical of self and others. Gentle, kind, a hard worker. Intense inner power. Needs a lot of freedom.

Bart, 5- Sparkling emotional outlook. Bold, courageous, a bit stubborn. Intense inner power. Dynamic, very busy lifestyle.

Barth, 4- Natural business aptitude. Natural teaching ability. Gentle, kind, a hard worker. Dynamic, very busy lifestyle. Self-reliant, successful.

Bartholomew, 6- Creative in a practical way. Pioneer and risk taker. Diligent, helpful. Dynamic, busy lifestyle. Self-reliant, successful. Natural counselor and healer. Frequent traveler. Musically talented. Systematic, organized. A free spirit, very adaptable. Likes to meet new people.

Bartley, 11- Good business partner. Intuitive, perceptive. Intense inner power. Dynamic, busy lifestyle. Strong verbal skills. A free spirit, very adaptable. Needs a lot of freedom.

Barton, 7- Quietly supportive. Not easily influenced. Gentle, kind, a hard worker. Dynamic, busy lifestyle. Natural counselor and healer. Original and unconventional.

Basil, 7- Quietly supportive. Not easily influenced. Charming and devoted. Artistic, having good taste. Strong verbal skills.

Baxter, 7- Quietly supportive. Not easily influenced. Artistic, sensual and perceptive. Dynamic, busy lifestyle. A free spirit, very adaptable. Gentle, kind, a hard worker.

Bea, 8- Enjoys luxury items. Original and creative. Resolute and purposeful.

Beatrice, 9- Generous and caring. Enjoys giving gifts. Bold, courageous, a bit stubborn. Dynamic, busy lifestyle. Gentle, kind, a hard worker. Artistic, having good taste. Self-expressive, cheerful. Likes to entertain.

Beau, 11- Good business partner. Keenly perceptive. Independent, critical of self and others. Attractive and charming.

Beaufort, 7- Quietly supportive. Not easily fooled. Independent, critical of self and others. Attractive and charming. Self-sacrificing, loving. Natural counselor and healer. Gentle, kind, a hard worker. Dynamic, busy lifestyle.

Beauregard, 10- Anticipates next move. Likes change and variety. Independent, critical of self and others. Attractive and charming. Gentle, kind, a hard worker. Loves adventure and excitement. Scientific and philosophical. Bold, courageous, a bit stubborn. Tendency to lose items. Down-to-earth, faithful.

Becca, 5- Sparkling emotional outlook. Physical and passionate. Self-expressive, cheerful. Optimistic and outspoken. Bright, adventuresome.

Becky, 10- Anticipates next move. Likes change and variety. Inspiring and creative. Strong desire to succeed. Needs a lot of freedom.

Behrang, 10- Anticipates next move. Likes change and variety. Self-reliant, successful. Gentle, kind, a hard worker. Independent, critical of self and others. Original and unconventional. Scientific and philosophical.

Behrooz, 8- Enjoys luxury items. Original and creative. Great judge of character. Intense inner power. Natural counselor and healer. Respects rules. Uses common sense.

Behzad, 10- Anticipates next move. Likes change and variety. Self-reliant, successful. Uses common sense. Independent, critical of self and others. Reliable, responsible.

Beldon, 7- Quietly supportive. Not easily fooled. Strong verbal skills. Reliable, responsible. Natural counselor and healer. Original and unconventional.

Belinda, 11- Good business partner. Keenly perceptive. Strong verbal skills. Artistic, having good taste. Original and unconventional. Natural authority. Resolute and purposeful.

Bella, 5- Sparkling emotional outlook. Likes change, very adaptable. Communicates skillfully. Ups and downs financially. Pioneer and risk taker.

Belle, 9- Generous and caring. Enjoys giving gifts. Strong verbal skills. Frequent traveler. A free spirit, very adaptable.

Ben, 3- Loyal and understanding. A free spirit, very adaptable. Romantic and creative.

Benny, 6- Creative in a practical way. A step ahead of others. Unconventional, opinionated. Romantic and sensual. Needs a lot of freedom.

Benedict, 8- Enjoys luxury items. Creative and original. Original and unconventional. Likes change and variety. Systematic, organized. Artistic, having good taste. Outgoing and cheerful. Dynamic, busy lifestyle.

Benita, 6- Creative in a practical way. A step ahead of others. Unconventional, opinionated. Artistic, having good taste. Dynamic, busy lifestyle. Pioneer and risk taker.

Benjamin, 5- Sparkling emotional outlook. Physical and passionate. Original, opinionated. Clever and talented. Bright, adventuresome. Domestic, hard working. Blessed in some ways. Creative, unconventional.

Benjie, 9- Generous and caring. Enjoys giving gifts. Original and unconventional. Clever and talented. Blessed in some ways. Loves adventure and excitement.

Benson, 6- Creative in a practical way. A step ahead of others. Romantic and original. Charming and devoted. Natural counselor and healer. Unconventional and opinionated.

Bentley, 11- Good business partner. Keenly perceptive. Original and unconventional. Dynamic, busy lifestyle. Communicates skillfully. Physical and passionate. Dislikes limitations.

Benton, 7- Quietly supportive. Not easily fooled. Original and unconventional. Dynamic, busy lifestyle. Natural counselor and healer. Creative and opinionated.

Berkley, 6- Creative in a practical way. A step ahead of others. Gentle, kind, a hard worker. Strong desire to succeed. Communicates skillfully. Physical and passionate. Dislikes limitations.

Bernadette, 22- Good business partner. Has big plans and ideas. Strives to improve humanity. Original and unconventional. Not easily influenced. Reliable, responsible. Physical and passionate. Dynamic, busy lifestyle. Sensitive and easily hurt. Loves adventure and excitement.

Bernadine, 9- Generous and caring. Enjoys giving gifts. Gentle, kind, a hard worker. Original and unconventional. Helpful, sincere. Reliable, responsible. Blessed in some ways. Romantic and sensual. A free spirit, very adaptable.

Bernard, 8- Enjoys luxury items. Original and creative. Uses good judgment. Romantic, sensual. Resolute and purposeful. Tendency to lose items. Has natural authority.

Bernie, 8- Enjoys luxury items. Original and creative. Intense inner power. Original and unconventional. Blessed in some ways. Physical and passionate.

Bernice, 11- Good business partner. Keenly perceptive. Gentle, kind, a hard worker. Original and unconventional. Artistic, having good taste. Self-expressive, cheerful. Physical and passionate.

Bert, 9- Generous and caring. Enjoys giving gifts. Diligent, helpful. Dynamic, busy lifestyle.

Bertha, 9- Generous and caring. Enjoys giving gifts. Considerate and kind. Dynamic, busy lifestyle. Great judge of character. Not easily influenced.

Bertie, 5- Sparkling emotional outlook. Physical and passionate. Intense inner power. Dynamic, busy lifestyle. Artistic, having good taste. Keenly perceptive.

Beryl, 8- Enjoys luxury items. Original and creative. Intense inner power. Needs a lot of freedom. Strong verbal skills.

Bess, 9- Generous and caring. Enjoys giving gifts. Charming and devoted. Impulsive and extreme.

Bessie, 5- Sparkling emotional outlook. Physical and passionate. Charming and devoted. Impulsive and extreme. Blessed in some ways. Keenly perceptive.

Beth, 8- Enjoys luxury items. Original and creative. Dynamic, busy lifestyle. Great judge of character.

Betsy, 8- Enjoys luxury items. Original and creative. Dynamic, busy lifestyle. Charming and devoted. Needs a lot of freedom.

Bette, 7- Quietly supportive. Not easily fooled. Dynamic, busy lifestyle. Sensitive and easily hurt. Physical and passionate.

Betty, 9- Generous and caring. Enjoys giving gifts. Dynamic, busy lifestyle. Sensitive and easily hurt. Dislikes limitations.

Beulah, 22- Good business partner. Has big plans and ideas. Attractive and charming. Strong verbal skills. Resolute and purposeful. Self-reliant, successful.

Beverly, 8- Enjoys luxury items. Original and creative. Intuitive and inspired. Likes change and variety. Gentle, kind, a hard worker. Strong verbal skills. Dislikes limitations.

Bevis, 3- Loyal and understanding. A free spirit, very adaptable. Strong imagination. Blessed in some ways. Charming and devoted.

Bian, 8- Enjoys luxury items. Original and creative. Not easily influenced. Romantic, opinionated.

Bianca, 3- Loyal and understanding. Blessed in some ways. Pioneer and risk taker. Original and unconventional. Self-expressive, cheerful. Bold, courageous, a bit stubborn.

Bibi, 22- Good business partner. Considerate, understanding. Emotional and sensitive. Artistic, having good taste.

Bill, 8- Enjoys luxury items. Blessed in some ways. Strong verbal skills. Financial ups and downs.

Billie, 4- Natural business aptitude. Considerate, understanding. Communicates skillfully. Frequent traveler. Artistic, having good taste. A free spirit, very adaptable.

Billy, 6- Creative in a practical way. Artistic, having good taste. Strong verbal skills. Frequent traveler. Dislikes limitations.

Bina, 8- Enjoys luxury items. Practical when giving. Romantic, sensual. Independent, critical of self and others.

Bing, 5- Sparkling emotional outlook. Idealistic, humanitarian. Romantic, sensual. Scientific and philosophical.

Binh, 6- Creative in a practical way. Blessed in some ways. Original, opinionated. Great judge of character.

Binti, 9- Generous and caring. Artistic, having good taste. Original and unconventional. Dynamic, busy lifestyle. Idealistic and humanitarian.

Biolulfo, 11- Good business partner. Blessed in some ways. Natural counselor and healer. Strong verbal skills. Attractive and charming. Frequent traveler. Self-sacrificing, loving. May have musical abilities.

Birdie, 11- Good business partner. Considerate, understanding. Gentle, kind, a hard worker. Reliable, responsible. Artistic, having good taste. A free spirit, very adaptable.

Bishop, 6- Creative in a practical way. Idealistic, humanitarian. Charming and devoted. Great judge of character. Natural counselor and healer. Intelligent and knowledgeable.

Bjorn, 5- Sparkling emotional outlook. Clever and talented. Natural counselor and healer. Intense inner power. Creative, opinionated.

Blade, 6- Creative in a practical way. Frequent traveler. Pioneer and risk taker. Workaholic, determined. Likes to entertain.

Blaine, 7- Quietly supportive. Strong verbal skills. Resolute and purposeful. Blessed in some ways. Original and unconventional. A free spirit, very adaptable.

Blair, 6- Creative in a practical way. Easy going attitude. Pioneer and risk taker. Blessed in some ways. Gentle, kind, a hard worker.

Blake, 22- Good business partner. Frequent traveler. Not easily influenced. Strong desire to succeed. A free spirit, very adaptable.

Blanca, 6- Creative in a practical way. Easy going attitude. Resolute and purposeful. Original and unconventional. Self-expressive, cheerful. Pioneer and risk taker.

Blanche, 9- Generous and caring. Strong verbal skills. Not easily influenced. Original and unconventional. Self-expressive, cheerful. Great judge of character. A free spirit, very adaptable.

Blane, 7- Quietly supportive. Intellectually sound. Independent, critical of self and others. Original and unconventional. A free spirit, very adaptable.

Blayne, 5- Sparkling emotional outlook. Communicates skillfully. Independent, critical of self and others. Highly perceptive. Original, unconventional. A free spirit, very adaptable.

Bliss, 7- Quietly supportive. Intellectually sound. Blessed in some ways. Charming and devoted. Impulsive and extreme.

Blossom, 5- Sparkling emotional outlook. Frequent traveler. Natural counselor and healer. Charming and devoted. Impulsive and extreme. Has musical talent. Domestic and hardworking.

Blythe, 9- Generous and caring. Strong verbal skills. Needs a lot of freedom. Dynamic, busy lifestyle. Great judge of character. Loves adventure and excitement.

Bo, 8- Enjoys luxury items. Natural counselor and healer. Successful.

Bob, 10- Anticipates next move. Ambitious and innovative. Good mediator.

Bobbi, 3- Loyal and understanding. Likes harmony and beauty. Emotional and sensitive. May be psychic. Artistic, having good taste.

Bobbie, 8- Enjoys luxury items. Competitive in business. Emotional and sensitive. May be psychic. Artistic, having good taste. Physical and passionate.

Bobby, 10- Anticipates next move. Natural counselor and healer. Emotional and sensitive. Friendly, but shy. Needs a lot of freedom.

Boden, 22- Good business partner. Creates group harmony. Workaholic, determined. A free spirit, very adaptable. Original and unconventional.

Bogart, 9- Generous and caring. Transforms others with love. Scientific and philosophical. Pioneer and risk taker. Gentle, kind, a hard worker. Dynamic, busy lifestyle.

Bonita, 7- Quietly supportive. Respects rules. Original and unconventional. Blessed in some ways. Dynamic, busy lifestyle. Independent, critical of self and others.

Bonne, 5- Sparkling emotional outlook. Versatile in service. Original and unconventional. Romantic, sensual. A free spirit, very adaptable.

Bonnie, 5- Sparkling emotional outlook. Natural counselor and healer. Original and opinionated. Romantic, sensual. Artistic, having good taste. A free spirit, very adaptable.

Boone, 6- Creative in a practical way. May have musical abilities. Magnetic personality. Original and unconventional. A free spirit, very adaptable.

Boris, 9- Generous and caring. Natural counselor and healer. Gentle, kind, a hard worker. Blessed in some ways. Charming and devoted.

Boswell, 7- Quietly supportive. Open to opportunities. Charming and devoted. Likes to meet new people. A free spirit, very adaptable. Strong verbal skills. Frequent traveler.

Bosworth, 3- Loyal and understanding. Natural counselor and healer. Charming and devoted. Likes to meet new people. Respects rules. Gentle, kind, a hard worker. Dynamic, busy lifestyle. Great judge of character.

Bowie, 9- Generous and caring. Transforms others with love. Likes to meet new people. Artistic, having good taste. A free spirit, very adaptable.

Boyce, 5- Sparkling emotional outlook. Natural counselor and healer. Needs a lot of freedom. Self-expressive, cheerful. Physical and passionate.

Boyd, 10- Anticipates next move. Natural counselor and healer. Dislikes limitations. Workaholic, determined.

Brad, 7- Quietly supportive. Gentle, kind, a hard worker. Not easily influenced. Domestic, responsible.

Braden, 8- Enjoys luxury items. Diligent, helpful. Resolute and purposeful. Reliable, responsible. Physical, passionate. Creative and opinionated.

Bradford, 5- Sparkling emotional outlook. Gentle, kind, a hard worker. Bight, adventuresome. Down-to-earth, faithful. Self-sacrificing, loving. Natural counselor and healer. Tendency to lose items. Workaholic, determined.

Bradley, 4- Natural business aptitude. Diligent, helpful. Excellent teaching skills. Systematic, organized. Communicates skillfully. Loves adventure and excitement. Highly perceptive.

Brady, 5- Sparkling emotional outlook. Gentle, kind, a hard worker. Not easily influenced. Has a natural authority. Needs a lot of freedom.

Bram, 7- Quietly supportive. Diligent, helpful. Not easily influenced. Domestic, hard working.

Bramwell, 5- Sparkling emotional outlook. Intense inner power. Not easily influenced. Domestic, hard working. Likes to meet new people. A free spirit, very adaptable. Strong verbal skills. Financial ups and downs.

Brandon, 5- Sparkling emotional outlook. Gentle, kind, a hard worker. Bright, adventuresome. Original and opinionated. Reliable, responsible. Natural counselor and healer. Romantic, sensual.

Brandy, 10- Anticipates next move. Diligent, helpful. Independent, critical of self and others. Original and unconventional. Reliable, responsible. Needs a lot of freedom.

Brant, 10- Anticipates next move. Diligent, helpful. Independent, critical of self and others. Original and unconventional. Dynamic, very busy lifestyle.

Brawley, 5- Sparkling emotional outlook. Intense inner power. Bright, adventuresome. Likes to meet new people. Strong verbal skills. Physical, passionate. Needs a lot of freedom.

Breanna, 10- Anticipates next move. Hard working, diligent. A free spirit, very adaptable. Independent, critical of self and others. Romantic and sensual. Creative and opinionated. Bold, courageous, a bit stubborn.

Bree, 3- Loyal and understanding. Gentle, kind, a hard worker. A free spirit, very adaptable. Physical and passionate

Bren, 3- Loyal and understanding. Gentle, kind, a hard worker. A free spirit, very adaptable. Romantic and sensual.

Brenda, 8- Enjoys luxury items. Intense inner power. Physical and passionate. Creative, opinionated. Reliable, responsible. Resolute and purposeful.

Brenna, 9- Generous and caring. Gentle, kind, a hard worker. A free spirit, very adaptable. Romantic and sensual. Creative and opinionated. Helpful, sincere.

Brent, 5- Sparkling emotional outlook. Gentle, kind, a hard worker. Physical and passionate. Creative, opinionated. Dynamic, busy lifestyle.

Bret, 9- Generous and caring. Gentle, kind, a hard worker. A free spirit, very adaptable. Dynamic, busy lifestyle.

Brett, 20- Emotional, sensitive. Diligent, helpful. A free spirit, very adaptable. Dynamic, busy lifestyle. Sensitive and easily hurt.

Brewster, 11- Good business partner. Idealistic, humanitarian. A free spirit, very adaptable. Likes to meet new people. Charming and devoted. Dynamic, busy lifestyle. Loves adventure and excitement. Tendency to lose items.

Brian, 8- Enjoys luxury items. Gentle, kind, a hard worker. Blessed in some ways. Resolute and purposeful. Romantic and opinionated.

Brianna, 5- Sparkling emotional outlook. Intense inner power. Artistic, having good taste. Not easily influenced. Original and unconventional. Romantic and sensual. Pioneer and risk taker.

Brice, 10- Anticipates next move. Diligent, helpful. Blessed in some ways. Self-expressive, cheerful. Likes change and variety.

Bridget, 11- Good business partner. Idealistic, humanitarian. Blessed in some ways. Reliable, responsible. Scientific and philosophical. A free spirit, very adaptable. Dynamic, busy lifestyle.

Brigette, 5- Sparkling emotional outlook. Gentle, kind, a hard worker. Blessed in some ways. Scientific and philosophical. A free spirit, very adaptable. Dynamic, busy lifestyle. Sensitive and easily hurt. Physical and passionate.

Brie, 7- Quietly supportive. Gentle, kind, a hard worker. Blessed in some ways. Not easily fooled.

Brieta, 10- Anticipates next move. Diligent, helpful. Works for group effort. A free spirit, very adaptable. Dynamic, busy lifestyle. Independent, critical of self and others.

Brietta, 3- Loyal and understanding. Optimistic, very kind. Artistic, having good taste. A free spirit, very adaptable. Dynamic, busy lifestyle. Sensitive and easily hurt. Aims to please.

Brienna, 9- Generous and caring. Gentle, kind, a hard worker. Blessed in some ways. A free spirit, very adaptable. Original and unconventional. Romantic and sensual. Helpful, sincere.

Brina, 8- Enjoys luxury items. Diligent, helpful. Practical when giving. Creative, opinionated. Resolute and purposeful.

Brita, 5- Sparkling emotional outlook. Gentle, kind, a hard worker. Artistic, having good taste. Dynamic, busy lifestyle. Bright, adventuresome.

Britney, 3- Loyal and understanding. Gentle, kind, a hard worker. Blessed in some ways. Dynamic, busy lifestyle. Romantic, sensual. A free spirit, very adaptable. Needs a lot of freedom.

Brodie, 8- Enjoys luxury items. Intense inner power. Natural counselor and healer. Reliable and responsible. Artistic, having good taste. Physical and passionate.

Broderick, 4- Natural business aptitude. Strong and healthy. Assumes responsibility. Systematic, organized. Physical and passionate. Tendency to lose items. Artistic, having good taste. Inspiring, very creative. Strong desire to succeed.

Bron, 22- Good business partner. Diligent, helpful. Natural counselor and healer. Original and unconventional.

Bronson, 7- Quietly supportive. Intense inner power. Natural counselor and healer. Original and unconventional. Charming and devoted. Magnetic personality. Romantic and sensual.

Brook, 7- Quietly supportive. Gentle, kind, a hard worker. Natural counselor and healer. Magnetic personality. Strong desire to succeed.

Brooke, 3- Loyal and understanding. Optimistic, very kind. Natural counselor and healer. Magnetic personality. Strong desire to succeed. A free spirit, very adaptable.

Bruce, 22- Good business partner. Diligent, helpful. Attractive and charming. Optimistic and outspoken. A free spirit, very adaptable.

Brucia, 9- Generous and caring. Sometimes naive. Youthful, appealing. Self-expressive, cheerful. Blessed in some ways. Resolute and purposeful.

Bruno, 7- Quietly supportive. Gentle, kind, a hard worker. Attractive and charming. Original and unconventional. Natural counselor and healer.

Bryan, 6- Creative in a practical way. Diligent, helpful. Needs a lot of freedom. Pioneer and risk taker. Original and unconventional.

Bryanna, 30- Loyal and understanding. Gentle, kind, a hard worker. Needs a lot of freedom. Pioneer and risk taker. Romantic and sensual. Creative, opinionated. Bold, courageous, a bit stubborn.

Bryant, 8- Enjoys luxury items. Intense inner power. Needs a lot of freedom. Resolute and purposeful. Romantic, sensual. Dynamic, busy lifestyle.

Bryce, 8- Enjoys luxury items. Diligent, helpful. Dislikes restrictions. Self-expressive, cheerful. Physical and passionate.

Bryna, 6- Creative in a practical way. Diligent, helpful. Needs a lot of freedom. Original and unconventional. Not easily influenced.

Bud, 9- Generous and caring. Attractive and charming. Reliable and responsible.

Buddy, 20- Emotional, sensitive. Socially charming. Practical, conservative. Down-to-earth, domestic. Needs a lot of freedom.

Bunny, 22- Good business partner. Creative, intuitive. Original and unconventional. Romantic, sensual. Stylish and refined.

Burke, 30- Loyal and understanding. Attractive and charming. Gentle, kind, a hard worker. Strong desire to succeed. A free spirit, very adaptable.

Burl, 8- Enjoys luxury items. Slow to make decisions. Intense inner power. Strong verbal skills.

Burt, 7- Quietly supportive. Attractive and charming. Gentle, kind, a hard worker. Dynamic, busy lifestyle.

Burton, 9- Generous and caring. Go with the flow attitude. Idealistic, humanitarian. Dynamic, busy lifestyle. Natural counselor and healer. Original and unconventional.

Busby, 6- Creative in a practical way. Very lucky. Can be moody. Affectionate and friendly. Dislikes limitations.

Buzz, 3- Loyal and understanding. Attractive and charming. Uses common sense. Excellent mediator.

Byford, 7- Quietly supportive. Needs a lot of freedom. Self-sacrificing, loving. Natural counselor and healer. Gentle, kind, a hard worker. Reliable and responsible.

Byram, 5- Sparkling emotional outlook. Stylish and refined. Intense inner power. Bright, adventuresome. Systematic, organized.

Byron, 11- Good business partner. Needs a lot of freedom. Gentle, kind, a hard worker. Natural counselor and healer. Original and unconventional.

> "Poor little orphan, and her Miss Gulch troubles. Gosh all hemlock—you know, she ought to have somebody to play with."
> ~*Excerpted from "The Wizard of Oz"*
> *Used with permission*

C

IF A NAME BEGINS with C, has more than one C, or ends with a C, this person is cheerful, self-expressive, creative and likable.

"C" is for communication. The C individual excels in the art of communication. They want to be sure the lines of communication are clear; and that everyone understands one another. They are exceptionally gifted in the area of writing, holding conversations, the entertainment industry, theatre, or any area in the field of communication or transportation. Because this letter is ruled by the number 3, most people with a C anywhere in their first name are a little "car happy." C people usually love their vehicles as well as other people's vehicles. This letter likes to go places, fast. Oddly enough, as much as they like to go fast, they are a little slow about making decisions. This letter, as well as the other number 3 ruled letters, L and U like to intellectualize their experiences making it difficult for them to make up their minds.

The typical C is a social delight and has the keen ability to not only hold their end of a conversation, but to listen well too. They have a great sense of humor. Carol Burnett, Charlie Chaplin and Cloris Leechman all have a comical, animated sense of humor. Even Comedian Lucille O'Ball has a C in her name. This letter rules the "natural comedian." We can recognize a C personality at the super market. They're the one that tells a joke at just the right moment that makes everyone laugh. Their sense of humor eases most tense situations. C's have a "stage presence" about them. It's as if they are putting on a performance all the time. It's a youthful letter; remember child starts with "C." There's a little child in all "C" people.

Those with names that begin with C are often extravagant and melodramatic. This letter needs a creative outlet or the C person can become moody and overly dramatic. This letter, as well as it's siblings, L and U are rich in imagination. If carried too far, this letter is known to exaggerate to the point of outright lying.

C is the 3rd letter of the alphabet, so C is similar to the number 3 vibration. 3 in numerology rules balance. Picture a teeter-totter going up and down. If we stood in the middle of the teeter-totter, we wouldn't move up or down. We would remain steady while the two sides of the teeter-totter moved up and down. The C or 3 ruled individual also needs to go in the middle for balance. They should go within themselves and meditate to achieve this balance. Escapist tendencies are not uncommon to the C, but if the C person practices meditation they will be more balanced and more able to apply themselves to a steady path toward inner peace. People in their lives can pull them up or down; they need to find their middle so this doesn't happen. The bible says, "Thy body is thy temple, worship within it." What a perfect passage for this letter to remember. C's or 3's that don't achieve this balance often scatter their energies and express little sense of purpose.

The typical C will make many short trips around town. Their housing situation may be temporary. C's usually experience many ups and downs financially. This letter often adopts the saying, "I'm spending my children's inheritance." If they have money, they spend it, if not, they don't. It's a cheerful, happy-go-lucky letter and hardly serious about life. Fortunately, what they lack in concern for money, they make up for in luck. Along with letters L and U, C people tend to strike it rich in the lottery, inheritance, or with just plain dumb luck. Another special bonus is they tend to bounce back rapidly from physical and mental setbacks. C first names have a go with the flow, easy going manner. Some may appear too easy-going with a devil-may-care attitude. And there is a reason Chatty Cathy starts with the letter C. Some C names will talk your ear off!

Speaking of talking, another interesting observation about people with letters ruled by the number 3 is their mouth. People with the letters C, L, or U in their names seem to have an interesting mouth. It's either too big for their face, or a noticeable space between their teeth, a cute lisp, or an attractive overbite. This is also true of those with intensity 3's and power number 3's. There's just something about their mouth.

Similar to the 3rd sign of the zodiac, Gemini; the C personality usually can't resist painting a story a little more colorful than it actually is. We should say to all those 3 ruled people out there, "I've told you a million times not to exaggerate!" They can be storytellers. This is also true of those with a power number or intensity number 3.

C ruled people make excellent sales persons, writers, comedians, and work well in the transportation industry, and any area of the communication industry. They are good with words and people. C types know how to make people feel comfortable and at ease. They have good manners and look almost as well dressed as those with an E in their name.

Those born with CH in the beginning of their names are young and sexy. Just look at how young and sexy Cher is. Long after she's gone people will remember her youthful appearance as well as her sex appeal. The C is youthful and the Scorpio-like H makes for quite a combination. Christian Slater also looks young and sexy on or off screen. CH people tend to think and act young, but also have a touch of Scorpio blended in their personality. Another person is Cheryl Tiegs. Imagine; she's over 50 years old, graces the cover of the 2004 Sports Illustrated in her swim suit, and looks great! She'll always be young and sexy somehow. Charlie Sheen is another remarkably young looking older actor.

Charlie Chaplin, although today not considered "young and sexy," still had the Gemini/Scorpio influence of his first two letters. The 3rd letter of the alphabet has a natural talent for comedy. The H or 8th letter has everything to do with control just like Scorpio does. Charlie at a very early age controlled the stage and brought laughter to many during the depression when happiness was a rare commodity. And typical to the H in his name; he made out quite well financially when most of the world was struggling. The H helped him master the material side of life, with the letter C in a fun way.

If there were a letter that symbolized the "salt of the earth," or the "spice of life," it would have to be "C" food would be bland without spices and the world would be boring without "C" or 3 vibration types. Their sparking emotional outlook and vibrant, witty personalities can be like a cold drink on a hot day. Very refreshing indeed. The entertainment industry is full of "C's."

Some more famous C names: Christopher Walker, Cary Grant, Christine Aguilara, Cloris Leechman, Conan O'Brien, Carol Channing, Chubby Checkers, Christopher Reeves, Carrie Fisher, Charlize Theron, Christina Applegate, Celine Dion, Clark Gable, Christy Brinkley, Chevy Chase, Cecil B. DeMille, Chuck Berry, Charlton Heston, Charles Bronson, Cameron Diaz, Clint Eastwood, Cindy Crawford, Carl Reiner, Catherine Zeta-Jones, Cesar Chavez, Condoleezza Rice, Carmen Electra and Cate Blanchett.

Quick Reference of "C" Names

Cadence, 8- Ups and downs financially. Resolute and purposeful. Reliable, responsible. Physical and passionate. Original and unconventional. Self-expressive, cheerful. Loves adventure and excitement.

Caesar, 11- Inspiring and highly creative. Intuitive, perceptive. A free spirit, very adaptable. Charming and devoted. Bold, courageous, a bit stubborn. Gentle, kind, a hard worker.

Cahil, 6- Mellow, yet tactful. Pioneer and risk taker. Great judge of character. Blessed in some ways. Strong verbal skills.

Cain, 9- Artistically creative. Helpful, sincere. Blessed in some ways. Original and unconventional.

Caitlin, 5- Quick sense of humor. Bright, adventuresome. Enjoys giving to others. Dynamic, busy lifestyle. Strong verbal skills. Artistic, having good taste. Romantic, opinionated.

Cal, 7- Sees the irony in situations. Not easily influenced. Strong verbal skills.

Calandra, 9- Artistically creative. Independent, critical of self and others. Frequent traveler. Bold, courageous, a bit stubborn. Original and unconventional. Reliable, responsible. Gentle, kind, hard worker. Pioneer and risk taker.

Caldwell, 9- Artistically creative. Helpful, sincere. Communicates skillfully. Reliable, responsible. Likes to meet new people. A free spirit, very adaptable. Frequent traveler. Slow to make decisions.

Caleb, 5- Quick sense of humor. Bright, adventuresome. Strong verbal skills. A free spirit, very adaptable. Affectionate, social.

Calhoun, 11- Inspiring and highly creative. Intuitive, perceptive. Strong verbal skills. Great judge of character. Natural counselor and healer. Attractive and charming. Original and unconventional.

Calista, 11- Inspiring and highly creative. Intuitive, perceptive. Strong verbal skills. Blessed in some ways. Charming and devoted. Dynamic, busy lifestyle. Bold, courageous, a bit stubborn.

Calixto, 30- Cheerful, light hearted. Aims to please. Communicates skillfully. Blessed in some ways. Artistic, sensual, perceptive. Dynamic, busy lifestyle. Natural counselor and healer.

Calla, 11- Inspiring and highly creative. Intuitive, perceptive. Strong verbal skills. Frequent traveler. Bold, courageous, a bit stubborn.

Calum, 5- Quick sense of humor. Bright, adventuresome. Optimistic, outspoken. Attractive and charming. Domestic, hard working.

Calvert, 9- Artistically creative. Helpful, sincere. Strong verbal skills. Intuitive and inspired. A free spirit, very adaptable. Gentle, kind, a hard worker. Dynamic, busy lifestyle.

Calvin, 7- Sees the irony in situations. Not easily influenced. Frequent traveler. A little eccentric. Blessed in some ways. Original and unconventional.

Calypso, 10- Great verbal expressions. Independent, critical of self and others. Strong verbal skills. Needs a lot of freedom. Intelligent and knowledgeable. Charming and devoted. Natural counselor and healer.

Cam, 8- Ups and downs financially. Resolute and purposeful. Domestic and hardworking.

Camella, 20- Has a sociable demeanor. Reads people easily. Domestic and hardworking. A free spirit, very adaptable. Strong verbal skills. Frequent traveler. Bold, courageous, a bit stubborn.

Cameo, 10- Great verbal expressions. Independent, critical of self and others. Domestic and hardworking. A free spirit, very adaptable. Natural counselor and healer.

Cameron, 6- Mellow, yet tactful. Pioneer and risk taker. Systematic and organized. A free spirit, very adaptable. Gentle, kind, a hard worker. Natural counselor and healer. Original and unconventional.

Camilla, 6- Mellow, yet tactful. Pioneer and risk taker. Domestic and hardworking. Blessed in some ways. Strong verbal skills. Frequent traveler. Bold, courageous, a bit stubborn.

Camille, 10- Great verbal expressions. Independent, critical of self and others. Domestic and hardworking. Blessed in some ways. Strong verbal skills. Frequent traveler. A free spirit, very adaptable.

Campbell, 10- Great verbal expressions. Independent, critical of self and others. Domestic and hardworking. Intelligent and knowledgeable. Affectionate, loyal. A free spirit, very adaptable. Strong verbal skills. Frequent traveler.

Candace, 22- Inspiring and highly creative. Resolute and purposeful. Original and unconventional. Reliable, responsible. Bold, courageous, a bit stubborn. Optimistic and outspoken. A free spirit, very adaptable.

Candi, 22- Inspiring and highly creative. Resolute and purposeful. Original and unconventional. Reliable, responsible. Blessed in some ways.

Candice, 30- Cheerful, lighthearted. Pioneer and risk taker. Creative, opinionated. Reliable, responsible. Blessed in some ways. Optimistic and outspoken. A free spirit, very adaptable.

Candida, 9- Artistically creative. Hard working, helpful. Original and unconventional. Reliable, responsible. Blessed in some ways. Down-to-earth, faithful. Bold, courageous, a bit stubborn.

Candido, 5- Quick sense of humor. Bright, adventuresome. Romantic, sensual. Reliable, responsible. Blessed in some ways. Workaholic, determined. Natural counselor and healer.

Candie, 9- Artistically creative. Pioneer and risk taker. Physical and passionate. Reliable, responsible. Artistic, having good taste. A free spirit, very adaptable.

Candy, 20- Has a sociable demeanor. Reads people easily. Original and unconventional. Reliable, responsible. Needs a lot of freedom.

Canute, 10- Great verbal expressions. Independent, critical of self and others. Original and unconventional. Charming and attractive. Dynamic, busy lifestyle. A free spirit, very adaptable.

Caprice, 10- Great verbal expressions. Independent, critical of self and others. Intelligent and knowledgeable. Gentle, kind, a hard worker. Blessed in some ways. Outgoing, youthful outlook. A free spirit, very adaptable.

Cara, 5- Quick sense of humor. Bright, adventuresome. Gentle, kind, a hard worker. Pioneer and risk taker.

Carey, 7- Sees the irony in situations. Not easily influenced. Gentle, kind, a hard worker. Loves adventure and excitement. Needs a lot of freedom.

Carie, 9- Artistically creative. Helpful, sincere. Gentle, kind, a hard worker. Artistic, having good taste. A free spirit, very adaptable.

Carin, 9- Artistically creative. Helpful, sincere. Gentle, kind, a hard worker. Considerate, understanding. Original, opinionated.

Carissa, 7- Sees the irony in situations. Not easily influenced. Gentle, kind, a hard worker. Blessed in some ways. Charming and devoted. Impulsive and extreme. Bold, courageous, a bit stubborn.

Carita, 7- Sees the irony in situations. Not easily influenced. Diligent, helpful. Blessed in many ways. Dynamic, busy lifestyle. Bold, courageous, a bit stubborn.

Carl, 7- Sees the irony in situations. Not easily influenced. Gentle, kind, a hard worker. Strong verbal skills.

Carla, 8- Ups and downs financially. Resolute and purposeful. Intense inner power. Communicates skillfully. Bold, courageous, a bit stubborn.

Carleton, 7- Sees the irony in situations. Not easily influenced. Gentle, kind, a hard worker. Strong verbal skills. A free spirit, very adaptable. Dynamic, busy lifestyle. Natural counselor and healer. Original and unconventional.

Carlin, 30- Cheerful, lighthearted. Aims to please. Gentle, kind, a hard worker. Strong verbal skills. Blessed in some ways. Original and unconventional.

Carlie, 30- Cheerful, lighthearted. Aims to please. Gentle, kind, a hard worker. Strong verbal skills. Blessed in some ways. A free spirit, very adaptable.

Carlisle, 7- Sees the irony in situations. Not easily influenced. Gentle, kind, a hard worker. Strong verbal skills. Blessed in some ways. Charming and devoted. Frequent traveler. A free spirit, very adaptable.

Carlo, 4- Happily takes care of business. Resolute and purposeful. Diligent, helpful. Strong verbal skills. Natural counselor and healer.

Carlos, 5- Quick sense of humor. Bright, adventuresome. Intense inner power. Communicates skillfully. Natural counselor and healer. Charming and devoted.

Carlotta, 9- Artistically creative. Pioneer and risk taker. Gentle, kind, a hard worker. Strong verbal skills. Natural counselor and healer. Dynamic, busy lifestyle. Sensitive and easily hurt. Bold, courageous, a bit stubborn.

Carly, 5- Quick sense of humor. Bright, adventuresome. Intense inner power. Communicates skillfully. Needs a lot of freedom.

Carma, 9- Artistically creative. Helpful, sincere. Gentle, kind, a hard worker. Systematic, organized. Pioneer and risk taker.

Carmel, 7- Sees the irony in situations. Not easily influenced. Gentle, kind, a hard worker. Systematic, organized. A free spirit, very adaptable. Strong verbal skills.

Carmela, 8- Ups and downs financially. Resolute and purposeful. Intense inner power. Systematic, organized. Physical and passionate. Strong verbal skills. Bold, courageous, a bit stubborn.

Carmelita, 10- Great verbal expressions. Independent, critical of self and others. Gentle, kind, a hard worker. Systematic, organized. A free spirit, very adaptable. Strong verbal skills. Blessed in some ways. Dynamic, busy lifestyle. Bold, courageous, a bit stubborn.

Carmen, 9- Artistically creative. Helpful, sincere. Gentle, kind, a hard worker. Systematic, organized. A free spirit, very adaptable. Romantic, opinionated.

Carmenata, 4- Happily takes care of business. Natural teaching ability. Gentle, kind, a hard worker. Systematic, organized. A free spirit, very adaptable. Original and unconventional. Bold, courageous, a bit stubborn. Dynamic, busy lifestyle. Pioneer and risk taker.

Carmine, 9- Artistically creative. Pioneer and risk taker. Gentle, kind, a hard worker. Systematic, organized. Blessed in some ways. Original and unconventional. A free spirit, very adaptable.

Carney, 30- Cheerful, lighthearted. Aims to please. Diligent, helpful. Original and unconventional. Loves adventure and excitement. Needs a lot of freedom.

Carol, 22- Inspiring and highly creative. Resolute and purposeful. Gentle, kind, a hard worker. Natural counselor and healer. Communicates skillfully.

Carola, 5- Quick sense of humor. Bright, adventuresome. Intense inner power. Natural counselor and healer. Strong verbal skills. Bold, courageous, a bit stubborn.

Carole, 9- Artistically creative. Helpful, sincere. Gentle, kind, a hard worker. Natural counselor and healer. Strong verbal skills. A free spirit, very adaptable.

Carolina, 10- Great verbal expressions. Independent, critical of self and others. Diligent, helpful. Natural counselor and healer. Strong verbal skills. Blessed in some ways. Original and unconventional. Bold, courageous, a bit stubborn.

Caroline, 5- Quick sense of humor. Bright, adventuresome. Gentle, kind, a hard worker. Natural counselor and healer. Strong verbal skills. Blessed in some ways. Original and unconventional. A free spirit, very adaptable.

Carolyn, 7- Sees the irony in situations. Not easily influenced. Diligent, helpful. An opportunist. Strong verbal skills. Needs a lot of freedom. Original and unconventional.

Caron, 6- Mellow, yet tactful. Pioneer and risk taker. Gentle, kind, a hard worker. Natural counselor and healer. Creative, opinionated.

Carrie, 9- Artistically creative. Helpful, sincere. Intense inner power. A bit of a bully. Blessed in some ways. A free spirit, very adaptable.

Carroll, 7- Sees the irony in situations. Not easily influenced. Diligent, helpful. Tendency to lose items. An opportunist. Strong verbal skills. Slow to make decisions.

Carson, 7- Sees the irony in situations. Independent, critical of self and others. Diligent, helpful. Charming and devoted. An opportunist. Original and unconventional.

Carter, 11- Inspiring and highly creative. Intuitive, perceptive. Diligent, helpful. Dynamic, busy lifestyle. A free spirit, very adaptable. Tendency to lose items.

Carver, 4- Happily takes care of business. Natural teaching ability. Gentle, kind, a hard worker. Intuitive and inspired. A free spirit, very adaptable. Tendency to lose items.

Cary, 11- Inspiring and highly creative. Intuitive, perceptive. Diligent, helpful. Needs a lot of freedom.

Caryl, 5- Quick sense of humor. Bright, adventuresome. Gentle, kind, a hard worker. Dislikes restrictions. Optimistic and outspoken.

Caryn, 7- Sees the irony in situations. Not easily influenced. Diligent, helpful. Needs a lot of freedom. Original and unconventional.

Casey, 8- Ups and downs financially. Resolute and purposeful. Charming and devoted. Physical and passionate. Needs a lot of freedom.

Cash, 4- Happily takes care of business. Natural teaching ability. Charming and devoted. Great judge of character.

Casie, 10- Great verbal expressions. Independent, critical of self and others. Charming and devoted. Blessed in some ways. A free spirit, very adaptable.

Casper, 8- Ups and downs financially. Resolute and purposeful. Charming and devoted. Intelligent and knowledgeable. A free spirit, very adaptable. Gentle, kind, a hard worker.

Cass, 6- Mellow, yet tactful. Pioneer and risk taker. Charming and devoted. Intense and extreme.

Cassandra, 8- Ups and downs financially. Resolute and purposeful. Charming and devoted. Intense and extreme. Bold, courageous, a bit stubborn. Original and unconventional. Reliable, responsible. Gentle, kind, a hard worker. Independent, critical of self and others.

Cassidy, 8- Ups and downs financially. Resolute and purposeful. Charming and devoted. Intense and extreme. Blessed in some ways. Reliable, responsible. Needs a lot of freedom.

Cassie, 11- Inspiring and highly creative. Intuitive, perceptive. Very charismatic. Intense and extreme. Blessed in some ways. A free spirit, very adaptable.

Cassius, 10- Great verbal expressions. Independent, critical of self and others. Loving and devoted. Intense and extreme. Blessed in some ways. Attractive and charming. Impulsive and extreme.

Castel, 6- Mellow, yet tactful. Pioneer and risk taker. Charming and devoted. Dynamic, busy lifestyle. A free spirit, very adaptable. Strong verbal skills.

Cat, 6- Mellow, yet tactful. Pioneer and risk taker. Dynamic, busy lifestyle.

Catherine, 11- Inspiring and highly creative. Intuitive, perceptive. Dynamic, busy lifestyle. Great judge of character. A free spirit, very adaptable. Gentle, kind, a hard worker. Blessed in some ways. Original and unconventional. Physical and passionate.

Cathleen, 5- Quick sense of humor. Bright, adventuresome. Dynamic, busy lifestyle. Great judge of character. Strong verbal skills. A free spirit, very adaptable. Physical and passionate. Creative, opinionated.

Cato, 3- Quick sense of humor. Aims to please. Dynamic, busy lifestyle. Natural counselor and healer.

Cavell, 10- Great verbal expressions. Independent, critical of self and others. Intuitive and inspired. A free spirit, very adaptable. Strong verbal skills. Frequent traveler.

Cecil, 5- Quick sense of humor. Physical and passionate. Spontaneous, lighthearted. Blessed in some ways. Ups and downs financially.

Cecile, 10- Great verbal expressions. A free spirit, very adaptable. Self-expressive, cheerful. Blessed in some ways. Strong verbal skills. Likes change and variety.

Cecilia, 6- Mellow, yet tactful. A step ahead of others. Inspiring and creative. Blessed in some ways. Strong verbal skills. Artistic, having good taste. Pioneer and risk taker.

Cecily, 30- Cheerful, lighthearted. A free spirit, very adaptable. Optimistic, outspoken. Blessed in some ways. Communicates skillfully. Needs a lot of freedom.

Cedric, 6- Mellow, yet tactful. Physical, passionate. Natural authority. Gentle, kind, a hard worker. Artistic, having good taste. Creative and inspiring.

Celeste, 6- Mellow, yet tactful. A free spirit, very adaptable. Strong verbal skills. Physical and passionate. Charming and devoted. Dynamic, busy lifestyle. Loves adventure and excitement.

Celia, 3- Cheerful, lighthearted. Likes to entertain. Slow to make decisions. Artistic, having good taste. Pioneer and risk taker.

Celina, 8- Ups and downs financially. Original and creative. Strong verbal skills. Blessed in some ways. Original and unconventional. Resolute and purposeful.

Celine, 30- Cheerful, lighthearted. Likes change and variety. Communicates skillfully. Blessed in some ways. Romantic, sensual. A free spirit, very adaptable.

Cerise, 5- Great sense of humor. Physical and passionate. Gentle, kind, a hard worker. Blessed in some ways. Charming and devoted. Tendency to overindulge.

Cesar, 10- Great verbal expressions. A free spirit, very adaptable. Charming and devoted. Independent, critical of self and others. Gentle, kind, a hard worker.

Chad, 7- Sees the irony in situations. Great judge of character. Independent, critical of self and others. Reliable, responsible.

Chambrea, 6- Mellow, yet tactful. Creative and original. Resolute and purposeful. Domestic, hard working. Friendly, but shy. Diligent, helpful. A free spirit, very adaptable. Bold, courageous, a bit stubborn.

Chance, 7- Sees the irony in situations. Great judge of character. Bold, courageous, adventuresome. Original and unconventional. Outgoing, youthful outlook. A free spirit, very adaptable.

Chancelor, 7- Sees the irony in situations. Great judge of character. Bold, courageous, adventuresome. Original and unconventional. Outgoing, youthful outlook. A free spirit, very adaptable. Strong verbal skills. Natural counselor and healer. Gentle, kind, a hard worker.

Chandler, 11- Inspiring and highly creative. Self-reliant, successful. Intuitive, perceptive. Original and unconventional. Reliable, responsible. Strong verbal skills. A free spirit, very adaptable. Intense inner power.

Chandra, 4- Happily takes care of business. Relies on own judgment. Natural teaching ability. Original and unconventional. Systematic, organized. Gentle, kind, a hard worker. Bold, courageous, a bit stubborn.

Chan-ho, 4- Happily takes care of business. Great judge of character. Natural teaching ability. Original and unconventional. Self-reliant, successful. Natural counselor and healer.

Channing, 7- Sees the irony in situations. Self-reliant, successful. Not easily influenced. Original and unconventional. Romantic, sensual. Blessed in some ways. Creative, opinionated. Scientific and philosophical.

Chaplin, 9- Artistically creative. Self-reliant, successful. Hard working, helpful. Intelligent and knowledgeable. Strong verbal skills. Blessed in some ways. Original and unconventional.

Charity, 3- Cheerful, light hearted. Relies on own judgment. Pioneer and risk taker. Gentle, kind, a hard worker. Blessed in some ways. Dynamic, busy lifestyle. Needs a lot of freedom.

Charlene, 3- Cheerful, light hearted. Relies on own judgment. Pioneer and risk taker. Gentle, kind, a hard worker. Strong verbal skills. A free spirit, very adaptable. Original and unconventional. Tendency to overindulge.

Charles, 30- Cheerful, light hearted. Self-reliant, successful. Pioneer and risk taker. Gentle, kind, a hard worker. Strong verbal skills. A free spirit, very adaptable. Charming and devoted.

Charley, 9- Artistically creative. Influential, successful. Hard working, helpful. Intense inner power. Frequent traveler. Loves adventure and excitement. Needs a lot of freedom.

Charlie, 11- Inspiring and highly creative. Self-reliant, successful. Intuitive, perceptive. Gentle, kind, a hard worker. Strong verbal skills. Blessed in some ways. A free spirit, very adaptable.

Charlize, 10- Great verbal expressions. Relies on own judgment. Independent, critical of self and others. Gentle, kind, a hard worker. Strong verbal skills. Blessed in some ways. Uses common sense. A free spirit, very adaptable.

Charlotte, 3- Cheerful, light hearted. Financial ups and downs. Pioneer and risk taker. Gentle, kind, a hard worker. Strong verbal skills. Natural counselor and healer. Dynamic, busy lifestyle. Sensitive and easily hurt. A free spirit, very adaptable.

Charlton, 10- Great verbal expressions. Sometimes a loner. Independent, critical of self and others. Gentle, kind, a hard worker. Communicates skillfully. Dynamic, busy lifestyle. Natural counselor and healer. Romantic, opinionated.

Charmaine, 9- Artistically creative. Great judge of character. Not easily influenced. Gentle, kind, a hard worker. Systematic, organized. Bold, courageous, a bit stubborn. Blessed in some ways. Original and unconventional. A free spirit, very adaptable.

Chas, 4- Happily takes care of business. Great judge of character. Independent, critical of self and others. Charming and devoted.

Chase, 9- Artistically creative. Self-reliant, successful. Hard working and helpful. Charming and devoted. A free spirit, very adaptable.

Chauncey, 8- Ups and downs financially. Appreciates quality. Resolute and purposeful. Attractive and charming. Original and unconventional. Physical and passionate. Needs a lot of freedom.

Che, 7- Sees the irony in situations. Great judge of character. A free spirit, very adaptable.

Chelsea, 8- Ups and downs financially. Appreciates quality. Physical and passionate. Communicates skillfully. Charming and devoted. Original and creative. Resolute and purposeful.

Chen, 3- Cheerful, light hearted. Financial ups and downs. Physical and passionate. Original and opinionated.

Cheol-soo, 11- Inspiring and highly creative. Great judge of character. A free spirit, very adaptable. Natural counselor and healer. Strong verbal skills. Charming and devoted. Good parental skills. Has musical talent.

Cher, 7- Sees the irony in situations. Great judge of character. A free spirit, very adaptable. Gentle, kind, a hard worker.

Cherie, 3- Cheerful, light hearted. Financial ups and downs. A free spirit, very adaptable. Gentle, kind, a hard worker. Blessed in some ways. Physical and passionate.

Cherilyn, 4- Happily takes care of business. Great judge of character. Loves adventure and excitement. Gentle, kind, a hard worker. Blessed in some ways. Strong verbal skills. Needs a lot of freedom. Original and unconventional.

Cherry, 5- Quick sense of humor. Creative and original. Physical and passionate. Gentle, kind, a hard worker. Could be forgetful. Needs a lot of freedom.

Cheryle, 4- Happily takes care of business. Great judge of character. Loves adventure and excitement. Gentle, kind, a hard worker. Needs a lot of freedom. Strong verbal skills. Physical and passionate.

Chester, 6- Mellow, yet tactful. Creative and original. A free spirit, very adaptable. Charming and devoted. Dynamic, busy lifestyle. Loves adventure and excitement. Gentle, kind, a hard worker.

Chet, 9- Artistically creative. Self-reliant, successful. A free spirit, very adaptable. Dynamic, busy lifestyle.

Chevy, 9- Artistically creative. Original, perceptive. A free spirit, very adaptable. Intuitive and inspired. Needs a lot of freedom.

Cheyenne, 7- Sees the irony in situations. Great judge of character. A free spirit, very adaptable. Needs a lot of freedom. Tendency to overindulge. Romantic and sensual. Original and unconventional. Loves adventure and excitement.

Chile, 10- Great verbal expressions. Makes and loses money easily. Artistic, having good taste. Communicates skillfully. Loves adventure and excitement.

China, 8- Ups and downs financially. Self-reliant, successful. Blessed in some ways. Original and unconventional. Resolute and purposeful.

Chiquita, 7- Sees the irony in situations. Great judge of character. Blessed in some ways. Attracts wealth. Youthful, appealing. Artistic, having good taste. Dynamic, busy lifestyle. Independent, critical of self and others.

Chloe, 7- Sees the irony in situations. Great judge of character. Strong verbal skills. Natural counselor and healer. A free spirit, very adaptable.

Chloris, 3- Cheerful, light hearted. Financial ups and downs. Frequent traveler. Parental nature. Gentle, kind, a hard worker. Blessed in some ways. Charming and devoted.

Choong-Wan, 10- Great verbal expressions. Self-reliant, successful. Natural counselor and healer. Has musical abilities. Original and unconventional. Scientific and philosophical. Likes to meet new people. Independent, critical of self and others. Romantic, sensual.

Chris, 30- Cheerful, light hearted. Financial ups and downs. Gentle, kind, a hard worker. Blessed in some ways. Charming and devoted.

Christa, 6- Mellow, yet tactful. Creative and original. Hard working and kind. Blessed in some ways. Charming and devoted. Dynamic, busy lifestyle. Pioneer and risk taker.

Christal, 9- Artistically creative. Great judge of character. Intense inner power. Forgive and be happy. Charming and devoted. Dynamic, busy lifestyle. Not easily influenced. Strong verbal skills.

Christian, 11- Inspiring and highly creative. Self-reliant, successful. Gentle, kind, a hard worker. Blessed in some ways. Charming and devoted. Dynamic, busy lifestyle. Artistic, having good taste. Independent, critical of self and others. Original and unconventional.

Christina, 11- Inspiring and highly creative. Self-reliant, successful. Gentle, kind, a hard worker. Blessed in some ways. Charming and devoted. Dynamic, busy lifestyle. Artistic, having good taste. Original and unconventional. Resolute and purposeful.

Christine, 6- Mellow, yet tactful. Creative and original. Gentle, kind, a hard worker. Blessed in some ways. Charming and devoted. Dynamic, busy lifestyle. Artistic, having good taste. Romantic, sensual. A step ahead of others.

Chrissy, 11- Inspiring and highly creative. Self-reliant, successful. Gentle, kind, a hard worker. Blessed in some ways. Charming and devoted. Impulsive and extreme. Needs a lot of freedom.

Christopher, 4- Happily takes care of business. Great judge of character. Gentle, kind, a hard worker. Blessed in some ways. Charming and devoted. Dynamic, busy lifestyle. Natural counselor and healer. Intelligent and knowledgeable. Self-reliant, successful. A free spirit, very adaptable. Intense inner power

Chuck, 10- Great verbal expressions. Self-reliant, successful. Attractive and charming. Self-expressive, cheerful. Strong desire to succeed.

Chuy, 3- Cheerful, light hearted. Creative and original. Attractive and charming. Needs a lot of freedom.

Cicero, 8- Ups and downs financially. Blessed in some ways. Optimistic, outspoken. Physical and passionate. Intense inner power. Natural counselor and healer.

Cicily, 7- Sees the irony in situations. Blessed in some ways. Spontaneous, cheerful. Artistic, having good taste. Slow to make decisions. Needs a lot of freedom.

Cindy, 10- Great verbal expressions. Blessed in some ways. Original and unconventional. Reliable, responsible. Needs a lot of freedom.

Claire, 30- Cheerful, light hearted. Communicates skillfully. Independent, critical of self and others. Blessed in some ways. Gentle, kind, a hard worker. A free spirit, very adaptable.

Clara, 8- Ups and downs financially. Recuperates quickly. Not easily influenced. Intense inner power. Bold, courageous, a bit stubborn.

Clare, 3- Cheerful, light hearted. Communicates skillfully. Independent, critical of self and others. Gentle, kind, a hard worker. A free spirit, very adaptable.

Clarence, 7- Sees the irony in situations. Strong verbal skills. Independent, critical of self and others. Gentle, kind, a hard worker. A free spirit, very adaptable. Original and unconventional. Optimistic and outspoken. Tendency to overindulge.

Clareta, 6- Mellow, yet tactful. Frequent traveler. Pioneer and risk taker. Diligent, helpful. A free spirit, very adaptable. Dynamic, very busy lifestyle. Bold, courageous, a bit stubborn.

Clarice, 6- Mellow, yet tactful. Frequent traveler. Pioneer and risk taker. Diligent, helpful. Blessed in some ways. Inspiring and creative. A step ahead of others.

Clarissa, 10- Great verbal expressions. Strong verbal skills. Independent, critical of self and others. Gentle, kind, a hard worker. Blessed in some ways. Charming and devoted. Impulsive and extreme. Bold, courageous, a bit stubborn.

Clark, 9- Artistically creative. Frequent traveler. Pioneer and risk taker. Gentle, kind, a hard worker. Strong desire to succeed.

Claud, 5- Quick sense of humor. Moves and travels often. Bold, courageous, a bit stubborn. Attractive and charming. Reliable and responsible.

Claude, 10- Great verbal expressions. Strong verbal skills. Independent, critical of self and others. Attractive and charming. Reliable, responsible. A free spirit, very adaptable.

Claudell, 7- Sees the irony in situations. Strong verbal skills. Not easily influenced. Attractive and charming. Reliable, responsible. A free spirit, very adaptable. Frequent traveler. Slow to make decisions.

Claudia, 6- Mellow, yet tactful. Frequent traveler. Independent, critical of self and others. Attractive and charming. Reliable, responsible. Blessed in some ways. Bold, courageous, a bit stubborn.

Clay, 5- Quick sense of humor. Moves and travels often. Independent, critical of self and others. Needs a lot of freedom.

Clayton, 9- Artistically creative. Strong verbal skills. Pioneer and risk taker. Needs a lot of freedom. Dynamic, busy lifestyle. Natural counselor and healer. Original and unconventional.

Clem, 6- Mellow, yet tactful. Frequent traveler. A free spirit, very adaptable. Domestic, hard working.

Clement, 9- Artistically creative. Strong verbal skills. A free spirit, very adaptable. Domestic, hard working. Loves adventure and excitement. Original and unconventional. Dynamic, a busy lifestyle.

Clementine, 10- Great verbal expressions. Frequent traveler. A free spirit, very adaptable. Domestic, hard working. Loves adventure and excitement. Original and unconventional. Dynamic, a busy lifestyle. Blessed in some ways. Romantic, sensual. Tendency to overindulge.

Cleo, 8- Ups and downs financially. Appreciates quality. Physical and passionate. Natural counselor and healer.

Cleopatra, 10- Great verbal expressions. Optimistic, outspoken. A free spirit, very adaptable. Natural counselor and healer. Intelligent and knowledgeable. Independent, critical of self and others. Dynamic, busy lifestyle. Gentle, kind, a hard worker. Bold, courageous, a bit stubborn.

Cliff, 9- Artistically creative. Strong verbal skills. Blessed in some ways. Self-sacrificing, loving. Easy going nature.

Clifford, 10- Great verbal expressions. Optimistic, outspoken. Blessed in some ways. Self-sacrificing, loving. Very considerate. Natural counselor and healer. Gentle, kind, a hard worker. Reliable, responsible.

Clifton, 7- Sees the irony in situations. Strong verbal skills. Blessed in some ways. Self-sacrificing, loving. Dynamic, busy lifestyle. Natural counselor and healer. Original and unconventional.

Clint, 22- Inspiring and highly creative. Travels frequently. Blessed in some ways. Romantic and opinionated. Dynamic, busy lifestyle.

Clinton, 6- Mellow, yet tactful. Optimistic and outspoken. Artistic, having good taste. Original and unconventional. Dynamic, busy lifestyle. Natural counselor and healer. Romantic and sensual.

Clive, 6- Mellow, yet tactful. Optimistic and outspoken. Artistic, having good taste. Intuitive and inspired. A free spirit, very adaptable.

Clovis, 8- Ups and downs financially. Recuperates quickly. Natural counselor and healer. Intuitive and inspired. Blessed in some ways. Charming and devoted.

Clyde, 22- Inspiring and highly creative. Strong verbal skills. Needs a lot of freedom. Reliable, responsible. Loves adventure and excitement.

Coby, 9- Artistically creative. Creates group harmony. Affectionate, social. Needs a lot of freedom.

Cody, 20- Has a sociable demeanor. Respects rules. Reliable and responsible. Needs a lot of freedom.

Colan, 9- Artistically creative. Creates group harmony. Strong verbal skills. Independent, critical of self and others. Original and unconventional.

Colbert, 30- Cheerful, light hearted. Natural counselor and healer. Communicates skillfully. Friendly, but shy. A free spirit, very adaptable. Gentle, kind a hard worker. Dynamic, busy lifestyle.

Colby, 3- Cheerful, light hearted. Natural counselor and healer. Communicates skillfully. Affectionate, social. Needs a lot of freedom.

Cole, 7- Sees the irony in situations. Open to opportunities. Strong verbal skills. A free spirit, very adaptable.

Colette, 7- Sees the irony in situations. Open to opportunities. Strong verbal skills. A free spirit, very adaptable. Dynamic, busy lifestyle. A force of nature. Tendency to overindulge.

Colin, 8- Ups and downs financially. Competitive in business. Communicates skillfully. Blessed in some ways. Original and unconventional.

Colleen, 30- Cheerful, light hearted. Natural counselor and healer. Optimistic, outspoken. Frequent traveler. A free spirit, very adaptable. Tendency to overindulge. Romantic and sensual.

Collier, 11- Inspiring and highly creative. Open to opportunities. Strong verbal skills. Frequent traveler. Considerate, understanding. Likes to entertain. Gentle, kind, a hard worker.

Conan, 20- Has a sociable demeanor. Natural counselor and healer. Creative and opinionated. Perceptive, reads people easily. Romantic and sensual.

Concepcion, 7- Sees the irony in situations. Open to opportunities. Original and unconventional. Optimistic, outspoken. A free spirit, very adaptable. Intelligent and knowledgeable. Outgoing, youthful outlook. Blessed in some ways. Natural counselor and healer. Romantic and sensual.

Conception, 6- Mellow, yet tactful. Natural counselor and healer. Original and unconventional. Inspiring and creative. A free spirit, very adaptable. Intelligent and knowledgeable. Dynamic, busy lifestyle. Blessed in some ways. May have musical abilities. Romantic and sensual.

Condoleezza, 9- Artistically creative. Creates group harmony. Original and romantic. Reliable, responsible. Nurturing, loving. Strong verbal skills. A free spirit, very adaptable. Loves adventure and excitement. Uses common sense. Is a great mediator. Resolute and purposeful.

Condolisa, 11- Inspiring and highly creative. Open to opportunities. Original and unconventional. Reliable, responsible. Nurturing, loving. Strong verbal skills. Blessed in some ways. Charming and devoted. Resolute and purposeful.

Conner, 6- Mellow, yet tactful. Natural counselor and healer. Original and unconventional. Creative, opinionated. A free spirit, very adaptable. Gentle, kind, a hard worker.

Connie, 6- Mellow, yet tactful. Natural counselor and healer. Original and unconventional. Creative, opinionated. Blessed in some ways. A free spirit, very adaptable.

Connor, 7- Sees the irony in situations. Open to opportunities. Original and unconventional. Romantic and sensual. May have musical abilities. Gentle, kind, a hard worker.

Conrad, 10- Great verbal expressions. Self-sacrificing, devoted. Romantic, opinionated. Intense inner power. Independent, critical of self and others. Reliable and responsible.

Conroy, 9- Artistically creative. Creates group harmony. Original and unconventional. Gentle, kind, a hard worker. Respects rules. Needs a lot of freedom.

Constance, 4- Happily takes care of business. Respects rules. Original and unconventional. Charming and devoted. Dynamic, busy lifestyle. Independent, critical of self and others. Romantic and sensual. Inspiring and very creative. A free spirit, very adaptable.

Consuelo, 5- Quick sense of humor. Natural counselor and healer. Romantic, opinionated. Charming and devoted. Creative, intuitive. A free spirit, very adaptable. Strong verbal skills. May have musical abilities.

Conway, 9- Artistically creative. Creates group harmony. Original and unconventional. Likes to meet new people. Pioneer and risk taker. Needs a lot of freedom.

Cooper, 9- Artistically creative. Creates group harmony. Nurturing, loving. Intelligent, knowledgeable. A free spirit, very adaptable. Gentle, kind, a hard worker.

Cora, 10- Great verbal expressions. Self-sacrificing, devoted. Gentle, kind, a hard worker. Independent, critical of self and others.

Coral, 22- Inspiring and highly creative. Natural counselor and healer. Gentle, kind, a hard worker. Resolute and purposeful. Strong verbal skills.

Corbin, 7- Sees the irony in situations. Open to opportunities. Gentle, kind, a hard worker. Friendly, loyal. Artistic, having good taste. Original and unconventional.

Coretta, 10- Great verbal expressions. Self-sacrificing, devoted. Intense inner power. Loves adventure and excitement. Dynamic, busy lifestyle. Needs to slow down. Bold, courageous, a bit stubborn.

Corey, 30- Cheerful, light hearted. Natural counselor and healer. Intense inner power. A free spirit, very adaptable. Dislikes limitations.

Corinne, 6- Mellow, yet tactful. Natural counselor and healer. Diligent, helpful. Considerate, understanding. Original and unconventional. Romantic, sensual. Likes to entertain.

Corliss, 5- Quick sense of humor. Enjoys working. Intense inner power. Strong verbal skills. Artistic, having good taste. Charming and devoted. Intense and Extreme.

Cornel, 4- Happily takes care of business. Respects rules. Gentle, kind, a hard worker. Original and unconventional. A free spirit, very adaptable. Strong verbal skills.

Cornelia, 5- Quick sense of humor. Natural counselor and healer. Gentle, kind, a hard worker. Original and unconventional. Physical and passionate. Strong verbal skills. Blessed in some ways. Independent, critical of self and others.

Cornelius, 8- Ups and downs financially. Competitive in business. Intense inner power. Creative, opinionated. Physical, passionate. Optimistic, outspoken. Artistic, having good taste. Attractive and charming. Many mood swings.

Courtney, 4- Happily takes care of business. Respects rules. Attractive and charming. Gentle, kind, a hard worker. Dynamic, busy lifestyle. Original, unconventional. Loves adventure and excitement. Needs a lot of freedom.

Cory, 7- Sees the irony in situations. Open to opportunities. Gentle, kind, a hard worker. Needs a lot of freedom.

Craig, 11- Inspiring and highly creative. Intense inner power. Not easily influenced. Blessed in some ways. Scientific and philosophical.

Cris, 22- Inspiring and highly creative. Gentle, kind, a hard worker. Blessed in some ways. Charming and devoted.

Cristo, 30-Cheerful, light hearted. Gentle, kind, a hard worker. Blessed in some ways. Charming and devoted. Dynamic, busy lifestyle. Natural counselor and healer.

Crystal, 8- Ups and downs financially. Intense inner power. Needs a lot of freedom. Charming and devoted. Dynamic, busy lifestyle. Resolute and purposeful. Strong verbal skills.

Cullen, 22- Inspiring and highly creative. Attractive and charming. Strong verbal skills. Frequent traveler. Likes to entertain. Romantic, sensual.

Culver, 9- Artistically creative. Attractive and charming. Strong verbal skills. Intuitive and inspired. A free spirit, very adaptable. Gentle, kind, hard worker.

Curt, 8- Ups and downs financially. Attractive and charming. Intense inner power. Dynamic, busy lifestyle.

Curtis, 9- Artistically creative. Attractive and charming. Gentle, kind, a hard worker. Dynamic, busy lifestyle. Blessed in some ways. Many mood swings.

Cyndi, 10- (Same as Cindy)

Cynthia, 8- Ups and downs financially. Dislikes limitations. Romantic, sensual. Dynamic, busy lifestyle. Self-reliant, successful. Artistic, having good taste. Resolute and purposeful.

Cyrena, 30- Cheerful, light hearted. Needs a lot of freedom. Gentle, kind, a hard worker. Tendency to overindulge. Romantic, sensual. Pioneer and risk taker.

Cyril, 4- Happily takes care of business. Needs a lot of freedom. Gentle, kind, a hard worker. Blessed in some ways. Strong verbal skills.

Cyrilla, 8- Ups and downs financially. Dislikes limitations. Intense inner power. Blessed in some ways. Strong verbal skills. Frequent traveler. Independent, critical of self and others.

Cyrinda, 11- Inspiring and highly creative. Stylish and refined. Gentle, kind, a hard worker. Artistic, having good taste. Original and unconventional. Reliable, responsible. Resolute and purposeful.

Cyrus, 5- Quick sense of humor. Needs a lot of freedom. Gentle, kind, a hard worker. Attractive and charming. Impulsive and extreme.

> "Here, here, what's all this jabber-wapping when there's work to be done? I know three shiftless farm hands that'll be out of a job before they know it!"
> ~Excerpted from "The Wizard of Oz"
> Used with permission

D

IF A NAME BEGINS with D, has more than one D, or ends with a D, this person is down-to-earth, systematic, practical and organized.

If you want to get something done, give it to a "D" person. They're very responsible and efficient about everything they do. Even when they are planning a fun trip, they seem so business-like, it's difficult to imagine them actually having fun. The fun part of a trip for a D person might very well be in the planning and taking care of all the last minute details and obligations. It's not that they are "stick-in-the-muds" it's just that they enjoy being efficient; it's their nature, that's all.

D's are almost as hard driven as A's. They're more domesticated, as the D is the fourth letter in the alphabet; ruled by the number 4. The number 4 vibration rules work and family. So consequently the D person is all about work and family. Hard work is complementary to their nature. The typical D ruled person is fine with the chores the rest of us find difficult. They don't mind weeding the garden, cleaning out the storage, paying the bills, and cooking dinner. Most consider themselves lucky to be married to a D named person for this reason. The letters D, M and V are all ruled by the number 4. Anyone with the letters D, M or V anywhere in their name will be task oriented, down-to-earth, systematic and practical.

In astrology we like to see a little earth in a chart to help ground a person so the person actually gets something done during their short time on earth. This is also true of a name. One 4 ruled letter could give a name just enough ability to get something accomplished during their lifetime. D's are earthy, goal oriented, shrewd and similar to Capricorns, yet they are as domesticated and security oriented as Cancer the crab.

A person with the name of "David" would have three 4-ruled letters in his name. Not only would he have a 4 intensity number, but also a 4 power number. It is possible to have too much of a good thing with this much 4 in a name. The numbers 4 and 8 are karmic. These numbers attract hard lessons in life to the ones who have them in their names. A little 7 year old girl, Danielle Van Dam disappeared on 2/2/2002. If we add up the date she disappeared it adds up to 8, a karmic number. Her name has four "4" ruled letters. Her mother, Brenda Van Dam also has four "4" ruled letters, Danielle's father, Damon Van Dam has five "4" ruled letters. And last but not least, David Westerfield, the man who was convicted of the crime with DNA evidence also has four "4" ruled letters in his first name. Danielle's 2 brothers' names also started with "D." They thought they would find Danielle's body in the desert, but found her on Dehesa Rd. And let's not forget the bar that got so much publicity during the trial, "Dad's." Too many D names added up to disaster and death. Although Danielle's parents won the case, no one mentioned above really won. They all lost, didn't they? The lessons brought about by karmic numbers can be harsh and brutal.

Look at the name Saddam Hussein. This terrorist leader has all 1's and 4's in his first name. How harsh is that? Almost as harsh as Adolf Hitler; the A and D in the front of his name was enough to earn this man a reputation for harsh and cruel behavior.

Before deciding to change little David's name to Barney, consider the fact that no matter how many harsh letters in a name, heredity and upbringing can have an overwhelming affect on a person's potential. The 4 ruled, similar to the 1 ruled, have a bully in their head driving them to do their best. They make wonderful teachers, accountants, lawyers, government officials, and managers. Most D's are workaholics, driven by contempt for anyone who is lazy, phony or unpredictable. They aren't as easily put off as some of the other letters. This 4 ruled letter has follow-through ability. Next time when going to an award ceremony, observe how many people win awards that have the letters D or M or V in their name. Almost every award winner does, or they have a 4 power number.

The D in Arnold Schwarzenegger's name was enough to make him play the role of terminator well. If a D appears anywhere in a name it gives the person the ability to systematically size up any situation. It's sort of a human computer effect. D names can enter a room, look around, assess and know what's right or wrong about it. If Arnold does well as governor of California, it's because of the D in his name. D is also for determination.

Another interesting observation about D's and other 4-ruled letters is the skin color of the person with this influence. It seems even a hidden 4 can denote a darker skin coloring. The name Jose adds up to a 4 power number, and most Jose's are dark skinned. The more 4-ruled letters or number 4 influence in a name, the darker the skin, in most cases. Even hidden 4's can explain why a person has dark skin.

A softer D type would be the late Princess Di. She suffered some of the problems of the number 4 vibration such as depression and hardships in her marriage. The I in her name made her a humanitarian. People looked up to her, right or wrong. She was blessed, but the I made her not happy unless able to forgive others for wrong doings toward her. Her power number added up to the unlucky 13 which condensed down to a 4. She was a natural teacher and taught the world a thing or two about compassion. She was down to earth, yet elegant, a combination only Princess Di could pull off.

Anyone married to a D that likes having a roof over their head and the bills paid on time can sleep well. The D person is one of the most shrewd and determined letters in the alphabet. Those married to a D are in for a special bonus. Cheating goes against their grain, if they are a typical D person. It's not that they aren't capable of cheating on their partner, it's that after they have invested time and money into their relationship, why chance it? Gamblers they're not. We won't find many D types throwing money away in the casinos either. And we won't find many D types throwing away a relationship they have invested in. It just isn't practical; it's non productive and wasteful.

Some other famous D names are: Daryl Hannah, David Letterman, Dean Martin, David Carradine, Dan Akroyd, Donald Trump, Davie Crockett, Debbie Reynolds, Dan Rather, Duke Cunningham, Dionne Warwick, Diana Ross, Dennis Quaid, Dave Mathews, Demi Moore, Dennis Hopper, Dustin Hoffman, Donny Osmond, Dana Carvey, Della Reese, Dom Deluise, Donald Sutherland, Don Henley and Dolly Parton.

Quick Reference of "D" Names

Dacha, 8- Reliable, responsible. Not easily influenced. Optimistic, outspoken. Great judge of character. Bold, courageous, a bit stubborn.

Daffodil, 3- Serious, yet fun-loving. Aims to please. Self-sacrificing, loving. High moral standards. Natural counselor and healer. Down-to-earth, faithful. Blessed in some ways. Strong verbal skills.

Daffi, 8- Reliable, responsible. Resolute and purposeful. Self-sacrificing, loving. High moral standards. Artistic, having good taste.

Daffy, 6- Creative problem solver. Pioneer and risk taker. Self-sacrificing, loving. Service oriented. Needs a lot of freedom.

Daghlawi, 11- Workaholic, determined. Intuitive, perceptive. Scientific and philosophical. Self-reliant, successful. Strong verbal skills. Bold, courageous, a bit stubborn. Likes to meet new people. Blessed in some ways.

Dagmar, 8- Reliable, responsible. Resolute and purposeful. Scientific and philosophical. Domestic, hard working. Resolute and purposeful. Intense inner power.

Dahlia, 8- Reliable, responsible. Resolute and purposeful. Self-reliant, successful. Strong verbal skills. Artistic, having good taste. Bold, courageous, a bit stubborn.

Daisie, 11- Workaholic, determined. Intuitive, perceptive. Artistic, having good taste. Charming and devoted. Blessed in some ways. Likes to entertain.

Daisy, 22- Workaholic, determined. Ambitious leader, great vision. Artistic, having good taste. Charming and devoted. Dislikes limitations.

Dakota, 7- Systematic, organized. Not easily influenced. Strong desire to succeed. Natural counselor and healer. Dynamic, busy lifestyle. Bold, courageous, a bit stubborn.

Dale, 4- Down-to-earth, faithful. Natural teaching ability. Strong verbal skills. A free spirit, very adaptable.

Daleen, 5- Enjoys working. Bright, adventuresome. Communicates skillfully. A free spirit, very adaptable. Tendency to overindulge. Romantic, sensual.

Dalin, 22- Workaholic, determined. Ambitious leader, great vision. Frequent traveler. Blessed in some ways. Creative, opinionated.

Dallan, 8- Reliable, responsible. Resolute and purposeful. Strong verbal skills. Ups and downs financially. Self-motivated, determined. Romantic, sensual.

Dallas, 4- Down-to-earth, faithful. Natural teaching ability. Strong verbal skills. Frequent traveler. Bold, courageous, a bit stubborn. Charming and devoted.

Dalton, 3- Serious, yet fun-loving. Aims to please. Communicates skillfully. Dynamic, busy lifestyle. Natural counselor and healer. Romantic, sensual.

Damian, 6- Creative problem solver. Pioneer and risk taker. Systematic, organized. Artistic, having good taste. Pioneer and risk taker. Original and unconventional.

Damien, 10- Natural authority. Independent, critical of self and others. Domestic, hard working. Blessed in some ways. A free spirit, very adaptable. Creative, opinionated.

Damon, 20- Practical, conservative. Reads people easily. Desires financial security. Natural counselor and healer. Romantic, sensual.

Dan, 10- Natural authority. Independent, critical of self and others. Creative, opinionated.

Dana, 11- Workaholic, determined. Intuitive, perceptive. Romantic, sensual Bold, courageous, a bit stubborn.

Daniel, 9- Trustworthy, dependable. Helpful, sincere. Original and unconventional. Blessed in some ways. A free spirit, very adaptable. Communicates skillfully.

Daniela, 10- Natural authority. Independent, critical of self and others. Original and unconventional. Blessed in some ways. Loves adventure and excitement. Frequent traveler. Bold, courageous, a bit stubborn.

Danielle, 8- Reliable, responsible. Resolute and purposeful. Creative, opinionated. Artistic, having good taste. A free spirit, very adaptable. Strong verbal skills. Frequent traveler. Physical and passionate.

Danilo, 10- Natural authority. Independent, critical of self and others. Original and unconventional. Blessed in some ways. Strong verbal skills. Natural counselor and healer.

Danita, 22- Workaholic, determined. Ambitious leader, great vision. Romantic, opinionated. Blessed in some ways. Dynamic, busy lifestyle. Resolute and purposeful

D'Anna, 7- Systematic, organized. Not easily influenced. Original and unconventional. Romantic, sensual. Bold, courageous, a bit stubborn.

Dannen, 7- Systematic, organized. Not easily influenced. Original and unconventional. Romantic, sensual. Tendency to overindulge. Creative, opinionated.

Danny, 22- Workaholic, determined. Ambitious leader, great vision. Original and unconventional. Creative, opinionated. Needs a lot of freedom.

Dante, 8- Reliable, responsible. Resolute and purposeful. Original and unconventional. Dynamic, very busy lifestyle. Physical and passionate.

Daphne, 30- Serious, yet fun-loving. Aims to please. Intelligent and knowledgeable. Great judge of character. Romantic and sensual. A free spirit, very adaptable.

Dar, 5- Enjoys working. Bright, adventuresome. Gentle, kind, a hard worker.

Dara, 6- Creative problem solver. Pioneer and risk taker. Compassionate, understanding. Natural authority.

Darby, 5- Enjoys working. Bright, adventuresome. Intense inner power. Affectionate, social. Needs a lot of freedom.

Darcie, 4- Down-to-earth, faithful. Natural teaching ability. Gentle, kind, a hard worker. Self-expressive, cheerful. Blessed in some ways. A free spirit, very adaptable.

Darcy, 6- Creative problem solver. Pioneer and risk taker. Compassionate, understanding. Optimistic, cheerful. Needs a lot of freedom.

Darei, 10- Natural authority. Independent, critical of self and others. Gentle, kind, a hard worker. A free spirit, very adaptable. Blessed in some ways.

Daria, 6- Creative problem solver. Pioneer and risk taker. Compassionate, understanding. Artistic, having good taste. Self-motivated, determined.

Dariel, 4- Down-to-earth, faithful. Natural teaching ability. Compassionate, understanding. Blessed in some ways. A free spirit, very adaptable. Communicates skillfully.

Darius, 9- Trustworthy, dependable. Helpful, sincere. Intense inner power. Blessed in some ways. Attractive and charming. Loving and devoted.

Darleen, 5- Enjoys working. Bright, adventuresome. Gentle, kind, a hard worker. Great verbal skills. A free spirit, very adaptable. Tendency to overindulge. Romantic, sensual.

Darlene, 5- (Same as Darleen)

Darlin, 4- Down-to-earth, faithful. Natural teaching ability. Gentle, kind, a hard worker. Strong verbal skills. Blessed in some ways. Romantic, sensual.

Darrah, 5- Enjoys working. Bright, adventuresome. Gentle, kind, a hard worker. Tendency to lose items. Pioneer and risk taker. Self-reliant, successful.

Darrel, 4- Down-to-earth, faithful. Natural teaching ability. Gentle, kind, a hard worker. Tendency to lose items. A free spirit, very adaptable. Strong verbal skills.

Darrell, 7- Systematic, organized. Not easily influenced. Intense inner power. Tendency to lose items. A free spirit, very adaptable. Strong verbal skills. Frequent traveler.

Darren, 6- Creative problem solver. Pioneer and risk taker. Gentle, kind, a hard worker. Could be forgetful. A free spirit, very adaptable. Original, unconventional.

Daryl, 6- Creative-problem solver. Pioneer and risk taker. Gentle, kind, a hard worker. Needs a lot of freedom. Strong verbal skills.

DaShaun, 5- Enjoys working. Bright, adventuresome. Charming and devoted. Self-reliant, successful. Bold, courageous, a bit stubborn. Very lucky. Physical and passionate.

Dave, 5- Enjoys working. Bright, adventuresome. Intuitive and inspired. Physical and passionate.

David, 22- Work-a-holic, determined. Ambitious leader, great vision. Intuitive and inspired. Artistic, having good taste. Down-to-earth, faithful.

Davie, 5- Enjoys working. Bright, adventuresome. Intuitive and inspired. Artistic, having good taste. Physical and passionate.

Davy, 7- Systematic, organized. Not easily influenced. Intuitive and inspired. Needs a lot of freedom.

Dawn, 6- Creative-problem solver. Pioneer and risk taker. Likes to meet new people. Original and unconventional.

Dean, 6- Creative-problem solver. A step ahead of others. Pioneer and risk taker. Romantic, opinionated.

Deane, 20- Practical, conservative. Social and entertaining. Resolute and purposeful. Romantic, sensual. A free spirit, very adaptable.

Deandra, 11- Workaholic, determined. Physical and passionate. Intuitive, perceptive. Creative, opinionated. Down-to-earth, faithful. Gentle, kind, a hard worker. Bold, courageous, a bit stubborn.

Deanna, 3- Serious, yet fun-loving. A free spirit, very adaptable. Self-motivated, independent. Original and unconventional. Romantic, sensual. Pioneer and risk taker.

Deb, 11- Workaholic, determined. Intuitive, perceptive. Affectionate, social.

Debbie, 9- Trustworthy, dependable. Enjoys giving gifts. Loyal, understanding. Emotional, sensitive. Blessed in some ways. Physical and passionate.

Debby, 20- Practical, conservative. Likes to entertain. Affectionate, social. Emotional, sensitive. Needs a lot of freedom.

Debora, 9- Trustworthy, dependable. Enjoys giving gifts. Loyal, understanding. Natural counselor and healer. Gentle, kind, a hard worker. Helpful, sincere.

Deborah, 8- Reliable, responsible. Original and creative. Friendly, but shy. Natural counselor and healer. Intense inner power. Bold, courageous, a bit stubborn. Great judge of character.

Debra, 3- Serious, yet fun-loving. A free spirit, very adaptable. Social, affectionate. Gentle, kind, a hard worker. Creative, aims to please.

Dede, 9- Trustworthy, dependable. Enjoys giving gifts. Domestic, responsible. Physical, passionate.

Dejuan, 10- Natural authority. Likes change and variety. Clever and talented. Attractive and charming. Self-motivated, purposeful. Romantic, sensual.

Dee, 5- Enjoys working. Physical and passionate. Perceptive, socially adept.

Deedee, 10- Natural authority. Likes change and variety. Perceptive, socially adept. Down-to-earth, practical. Likes to entertain. Physical and passionate.

Deidre, 9- Trustworthy, dependable. Enjoys giving gifts. Artistic, having good taste. Workaholic, shrewd, determined. Tendency to lose things. Physical, passionate.

Delano, 6- Creative-problem solver. A step ahead of others. Strong verbal skills. Pioneer and risk taker. Original and unconventional. Natural counselor and healer.

Delia, 22- Workaholic, determined. Has big plans and ideas. Frequent traveler. Blessed in some ways. Independent, self-motivated.

Delight, 11- Workaholic, determined. Keenly perceptive. Strong verbal skills. Artistic, having good taste. Willpower and determination. Great judge of character. Dynamic, busy lifestyle.

Delilah, 6- Creative problem solver. A step ahead of others. Financial ups and downs. Blessed in some ways. Frequent traveler. Pioneer and risk taker. Great judge of character.

Della, 7- Systematic, organized. Not easily fooled. Strong verbal skills. Frequent traveler. Resolute and purposeful.

Deloris, 10- Natural authority. Likes change and variety. Strong verbal skills. Natural counselor and healer. Gentle, kind, a hard worker. Blessed in some ways. Charming and devoted.

Delphine, 10- Natural authority. Likes change and variety. Frequent traveler. Intelligent and knowledgeable. Self-reliant, successful. Blessed in some ways. Romantic, sensual. Loves adventure and excitement.

Delta, 6- Creative-problem solver. A step ahead of others. Strong verbal skills. Dynamic, busy lifestyle. Pioneer and risk taker.

Demetra, 30- Serious, yet fun-loving. A free spirit, very adaptable. Domestic, hard working. Likes to entertain. Dynamic, busy lifestyle. Tendency to lose things. Independent, self-motivated.

Demetria, 3- Serious, yet fun-loving. A free spirit, very adaptable. Domestic, hard working. Likes to entertain. Dynamic, busy lifestyle. Tendency to lose things. Blessed in some ways. Independent, self-motivated.

Demetrius, 6- Creative-problem solver. A step ahead of others. Tolerant, endures hardships. Adaptable to change. Dynamic, busy lifestyle. Diligent, helpful. Considerate, understanding. Youthful, appealing. Charming and devoted.

Demi, 22- Workaholic, determined. A free spirit, very adaptable. Energetic, hard working. Blessed in some ways.

Demitra, 7- Systematic, organized. Not fooled easily. Domestic, hard working. Artistic, having good taste. Dynamic, busy lifestyle. Self-sacrificing, helpful. Independent, critical of self and others.

Demmie, 4- Down-to-earth, faithful. A free spirit, very adaptable. Energetic, hard working. Tolerant, endures hardships. Blessed in some ways. Physical and passionate.

Dena, 6- Creative problem solver. A step ahead of others. Romantic, sensual, perceptive. Independent, ambitious.

Denise, 11- Workaholic, determined. Physical and passionate. Opinionated, original. Blessed in some ways. Charming and devoted. Learns through experiences.

Deniz, 4- Down-to-earth, faithful. Accesses quickly. Romantic, sensual. Blessed in some ways. Uses common sense.

Dennis, 11- Workaholic, determined. Intuitive, perceptive. Original and unconventional. Romantic and sensual. Blessed in some ways. Charming and devoted.

Denny, 8- Reliable, responsible. Original and creative. Romantic, sensual. Unconventional, opinionated. Needs a lot of freedom.

Denton, 9- Trustworthy, dependable. Enjoys giving gifts. Creative, opinionated. Dynamic, very busy lifestyle. Natural counselor and healer. Romantic and sensual.

Denver, 5- Enjoys working. Physical and passionate. Original and opinionated. Intuitive and inspired. A free spirit, very adaptable. Gentle, kind, a hard worker.

Denys, 22- Workaholic, determined. Has big plans and ideas. Opinionated and unconventional. Needs a lot of freedom. Charming and devoted.

Denzel, 30- Serious, yet fun-loving. A free spirit, very adaptable. Romantic, sensual. Uses common sense. Likes change and variety. Communicates skillfully.

Derek, 7- Systematic, organized. Not easily fooled. Gentle, kind, a hard worker. Likes change and variety. Strong desire to succeed.

Dermot, 30- Serious, yet fun-loving. A free spirit, very adaptable. Intense inner power. Domestic, hard working. Natural counselor and healer. Dynamic, busy lifestyle.

Derrick, 5- Enjoys working. Physical and passionate. Gentle, kind, a hard worker. Intense inner power. Artistic, having good taste. Self-expressive, cheerful. Strong desire to succeed.

Derwin, 10- Natural authority. Likes change and variety. Diligent, helpful. Likes to meet new people. Humanitarian, emotional. Original and unconventional.

Desiree, 11- Workaholic, determined. Intuitive, perceptive. Charming and devoted. Artistic, having good taste. Intense inner power. Physical and passionate. Loves adventure and excitement.

Desi, 10- Natural authority. Likes change and variety. Charming and devoted. Blessed in some ways.

Desma, 6- Creative problem solver. A step ahead of others. Devoted, loving. Domestic, hard working. Independent, ambitious.

Desmond, 11- Workaholic, determined. Intuitive, perceptive. Charming and devoted. Domestic, hard working. Natural counselor and healer. Creative, opinionated. Down-to-earth, faithful.

Destiny, 6- Creative problem solver. A step ahead of others. Passionate, loving. Dynamic, busy lifestyle. Artistic, having good taste. Original, opinionated. Needs a lot of freedom.

Deva, 5- Enjoys working. Physical and passionate. Intuitive and inspired. Independent, pioneer and risk taker.

Devin, 9- Trustworthy, dependable. Enjoys giving gifts. Strong imagination. Blessed in some ways. Original and unconventional.

Devon, 6- Creative problem solver. A step ahead of others. Intuitive and inspired. Natural counselor and healer. Unconventional, opinionated.

Devona, 7- Systematic, organized. Not easily fooled. Strong imagination. Creates group harmony. Original and unconventional. Not easily fooled.

Dewey, 8- Reliable, responsible. Original and creative. Likes to meet new people. Physical and passionate. Needs a lot of freedom.

Dexter, 4- Down-to-earth, faithful. A free spirit, very adaptable. Artistic, sensual, perceptive. Dynamic, busy lifestyle. Loves adventure and excitement. Gentle, kind, a hard worker.

Dextra, 9- Trustworthy, dependable. Adaptable to change. Artistic, sensual, perceptive. Dynamic, busy lifestyle. Intense inner power. Pioneer and risk taker.

Di, 4- Down-to-earth, faithful. Teaches kindness. Desires financial security.

Diana, 20- Practical, conservative. Emotional, considerate. Reads people easily. Original and creative. Bold, courageous, a bit stubborn.

Diane, 6- Creative problem solver. Artistic, having good taste. Resolute and purposeful. Original and opinionated. A free spirit, very adaptable.

Dick, 9- Trustworthy, dependable. Idealistic and humanitarian. Self-expressive, cheerful. Strong desire to succeed.

Didi, 8- Reliable, responsible. Blessed in some ways. Down-to-earth, faithful. Artistic, having good taste.

Diego, 4- Down-to-earth, faithful. Idealistic and humanitarian. Loves adventure and excitement. Has willpower and determination. Natural counselor and healer.

Dierdre, 9- Trustworthy, dependable. Artistic, having good taste. Likes to entertain. Gentle, kind, a hard worker. Domestic, responsible. Tendency to lose items. A free spirit, very adaptable.

Digna, 8- Reliable, responsible. Blessed in some ways. Stylish and refined. Romantic, sensual. Resolute and purposeful.

Dillon, 30- Serious, yet fun-loving. Blessed in some ways. Strong verbal skills. Financial ups and downs. Natural counselor and healer. Original and unconventional.

Dimitra, 11- Workaholic, determined. Considerate, understanding. Domestic, hard working. Artistic, having good taste. Dynamic, busy lifestyle. Could be forgetful. Ambitious, self-motivated.

Dinah, 9- Trustworthy, dependable. Idealistic and humanitarian. Original and unconventional. Bold, courageous, a bit stubborn. Great judge of character.

Dion, 6- Creative problem solver. Artistic, having good taste. Natural counselor and healer. Original and unconventional.

Dione, 11- Workaholic, determined. Considerate, understanding. Loving and nurturing. Original and unconventional. Loves adventure and excitement.

Dionisio, 4- Down-to-earth, faithful. Blessed in some ways. Natural counselor and healer. Romantic, sensual. Idealistic and humanitarian. Charming and devoted. Artistic, having good taste. May have musical abilities.

Dirk, 6- Creative problem solver. Considerate, understanding. Diligent and helpful. Strong desire to succeed.

Dixie, 6- Creative problem solver. Blessed in some ways. Artistic, sensual, perceptive. Idealistic and humanitarian. Adaptable to change.

Dixon, 30- Serious, yet fun-loving. Blessed in some ways. Artistic, sensual, perceptive. Natural counselor and healer. Original and unconventional.

D.J., 5- Enjoys working. Very clever and talented. Freedom loving.

Dodi, 5- Enjoys working. Natural counselor and healer. Down-to-earth, faithful. Artistic, having good taste.

Dodong, 5- Enjoys working. Natural counselor and healer. Hardworking, faithful. May have musical abilities. Romantic, sensual. Willpower and determination.

Dolan, 10- Natural authority. Natural counselor and healer. Strong verbal skills. Independent, critical of self and others. Original and unconventional.

Dolley, 10- Natural authority. Natural counselor and healer. Strong verbal skills. Frequent traveler. Loves adventure and excitement. Needs a lot of freedom.

Dollie, 30- Serious, yet fun-loving. Good parenting abilities. Communicates skillfully. Financial ups and downs. Blessed in some ways. A free spirit, very adaptable.

Dolly, 5- Enjoys working. Creates group harmony. Strong verbal skills. Ups and downs financially. Dislikes limitations.

Dolores, 7- Systematic, organized. Natural counselor and healer. Frequent traveler. May have musical abilities. Intense inner power. Likes change, very adaptable. Charming and devoted.

Dom, 5- Enjoys working. Natural counselor and healer. Domestic, faithful, hard working.

Dominic, 4- Down-to-earth, faithful. Respects rules. Domestic, hard working. Blessed in some ways. Romantic, sensual. Artistic, having good taste. Optimistic, cheerful.

Dominica, 5- Enjoys working. Natural counselor and healer. Domestic, hard working. Blessed in some ways. Romantic, sensual. Artistic, having good taste. Loyal, understanding. Pioneer and risk taker.

Dominick, 6- Creative problem solver. Loving and nurturing. Domestic, hard working. Blessed in some ways. Creative, opinionated. Artistic, having good taste. Self-expressive, cheerful. Strong desire to succeed.

Dominique, 8- Reliable, responsible. Natural counselor and healer. Domestic, hard working. Blessed in some ways. Creative, opinionated. Artistic, having good taste. Attracts wealth. Attractive and charming. Likes change, very adaptable.

Don, 6- Creative problem solver. Nurturing, loving, responsible. Original and unconventional.

Donald, 5- Enjoys working. Natural counselor and healer. Original and unconventional. Pioneer and risk taker. Strong verbal skills. Down-to-earth, faithful.

Donalt, 3- Serious, yet fun-loving. Create group harmony. Romantic, sensual. Pioneer and risk taker. Strong verbal skills. Dynamic, busy lifestyle.

Donn, 20- Practical, conservative. Natural counselor and healer. Romantic, sensual. Creative and opinionated.

Donna, 3- Serious, yet fun-loving. Good parenting skills. Creative, opinionated. Romantic, sensual. Bold, courageous, a bit stubborn.

Donnell, 4- Down-to-earth, faithful. Natural counselor and healer. Original and unconventional. Creative, opinionated. Physical and passionate. Strong verbal skills. Frequent traveler.

Donny, 9- Trustworthy and dependable. Creates group harmony. Creative, opinionated. Romantic, sensual. Needs a lot of freedom.

Donovan, 4- Down-to-earth, faithful. Natural counselor and healer. Original and unconventional. Strong parental skills. Intuitive and inspired. Independent, critical of self and others. Romantic and sensual.

Dooley, 4- Down-to-earth, faithful. Strong parenting skills. May have musical abilities. Frequent traveler. Adaptable to change. Needs a lot of freedom.

Dora, 20- Practical, conservative. Creates group harmony. Gentle, kind, a hard worker. Not easily influenced.

Doreen, 7- Systematic, organized. Respects rules. Diligent, helpful. Physical, passionate. A free spirit, very adaptable. Creative, opinionated.

Dori, 10- Natural authority. Self-sacrificing, devoted. Intense inner power. Artistic, having good taste.

Doria, 11- Workaholic, determined. Natural counselor and healer. Gentle, kind, a hard worker. Blessed in some ways. Independent, critical of self and others.

Dorian, 7- Systematic, organized. Respects rules. Intense inner power. Blessed in some ways. Independent, critical of self and others. Creative, opinionated.

Dorie, 6- Creative problem solver. Strong parenting skills. Gentle, kind, a hard worker. Blessed in some ways. A free spirit, very adaptable.

Dorien, 11- Workaholic, determined. Creates group harmony. Intense inner power. Artistic, having good taste. Physical, passionate. Creative, opinionated.

Doris, 11- Workaholic, determined. Creates group harmony. Intense inner power. Blessed in some ways. Charming and devoted.

Dorothea, 5- Enjoys working. Respects rules. Intense inner power. May have musical abilities. Dynamic, busy lifestyle. Likes to delegate. Enjoys entertaining. Not easily influenced.

Dorothy, 6- Creative problem solver. Natural counselor and healer. Highly emotional. May have musical abilities. Dynamic, busy lifestyle. Great judge of character. Needs a lot of freedom.

Dorrie, 6- Creative problem solver. Nurturing and loving. Gentle, kind, a hard worker. Tendency to lose items. Blessed in some ways. A free spirit, very adaptable.

Dorry, 8- Reliable, responsible. Natural counselor and healer. Intense inner power. Highly emotional. Needs a lot of freedom.

Dory, 8- Reliable, responsible. Natural counselor and healer. Gentle, kind, a hard worker. Needs a lot of freedom.

Dot, 3- Serious, yet fun-loving. Creates group harmony. Dynamic, busy lifestyle.

Dottie, 10- Natural authority. Natural counselor and healer. Dynamic, busy lifestyle. Sensitive and easily hurt. Artistic, having good taste. Likes to entertain.

Dotty, 3- Serious, yet fun-loving. Creates group harmony. Dynamic, busy lifestyle. Sensitive and easily hurt. Needs a lot of freedom.

Doug, 20- Practical, conservative. Natural counselor and healer. Attractive and charming. Scientific and philosophical.

Douglas, 7- Systematic, organized. Respects rules. Attractive and charming. Scientific and philosophical. Strong verbal skills. Not easily influenced. Many mood swings.

Doyle, 7- Systematic, organized. Respects rules. Needs a lot of freedom. Frequent traveler. Loves adventure and excitement.

Do-young, 11- Workaholic, determined. Creates group harmony. Needs a lot of freedom. May have musical abilities. Attractive and charming. Original and unconventional. Scientific and philosophical.

Drake, 30- Serious, yet fun-loving. Gentle, kind, a hard worker. Independent, critical of self and others. Strong desire to succeed. Loves adventure and excitement.

Drew, 5- Enjoys working. Diligent, helpful. Physical, passionate. Friendly, adaptable to change.

Duane, 9- Trustworthy, dependable. Attractive and charming. Independent, critical of self and others. Original and unconventional. A free spirit, very adaptable.

Dude, 7- Systematic, organized. Attractive and charming. Down-to-earth, faithful. A free spirit, very adaptable.

Dudley, 8- Reliable, responsible. Attractive and charming. Down-to-earth, faithful. Strong verbal skills. Physical, passionate. Dislikes limitations.

Dugan, 20- Practical, conservative. Attractive and charming. Scientific and philosophical. Independent, critical of self and others. Original and unconventional.

Duke, 5- Enjoys working. Attractive and charming. Strong desire to succeed. A free spirit, very adaptable.

Duncan, 3- Serious, yet fun-loving. Slow to make decisions. Original and unconventional. Self-expressive, cheerful. Independent, critical of self and others. Romantic and sensual.

Dunstan, 3- Serious, yet fun-loving. Slow to make decisions. Original and unconventional. Charming and devoted. Dynamic, busy lifestyle. Pioneer and risk taker. Romantic and sensual.

Durand, 8- Reliable, responsible. Attractive and charming. Intense inner power. Resolute and purposeful. Romantic, sensual. Down-to-earth, faithful.

Durant, 6- Creative problem solver. Youthful, appealing. Gentle, kind, a hard worker. Independent, critical of self and others. Original and unconventional. Dynamic, very busy lifestyle.

Dustin, 6- Creative problem solver. Youthful, appealing. Charming and devoted. Dynamic, busy lifestyle. Blessed in some ways. Original and opinionated.

Dusty, 8- Reliable, responsible. Attractive and charming. Many mood swings. Dynamic, busy lifestyle. Needs a lot of freedom.

Dutch, 20- Practical, conservative. Attractive and charming. Dynamic, busy lifestyle. Loyal and understanding. Excellent judge of character.

Dwane, 20- Practical, conservative. Likes to meet new people. Independent, critical of self and others. Romantic, sensual. A free spirit, very adaptable.

Dwayne, 9- Trustworthy and dependable. Likes to meet new people. Pioneer and risk taker. Needs a lot of freedom. Romantic, sensual. Enjoys giving gifts.

Dwight, 8- Reliable, responsible. Likes to meet new people. Blessed in some ways. Scientific and philosophical. Excellent judge of character. Dynamic, busy lifestyle.

Dylan, 20- Practical, conservative. Dislikes limitations. Frequent traveler. Independent, critical of self and others. Romantic, sensual.

"Some place where there isn't any trouble. Do you suppose there is such a place, Toto? There must be. It's not a place you can get to by a boat or a train. It's far, far away—behind the moon—beyond the rain—"
~Excerpted from "The Wizard of Oz"
Used with permission

E

IF A NAME BEGINS with E, is the first vowel, has more than one E, or ends with an E, this person is a free spirit, adaptable to change, physical, passionate and loves adventure.

Those with names that begin with E enjoy giving more than receiving. It's important to remember that an E person delights in the reaction of others receiving a gift from them. Elvis Presley would take off jewelry and throw it to the audience. That's the E in his name, he loved surprising others. Even his famous "Graceland," where he lived, reflected a sort of freedom in its décor. Since Elvis begins with a vowel, he wore his heart's desire letter up front for the world to see. Speaking of world, his name adds up to a 22 power number. This means he was a master on the global playing field. 22 is a master number and gives the bearer an ability to be big on an international level. The world knows and loves Elvis. Almost everyone around the world has heard of him.

E represents the "change" aspect of a personality. E is the 5th letter and 5 rules change. This 5 ruled letter often changes circumstances beyond our control. An E anywhere in a name gives the bearer the feeling that; "The only thing constant in life is change." Often change is a blessing for anyone with the 5th vibration ruled letters E, N, or W in their name. Similar to cats, they generally land on their feet.

E's are also excellent dressers, if not a bit flashy. They seem to remember the hair, earrings and make up. Both male and female under the E's influence won't mind getting ready for a date. They'll look good, smell good, and feel good. E's are into the 5 senses: feel, sound, touch, smell and sight. This makes the E very sensual. They'll want to have all the effects, lighting, candle scents, music, and atmosphere just right. This letter, next to N, W and X is one of the sexiest of letters. Elvis was one of the biggest heart throbs of all time. "The Beatles" had an E first vowel. The Beatles weren't all that sexy by themselves, but as a group under a name with an E first vowel, well, the girls went crazy over them.

E names as well as N names tend to fall in and out of love often, especially early in life. Yet, if they are lucky enough to find the right mate, their marriage is the model of happiness. The paradox of this letter is that they have a strong sex drive and they love their freedom. So in order to stay happy in a relationship with this 5 ruled letter, one must allow the person with the E in their name freedom, without suspicion or jealousy. This is a tall order because E named people are so desirable and sexy. The typical E will run the other way when jealousy is displayed. Not to hold on too tightly is the key to staying with an E. Patience is also a virtue; ask Shannon Tweed, long time girlfriend of Rock Star, Gene Simmons from Kiss. Fortunately she has plenty of 5-ruled letters in her own name, which aids in compatibility and understanding.

This letter is similar to the astrological sign of Leo in the way of romance and creativity; yet also has qualities of Aquarius in that they enjoy their friends and freedom. This is truly one of the most fun and exciting letters to have in a name. E people light up the room with their smile. The person with this letter anywhere in their name will adapt easily to change. Some fit in well with the military because change in residence is most likely. This letter, as well as N and W, are capable of roll reversal. It's not uncommon for the wife to go to work and leave the husband home to take care of the kids. This letter is not afraid to defy the natural order of things. Different and unusual is their wavelength. E's also manage to look as if they are listening, when they are really a million miles away. Don't underestimate their power of concentration. Often while they are nodding their head as if listening to you, they are solving a problem that has been perplexing their co-workers for weeks.

E is for entertainment. The E person could be bored to tears in a humdrum routine. They're versatile, adventurous and freedom oriented. An E anywhere in a person's name will give them the edge in interior decorating. E names have a natural flair, or at the very least, an interesting concept and are one of the best dressed of all the letters. Also, E's can wrap a gift better than any other letter in the alphabet.

Emeril Lagasse, Chef, Restaurateur, television personality and author of 8 cook books, so far exemplifies his E name by popularizing the word, "Bam!" Such an exciting word for this Chef with two E's in his name. He's very domestic and hard working with his first consonant M. Still, two E's give him an intensity 5, so he loves excitement, change and variety. No doubt all his recipes are a delight to the senses. He's unorthodox and different from any other chef to say the least. Also, the R and I give him an intensity 9, so he's very much a humanitarian with friends of all race and color. His name sums-up to a power number 8, so he's a survivor and will no doubt receive financial rewards in this lifetime.

Elvira, "Mistress of the Dark" or "The Queen of Halloween" also seems to fit her name well. Although her real name is Cassandra Peterson, both the letters C and L give way to a natural comedian. Her character is funny, sexy and delivers one-liners in a low cut black skin tight evening gown. With an E first name she can get away with being "shocking" better than most. Also the 5 ruled E next to the 3 ruled L adds up to a hidden 8 which is also comfortable with Halloween. 8 rules the 8th astrological sign of Scorpio and goes without saying, the sexiest of influences. Also this hidden 8 is a little frightening or scary, but with the E and L it's delivered in a crazy-fun way. She also never ages! This can be attributed to the C in her birth name; or the L in Elvira. C's and L's are ruled by the number 3 and have a youthful appearance for much longer than the other letters, except for the letter U which is also ruled by the number 3.

Too much of this letter in a name could give one a tendency to overindulge. Many E names are candidates for Jenny Craig. Who better to understand a tendency to overindulge than an intensity 5 name like Jenny? Weight Watchers also has two 5 ruled letters in the beginning of its name. An abundance of this letter, or the letter N or W in a name can also promote a desire for escapism. The escapist tendencies could fall into many categories including television, books, and overeating; however, sadly some fall into dangerous forms of escapism such as drugs and alcohol. Furthermore, a 5 intensity number can cause a person to be preoccupied with sex. This letter, as well as other 5 ruled letters, can get burned out easily by overdoing and over-indulging. This usually has to do with certain foods, driving, sex, people, hobbies, a particular job or any activity on which they get hooked. This letter along with the 5 ruled letters N and W need to adopt the attitude, "moderation in everything!"

The 5-ruled knows how to motivate others and seem to have some teaching ability. Some can master the art of communication better than a C or L person! Their sense of humor can be spontaneous and highly acute. The typical E is very intelligent and good with their hands. They seem to have some mechanical ability. Some can hit the T.V. just right so it stops making that noise. E's make excellent salespersons, politicians, public-relations persons, lawyers and teachers. Some E's succeed in more shocking careers such as strip tease clubs or rock and roll bands. Gene Simmons of Kiss has 2 E's in his name. Anyone with an E in their name is bound to be more colorful. Often E's are gamblers, playing for high stakes with a great enthusiasm which others find attractive. Their desire to gamble or take chances can backfire, causing them to take another course of action. That's okay, because who's better equipped to adapt to change than an E person? It complements their nature. For them, life's an adventure waiting to happen.

Other famous people whose names begin with E are Elizabeth Taylor, Elton John, Ernest Hemmingway, Elijah Wood, Elizabeth Hurley, Edgar Allan Poe, Ellen Bernstein, Eddie Murphy, Evita Peron, Eleanor Roosevelt, Eve Arden, Esther Williams, Eminem, Enya, Edgar Cayce, Ethel Murman, Eartha Kitt, Eric Clapton, Eva Gabor, Ed McMahon, Ed Sullivan, Efrem Zimbalist, Jr., Elizabeth Montgomery, Elle Macpherson, Elizabeth-The Queen Mother, Ellen DeGeneres, Elliott Gould, Elvis Costello, Evel Knievel and Errol Flynn.

Quick Reference of "E" Names

Earl, 9- True humanitarian. Resolute and purposeful. Gentle, kind, a hard worker. Strong verbal skills.

Earle, 5- Physical and passionate. Bold, adventuresome. Intense inner power. Frequent traveler. Loves excitement and change.

Earlene, 6- A step ahead of others. Pioneer and risk taker. Gentle, kind, a hard worker. Strong verbal skills. Physical and passionate. Original and unconventional. Loves adventure and excitement.

Earline, 10- Likes change and variety. Self-motivated, courageous. Diligent, helpful. Strong verbal skills. Blessed in some ways. Original and opinionated. Loves adventure and excitement.

Eartha, 8- Original and creative. Bold, courageous, a bit stubborn. Intense inner power. An excellent mediator. Self-reliant, successful. Pioneer and risk taker.

Easter, 5- Physical and passionate. Pioneer and risk taker. Charming and devoted. Dynamic, busy lifestyle. Loves freedom and adventure. Considerate and kind.

Eaton, 10- Likes change and variety. Independent, critical of self and others. Dynamic, busy lifestyle. Natural counselor and healer. Original and opinionated.

Ebba, 10- Likes change and variety. Emotional and sensitive. Affectionate and loyal. Not easily influenced.

Eben, 8- Original and creative. Loyal and understanding. Physical and passionate. Unconventional, opinionated.

Ebenezer, 8- Original and creative. Great mediator. Physical and passionate. Unconventional, opinionated. Loves adventure and excitement. Uses common sense. Needs change and variety. Intense inner power.

Ebrahim, 11- Keenly perceptive. Friendly, but shy. Gentle, kind, a hard worker. Reads people easily. Great judge of character. Blessed in some ways. Systematic and organized.

Echo, 22- Has big plans. Optimistic, outspoken. Excellent judge of character. Has musical abilities.

Ed, 9- True humanitarian. Down-to-earth, faithful. A natural teacher.

Eda, 10- Likes change and variety. Natural authority and leader. Independent, critical of self and others.

Edan, 6- A step ahead of others. Reliable, responsible. Pioneer and risk taker. Romantic and sensual.

Edana, 7- Not easily fooled. Down-to-earth, faithful. Independent, critical of self and others. Original and unconventional. Bold, courageous, a bit stubborn.

Eddie, 9- True humanitarian. Reliable, responsible. Down-to-earth, faithful. Artistic, having good taste. A free spirit, very adaptable.

Ede, 5- Physical and passionate. Quick problem solver. Loves adventure and excitement..

Eden, 10- Likes change and variety. Natural authority. A free spirit, very adaptable. Romantic, sensual.

Edgar, 8- Original and creative. Systematic, organized. Willpower and determination. Not easily influenced. Intense inner power.

Edgardo, 9- True humanitarian. Reliable, responsible. Scientific and philosophical. Natural authority. Gentle, kind, a hard worker. Down-to-earth, faithful. Natural counselor and healer.

Edie, 5- Physical and passionate. Systematic, organized. Blessed in some ways. A free spirit, very adaptable.

Edina, 6- A step ahead of others. Reliable, responsible. Artistic, having good taste. Creative, opinionated. Pioneer and risk taker.

Edison, 30- A free spirit, very adaptable. Creative problem solver. Blessed in some ways. Charming and devoted. Natural counselor and healer. Romantic, opinionated.

Edith, 10- Likes change and variety. A natural authority. Artistic, having good taste. Dynamic, busy lifestyle. Excellent, judge of character.

Edmond, 10- Likes change and variety. Practical and determined. Domestic, hardworking. Natural counselor and healer. Creative, opinionated. Down-to-earth, faithful.

Edmund, 7- Not easily fooled. Systematic, organized. Domestic, hardworking. Attractive and charming. Original and unconventional. Down-to-earth, faithful.

Edna, 6- A step ahead of others. Reliable, responsible. Creative, opinionated. Pioneer and risk taker.

Edsel, 9- True humanitarian. Natural authority. Charming and devoted. Physical and passionate. Strong verbal skills.

Eduardo, 5- Physical and passionate. Systematic, organized. Attractive and charming. Not easily influenced. Intense inner power. Down-to-earth, practical. Natural counselor and healer.

Edward, 10- Likes change and variety. Creative problem solver. Enjoys meeting new people. Independent, critical of self and others. Gentle, kind, a hard worker. Down-to-earth, practical.

Edwin, 10- Likes change and variety. Creative problem solver. Enjoys meeting new people. Blessed in some ways. Romantic, sensual.

Edwina, 11- Keenly perceptive. Natural authority. Creative and determined. Blessed in some ways. Original and unconventional. Reads people easily.

Efrem, 11- Keenly perceptive. Self-sacrificing, loving. Intense inner power. Loves adventure and excitement. Domestic, hardworking.

Efren, 30- A free spirit, very adaptable. Self-sacrificing, loving. Gentle, kind, a hard worker. Physical and passionate. Original and opinionated.

Effie, 4- Accesses quickly. Self-sacrificing, loving. High moral standards. Artistic, having good taste. Likes change and variety.

Egan, 9- True humanitarian. Scientific and philosophical. Pioneer and risk taker. Original and unconventional.

Egbert, 30- A free spirit, very adaptable. Philosophical and scientific. Friendly and affectionate. Likes to entertain. Gentle, kind, a hard worker. Dynamic, busy lifestyle.

Egill, 9- True humanitarian. Scientific, philosophical. Idealistic and humanitarian. Strong verbal skills. Frequent traveler.

Egon, 5- Physical and passionate. Extremely intelligent. Nurturing, loving. Creative and opinionated.

Eileen, 5- Physical and passionate. Blessed in some ways. Communicates skillfully. Tendency to overindulge. A free spirit, very adaptable. Creative and opinionated.

Eirene, 11- Keenly perceptive. Artistic, having good taste. Gentle, kind, a hard worker. Good entertainer. Original and unconventional. Physical, passionate.

Elaina, 6- A step ahead of others. Strong verbal skills. Independent, critical of self and others. Blessed in some ways. Creative and original. Bold, courageous, a bit stubborn.

Elaine, 10- Likes change and variety. Strong verbal skills. Independent, critical of self and others. Artistic, having good taste. Romantic, sensual. Social, friendly.

Elan, 5- Physical and passionate. Communicates skillfully. Self-motivated, stubborn. Original and unconventional.

Elayne, 8- Original and creative. Frequent traveler. Resolute and purposeful. Needs a lot of freedom. Unconventional, opinionated. Physical and passionate.

Elberta, 9- True humanitarian. Strong verbal skills. Friendly, but shy. A free spirit, very adaptable. Gentle, kind, a hard worker. Dynamic, busy lifestyle. Independent, critical of self and others.

Elden, 22- Has big plans. Frequent traveler. Systematic, organized. Physical and passionate. Original and unconventional.

Eldon, 5- Physical and passionate. Strong verbal skills. Reliable, responsible. Natural counselor and healer. Creative, opinionated.

Eldora, 10- Likes change and variety. Frequent traveler. Systematic, organized. Loving and nurturing. Gentle, kind, a hard worker. Independent, critical of self and others.

Eldrick, 8- Original and creative. Communicates skillfully. Reliable, responsible. Intense inner power. Blessed in some ways. Self-expressive, cheerful. Strong desire to succeed.

Eldridge, 10- Likes change and variety. Strong verbal skills. Systematic, organized. Gentle, kind, a hard worker. Blessed in some ways. Down-to-earth, faithful. Stylish and refined. Physical and passionate.

Eleanor, 7- Not easily fooled. Strong verbal skills. Physical and passionate. Resolute and purposeful. Original and opinionated. Natural counselor and healer. Gentle, kind, a hard worker.

Eleazar, 5- Physical and passionate. Ups and downs financially. Loves adventure and excitement. Pioneer and risk taker. A good mediator. Not easily influenced. Intense inner power.

Elecio, 4- Accesses quickly. Communicates skillfully. Physical and passionate. Self-expressive, cheerful. Blessed in some ways. Natural counselor and healer.

Electra, 10- Likes change and variety. Frequent traveler. Physical and passionate. Optimistic, outspoken. Dynamic, busy lifestyle. Gentle, kind, a hard worker. Independent, critical of self and others.

Elena, 10- Likes change and variety. Strong verbal skills. Physical and passionate. Original and unconventional. Independent, critical of self and others.

Eleni, 9- True humanitarian. Frequent traveler. Loves adventure and excitement. Creative and opinionated. Blessed in some ways.

Elese, 10- Likes change and variety. Strong verbal skills. Physical and passionate. Charming and devoted. Loves adventure and excitement.

Elexa, 20- Social and entertaining. Communicates well. Physical and passionate. Artistic, sensual, perceptive. Reads people easily.

Elfreda, 6- A step ahead of others. Strong verbal skills. Self-sacrificing, loving. Gentle, kind, a hard worker. Physical, passionate. Reliable, responsible. Pioneer and risk taker.

Elga, 7- Not easily fooled. Frequent traveler. Scientific and philosophical. Independent, courageous, bold.

Eli, 8- Original and creative. Recuperates quickly. Blessed in some ways.

Elia, 9- True humanitarian. Communicates skillfully. Forgive and be happy. Pioneer and risk taker.

Elias, 10- Likes change and variety. Strong verbal skills. Blessed in some ways. Independent, critical of self and others. Charming and devoted.

Elijah, 9- True humanitarian. Frequent traveler. Forgive and be happy. Clever and talented. Hard working, helpful, sincere. Excellent judge of character.

Elinore, 6- A step ahead of others. Strong verbal skills. Artistic, having good taste. Creative, opinionated. Natural counselor and healer. Gentle, kind, a hard worker. Physical and passionate.

Eliot, 7- Not easily fooled. Strong verbal skills. Blessed in some ways. Natural counselor and healer. Dynamic, busy lifestyle.

Elisa, 10- Likes change and variety. Frequent traveler. Considerate, understanding. Charming and devoted. Not easily influenced.

Elise, 5- Physical and passionate. Communicates skillfully. Blessed in some ways. Charming and devoted. A free spirit, adaptable to change.

Elisha, 9- True humanitarian. Strong verbal skills. Artistic, having good taste. Devoted, loving. Great judge of character. Pioneer and risk taker.

Elissa, 20- Social and entertaining. Communicates skillfully. Blessed in some ways. Charming and devoted. Impulsive and extreme. Independent, critical of self and others.

Elite, 6- A step ahead of others. Strong verbal skills. Artistic, having good taste. Dynamic, busy lifestyle. A free spirit, very adaptable.

Eliza, 8- Original and creative. Strong powers of recuperation. Blessed in some ways. Has common sense. Independent, critical of self and others.

Elizabeth, 7- Not easily fooled. Strong verbal skills. Blessed in some ways. Has common sense. Independent, critical of self and others. Friendly, but shy. Loves adventure and excitement. Dynamic, busy lifestyle. Excellent judge of character.

Ella, 3- A free spirit, very adaptable. Slow to make decisions. Communicates skillfully. Pioneer and risk taker.

Ellamay, 6- A step ahead of others. Skilled communicator. Frequent traveler. Independent, critical of self and others. Domestic, hard working. Pioneer and risk taker. Needs a lot of freedom.

Elle, 7- Not easily fooled. Has gift of gab. Listens well too. Loves freedom and adventure.

Ellen, 3- A free spirit, very adaptable. Has gift of gab. Listens well too. Tendency to overindulge. Romantic and sensual.

Ellery, 5- Physical and passionate. Communicates skillfully. Financial ups and downs. A free spirit, very adaptable. Gentle, kind, a hard worker. Needs a lot of freedom.

Ellie, 7- Not easily fooled. Strong verbal skills. Frequent traveler. Blessed in some ways. Physical and passionate.

Ellin, 7- Not easily fooled. Strong verbal skills. Frequent traveler. Blessed in some ways. Romantic and sensual.

Elliott, 30- A free spirit, very adaptable. Gift of gab. Listens well too. Blessed in some ways. Natural counselor and healer. Dynamic, busy lifestyle. Sensitive and easily hurt.

Ellis, 3- A free spirit, very adaptable. Gift of gab. Listens well too. Blessed in some ways. Charming and devoted.

Elma, 4- Accesses quickly. Strong powers of recuperation. Domestic, hard working. Resolute and purposeful.

Elmer, 8- Original and creative. Communicates skillfully. Desires financial security. Likes change and variety. Gentle, kind, a hard worker.

Elmira, 4- Accesses quickly. Strong powers of recuperation. Domestic, hard working. Artistic, having good taste. Diligent, thoughtful. Resolute and purposeful.

Elmo, 9- True humanitarian. Communicates skillfully. Systematic, organized. Natural counselor and healer.

Eloise, 11- Keenly perceptive. Strong verbal skills. Natural counselor and healer. Artistic, having good taste. Charming and devoted. Physical and passionate.

Elroy, 30- A free spirit, very adaptable. Slow to make decisions. Gentle, kind, a hard worker. Natural counselor and healer. Needs a lot of freedom.

Elsa, 10- Likes change and variety. Strong verbal skills. Charming and devoted. Independent, critical of self and others.

Elsbeth, 8- Original and creative. Recuperates quickly. Devoted and loving. Great mediator. Physical and passionate. Dynamic, busy lifestyle. Self-reliant, successful.

Elsie, 5- Physical and passionate. Frequent traveler. Charming and devoted. Artistic, having good taste. Likes change and variety.

Elton, 3- A free spirit, very adaptable. Slow to make decisions. Dynamic, busy lifestyle. Natural counselor and healer. Creative and opinionated.

Elvis, 22- Has big plans. Communicates skillfully. Intuitive and inspired. Blessed in some ways. Charming and devoted.

Elvina, 9- True humanitarian. Frequent traveler. Intuitive and inspired. Artistic, having good taste. Creative and opinionated. Pioneer and risk taker.

Elvira, 4- Accesses quickly. Strong powers of recuperation. Intuitive and inspired. Blessed in some ways. Gentle, kind, a hard worker. Resolute and purposeful.

Elwin, 9- True humanitarian. Communicates skillfully. Likes to meet new people. Considerate, understanding. Romantic and sensual.

Ely, 6- A step ahead of others. Communicates skillfully. Needs a lot of freedom.

Elyce, 5- Physical and passionate. Frequent traveler. Dislikes limitations. Sense of humor. A free spirit, adaptable to change.

Elyse, 3- A free spirit, very adaptable. Slow to make decisions. Needs a lot of freedom. Charming and devoted. Physical and passionate.

Elysia, 8- Original and creative. Recuperates quickly. Dislikes limitations. Charming and devoted. Blessed in some ways. Independent, critical of self and others.

Em, 9- A true humanitarian. Systematic, organized. Generous, enjoys giving gifts.

Emanuel, 8- Original and creative. Domestic, hard working. Resolute and purposeful. Unconventional, opinionated. Attractive and charming. Physical and passionate. Communicates skillfully.

Emeril, 8- Original and creative. Domestic, hard working. Physical and passionate. Intense inner power. Blessed in some ways. Communicates skillfully.

Emerson, 8- Original and creative. Domestic, hard working. Likes variety and change. Intense inner power. Charming and devoted. Natural counselor and healer. Romantic, sensual.

Emery, 30- A free spirit, very adaptable. Systematic, organized. Loves adventure and excitement. Gentle, kind, a hard worker. Dislikes limitations.

Emil, 3- A free spirit, very adaptable. Systematic, hard working. Blessed in some ways. Communicates skillfully.

Emile, 8- Original and creative. Systematic, organized. Artistic, having good taste. Strong verbal skills. Likes change and variety.

Emilia, 4- Accesses quickly. Domestic, hard working. Blessed in some ways. Communicates skillfully. Artistic, having good taste. Not easily influenced.

Emily, 10- Likes change and variety. Systematic, organized. Blessed in some ways. Strong verbal skills. Dislikes limitations.

Eminem, 5- Physical and passionate. Domestic, hard working. Artistic, having good taste. Original and opinionated. A free spirit, very adaptable. Desires financial security.

Emlyn, 6- A step ahead of others. Systematic, organized. Communicates skillfully. Dislikes limitations. Romantic, opinionated.

Emma, 5- Physical and passionate. Domestic, hard working. Desires financial security. Self-motivated, determined.

Emmanuel, 30- A free spirit, very adaptable. Domestic, hard working. Desires financial security. Independent, critical of self and others. Original and unconventional. Attractive and charming. Escapist tendencies. Strong verbal skills.

Emmet, 20- Social and entertaining. Domestic, hard working. Desires financial security. Physical, passionate. Dynamic, busy lifestyle.

Emory, 4- Accesses quickly. Domestic, hard working. Natural counselor and healer. Diligent, helpful. Dislikes limitations.

Engelbert, 7- Not easily fooled. Creative, opinionated. Extremely intelligent. A free spirit, very adaptable. Strong verbal skills. Friendly, but shy. Physical and passionate. Gentle, kind, a hard worker. Dynamic, busy lifestyle.

Enid, 5- Physical and passionate. Original and unconventional. Considerate and understanding. Reliable, responsible.

Enrico, 10- Likes change and variety. Creative, opinionated. Gentle, kind, a hard worker. Artistic, having good taste. Cheerful, lighthearted. Natural counselor and healer.

Enya, 9- True humanitarian. Romantic, opinionated. Needs a lot of freedom. Pioneer and risk taker.

Ephraim, 7- Not easily fooled. Intelligent and knowledgeable. Excellent judge of character. Gentle, kind, a hard worker. A natural authority. Blessed in some ways. Desires financial security.

Ephrem, 11- Keenly perceptive. Intelligent and knowledgeable. Excellent judge of character. Gentle, kind a hard worker. Physical and passionate. Desires financial security.

Epifanio, 3- A free spirit, very adaptable. Level headed. Blessed in some ways. Self-sacrificing, loving. Pioneer and risk taker. Original and unconventional. Artistic, having good taste. Natural counselor and healer.

Epsilon, 9- True humanitarian. Intelligent and knowledgeable. Charming and devoted. Blessed in some ways. Strong verbal skills. Natural counselor and healer. Original and unconventional.

Erasmus, 6- A step ahead of others. Intense inner power. Pioneer and risk taker. Charming and devoted. Domestic, hard working. Attractive, youthful. Impulsive and extreme.

Eric, 8- Original and creative. Gentle, kind, a hard worker. Considerate, understanding. Self-expressive, cheerful.

Erica, 9- True humanitarian. Understanding, helpful. Artistic, having good taste. Self-expressive, cheerful. Pioneer and risk taker.

Erik, 7- Not easily fooled. Diligent, helpful. Blessed in some ways. Strong desire to succeed.

Erika, 8- Original and creative. Gentle, kind, a hard worker. Idealistic, humanitarian. Strong desire to succeed. Independent, critical of self and others.

Erin, 10- Likes change and variety. Compassionate, understanding. Blessed in some ways. Romantic, opinionated.

Erle, 22- Has big plans. Gentle, kind, a hard worker. Frequent traveler. Physical and passionate.

Erma, 10- Likes change and variety. Diligent, helpful. Domestic, hard working. Independent, critical of self and others.

Erna, 20- Social and entertaining. Compassionate, understanding. Romantic, opinionated. Resolute and purposeful.

Ernest, 9- True humanitarian. Considerate, helpful. Original and unconventional. Physical and passionate. Charming and devoted. Dynamic, busy lifestyle.

Ernestine, 10- Likes change and variety. Gentle, kind, a hard worker. Original and unconventional. Physical and passionate. Charming and devoted. Dynamic, busy lifestyle. Blessed in some ways. Creative and opinionated. Loves adventure and excitement.

Ernesto, 6- A step ahead of others. Gentle, kind, a hard worker. Original and unconventional. Physical and passionate. Charming and devoted. Dynamic, busy lifestyle. Natural counselor and healer.

Errol, 5- Physical and passionate. Intense inner power. Could be forgetful. Natural counselor and healer. Strong verbal skills.

Erwin, 6- A step ahead of others. Gentle, kind, a hard worker. Likes to meet new people. Artistic, having good taste. Romantic, opinionated.

Erwina, 7- Not easily fooled. Hard working and kind. Likes to meet new people. Blessed in some ways. Creative, opinionated. Self-motivated, determined.

Esau, 10- Likes change and variety. Charming and devoted. Independent, critical of self and others. Attractive, youthful.

Eskel, 7- Not easily fooled. Charming and devoted. Strong desire to succeed. Physical and passionate. Communicates skillfully.

Esmeralda, 6- A step ahead of others. Charming and devoted. Systematic, organized. Physical and passionate. Gentle, kind, hard worker. Independent, critical of self and others. Strong verbal skills. Reliable, responsible. Bold, courageous, a bit stubborn.

Estella, 20- Social and entertaining. Charming and devoted. Dynamic, busy lifestyle. Physical and passionate. Strong verbal skills. Financial ups and downs. Perceptive, reads people easily.

Estelle, 6- A step ahead of others. Devoted and loving. Dynamic, busy lifestyle. Physical and passionate. Strong verbal skills. Financial ups and downs. Loves adventure and excitement.

Estes, 5- Physical and passionate. Charming and devoted. Dynamic, busy lifestyle. Needs freedom and adventure. Intense and extreme.

Esther, 30- A free spirit, very adaptable. Charming and devoted. Dynamic, busy lifestyle. Excellent judge of character. Physical and passionate. Gentle, kind, a hard worker.

Ethan, 3- A free spirit, very adaptable. Dynamic, busy lifestyle. Financial ups and downs. Independent, critical of self and others. Romantic and sensual.

Ethel, 5- Physical and passionate. Dynamic, busy lifestyle. Original and creative. A free spirit, very adaptable. Strong verbal skills.

Etta, 10- Loves change and variety. Dynamic, busy lifestyle. Needs to slow down. Independent, critical of self and others.

Eugene, 30- A free spirit, very adaptable. Attractive and charming. Scientific and philosophical. Tendency to overindulge. Romantic and sensual. Loves adventure and excitement.

Eugenia, 8- Original and creative. Attractive and charming. Scientific and philosophical. Likes freedom and variety. Physical and passionate. Blessed in some ways. Self-motivated, successful.

Eulalee, 7- Not easily fooled. Attractive and charming. Excellent verbal skills. Pioneer and risk taker. Financial ups and downs. Physical and passionate. Needs change and variety.

Eun, 4- Accesses quickly. Attractive and charming. Romantic and opinionated.

Eun-hee, 4- Accesses quickly. Attractive and charming. Original and unconventional. Great judge of character. Physical and passionate. Loves adventure and excitement.

Eunice, 30- A free spirit, very adaptable. Youthful, appealing. Creative, opinionated. Artistic, having good taste. Great sense of humor. Loves freedom and adventure.

Eun-ju, 8- Original and creative. Attractive and charming. Original and unconventional. Clever and talented. Difficulty making decisions.

Eustace, 20- Social and entertaining. Attractive and charming. Devoted, loving. Dynamic, busy lifestyle. Perceptive, reads people easily. Self-expressive, cheerful. Physical and passionate.

Eva, 10- Likes change and variety. Intuitive and inspired. Independent, critical of self and others.

Evan, 6- A step ahead of others. Responsible, trustworthy. Self-motivated, independent. Romantic, opinionated.

Evangeline, 4- Accesses quickly. Strong imagination. Resolute and purposeful. Original and unconventional. Has willpower and determination. Physical and passionate. Strong verbal skills. Blessed in some ways. Creative, opinionated. A free spirit, very adaptable.

Eve, 5- Physical and passionate. Intuitive and inspired. Loves adventure and excitement.

Eveline, 9- True humanitarian. Has big plans and ideas. Needs change and variety. Communicates well. Artistic, having good taste. Creative, opinionated. Loves adventure and excitement.

Evelyn, 11- Keenly perceptive. Intuitive and inspired. Physical and passionate. Strong verbal skills. Needs a lot of freedom. Original and opinionated.

Everett, 5- Physical and passionate. Strong imagination. A free spirit, very adaptable. Gentle, kind, a hard worker. Likes to entertain. Dynamic, busy lifestyle. Social, affectionate.

Evita, 3- A free spirit, very adaptable. Intuitive and inspired. Blessed in some ways. Dynamic, busy lifestyle. Pioneer and risk taker.

Evona, 3- A free spirit, very adaptable. Responsible and trustworthy. Natural counselor and healer. Original and unconventional. Pioneer and risk taker.

Evonne, 30- A free spirit, very adaptable. Intuitive and inspired. Natural counselor and healer. Original and unconventional. Romantic, sensual. Needs change and variety.

Ewald, 9- True humanitarian. Likes to meet new people. Pioneer and risk taker. Communicates skillfully. Natural authority.

Ewan, 7- Not easily fooled. Creative and determined. Independent, self-motivated. Romantic and sensual.

Exene, 8- Original and creative. Artistic, sensual, perceptive. Tendency to overindulge. Unconventional and opinionated. Physical and passionate.

Ezekial, 6- A step ahead of others. Uses common sense. Physical and passionate. Sensitive, diplomatic. Blessed in some ways. Pioneer and risk taker. Strong verbal skills.

Ezekiel, 10- Likes change and variety. Uses common sense. Physical and passionate. Strong desire to succeed. Blessed in some ways. Loves adventure and excitement. Strong verbal skills.

Ezra, 5- Physical and passionate. An excellent mediator. Gentle, kind, a hard worker. Self-motivated, determined.

> "No, no—now don't tell me. They—they
> don't understand you at home. They don't
> appreciate you. You want to see other lands
> —big cities—big mountains—big oceans—"
> ~*Excerpted from "The Wizard of Oz"*
> *Used with permission*

F

IF A NAME BEGINS WITH F, has more than one F, or ends with an F, this person is loving, nurturing, able to counsel, can carry a tune, has a strong parental nature and is self-sacrificing.

The 6th letter rules love. Among the emotions F is capable of is jealousy, although not all F people are the jealous type. The devoted letter F person is a little more territorial than the other letters. Fidel Castro of Cuba has always been insistent on protecting and keeping his people in Cuba. The cartoon character, Fred Flintstone often showed a jealous streak when his wife, Wilma, was wooed by a good-looking movie star.

F people need someone to love. If they think the object of their affection is in danger of leaving them, they will take steps to protect what they feel is rightfully theirs. Or, as in the case of Farrah Faucett, when her husband, Lee Majors wasn't around for her to give her love to, she left him. It's important to let the F person have someone to love and take care of. Those whose names begin with F will need to have kids, pets, or at least a garden to love and nurture. It's not surprising the word flower and florist begin with the nurturing letter F. After all, gardens need lots of love, care and attention too.

We can often recognize an F person by their conversations. Everything they do is for their loved ones. They are one of the most responsible and duty bound of all the letters. Chances are you won't find Fiona or Frank out partying all night. You'll find them taking care of their loved ones, working to support them, thinking about them, talking about them, or doing something for them. If they have children, they are their whole world. If they don't have children, they will treat their pets like children. They often like to dress their pets up and take them everywhere. Some spend time tending to their gardens everyday. Similar to letters O and X, this letter can manage over large groups of people. I know one woman whose name starts with an F who thought of her business as a "child." She started, or gave birth to it, nurtured it, helped it to grow- so for some, a business can be like a child for them to love. Either way, this letter needs to give out love!

F types are magnetic. Fabio is quite attractive to most females; he's famous for it. Sure he's good-looking, but it's more than that. This 6 ruled letter makes people stop dead in their tracks and take notice. Franklin D. Roosevelt, the only president to serve 3 terms had that magnetic quality. Everyone felt "taken care of" under the democratic President Franklin D. Roosevelt. We already know Fidel Castro has had an alluring hold on his people for many decades. It's that loving, nurturing energy that Fidel gives out. People are drawn to him. The famous are also drawn to Fidel's magnetic personality. Jack Nicholson, Steven Spielberg and Robert Redford have all visited the long-time leader of Cuba. This love-ruled letter holds the power of attraction. Even the "F" word has something to do with love. Those who use the "F" word frequently may be drawn to the subject of love for some reason.

The F named person is a mother and father all wrapped-up in one. They are so nurturing and duty-bound they usually end up in managerial positions. That's why F people tend to navigate toward leadership positions early in life. When trying to decide among employees, as to which one to put in charge, consider a person with F in their name. They are all about service and duty. They don't need someone to hold their hand. They will take on all the duties and responsibilities one person can handle. The rest of the employees seem like mere children compared to the responsible, duty bound F named employee. Consequently, because they are so capable of handling the responsibility of managing large tasks, they resent having anyone look over their shoulder while doing so. Just leave them alone so they can work some miracles for you.

Before we get too carried away with all the wonderfulness of this 6-ruled letter of love, consider that F is one of the most meddlesome of all the letters. Sometimes they become jealous or try to interfere with other people's lives. Similar to the letter O, they could take what does not belong to them, if they are not taught early in life good moral values. Often the F ruled will find themselves in a power struggle between opposing parties. They often bring peace to a volatile situation, similar to the role of a parent. The F named person needs to learn to have an open mind in family disputes, without taking sides or interfering. This also includes their family at work and their family of friends. Similar to the letter "O," men with an F in their name can be drawn to the damsel in distress; and the woman with this letter can be drawn to a mama's boy's who needs lots of nurturing and care. Duty bound F tends to attract the meek and needy.

Another famous person whose name began with "F," is Florence Nightingale. She truly lived out this loving and nurturing vibration as the founder of the nursing profession. Not only did she have 2 letters in her name ruled by the number 6, but her name summed up to a 6 power number as well. She was born into a wealthy family in Italy and didn't have to work. Her parents couldn't understand why she chose a life of duty and service. With all that 6 energy in her name, how could she escape it? She was destined to sacrifice herself to the service and care of others. And as most F names, she excelled in providing a much needed service at that time. She was the "parent" of the nursing profession, as we know it today. That loving, caring, nurturing quality is the same quality that nurses aspire to be everyday. They are service oriented as should be.

Another fascinating F name is Frank Lloyd Wright. He has been described as a creative genius in the field of American architecture. F people create children of their minds and bodies. This 6th ruled letter desires to create. During Frank's lifetime he designed over 800 buildings! He was 92 years old when he died. He had never stopped working. F people are very devoted, but the R in his name made him a very hard worker. His first vowel, A, is responsible for his critical eye. The K at the end of his name gave him a strong desire to succeed. The N and power number 5 gave him a desire to change the existing order of things. His contribution was to build houses that looked as if they were a natural part of the place they were in. The 5 is adaptable to change—and so were his buildings. Although they were foreign, he designed them to adapt or fit into their environment in an aesthetically pleasing way. Today it's an honor to graduate from one of his schools.

This letter is similar to the astrological sign Virgo. Like Virgo, the F name tends to have a stocked medicine cabinet at home. They are natural counselors and healers, similar to the O names. Many are vegetarians and have their own herb garden. Don't hesitate to ask your F named friend for health advice, they are usually right on the money in diagnosing illness. This letter tends to have allergies and to be sensitive to odors and perfumes. They will be the first to complain if something smells bad. Some F names cannot tolerate perfume at all.

F people make excellent counselors, healers, teachers, social workers, singers, psychologists, gardeners, farmers, florists, also artists and designers. This letter has something musical about it. Similar to the letter O, F can go far in the music industry. Unfortunately, the F ruled person is usually too busy trying to make a living to pursue a career in music. So at the very least, we should consider our F named friends when we need good singers at our next karaoke party.

Other famous people with names that begin with F are: Flip Wilson, Fiona Apple, Fred Astaire, Fantasia Barrino, Franz Liszt, F. Scott Fitzgerald, Faith Hill, Fred McMurray, Frank Sinatra, Finola Hughes, Florence Henderson, Frances Fisher, Franklin Pierce, Frankie J., Federico Fellini, Frederic Chopin, Faith Evans, Francis Scott Key, Fernando Lamas, Frankie Avalon, Franz Ferdinand and Fats Domino.

Quick Reference of "F" Names

Fabia, 10- Wonderful leadership abilities. Independent, critical of self and others. Affectionate, social. Blessed in some ways. Not easily influenced.

Fabian, 6- Very devoted, loving. Pioneer and risk taker. Friendly, but shy. Artistic, having good taste. Independent, self-motivated. Romantic, sensual.

Fabio, 6- Very devoted, loving. Pioneer and risk taker. Friendly, but shy. Artistic, having good taste. Magnetic personality.

Fabiola, 10- Wonderful leadership abilities. Independent, critical of self and others. Loyal, understanding. Blessed in some ways. Natural counselor and healer. Strong verbal skills. Bold, courageous, a bit stubborn.

Fairleigh, 3- Lucky in timing. Pioneer and risk taker. Blessed in some ways. Gentle, kind, a hard worker. Communicates well. A free spirit, very adaptable. Artistic, having good taste. Scientific, philosophical. Self-reliant, successful.

Faith, 8- Likes competition. Resolute and purposeful. Blessed in some ways. Dynamic, busy lifestyle. Self-reliant, successful.

Fannie, 4- Responsible, duty bound. Independent, critical of self and others. Opinionated, original. Romantic, sensual. Blessed in some ways. A free spirit, very adaptable.

Fanny, 6- Very devoted, loving. Independent, self-motivated. Original and unconventional. Romantic, creative. Needs a lot of freedom.

Fantasia, 8- Likes competition. Not easily influenced. Creative, opinionated. Dynamic, busy lifestyle. Pioneer and risk taker. Charming and devoted. Blessed in some ways. Bold, courageous, a bit stubborn.

Fara, 8- Likes competition. Independent, critical of self and others. Gentle, kind, a hard worker. Bold, courageous, a bit stubborn.

Faris, 8- Likes competition. Not easily influenced. Intense inner power. Artistic, having good taste. Can be moody.

Farley, 4- Responsible, duty bound. Resolute and purposeful. Gentle, kind, a hard worker. Strong verbal skills. A free spirit, very adaptable. Dislikes limitations.

Farr, 7- Enjoys working alone. Not easily influenced. Intense inner power. Diligent, helpful, kind.

Farrah, 7- Enjoys working alone. Independent, critical of self and others. Gentle, kind, a hard worker. Tendency to lose items. Bold, courageous, a bit stubborn. Excellent judge of character.

Farrel, 6- Very devoted, loving. Pioneer and risk taker. Highly emotional. Diligent, hard working. A free spirit, very adaptable. Strong verbal skills.

Fatemeh, 4- Responsible, duty bound. Natural teaching ability. Dynamic, busy lifestyle. A free spirit, very adaptable. Domestic, hard working. Loves adventure and excitement. Self-reliant, successful.

Fatima, 5- Original, innovative. Bright, adventuresome. Dynamic, busy lifestyle. Blessed in some ways. Domestic, hard working. Pioneer and risk taker.

Faust, 4- Responsible, duty bound. Natural teaching ability. Attractive and charming. Prone to mood swings. Dynamic, busy lifestyle.

Fave, 7- Enjoys working alone. Not easily influenced. A brilliant mind. Likes change and variety.

Favian, 8- Likes competition. Resolute and purposeful. Intuitive and inspired. Blessed in some ways. Bold, courageous, a bit stubborn. Romantic, sensual.

Favor, 8- Likes competition. Resolute and purposeful. Strong imagination. Magnetic personality. Intense inner power.

Fawn, 8- Likes competition. Resolute and purposeful. Likes to meet new people. Romantic, sensual.

Fawna, 9- Easy going nature. Helpful, sincere. Likes to meet new people. Creative, opinionated. Not easily influenced.

Fay, 5- Original, innovative. Bright, adventuresome. Needs a lot of freedom.

Faye, 10- Wonderful leadership abilities. Independent, critical of self and others. Needs a lot of freedom. Loves adventure and excitement.

Federico, 11- Task or service oriented. A free spirit, very adaptable. Reliable, responsible. Likes to entertain. Gentle, kind, a hard worker. Blessed in some ways. Self-expressive, cheerful. Natural counselor and healer.

Fedora, 4- Responsible, duty bound. Likes change and variety. Down-to-earth, faithful. Natural counselor and healer. Gentle, kind, a hard worker. Resolute and purposeful.

Felice, 4- Responsible, duty bound. Physical and passionate. Strong verbal skills. Blessed in some ways. Self-expressive, cheerful. Loves adventure and excitement.

Felicia, 9- Easy going nature. A free spirit, very adaptable. Communicates well. Blessed in some ways. Self-expressive, cheerful. Artistic, having good taste. Pioneer and risk taker.

Feliciano, 11- Task or service oriented. Intuitive, perceptive. Frequent traveler. Blessed in some ways. Outgoing, youthful outlook. Artistic, having good taste. Bold, courageous, a bit stubborn. Romantic, sensual. Musically talented.

Felicity, 8- Likes competition. Original and creative. Financial ups and downs. Emotional, considerate. Self-expressive, cheerful. Artistic, having good taste. Dynamic, busy lifestyle. Needs a lot of freedom.

Felimon, 11- Task or service oriented. Intuitive, perceptive. Strong verbal skills. Blessed in some ways. Domestic, hard working. Natural counselor and healer. Creative, opinionated.

Felipe, 8- Likes competition. Original and creative. Strong verbal skills. Blessed in some ways. Intelligent and knowledgeable. Loves adventure and excitement.

Feliza, 5- Original, innovative. Physical and passionate. Ups and downs financially. Blessed in some ways. A great mediator. Bold, courageous, a bit stubborn.

Felix, 11- Task or service oriented. Intuitive, perceptive. Frequent traveler. Emotional, considerate. Artistic, sensual, perceptive.

Felton, 9- Easy going nature. Enjoys giving gifts. Strong verbal skills. Dynamic, busy lifestyle. Natural counselor and healer. Romantic, opinionated.

Femi, 6- Very devoted, loving. A step ahead of others. Domestic, hard working. Artistic, having good taste.

Fenton, 11- Task or service oriented. Intuitive, perceptive. Creative, opinionated. Dynamic, busy lifestyle. Natural counselor and healer. Romantic and sensual.

Ferdinand, 3- Lucky in timing. A free spirit, very adaptable. Gentle, kind, a hard worker. Reliable, responsible. Blessed in some ways. Original and unconventional. Pioneer and risk taker. Romantic, sensual. Down-to-earth, faithful.

Fergus, 4- Responsible, duty bound. Accesses quickly. Diligent, helpful. Scientific and philosophical. Attractive and charming. Loving and devoted.

Fermain, 3- Lucky in timing. A free spirit, very adaptable. Gentle, kind, a hard worker. Domestic, organized. Pioneer and risk taker. Blessed in some ways. Original and unconventional.

Fermin, 11- Task or service oriented. Intuitive, perceptive. Compassionate, understanding. Domestic, organized. Blessed in some ways. Original and unconventional.

Fern, 7- Enjoys working alone. Not easily fooled. Gentle, kind, a hard worker. Original, opinionated.

Fernando, 5- Original, innovative. Physical and passionate. Intense inner power. Creative and unconventional. Bold, courageous, a bit stubborn. Creative, opinionated. Problem solver. Natural counselor and healer.

Ferris, 3- Lucky in timing. A free spirit, very adaptable. Gentle, kind, a hard worker. Could be forgetful. Blessed in some ways. Charming and devoted.

Fidel, 9- Easy going nature. Artistic, having good taste. Natural authority, practical. Very entertaining, likes variety. Slow to make decisions.

Fielding, 3- Lucky in timing. Blessed in some ways. Likes to entertain. Slow to make decisions. Practical, reliable. Considerate, understanding. Creative, romantic. Scientific and philosophical.

Fifi, 30- Lucky in timing. Blessed in some ways. Great with plants, kids and animals. Creative with easy-going attitude.

Filbert, 9- Easy going nature. Artistic, having good taste. Strong verbal skills. Friendly, but shy. A free spirit, very adaptable. Gentle, kind, a hard worker. Dynamic, busy lifestyle.

Filmore, 6- Very devoted, loving. Artistic, having good taste. Frequent traveler. Domestic, hard working. Natural counselor and healer. Highly emotional. A free spirit, very adaptable.

Findlay, 8- Likes competition. Idealistic, humanitarian. Romantic, sensual. Workaholic, shrewd, determined. Strong verbal skills. Resolute and purposeful. Truth seeker.

Findley, 3- Lucky in timing. Artistic, having good taste. Creative, romantic. Reliable, responsible. Slow to make decisions. Loves adventure and excitement. Needs a lot of freedom.

Finley, 8- Likes competition. Blessed in some ways. Creative, opinionated. Frequent traveler. Physical and passionate. Dislikes limitations.

Finn, 7- Enjoys working alone. Humanitarian, Idealistic. Original and unconventional. Romantic, opinionated.

Fiona, 9- Easy going nature. Artistic, having good taste. Natural counselor and healer. Original and unconventional. Pioneer and risk taker.

Fionna, 5- Original, innovative. Blessed in some ways. Magnetic personality. Creative, opinionated. Romantic, sensual. Bold, courageous, a bit stubborn.

Fiorenza, 4- Responsible, duty bound. Blessed in some ways. Natural counselor and healer. Gentle, kind, a hard worker. Physical and passionate. Original and unconventional. Great judge of character. Pioneer and risk taker.

Fitch, 10- Wonderful leadership abilities. Artistic, having good taste. Dynamic, busy lifestyle. Self-expressive, cheerful. Excellent judge of character.

Fitzgerald, 9- Easy going nature. Idealistic, humanitarian. Needs to slow down. Uses common sense. Extremely intelligent. A free spirit, very adaptable. Gentle, kind, a hard worker. Independent, critical of self and others. Strong verbal skills. Reliable, responsible.

Fitzpatrick, 4- Responsible, duty bound. Artistic, having good taste. Dynamic, busy lifestyle. Uses common sense. Intelligent and knowledgeable. Independent, critical of self and others. Sensitive and easily hurt. Gentle, kind, a hard worker. Blessed in some ways. Self-expressive, cheerful. Strong desire to succeed.

Flavia, 6- Very devoted, loving. Strong verbal skills. Pioneer and risk taker. Intuitive and inspired. Blessed in some ways. Not easily influenced.

Flavian, 11- Task or service oriented. Communicates skillfully. Independent, critical of self and others. Intuitive and inspired. Artistic, having good taste. Bold, courageous, a bit stubborn. Original and unconventional.

Flavius, 9- Easy going nature. Strong verbal skills. Pioneer and risk taker. Intuitive and inspired. Blessed in some ways. Attractive, flirtatious. Charming and devoted.

Fleming, 3- Lucky in timing. Frequent traveler. A free spirit, very adaptable. Domestic, hard working. Blessed in some ways. Original and unconventional. Scientific and philosophical.

Fletch, 9- Easy going nature. Slow to make decisions. Adaptable, likes change. Dynamic, busy lifestyle. Self-expressive, cheerful. Excellent judge of character.

Fletcher, 5- Original, innovative. Strong verbal skills. A free spirit, very adaptable. Dynamic, busy lifestyle. Self-expressive, cheerful. Excellent judge of character. Tendency to overindulge. Gentle, kind, a hard worker.

Flint, 7- Enjoys working alone. Frequent traveler. Blessed in some ways. Original and unconventional. Dynamic, busy lifestyle.

Flo, 6- Very devoted, loving. Communicates skillfully. Magnetic personality.

Flora, 7- Enjoys working alone. Strong verbal skills. Natural counselor and healer. Intense inner power. Independent, critical of self and others.

Florence, 6- Very devoted, loving. Communicates skillfully. Natural counselor and healer. Gentle, kind, a hard worker. A free spirit, very adaptable. Romantic and creative. Self-expressive, cheerful. Likes change and variety.

Floyd, 8- Likes competition. Strong verbal skills. Natural counselor and healer. Needs a lot of freedom. Natural authority.

Flynn, 8- Likes competition. Frequent traveler. Dislikes limitations. Original and unconventional. Romantic, sensual.

Forbes, 11- Task or service oriented. Natural counselor and healer. Gentle, kind, a hard worker. Friendly, but shy. A free spirit, very adaptable. Charming and devoted.

Ford, 7- Enjoys working alone. Respects rules. Diligent, helpful. Practical and conservative.

Forrest, 11- Task or service oriented. Natural counselor and healer. Intense inner power. Tendency to lose items. A free spirit, very adaptable. Charming and devoted. Dynamic, busy lifestyle.

Forrester, 7- Enjoys working alone. Natural counselor and healer. Gentle, kind, a hard worker. Tendency to lose items. A free spirit, very adaptable. Charming and devoted. Dynamic, busy lifestyle. Loves adventure and excitement. Intense inner power.

Fortune, 9- Easy going nature. Natural counselor and healer. Gentle, kind, a hard worker. Dynamic, busy lifestyle. Attractive and charming. Original and unconventional. A free spirit, very adaptable.

Foster, 11- Task or service oriented. Has musical abilities. Charming and devoted. Dynamic, busy lifestyle. A free spirit, very adaptable. Gentle, kind, a hard worker.

Fostina, 30- Lucky in timing. Good parenting skills. Charming and devoted. Dynamic, busy lifestyle. Blessed in some ways. Resolute and purposeful.

Fran, 3- Lucky in timing. Diligent, helpful. Independent, critical of self and others. Romantic, opinionated.

Franc, 6- Very devoted, loving. Gentle, kind, a hard worker. Self-motivated, independent. Original and unconventional. Optimistic, cheerful.

Frances, 30- Lucky in timing. Intense inner power. Independent, critical of self and others. Romantic, opinionated. Self-expressive, cheerful. A free spirit, very adaptable. Charming and devoted.

Francine, 7- Enjoys working alone. Gentle, kind, a hard worker. Independent, critical of self and others. Original and unconventional. Self-expressive, cheerful. Blessed in some ways. Romantic, sensual. A free spirit, very adaptable.

Francis, 7- Enjoys working alone. Highly emotional. Independent, critical of self and others. Original and unconventional. Self-expressive, cheerful. Blessed in some ways. Charming and devoted.

Francisca, 11- Task or service oriented. Intense inner power. Independent, critical of self and others. Romantic, sensual. Outgoing, cheerful. Blessed in some ways. Charming and devoted. Inspiring and creative. Bold, courageous, a bit stubborn.

Franco, 30- Lucky in timing. Diligent, helpful. Independent, critical of self and others. Original and unconventional. Outspoken, cheerful. Natural counselor and healer.

Francois, 4- Responsible, duty bound. Gentle, kind, a hard worker. Independent, critical of self and others. Original and unconventional. Self-expressive, cheerful. Natural counselor and healer. Blessed in some ways. Charming and devoted.

Frank, 5- Original, innovative. Diligent, hardworking. Independent, critical of self and others. Creative and unconventional. Strong desire to succeed.

Frankie, 10- Wonderful leadership abilities. Highly emotional. Independent, critical of self and others. Romantic, original. Strong desire to succeed. Blessed in some ways. A free spirit, very adaptable.

Franklin, 4- Responsible, duty bound. Gentle, kind, a hard worker. Natural teaching ability. Original and unconventional. Strong desire to succeed. Frequent traveler. Blessed in some ways. Romantic, sensual.

Franz, 11- Task or service oriented. Highly emotional. Intuitive, perceptive. Original and unconventional. Uses common sense.

Fraser, 4- Responsible, duty bound. Gentle, kind, a hard worker. Natural teaching ability. Charming and devoted. A free spirit, very adaptable. Tendency to lose items.

Frasier, 4- Responsible, duty bound. Intense inner power. Natural teaching ability. Charming and devoted. Blessed in some ways. A free spirit, very adaptable. Tendency to lose items.

Frazer, 11- Task or service oriented. Emotional, considerate. Intuitive, perceptive. Good mediator. A free spirit, very adaptable. Tendency to lose things.

Frazier, 11- Task or service oriented. Emotional, considerate. Intuitive, perceptive. Good mediator. Blessed in some ways. Likes change and variety. Tendency to lose items.

Fred, 6- Very devoted, loving. Gentle, kind, a hard worker. A step ahead of others. Reliable, responsible.

Freda, 7- Enjoys working alone. Intense inner power. Not easily fooled. Reliable, responsible. Bold, courageous, a bit stubborn.

Freddie, 6- Very devoted, loving. Diligent, helpful. A step ahead of others. Natural authority. Down-to-earth, faithful. Blessed in some ways. Physical, passionate.

Frederic, 5- Original, innovative. Intense inner power. Physical and passionate. Creative problem solver. Loves adventure and excitement. Tendency to lose items. Blessed in some ways. Optimistic, sense of humor.

Frederica, 6- Very devoted, loving. Diligent, helpful. A step ahead of others. Faithful, down-to-earth. Likes to entertain. Tendency to lose items. Blessed in some ways. Self-expressive, cheerful. Bold, courageous, a bit stubborn.

Frederick, 7- Enjoys working alone. Gentle, kind, a hard worker. Not easily fooled. Reliable, responsible. Loves adventure and excitement. Tendency to lose items. Blessed in some ways. Self-expressive, cheerful. Strong desire to succeed.

Fredric, 9- Easy going nature. Emotional, considerate. Enjoys giving gifts. Down-to-earth, faithful. Intense inner power. Blessed in some ways. Inspiring, very creative.

Freeman, 8- Likes competition. Diligent, helpful. Creative, original. Physical, passionate. Desires financial security. Resolute and purposeful. Stubborn, opinionated.

Freemon, 4- Responsible, duty bound. Gentle, kind, a hard worker. Accesses quickly. Physical, passionate. Systematic, organized. Natural counselor and healer. Original and unconventional.

Freida, 7- Enjoys working alone. Intense inner power. Not easily fooled. Blessed in some ways. Reliable, responsible. Bold, courageous, a bit stubborn.

Fremont, 10- Wonderful leadership abilities. Gentle, kind, a hard worker. Likes change and variety. Systematic, organized. Respects rules. Original and unconventional. Dynamic, busy lifestyle.

Frida, 11- Task or service oriented. Sensitive, emotional. Considerate, understanding. Reliable, responsible. Independent, critical of self and others.

Friday, 9- Easy going nature. Intense inner power. Artistic, having good taste. Reliable, responsible. Pioneer and risk taker. Needs a lot of freedom.

Fritz, 7- Enjoys working alone. Gentle, kind, a hard worker. Blessed in some ways. Dynamic, busy lifestyle. Uses common sense.

Fuller, 11- Task or service oriented. Attractive and charming. Communicates skillfully. Ups and downs financially. A free spirit, very adaptable. Gentle, kind, a hard worker.

> "Better get under cover, Sylvester--
> there's a storm blowing up—a whopper, to
> speak in the vernacular of the peasantry.
> Poor little kid—I hope she gets home all
> right."
>
> ~*Excerpted from "The Wizard of Oz"*
> *Used with permission*

G

IF A NAME BEGINS WITH G, has more than one G, or ends with a G, this person is a truth seeker, spiritual, psychic, scientific, philosophical and needs periodic solitude.

G is ruled by the number 7 vibration. The number 7 ruled letters are spiritual. There's a Neptunian feel to the 7th letter of the alphabet. G names often prefer to live by water. G's are a little more psychic than most. They are also photogenic and seem to perform well in front of a camera or on the silver screen. They tend to have style and are more refined than the rest of us. Even though Lady Godiva was forced to ride naked on a horse down the middle of town, she managed to do it with style.

Unfortunately this is one of those letters that is prone to negative forms of escapism. Not all people with a G in their name are susceptible to alcohol or drug addictions. Heredity is a factor as with all the letters. If the G named person came from a family of alcohol or drug addictions, they may also be prone to the same. Alcohol is often referred to as "spirits." Spiritualism and spirits are ruled by the same vibration. It won't be hard to tell which side of the line your G friends are on. I once knew a Gregg that suffered from drug and alcohol addiction. If his parents only knew that a name with 3 G's in it might lead to escapist tendencies, they may have named him differently. If Gregg came from a family with strong religious beliefs, he may have turned to the spirit of God instead. Or if from a family of rocket scientists, he would take on a similar role, as this letter is so scientific. On the same note, names with G need to recognize the difference between reality and illusion. This letter is so spiritual, some are dreamers and some are doers, they're either one or the other, no in between. Young people with this letter need to be guided early in life so they don't waste their potential. G is one of the most willful and determined of all the letters.

G's need to have faith in order to be happy. If the G named person doesn't have a solid relationship with God, then they can become wrapped up in their own egos. This letter, along with the letters P and Y tend to have an overly inflated opinion of themselves unless grounded with a solid belief in a higher source. As the saying goes; we have those who believe in God, and those that think they are God. To have faith in God—this is their lesson. G named people won't truly be happy unless they have faith.

A typical G person has a strong desire for knowledge and truth; however, their fine mind needs to recognize the difference between reality and illusion. They could be drawn to the scientific, technological fields; or they could be dreamers, never accomplishing any of their dreams. Again, heredity is a factor. Either one will insist upon the truth and will have a strong dislike for anything other than the truth. Similar to the letters P and Y, if a G named person doesn't like someone, they can't pretend to like them. That would fall into the category of "not being truthful," which is against their code of ethics. They'll be down-right stubborn about this too.

G is also for genius. The typical G will approach a problem in a detached analytical sort of way. They are among the most visionary of letters. G's make great inventors, researchers, investigators, technicians, watchmakers, philosophers and theologians. They also perform well in the television and movie industry. This spiritual letter needs to recharge it's batteries from time to time. The typical G will get cranky if not allowed their own space for sleep and meditation.

The famous Gwyneth Paltrow has two 7 ruled letters in her name. She has three 5 ruled letters as well, giving her more social qualities than most G names. Plus her name adds up to a 3 power number. 3 power numbers are youthful, lucky and easy going. This actress is extremely intelligent with all those 7's and 5's in her name. Still the two 7's influence her ability to look good on camera. The intensity 5 helps her adapt to change more easily. 'Bet she can escape the paparazzi better than most. It's well known she likes to spend her free time in Europe. She was quoted in a popular magazine article in 2003 as preferring the company of Europeans to Americans. She said Europeans like to talk about philosophy, art, and other cultural matters, and gave an example of how "stupid" American conversations can be. She seeks knowledge and truth above all else. She's stylish, refined, elegant and polished. Gwyneth gives a wonderful example of this 7th letter influence.

Another famous G name is the late actor Gregory Peck. The 2 G's in his name were responsible for giving him style and grace. It also helped him look good on camera. The 2 R's gave him the upper hand in a game of intimidation. R's can be bullies, but the G's helped him do it with style. Plus the E as his first vowel gave him sex appeal and a love of adventure. The intensity 7 kept his private life private.

Mahatma Gandhi, better known as Gandhi, one of the great master teachers on earth demonstrated style and grace during his peaceful resistance from British rule. This spiritual soul showed how non-violence was more powerful than violence. Furthermore, he did it with style.

Geraldo Rivera joined Fox News in 2001 as a war correspondent. To no surprise, as dangerous as his job was, it fit in perfectly with his name. His name adds up to an 8 power number, which rules death among other things. Often 8 power numbers have a brush with death or have dealings with death during their lifetime. Often his assignments are dangerous or death related. G names are truth seekers, G added to E equals a hidden 3 which rules communication. The L also rules communication as it too is ruled by 3, so this man has a double dose of the number that makes for a great news correspondent.

This spiritual letter is similar to the astrological sign, Pisces the fish. Some G names appear to "swim" across a room. It's entertaining to watch how smoothly they glide from one place to another. Also, some are known to "drink like a fish." Our nautical friends tend to either need more sleep than most, or have sleeping disorders from too much mental activity.

Still, our philosophical and very knowledgeable friends have much to offer the world even if they sometimes feel as if they don't fit in. The world can learn much from these highly spiritual souls.

Have you ever gone fishing? The key to hooking one of these stylish, dreamy fish into falling in love is to let them chase you until you catch them. Be elusive, but not too elusive, as they need to know the truth. Be honest, don't lie or they'll never, and I do mean never, trust you again.

Some more famous G names: Gloria Estefan, Goldie Hawn, Gladys Knight, Greta Garbo, Garth Brooks, Geena Davis, Garfield, Glenn Close, Gwen Stephani, Gregory Hines, Princess Grace of Monaco, George Pappard, Golda Meir, Grace Kelly, Gabe Kaplan, Graham Nash, Gordon Lightfoot, Glenn Frey,

Grocho Marx, Gene Hackman, Gilda Radner, Gina Lollobrigida, Gypsy Rose Lee, Guy Lombardo and George Clooney.

Quick Reference of "G" Names

Gabey, 22- Vision brings wealth. Ambitious leader. Affectionate, social. Loves adventure and excitement. Needs a lot of freedom.

Gabe, 6- Appreciates nature's beauty. Pioneer and risk taker. Good mediator. A free spirit, very adaptable.

Gabi, 10- A thinker, determined. Independent, critical of self and others. Friendly, but shy. Blessed in some ways.

Gabie, 6- Appreciates nature's beauty. Pioneer and risk taker. Friendly, but shy. Artistic, having good taste. Loves adventure and excitement.

Gable, 9- Quiet and reflective. Helpful, sincere. Loyal and understanding. Strong verbal skills. A free spirit, very adaptable.

Gabriel, 9- Quiet and reflective. Helpful, sincere. Friendly, but shy. Gentle, kind, a hard worker. Blessed in some ways. A free spirit, very adaptable. Communicates skillfully.

Gabriela, 10- A thinker, determined. Independent, critical of self and others. Social, loyal. Gentle, kind, a hard worker. Blessed in some ways. A free spirit, very adaptable. Strong verbal skills. Bold, courageous, a bit stubborn.

Gabrielle, 8- Willpower, determination. Resolute and purposeful. Friendly, but shy. Gentle, kind, a hard worker. Blessed in some ways. A free spirit, very adaptable. Strong verbal skills. Frequent traveler. Physical and passionate.

Gabriella, 4- Into family life. Natural teaching ability. Friendly, but shy. Gentle, kind, a hard worker. Blessed in some ways. A free spirit, very adaptable. Strong verbal skills. Frequent traveler. Bold, courageous, a bit stubborn.

Gaby, 8- Willpower, determination. Resolute and purposeful. Friendly, but shy. Needs a lot of freedom.

Gael, 7- Enjoys alone time. Not easily influenced. A free spirit, very adaptable. Great communication skills.

Gaelle, 6- Appreciates nature's beauty. Pioneer and risk taker. A free spirit, very adaptable. Strong verbal skills. Ups and downs financially. Physical and passionate.

Gail, 20- Sensitive and psychic. Reads people easily. Blessed in some ways. Communicates skillfully.

Gale, 7- Enjoys alone time. Not easily influenced. Great communication skills. A free spirit, very adaptable.

Galen, 3- Intelligent conversationalist. Aims to please. Strong verbal skills. A free spirit, very adaptable. Romantic, opinionated.

Gallagher, 8- Willpower, determination. Resolute and purposeful. Strong verbal skills. Financial ups and downs. Bold, courageous, a bit stubborn. Extremely intelligent. Excellent judge of character. A free spirit, very adaptable. Gentle, kind, a hard worker.

Gannon, 11- Vision brings wealth. Intuitive, perceptive. Original and unconventional. Romantic, sensual. Natural counselor and healer. Creative, opinionated.

Gardenia, 5- Extremely bright. Bold, adventuresome. Gentle, kind, a hard worker. Reliable, responsible. A free spirit, very adaptable. Original and unconventional. Blessed in some ways. Bold, courageous, a bit stubborn.

Garett, 8- Willpower, determination. Resolute and purposeful. Gentle, kind, a hard worker. Physical and passionate. Dynamic, very busy lifestyle. Sensitive and easily hurt.

Garfield, 8- Willpower, determination. Resolute and purposeful. Intense inner power. Self-sacrificing, loving. Blessed in some ways. A free spirit, very adaptable. Strong verbal skills. Natural authority.

Garland, 30- Intelligent conversationalist. Aims to please. Considerate, kind. Strong verbal skills. Bold, courageous, a bit stubborn. Original and unconventional. Reliable, responsible.

Garner, 9- Quiet and reflective. Helpful, sincere. Diligent, hard working. Creative and opinionated. A free spirit, very adaptable. Tendency to lose items.

Garnet, 11- Vision brings wealth. Intuitive, perceptive. Gentle, kind, a hard worker. Original and unconventional. A free spirit, very adaptable. Dynamic, busy lifestyle.

Garrett, 8- Willpower, determination. Resolute and purposeful. Intense inner power. Tendency to lose items. A free spirit, very adaptable. Dynamic, very busy lifestyle. Sensitive and easily hurt.

Garrick, 4- Into family life. Natural teaching ability. Gentle, kind, a hard worker. Intense inner power. Blessed in some ways. Self-expressive, cheerful. Strong desire to succeed.

Garth, 9- Quiet and reflective. Helpful, sincere. Gentle, kind, a hard worker. Dynamic, busy lifestyle. Excellent judge of character.

Garton, 30- Intelligent conversationalist. Aims to please. Considerate, kind. Dynamic, busy lifestyle. Natural counselor and healer. Original and unconventional.

Garvey, 6- Appreciates nature's beauty. Pioneer and risk taker. Gentle, kind, a hard worker. Intuitive and inspired. Loves adventure and excitement. Needs a lot of freedom.

Gary, 6- Appreciates nature's beauty. Pioneer and risk taker. Gentle, kind, a hard worker. Needs a lot of freedom.

Garry, 6- Appreciates nature's beauty. Pioneer and risk taker. Intense inner power. Tendency to lose items. Needs a lot of freedom.

Gaston, 22- Vision brings wealth. Ambitious leader. Charming and devoted. Dynamic, busy lifestyle. Natural counselor and healer. Original and romantic.

Gavan, 9- Quiet and reflective. Helpful, sincere. Intuitive and inspired. Bold, courageous, a bit stubborn. Original and unconventional.

Gavin, 8- Willpower, determination. Resolute and purposeful. Intuitive and inspired. Blessed in some ways. Original and unconventional.

Gay, 6- Appreciates nature's beauty. Pioneer and risk taker. Needs a lot of freedom.

Gaye, 20- Sensitive and psychic. Reads people easily. Needs a lot of freedom. Loves adventure and excitement.

Gayle, 5- Extremely bright. Bold, adventuresome. Needs a lot of freedom. Strong verbal skills. Loves adventure and excitement.

Gaylord, 10- A thinker, determined. Independent, critical of self and others. Needs a lot of freedom. Communicates skillfully. Natural counselor and healer. Gentle, kind, a hard worker. Reliable, responsible.

Gaynor, 8- Willpower, determination. Resolute and purposeful. Needs a lot of freedom. Original and unconventional. Natural counselor and healer. Gentle, kind, a hard worker.

Gazella, 10- A thinker, determined. Independent, critical of self and others. Uses common sense. A free spirit, very adaptable. Strong verbal skills. Frequent traveler. Bold, courageous, a bit stubborn.

Gem, 7- Enjoys alone time. Not easily influenced. Domestic, hard working.

Gemma, 3- Intelligent conversationalist. A free spirit, very adaptable. Domestic, hard working. Systematic, organized. Natural teaching ability.

Geena, 5- Extremely bright. Physical and passionate. Perceptive, socially adept. Original and opinionated. Self-motivated, a pioneer.

Gena, 9- Quiet and reflective. Enjoys giving gifts. Original and opinionated. Helpful, sincere.

Genaro, 6- Appreciates nature's beauty. A step ahead of others. Romantic and opinionated. Pioneer and risk taker. Gentle, kind, a hard worker. Natural counselor and healer.

Gene, 22- Vision brings wealth. Has big plans and ideas. Original and opinionated. Loves adventure and excitement.

Genesis, 6- Appreciates nature's beauty. A step ahead of others. Original and opinionated. Physical and passionate. Charming and devoted. Blessed in some ways. Impulsive and extreme.

Geneva, 9- Quiet and reflective. Enjoys giving gifts. Creative and opinionated. Loves adventure and excitement. Intuitive and inspired. Independent, critical of self and others.

Genevieve, 4- Into family life. Accesses quickly. Original and unconventional. Loves adventure and excitement. Intuitive and inspired. Blessed in some ways. Physical and passionate. Strong imagination. Skilled interior decorator.

Genie, 4- Into family life. Accesses quickly. Original and unconventional. Blessed in some ways. Loves adventure and excitement.

Geof, 6- Appreciates nature's beauty. A step ahead of others. Nurturing, loving. Self-sacrificing, loving.

Geoff, 30- Intelligent conversationalist. A free spirit, very adaptable. Natural counselor and healer. Self-sacrificing, loving. High moral standards.

Geoffrey, 6- Appreciates nature's beauty. A step ahead of others. Nurturing and care giving. Self-sacrificing, loving. High moral standards. Gentle, kind, a hard worker. Loves adventure and excitement. Needs a lot of freedom.

Georg, 7- Enjoys alone time. Not easily fooled. Natural counselor and healer. Gentle, kind, a hard worker. Extremely intelligent, needs solitude.

George, 3- Intelligent conversationalist. A free spirit, very adaptable. Natural counselor and healer. Gentle, kind, a hard worker. Extremely intelligent. Loves adventure and excitement.

Georgette, 3- Intelligent conversationalist. A free spirit, very adaptable. Natural counselor and healer. Gentle, kind a hard worker. Extremely intelligent. Loves adventure and excitement. Dynamic, busy lifestyle. Sensitive and easily hurt. Physical and passionate.

Georgia, 8- Willpower, determination. Original, creative. Enjoys competition. Gentle, kind, a hard worker. Extremely intelligent. Blessed in some ways. Independent, critical of self and others.

Georgie, 3- Intelligent conversationalist. A free spirit, very adaptable. Natural counselor and healer. Gentle, kind, a hard worker. Extremely intelligent. Blessed in some ways. Loves adventure and excitement.

Georgiana, 5- Extremely bright. Physical and passionate. Natural counselor and healer. Intense inner power. An opportunist. Blessed in some ways. Independent, critical of self and others. Original, unconventional. Bold, courageous, a bit stubborn.

Georgina, 4- Into family life. Accesses quickly. Respects rules. Gentle, kind, a hard worker. Willpower and determination. Artistic, having good taste. Romantic, sensual. Independent, self-motivated.

Gerald, 11- Vision brings wealth. Keenly perceptive. Gentle, kind, a hard worker. Independent, critical of self and others. Strong verbal skills. Reliable, responsible.

Geraldine, 3- Intelligent conversationalist. A free spirit, very adaptable. Gentle, kind, a hard worker. Independent, critical of self and others. Strong verbal skills. Reliable, responsible. Blessed in some ways. Original and unconventional. Loves adventure and excitement.

Geraldo, 8- Willpower, determination. Original, creative. Gentle, kind, a hard worker. Self-motivated, a risk taker. Strong verbal skills. Practical, a problem solver. Enjoys competition.

Gerard, 8- Willpower, determination. Original, creative. Intense inner power. Bold, courageous, a bit stubborn. Tendency to lose items. Natural authority.

Gerda, 8- Willpower, determination. Original, creative. Intense inner power. Reliable, responsible. Resolute and purposeful.

Germain, 4- Into family life. Accesses quickly. Gentle, kind a hard worker. Desires financial security. Independent, critical of self and others. Blessed in some ways. Original and unconventional.

German, 4- Into family life. Accesses quickly. Gentle, kind, a hard worker. Systematic, organized. Resolute and purposeful. Romantic, sensual.

Geronimo, 6- Appreciates nature's beauty. Pioneer and risk taker. Intense inner power. Natural counselor and healer. Original and unconventional. Blessed in some ways. Domestic, hard working. Magnetic personality.

Gerry, 10- A thinker, determined. Likes change and variety. Gentle, kind a hard worker. Emotional, intense. Dislikes limitations.

Gertrude, 8- Willpower, determination. Original, creative. Gentle, kind, a hard worker. Dynamic, busy lifestyle. Emotional, intense. Attractive and charming. Reliable, responsible. Loves adventure and excitement.

Gervase, 11- Vision brings wealth. Keenly perceptive. Diligent, hard working. Intuitive and inspired. Independent, critical of self and others. Charming and devoted. Loves adventure and excitement.

Gibson, 30- Intelligent conversationalist. Understanding, thoughtful. Friendly, but shy. Charming and devoted. Natural counselor and healer. Original and unconventional.

Gideon, 9- Quiet and reflective. Blessed in some ways. Reliable, responsible. A free spirit, very adaptable. Natural counselor and healer. Original and unconventional.

Gifford, 11- Vision brings wealth. Idealistic, humanitarian. Self-sacrificing, loving. High moral standards. Natural counselor and healer. Gentle, kind, a hard worker. Reliable, responsible.

Gil, 10- A thinker, determined. Respectful, kind. Frequent traveler.

Gilbert, 10- A thinker, determined. Respectful, kind. Frequent traveler. Friendly, but shy. A free spirit, very adaptable. Diligent, hard working. Dynamic, busy lifestyle.

Gilberta, 11- Vision brings wealth. Idealistic, humanitarian. Communicates skillfully. Friendly, but shy. A free spirit, very adaptable. Gentle, kind, a hard worker. Dynamic, busy lifestyle. Independent, critical of self and others.

Gilda, 6- Appreciates nature's beauty. Artistic, having good taste. Strong verbal skills. Reliable, responsible. Independent, critical of self and others.

Giles, 7- Enjoys alone time. Blessed in some ways. Strong verbal skills. A free spirit, very adaptable. Charming and devoted.

Gillian, 10- A thinker, determined. Blessed in some ways. Strong verbal skills. Financial ups and downs. Artistic, having good taste. Independent, critical of self and others. Original and unconventional.

Gillianne, 11- Vision brings wealth. Idealistic, humanitarian. Communicates skillfully. Financial ups and downs. Artistic, having good taste. Independent, critical of self and others. Original and unconventional. Romantic, sensual. A free spirit, very adaptable.

Gilmore, 7- Enjoys alone time. Blessed in some ways. Strong verbal skills. Domestic, hard working. Natural counselor and healer. Gentle, kind, a hard worker. A free spirit, very adaptable.

Gilroy, 5- Extremely bright. Blessed in some ways. Strong verbal skills. Gentle, kind, a hard worker. Natural counselor and healer. Needs a lot of freedom.

Gina, 22- Vision brings wealth. Blessed in some ways. Original and unconventional. Resolute and purposeful.

Ginger, 6- Appreciates nature's beauty. Artistic, having good taste. Romantic, sensual. Extremely intelligent. A free spirit, very adaptable. Gentle, kind, a hard worker.

Ginny, 6- Appreciates nature's beauty. Artistic, having good taste. Creative, opinionated. Romantic, sensual. Needs a lot of freedom.

Giovanni, 10- A thinker, determined. Blessed in some ways. Natural counselor and healer. Intuitive and inspired. Independent, critical of self and others. Original and opinionated. Romantic, sensual. Artistic, having good taste.

Giovanny, 8- Willpower, determination. Blessed in some ways. Natural counselor and healer. Intuitive and inspired. Resolute and purposeful. Original and opinionated. Romantic, sensual. Needs a lot of freedom.

Giselle, 6- Appreciates nature's beauty. Creates group harmony. Charming and devoted. A free spirit, very adaptable. Strong verbal skills. Frequent traveler. A step ahead of others.

Gitta, 3- Intelligent conversationalist. Understanding, compassionate. Dynamic, busy lifestyle. Sensitive and easily hurt. Pioneer and risk taker.

Gladi, 6- Appreciates nature's beauty. Strong verbal skills. Independent, critical of self and others. Reliable, responsible. Blessed in some ways.

Gladys, 5- Extremely bright. Communicates skillfully. Bold, adventuresome. Reliable, responsible. Needs a lot of freedom. Charming and devoted.

Glen, 20- Sensitive and psychic. Communicates skillfully. A free spirit, very adaptable. Romantic, sensual.

Glenda, 7- Enjoys alone time. Travels frequently. Not easily fooled. Original and creative. Reliable, responsible. Not easily influenced.

Glenn, 7- Enjoys alone time. Travels frequently. Not easily fooled. Original and opinionated. Romantic, sensual.

Glenna, 8- Willpower, determination. Speaks their mind. A free spirit, very adaptable. Original and unconventional. Romantic, sensual. Resolute and purposeful.

Gloria, 8- Willpower, determination. Speaks their mind. Natural counselor and healer. Gentle, kind, a hard worker. Blessed in some ways. Resolute and purposeful.

Glorie, 3- Intelligent conversationalist. Strong verbal skills. Natural counselor and healer. Gentle, kind, a hard worker. Blessed in some ways. A free spirit, very adaptable.

Gloriana, 5- Extremely bright. Communicates skillfully. Natural counselor and healer. Gentle, kind, a hard worker. Blessed in some ways. Independent, critical of self and others. Original and unconventional. Bold, courageous, a bit stubborn.

Glory, 5- Extremely bright. Communicates skillfully. Natural counselor and healer. Gentle, kind, a hard worker. Needs a lot of freedom.

Glynis, 5- Extremely bright. Communicates skillfully. Needs a lot of freedom. Romantic, opinionated. Blessed in some ways. Charming and devoted.

Glynn, 9- Quiet and reflective. Strong verbal skills. Dislikes restrictions. Original and unconventional. Romantic, sensual.

Godfrey, 8- Willpower, determination. Enjoys competition. Reliable, responsible. Self-sacrificing, loving. Gentle, kind, a hard worker. A free spirit, very adaptable. Dislikes limitations.

Golda, 3- Intelligent conversationalist. Natural counselor and healer. Communicates skillfully. Creative problem solver. Pioneer and risk taker.

Goldie, 7- Enjoys alone time. Open to opportunities. Strong verbal skills. Workaholic, determined. Blessed in some ways. A free spirit, very adaptable.

Goran, 10- A thinker, determined. Natural counselor and healer. Gentle, kind, a hard worker. Independent, critical of self and others. Original and unconventional.

Gordon, 10- A thinker, determined. Natural counselor and healer. Gentle, kind, a hard worker. Reliable, responsible. May have musical abilities. Original and opinionated.

Gordy, 6- Appreciates nature's beauty. Nurturing, loving. Gentle, kind, a hard worker. Reliable, responsible. Needs a lot of freedom.

Gottfried, 5- Extremely bright. Natural counselor and healer. Dynamic, busy lifestyle. Sensitive and easily hurt. Warmhearted, compassionate. Intense inner power. Blessed in some ways. A free spirit, very adaptable. Reliable, responsible.

Grace, 7- Enjoys alone time. Gentle, kind, a hard worker. Not easily fooled. Self-expressive, cheerful. A free spirit, very adaptable.

Gracie, 7- Enjoys alone time. Gentle, kind a hard worker. Not easily fooled. Self-expressive, cheerful. Blessed in some ways. A free spirit, very adaptable.

Grady, 10- A thinker, determined. Hard working, diligent. Independent, critical of self and others. Reliable, responsible. Needs a lot of freedom.

Graham, 30- Intelligent conversationalist. Gentle, kind, a hard worker. Aims to please. Excellent judge of character. Bold, courageous, a bit stubborn. Desires financial security.

Graig, 6- Appreciates nature's beauty. Intense inner power. Pioneer and risk taker. Blessed in some ways. Extremely intelligent.

Granger, 7- Enjoys alone time. Gentle, kind, a hard worker. Not easily fooled. Original and unconventional. Extremely intelligent. A free spirit, very adaptable. Intense inner power.

Grant, 6- Appreciates nature's beauty. Diligent, hard working. Pioneer and risk taker. Original and unconventional. Dynamic, busy lifestyle.

Grayson, 9- Quiet and reflective. Gentle, kind, a hard worker. Helpful, sincere. Needs a lot of freedom. Charming and devoted. Natural counselor and healer. Original and unconventional.

Gredel, 6- Appreciates nature's beauty. Diligent, hard working. A step ahead of others. Reliable, responsible. Loves adventure and excitement. Strong verbal skills.

Greg, 10- A thinker, determined. Gentle, kind, a hard worker. Likes change and variety. Periodically needs solitude.

Gregg, 8- Willpower, determination. Intense inner power. Original and creative. Extremely intelligent. Periodically needs solitude.

Gregorio, 4- Into family life. Gentle, kind, a hard worker. Accesses quickly. Willpower and determination. Natural counselor and healer. Tendency to lose items. Blessed in some ways. Has musical talent.

Gregory, 5- Extremely bright. Intense inner power. Not easily fooled. Scientific, philosophical. Natural counselor and healer. Tendency to lose items. Needs a lot of freedom.

Greer, 8- Willpower, determination. Gentle, kind, a hard worker. Original and creative. Loves adventure and excitement. Tendency to lose items.

Greta, 6- Appreciates nature's beauty. Emotional, understanding. A step ahead of others. Dynamic, busy lifestyle. Pioneer and risk taker.

Gretchen, 8- Willpower, determination. Gentle, kind, a hard worker. Original and creative. Dynamic, busy lifestyle. Self-expressive, cheerful. Excellent judge of character. Loves adventure and excitement. Romantic, sensual.

Gretel, 4- Into family life. Natural teaching abilities. Accesses quickly. Dynamic, busy lifestyle. A free spirit, very adaptable. Strong verbal skills.

Griselda, 3- Intelligent conversationalist. Gentle, kind, a hard worker. Blessed in some ways. Charming and devoted. A free spirit, very adaptable. Strong verbal skills. Reliable, responsible. Pioneer and risk taker.

Grover, 4- Into family life. Has teaching ability. Natural counselor and healer. Intuitive and inspired. A free spirit, very adaptable. Tendency to lose items.

Guadalupe, 7- Enjoys alone time. Attractive and charming. Not easily influenced. Reliable, responsible. Bold, courageous, a bit stubborn. Strong verbal skills. Slow to make decisions. Intelligent and knowledgeable. A free spirit, very adaptable.

Guilana, 11- Vision brings wealth. Gracious, well mannered. Blessed in some ways. Slow to make decisions. Intuitive, perceptive. Original and unconventional. Bold, courageous, a bit stubborn.

Guiliana, 11- Vision brings wealth. Gracious, well mannered. Artistic, having good taste. Strong verbal skills. Blessed in some ways. Intuitive, perceptive. Original and unconventional. Bold, courageous, a bit stubborn.

Guillermo, 4- Into family life. Attractive and charming. Blessed in some ways. Strong verbal skills. Slow to make decisions. A free spirit, very adaptable. Gentle, kind, a hard worker. Systematic, organized. A natural counselor and healer.

Guinevere, 7- Enjoys alone time. Stylish and refined. Blessed in some ways. Original and unconventional. A free spirit, very adaptable. Intuitive and inspired. Tendency to overindulge. Gentle, kind, a hard worker. Loves adventure and excitement.

Gunny, 9- Quiet and reflective. Attractive and charming. Original and unconventional. Romantic, sensual. Needs a lot of freedom.

Gunther, 3- Intelligent conversationalist. Attractive and charming. Original and unconventional. Always coming and going. Excellent judge of character. A free spirit, very adaptable. Gentle, kind a hard worker.

Gus, 11- Vision brings wealth. Gracious, well mannered. Charming and devoted.

Gustaf, 20- Sensitive and psychic. Youthful, attractive. Charming and devoted. Dynamic, busy lifestyle. Independent, critical of self and others. Self-sacrificing, loving.

Gustave, 5- Extremely bright. Fun, flirtatious. Charming and devoted. Takes the initiative. Bold, adventuresome. Intuitive and inspired. A free spirit, very adaptable.

Gustavo, 6- Appreciates nature's beauty. Attractive and charming. Loving, duty bound. Socially busy. Independent, critical of self and others. Intuitive and inspired. Natural counselor and healer.

Guthrie, 7- Enjoys alone time. Attractive and charming. Dynamic, busy lifestyle. Excellent judge of character. Gentle, kind, a hard worker. Blessed in some ways. A free spirit, very adaptable.

Guy, 8- Willpower, determination. Attractive and charming. Needs a lot of freedom.

Gwen, 22- Vision brings wealth. Likes to meet new people. A free spirit, very adaptable. Original and unconventional.

Gwendolen, 9- Quiet and reflective. Likes to meet new people. Enjoys giving gifts. Creative and original. Reliable, responsible. Natural counselor and healer. Strong verbal skills. Likes change and variety. Romantic, sensual.

Gwendolyn, 11- Vision brings wealth. Likes to meet new people. Keenly perceptive. Original and unconventional. Reliable, responsible. Natural counselor and healer. Strong verbal skills. Needs a lot of freedom. Romantic, sensual.

Gweneth, 10- A thinker, determined. Implements original ideas. Likes change and variety. Opinionated and creative. Loves adventure and excitement. Dynamic, busy lifestyle. Excellent judge of character.

Gwyn, 6- Appreciates nature's beauty. Likes to meet new people. Needs a lot of freedom. Creative and romantic

Gwyneth, 3- Intelligent conversationalist. Expressive, outgoing. Dislikes restrictions. Romantic and opinionated. A free spirit, very adaptable. Dynamic, busy lifestyle. Excellent judge of character.

Gypsy, 11- Vision brings wealth. Needs a lot of freedom. Intelligent and knowledgeable. Charming and devoted. Highly perceptive.

> "Toto—I've a feeling we're not in Kansas anymore."
> ~*Excerpted from "The Wizard of Oz"*
> Used with permission

H

IF A NAME BEGINS WITH H, has more than one H, or ends with an H, this person enjoys rivalry, is an excellent judge of character, is original and creative, and likes delegating authority.

H is the 8th letter of the alphabet, ruled by the number 8. This number most resembles the 8th sign of the Zodiac, Scorpio. The number 8, in numerology, rules rewards and punishment. This 8th letter is considered karmic. It can sometimes be unlucky, but other times it will bring good fortune. This depends on the person who bears this letter in their name; it depends on the karma they brought to themselves.

The letter H is the Hercules of letters. Its very shape is structurally sound. Oddly enough, we have few female H names compared to male H names. This gives letter H a more masculine appeal. Many "Hillary Haters" bashed Hillary Clinton because of her strength of character. Most people can't understand a woman so well equipped to handle life's ups and downs. A person whose name has an H anywhere in it has survivor capabilities. Especially if the H is in the beginning of their name.

As with Dr. Jeckel and Mr. Hyde, Hyde was the strong one. Not all H people are scary; however, they seem to have tremendous strength and determination. H people aren't quitters. Most of us know Howard Hughes came from humble beginnings. H people seem to have a natural understanding of money, power and authority. Many corporate types have the letter H in their name somewhere. Even Martha Stewart has a little Hercules in her name. So she is well equipped to handle the ups and downs.

The most frightful day of the calendar, recognized as "Halloween," is appropriately named starting with an H. This Scorpio ruled letter is the queen of the occult. When looking up the word, "occult" in the dictionary, it's defined as; "beyond ordinary knowledge." So, it's to no surprise that our H ruled friends just seem to know things. As we dare to look into their eyes, it seems as if they know our very thoughts. Most of them sense this and intentionally wear sunglasses. They don't want us to feel uncomfortable as they look through us and examine our very souls.

The H person often suffers financial challenges. One of their lessons is to learn to manage their money and not let their money manage them. The H letter is comfortable in the banking or money market field. They make good administrators, top executives, brokers, collectors, art dealers, negotiators, builders, and entrepreneurs—anything "Scorpio-like." They are attracted to matters having to do with joint finances, taxes, insurance, goods of the dead, sex, restoration, making new of something old, and death. Famous Hollywood Madam, Heidi Fleiss fits right into this category. Her name with the Scorpio-like beginning, is most fitting for the sexual and material lessons learned.

8 rules letters H, Q and Z. Coincidently, the game "scrabble" gives a lot of points for those letters. H people need to remember, "what goes around comes around." What they give out, they will get back.

They must always remember to balance the material and spiritual sides of their nature. H names need to observe their own ability to give and take, punish and reward, serve and be served. This is their lesson.

In the 2002 film, "Die Another Day," Halle Berry was declared "the strongest Bond woman ever." With an H in the front of her name, she is the Hercules of women. She also came off strong in "X2:X-Men United," while demonstrating her special powers. It's not surprising to find this actress in a movie that has the word "Die" in it, as this Scorpio-like letter has everything to do with death.

Another famous H person who exhibited Scorpio-like behavior was Harry Houdini. He was the greatest magician of his time. Harry was known for his "death defying" tricks. When his mother died, he tried to contact her through séances, which is another Scorpio trait.

Hugh Grant, yet another famous H person, is as financially successful as most with not only one, but two H's in his name. In fact, Hugh's power number equals 8 as well, so his whole personality is rather Scorpio like. His first vowel, "U," makes him attractive and charming. The "G" in his first name makes him quite intelligent and philosophical. It also gives him style and good looks on camera. With half his first name ruled by the number 8, he's probably quite good at negotiating his own contracts. H types like to be in control. They can also evade issues better than any other letter, except Q and Z, which are also ruled by 8.

As Harry Houdini was able to escape death traps, our H name friends have a natural talent for escaping questions they don't want to answer. If they want you to know something, they'll let you know. They are in total control at all times. This is one of those "control freak" letters. Seldom does anyone with an H in their name ever let anything get beyond their control.

Hugh Hefner, of Playboy Magazine is a prime example of the letter H ruled by Scorpio. As mentioned before, this letter has something to do with sex. With all those H's in his name, he was born to go into the sex industry, or else he may have ended up in the stock market, insurance industry or some other Scorpio ruled business. Either way, Hugh and Heidi have a place in the sex industry.

Even though he's a fictional character, Harry Potter seems to fit his name as well. The whole witchcraft scene and the near death escapes give way to his H name. Plus the H and A add up to a hidden 9, then 2 R's ruled by the number 9 makes it difficult for him to forgive. 9's won't be happy unless they forgive others for what they've done against them. He always seems unhappy because of the past. The Y in his name makes him need a lot of freedom. So he's always running away from his guardians. Although this is only a character in a book or movie, his name still fits him perfectly!

The H influence is similar to a pot of boiling water. They appear as if about to boil over at any minute. So much energy bottled up inside of them. Yet in total control at all times … except for the times they blow off steam. In the event we are unable to escape the H's blowing off steam, we may take consolation in the fact that it only hurts for a minute. Once this volatile letter is allowed to vent, they usually forget about the whole matter within minutes. They won't brood for hours and days like the "F" and "O" letters. A little bit of heaven, a little bit of hell, our H ruled friends are a little of each.

Those daring enough to get emotionally involved with an H person may be pleasantly surprised. First of all, they've probably already sized you up the minute you walked through the door. So now all you have to do is convince them you'll be able to support them, (financially or emotionally) in the manner which they'd like to grow accustom to. They do like the finer things in life, and if they like you, then you're half-way there.

Some other famous people whose names start with H are: Hilary Duff, Howie Mandel, Hulk Hogan, Heather Locklear, Howard Stern, Hailey Mills, Harrison Ford, Harpo Marx, Henry Winkler, Huey Louis, Humphrey Bogart, Heidi Klum, Hilary Swank, Hugh Jackman, Hedda Hopper, Helen Keller, Henry Fonda,

Harvey Korman, Howard Cosell, Hedy Lamar, Ho Chi Minh, Helen Reddy, Herschel Walker, H.G Wells, Holly Hunter and Hank Williams, Jr.

Quick Reference of "H" Names

Habib, 22- Self-reliant, successful. Ambitious leader, great vision. Friendly, but shy. Blessed in some ways. Emotional, sensitive.

Hadden, 9- Likes helping others. Hard working, sincere. Reliable, responsible. Down-to-earth, faithful. A free spirit, very adaptable. Original and unconventional.

Haden, 5- A passionate soul. Bright, adventuresome. Enjoys hard work. Physical, passionate. Original and unconventional.

Hadlee, 8- Enjoys competition. Resolute and purposeful. Reliable, responsible. Strong verbal skills. A free spirit, very adaptable. Physical and passionate.

Hadley, 10- Sometimes a loner. Independent, critical of self and others. Reliable, responsible. Strong verbal skills. Loves adventure and excitement. Needs a lot of freedom.

Haidar, 5- A passionate soul. Bright, adventuresome. Blessed in some ways. Reliable, responsible. Bold, courageous, a bit stubborn. Gentle, kind, a hard worker.

Hailey, 6- Creative in business. Pioneer and risk taker. Blessed in some ways. Strong verbal skills. A free spirit, very adaptable. Dislikes limitations.

Hakeem, 7- Perceptive, psychic. Not easily influenced. Strong desire to succeed. A free spirit, very adaptable. Loves adventure and excitement. Domestic, hard working.

Hal, 3- Makes and loses money easily. Aims to please. Travels frequently.

Halbert, 30- Makes and loses money easily. Aims to please. Strong verbal skills. Friendly, but shy. A free spirit, very adaptable. Gentle, kind, a hard worker. Dynamic, busy lifestyle.

Hale, 8- Enjoys competition. Resolute and purposeful. Communicates skillfully. Physical, passionate.

Haley, 6- Creative in business. Pioneer and risk taker. Easy going attitude. A free spirit, very adaptable. Dislikes limitations.

Hall, 6- Creative in business. Pioneer and risk taker. Strong verbal skills. A frequent traveler.

Halle, 20- Excellent mediator. Reads people easily. Honest and sincere. Frequent traveler. A free spirit, very adaptable.

Halley, 9- Likes helping others. Hard working, sincere. Strong verbal skills. Frequent traveler. A free spirit, very adaptable. Dislikes limitations.

Hamidi, 8- Enjoys competition. Resolute and purposeful. Domestic, hard working. Blessed in some ways. Reliable, responsible. Idealistic, humanitarian.

Hamilton, 11- Self-reliant, successful. Intuitive, perceptive. Desires financial security. Blessed in some ways. Strong verbal skills. Dynamic, busy lifestyle. Natural counselor and healer. Original and opinionated.

Hamish, 4- Relies on own judgment. Natural teaching ability. Down to earth, practical. Blessed in some ways. Charming and devoted. Self-reliant, successful.

Hamlet, 5- A passionate soul. Bright, adventuresome. Domestic, hard working. Strong verbal skills. Physical and passionate. Dynamic, busy lifestyle.

Hamlin, 30- Makes and loses money easily. Aims to please. Domestic, hard working. Communicates skillfully. Blessed in some ways. Romantic, opinionated.

Hana, 6- Creative in business. Pioneer and risk taker. Romantic, sensual. Bold, courageous, a bit stubborn.

Hanako, 5- A passionate soul. Bright, adventuresome. Original and unconventional. Bold, courageous, a bit stubborn. Strong desire to succeed. Natural counselor and healer.

Hank, 7- Perceptive, psychic. Not easily influenced. Original and unconventional. Strong desire to succeed.

Hanna, 20- Excellent mediator. Reads people easily. Original and opinionated. Romantic, sensual. Bold, courageous, a bit stubborn.

Hannah, 10- Sometimes a loner. Independent, critical of self and others. Creative, opinionated. Romantic, sensual. Bold, courageous, a bit stubborn. Self-reliant, successful.

Hans, 6- Creative in business. Pioneer and risk taker. Original and unconventional. Charming and devoted.

Hansel, 5- A passionate soul. Bright, adventuresome. Creative, opinionated. Charming and devoted. A free spirit, very adaptable. Strong verbal skills.

Hara, 10- Sometimes a loner. Independent, critical of self and others. Diligent, hard working. Bold, courageous, a bit stubborn.

Harbin, 7- Perceptive, psychic. Not easily influenced. Gentle, kind, a hard worker. Friendly, but shy. Blessed in some ways. Original and unconventional.

Harden, 5- A passionate soul. Bright, adventuresome. Gentle, kind, a hard worker. Reliable, responsible. A free spirit, very adaptable. Original and unconventional.

Harding, 7- Perceptive, psychic. Not easily influenced. Spiritually motivated. Reliable, responsible. Blessed in some ways. Original, opinionated. Scientific and philosophical.

Hardy, 11- Self-reliant, successful. Intuitive, perceptive. Gentle, kind, a hard worker. Reliable, responsible. Needs a lot of freedom.

Hargrove, 4- Relies on own judgment. Natural teaching ability. Gentle, kind, a hard worker. Scientific and philosophical. Tendency to lose items. Nurturing, loving. Intuitive and inspired. A free spirit, very adaptable.

Harim, 4- Relies on own judgment. Natural teaching ability. Hard working, idealistic. Blessed in some ways. Systematic, organized.

Harlan, 9- Likes helping others. Hardworking, sincere. Gentle, kind, very diligent. Strong verbal skills. Bold, courageous, a bit stubborn. Original and unconventional.

Harley, 6- Creative in business. Pioneer and risk taker. Gentle, kind, a hard worker. Strong verbal skills. A free spirit, very adaptable. Dislikes limitations.

Harlow, 5- A passionate soul. Bright, adventuresome. Hard working, idealistic. Communicates skillfully. Natural counselor and healer. Likes to meet new people.

Harmony, 4- Relies on own judgment. Natural teaching ability. Gentle, kind, a hard worker. Domestic, hard working. Nurturing, loving. Original and unconventional. Needs a lot of freedom.

Harod, 10- Sometimes a loner. Independent, critical of self and others. Gentle, kind, a hard worker. Natural counselor and healer. Systematic, organized.

Harold, 4- Relies on own judgment. Natural teaching ability. Gentle, kind, a hard worker. Nurturing, loving. Strong verbal skills. Reliable, responsible.

Harper, 3- Makes and loses money easily. Aims to please. Optimistic and kind. Intelligent and knowledgeable. A free spirit, very adaptable. Tendency to lose items.

Harriet, 7- Perceptive, psychic. Not easily influenced. Spiritual, idealistic. Tendency to lose items. Blessed in some ways. A free spirit, very adaptable. Dynamic, busy lifestyle.

Harris, 10- Sometimes a loner. Independent, critical of self and others. Gentle, kind, a hard worker. Tendency to lose items. Blessed in some ways. Charming and devoted.

Harrison, 3- Makes and loses money easily. Aims to please. Optimistic, very kind. Intense inner power. Artistic, having good taste. Natural counselor and healer. Original and opinionated.

Harry, 7- Perceptive, psychic. Not easily influenced. Gentle, kind, a hard worker. Tendency to lose items. Needs a lot of freedom.

Harv, 22- Self-reliant, successful. Ambitious leader, great vision. Gentle, kind, a hard worker. Intuitive and inspired.

Harvey, 7- Perceptive, psychic. Not easily influenced. Gentle, kind, a hard worker. Intuitive and inspired. A free spirit, very adaptable. Dislikes limitations.

Hasana, 8- Enjoys competition. Resolute and purposeful. Charismatic, loving. Independent, critical of self and others. Original and unconventional. Pioneer and risk taker.

Hasina, 7- Perceptive, psychic. Not easily influenced. Charming and devoted. Blessed in some ways. Original and unconventional. Bold, courageous, a bit stubborn.

Hassan, 8- Enjoys competition. Resolute and purposeful. Charming and devoted. Impulsive and extreme. Resolute and purposeful. Original and unconventional.

Hattie, 9- Likes helping others. Hard working, sincere. Dynamic, busy lifestyle. Sensitive and easily hurt. Blessed in some ways. A free spirit, very adaptable.

Hatty, 20- Excellent mediator. Reads people easily. Socially active. Sensitive and easily hurt. Needs a lot of freedom.

Hawley, 11- Self-reliant, successful. Intuitive, perceptive. Likes to meet new people. Strong verbal skills. A free spirit, very adaptable. Dislikes limitations.

Hayden, 30- Makes and loses money easily. Aims to please. Needs a lot of freedom. Reliable, responsible. Loves adventure and excitement. Original and opinionated.

Hayes, 22- Self-reliant, successful. Ambitious leader, great vision. Needs a lot of freedom. Loves adventure and excitement. Charming and devoted.

Hazel, 7- Perceptive, psychic. Not easily influenced. Uses common sense. A free spirit, very adaptable. Strong verbal skills.

Heath, 6- Creative in business. A step ahead of others. Pioneer and risk taker. Dynamic, busy lifestyle. Self-reliant, successful.

Heather, 11- Self-reliant, successful. Keenly perceptive. Independent, critical of self and others. Dynamic, busy lifestyle. Self-reliant, successful. Loves adventure and excitement. Gentle, kind, a hard worker.

Hector, 6- Creative in business. A step ahead of others. Self-expressive, cheerful. Dynamic, busy lifestyle. Natural counselor and healer. Gentle, kind, a hard worker.

Hedda, 22- Self-reliant, successful. Has big plans and ideas. Shrewd and determined. Down-to-earth, faithful. Ambitious leader, great vision.

Heddy, 10- Sometimes a loner. Likes change and variety. Reliable, responsible. Down-to-earth, faithful. Needs a lot of freedom.

Hedy, 6- Creative in business. A step ahead of others. Systematic, organized. Needs a lot of freedom.

Heidi, 8- Enjoys competition. Original and creative. Blessed in some ways. Reliable, responsible. Artistic, having good taste.

Helaine, 9- Likes helping others. Enjoys giving gifts. Frequent traveler. Independent, hard working. Blessed in some ways. Original, creative. Physical and passionate.

Helen, 8- Enjoys competition. Original and creative. Strong verbal skills. Loves adventure and excitement. Original and unconventional.

Helena, 9- Likes helping others. Enjoys giving gifts. Strong verbal skills. Physical and passionate. Original, creative. Resolute and purposeful.

Helga, 6- Creative in business. A step ahead of others. Easy going attitude. Scientific and philosophical. Independent, critical of self and others.

Helki, 9- Likes helping others. Enjoys giving gifts. Communicates skillfully. Strong desire to succeed. Blessed in some ways.

Henley, 6- Creative in business. A step ahead of others. Original and unconventional. Strong verbal skills. Physical and passionate. Dislikes limitations.

Henrietta, 10- Sometimes a loner. Likes change and variety. Creative, opinionated. Gentle, kind, a hard worker. Blessed in some ways. Loves adventure and excitement. Dynamic, busy lifestyle. Sensitive and easily hurt. Independent, critical of self and others.

Henry, 7- Perceptive, psychic. Not easily fooled. Original and unconventional. Gentle, kind, a hard worker. Needs a lot of freedom.

Herald, 30- Makes and loses money easily. A free spirit, very adaptable. Gentle, kind, a hard worker. Independent, critical of self and others. Strong verbal skills. Reliable, responsible.

Herb, 6- Creative in business. A step ahead of others. Generous, helpful. Friendly, but shy.

Herbert, 4- Relies on own judgment. Accesses quickly. Gentle, kind, a hard worker. Friendly, buy shy. Loves adventure and excitement. Tendency to lose items. Dynamic, busy lifestyle.

Herm, 8- Enjoys competition. Original and creative. Intense inner power. Systematic, organized.

Herman, 5- A passionate soul. Adaptable to change. Gentle, kind, a hard worker. Systematic, organized. Bright, adventuresome. Original and unconventional.

Hermen, 9- Likes helping others. A free spirit, very adaptable. Gentle, kind, a hard worker. Systematic, organized. Tendency to overindulge. Original and unconventional.

Hermes, 5- A passionate soul. A free spirit, very adaptable. Intense inner power. Systematic, organized. Perceptive, reads people easily. Charming and devoted.

Hermie, 4- Relies on own judgment. Natural teaching ability. Diligent, helpful. Down-to-earth, faithful. Blessed in some ways. Loves adventure and excitement.

Hermosa, 7- Perceptive, psychic. Not easily fooled. Spiritually motivated. Systematic, organized. Natural counselor and healer. Charming and devoted. Independent, critical of self and others.

Hernando, 7- Perceptive, psychic. Not easily fooled. Spiritually motivated. Original and unconventional. Independent, self reliant. Romantic, sensual. Reliable, responsible. Natural counselor and healer.

Herro, 10- Sometimes a loner. A free spirit, very adaptable. Gentle, kind, a hard worker. Tendency to lose items. Natural counselor and healer.

Herrod, 5- A passionate soul. Loves adventure and excitement. Intense inner power. Tendency to lose items. Natural counselor and healer. Reliable, responsible.

Hester, 30- Makes and loses money easily. A free spirit, very adaptable. Charming and devoted. Dynamic, busy lifestyle. Physical and passionate. Intense inner power.

Hetti, 8- Enjoys competition. Physical and passionate. Dynamic, busy lifestyle. Sensitive and easily hurt. Blessed in some ways.

Hettie, 4- Relies on own judgment. A free spirit, very adaptable. Busy family life. Sensitive and easily hurt. Blessed in some ways. Loves adventure and excitement.

Hetty, 6- Creative in business. A step ahead of others. Dynamic, busy lifestyle. Sensitive and easily hurt. Needs a lot of freedom.

Hewe, 5- A passionate soul. A free spirit, very adaptable. Likes to meet new people. Loves adventure and excitement.

Hewett, 9- Likes helping others. Enjoys giving gifts. Likes to meet new people. Physical and passionate. Dynamic, busy lifestyle. Sensitive and easily hurt.

Hiatt, 22- Self-reliant, successful. Blessed in some ways. Resolute and purposeful. Dynamic, busy lifestyle. Sensitive and easily hurt.

Hilary, 10- Sometimes a loner. Works for group effort. Strong verbal skills. Independent, critical of self and others. Gentle, kind, a hard worker. Needs a lot of freedom.

Hillary, 4- Relies on own judgment. Blessed in some ways. Strong verbal skills. Frequent traveler. Resolute and purposeful. Gentle, kind, a hard worker. Needs a lot of freedom.

Hilda, 7- Perceptive, psychic. Needs alone time. Frequent traveler. Systematic, organized. Independent, critical of self and others.

Hildegard, 5- A passionate soul. Blessed in some ways. Communicates skillfully. Reliable, responsible. A free spirit, very adaptable. Scientific, philosophical. Independent, critical of self and others. Gentle, kind, a hard worker. Down-to-earth.

Hildie, 11- Self-reliant, successful. Idealistic, humanitarian. Strong verbal skills. Reliable, responsible. Artistic, having good taste. A free spirit, very adaptable.

Hildy, 4- Relies on own judgment. Blessed in some ways. Strong verbal skills. Reliable, responsible. Needs a lot of freedom.

Hilton, 6- Creative in business. Artistic, having good taste. Communicates skillfully. Dynamic, busy lifestyle. Natural counselor and healer. Original and unconventional.

Hines, 10- Sometimes a loner. Respectful, kind. Original and unconventional. A free spirit, very adaptable. Charming and devoted.

Hiram, 4- Relies on own judgment. Blessed in some ways. Gentle, kind, a hard worker. Independent, critical of self and others. Systematic, organized.

Hobart, 10- Sometimes a loner. Natural counselor and healer. Friendly, but shy. Independent, critical of self and others. Gentle, kind, a hard worker. Dynamic, busy lifestyle.

Hogan, 9- Likes helping others. Creates group harmony. Scientific, philosophical. Independent, critical of self and others. Original and unconventional.

Holbrook, 6- Creative in business. Nurturing, loving. Communicates skillfully. Friendly, but shy. Gentle, kind, a hard worker. Musically talented. Magnetic personality. Strong desire to succeed.

Holden, 4- Relies on own judgment. Natural counselor and healer. Strong verbal skills. Reliable, responsible. A free spirit, very adaptable. Original and unconventional.

Holley, 5- A passionate soul. Natural counselor and healer. Strong verbal skills. Frequent traveler. Physical and passionate. Dislikes limitations.

Hollie, 7- Perceptive, psychic. Open to opportunities. Strong verbal skills. Frequent traveler. Blessed in some ways. A free spirit, very adaptable.

Hollis, 30- Makes and loses money easily. Has creative solutions. Communicates skillfully. Travels frequently. Artistic, having good taste. Charming and devoted.

Holly, 9- Likes helping others. Creates group harmony. Strong verbal skills. Frequent traveler. Needs a lot of freedom.

Holmes, 9- Likes helping others. Creates group harmony. Strong verbal skills. Domestic, hard working. A free spirit, very adaptable. Charming and devoted.

Homa, 10- Sometimes a loner. Natural counselor and healer. Domestic, hard working. Independent, critical of self and others.

Homer, 5- A passionate soul. Nurturing, loving. Systematic, organized. A free spirit, very adaptable. Gentle, kind, a hard worker.

Honey, 4- Relies on own judgment. Practical and duty bound. Romantic, opinionated. Accesses quickly. Needs a lot of freedom.

Hong, 8- Enjoys competition. Natural counselor and healer. Original and unconventional. Scientific and philosophical.

Honoria, 8- Enjoys competition. Magnetic personality. Romantic, opinionated. Natural counselor and healer. Intense inner power. Blessed in some ways. Resolute and purposeful.

Hope, 8- Enjoys competition. Natural counselor and healer. Intelligent and knowledgeable. A free spirit, very adaptable.

Horace, 5- A passionate soul. Magnetic personality. Gentle, kind, a hard worker. Independent, critical of self and others. Self-expressive, cheerful. A free spirit, very adaptable.

Horatio, 5- A passionate soul. Natural counselor and healer. Intense inner power. Independent, critical of self and others. Dynamic, busy lifestyle. Blessed in some ways. May have musical abilities.

Hortense, 5- A passionate soul. Magnetic personality. Gentle, kind, a hard worker. Dynamic, busy lifestyle. A free spirit, very adaptable. Original and unconventional. Charming and devoted. Tendency to overindulge.

Horton, 9- Likes helping others. Creates group harmony. Gentle, kind, a hard worker. Dynamic, busy lifestyle. May have musical abilities. Original and unconventional.

Hoshi, 5- A passionate soul. Natural counselor and healer. Charming and devoted. Self-reliant, successful. Blessed in some ways.

Hoshie, 10- Sometimes a loner. Self-sacrificing, loving. Charming and devoted. Self-reliant, successful. Blessed in some ways. A free spirit, very adaptable.

Hoshiko, 4- Relies on own judgment. Natural counselor and healer. Charming and devoted. Self-reliant, successful. Blessed in some ways. Strong desire to succeed. May have musical abilities.

Hossain, 4- Relies on own judgment. Natural counselor and healer. Charming and devoted. Impulsive and extreme. Independent, critical of self and others. Blessed in some ways. Original and unconventional.

Houston, 4- Relies on own judgment. Responsible, duty bound. Attractive and charming. Can be impulsive and extreme. Dynamic, busy lifestyle. May have musical abilities. Original and unconventional.

Howard, 6- Creative in business. Nurturing, loving. Likes to meet new people. Independent, critical of self and others. Gentle, kind, a hard worker. Reliable, responsible.

Howie, 6- Creative in business. Creates group harmony. Likes to meet new people. Blessed in some ways. A free spirit, very adaptable.

Hoyt, 5- A passionate soul. Natural counselor and healer. Needs a lot of freedom. Dynamic, busy lifestyle.

Hubert, 11- Self-reliant, successful. Attractive and charming. Friendly, but shy. A free spirit, very adaptable. Gentle, kind, a hard worker. Dynamic, busy lifestyle.

Huey, 5- A passionate soul. Fun, flirtatious. A free spirit, very adaptable. Dislikes limitations.

Hugh, 8-Enjoys competition. Attractive and charming. Scientific and philosophical. Self-reliant, successful.

Hughie, 4- Relies on own judgment. Attractive and charming. Scientific and philosophical. Self-reliant, successful. Blessed in some ways. A free spirit, very adaptable.

Hugo, 6- Creative in business. Charming, youthful. Scientific and philosophical. Natural counselor and healer.

Humbert, 6- Creative in business. Charming, youthful. Desires financial security. Friendly, but shy. A free spirit, very adaptable. Gentle, kind, a hard worker. Dynamic, busy lifestyle.

Hume, 20- Excellent mediator. Attractive and charming. Domestic, hardworking. Loves excitement and adventure.

Humphrey, 6- Creative in business. Charming, youthful. Desires financial security. Intelligent and knowledgeable. Self-reliant, successful. Intense inner power. A free spirit, very adaptable. Dislikes limitations.

Humfrey, 6- Creative in business. Charming, youthful. Domestic, hardworking. Self-sacrificing, loving. Intense inner power. A free spirit, very adaptable. Dislikes limitations.

Hunt, 9- Likes helping others. Attractive and charming. Original and unconventional. Dynamic, busy lifestyle.

Hunter, 5- A passionate soul. Attractive and charming. Creative, opinionated. Extremely social. A free spirit, very adaptable. Gentle, kind, a hard worker.

Huntley, 6- Creative in business. Charming, youthful. Original and unconventional. Dynamic, busy lifestyle. Strong verbal skills. Likes change and variety. Needs a lot of freedom.

Huntington, 7- Perceptive, psychic. Attractive and charming. Original and unconventional. Dynamic, busy lifestyle. Blessed in some ways. Romantic, sensual. Extremely intelligent. Sensitive and easily hurt. Natural counselor and healer. Creative and opinionated.

Hurley, 8- Enjoys competition. Attractive and charming. Gentle, kind, a hard worker. Strong verbal skills. A free spirit, very adaptable. Dislikes limitations.

Hutton, 8- Enjoys competition. Attractive and charming. Dynamic, busy lifestyle. Sensitive and easily hurt. Natural counselor and healer. Original and unconventional.

Huxford, 6- Creative in business. Charming, youthful. Artistic, sensual, perceptive. Self-sacrificing, loving. Natural counselor and healer. Gentle, kind, a hard worker. Reliable, responsible.

Huxley, 5- A passionate soul. Attractive and charming. Artistic, sensual, perceptive. Strong verbal skills. A free spirit, very adaptable. Dislikes limitations.

Hyacinth, 7- Perceptive, psychic. Needs a lot of freedom. Not easily fooled. Optimistic, outgoing. Blessed in some ways. Original and unconventional. Dynamic, busy lifestyle. Self-reliant, successful.

Hyatt, 20- Excellent mediator. Needs a lot of freedom. Independent, critical of self and others. Dynamic, busy lifestyle. Sensitive and easily hurt.

Hyde, 6- Creative in business. Dislikes limitations. Reliable, responsible. A free spirit, very adaptable.

Hy, 6- Creative in business. Needs a lot of freedom. Nurturing, loving.

Hyman, 7- Perceptive, psychic. Needs a lot of freedom. Domestic, hard working. Independent, critical of self and others. Original and unconventional.

Hymen, 11- Self-reliant, successful. Needs a lot of freedom. Desires financial security. A free spirit, very adaptable. Original and unconventional.

Hymie, 6- Creative in business. Needs a lot of freedom. Domestic, hard working. Blessed in some ways. Loves adventure and excitement.

Hyrum, 4- Relies on own judgment. Needs a lot of freedom. Gentle, kind, a hard worker. Attractive and charming. Domestic, goal oriented.

> "The little people who live in this land—
> it's Munchkin land, and you are their
> national heroine, my dear. It's all right—
> you may all come out and thank her. It's
> all right now—you may all come out."
> ~*Excerpted from "The Wizard of Oz"*
> *Used with permission*

I

IF A NAME BEGINS WITH I, is the first vowel, has more than one I, or ends with an I, this person is a humanitarian, blessed in some ways, and is artistic and creative.

The letter "I" is the 9th letter of the alphabet and influenced by the number 9 vibration. Its personality is similar to the astrological sign Sagittarius. Those with the letter I in their name, have a generous, broadminded attitude toward all of humanity. They tend to have friends and associates of all colors and backgrounds. The letter I is open minded, spiritual, charitable and tolerant of the differences of others. People with an I in the beginning of their name or as a first vowel are often recognized by their friendly, comfortable nature. Others feel safe when they're with an I person. It's that self-sacrificing, impersonal quality that everyone notices. They are the teachers and counselors that stay late to donate their time for the good of the whole. Often they are taken advantage of, but they will be the last to say anything about it. God notices though, and that's why they are more blessed than the rest of us.

Whether their name begins with an I or they have an I first vowel, people often go up to the I person in a grocery store to ask where something is. I's give the impression as if they know everything somehow. Life is much bigger and grander for an I person. It's difficult for the I person to narrow their attention down to just one or two people when they are use to spreading themselves far and wide to many people. So an I person can be a disappointment in a relationship, unless the other person also has an I or an R in their name. Another disappointment could be in their apparent lack of concern for material wealth. Spiritual development and greed don't go together in the mind of the I person.

Similar to Sagittarius, the I person is lucky. They often are blessed in some area of their life. Although they are apparently immune to the call for materialism, they often are blessed enough to marry into money, as our late Princess Di, with I as the first vowel in her name. I's are often born into money. First vowel Pricilla Presley, as well as Pricilla's and Elvis' daughter, Lisa Presley, were blessed by being born into money. Even though Elvis wasn't born into money, he was still blessed in some ways, just having an I in his name.

Sadly enough, this 9th letter of the alphabet usually suffers from the "poor little rich kid" syndrome. A sadness seems to be attached to those with an I influence. Although I first vowels and names are blessed in some ways, they often have old family pain that remains to haunt them. Many of them have "father issues." The I person will be happy if they can forgive the mistakes others have made against them. As spiritual as they are, forgiveness does not come easily for the I individual. As long as they are unable to forgive and forget, they will not truly be happy. They will remain tormented.

Those with the first letter of their name beginning with an I, or first vowel beginning with an I tend to have good taste in décor. It's not surprising to find these individuals in artistic careers, especially since they aren't materialistic. Often they live in humble surroundings while they pursue artistic endeavors.

Often people will follow those with an I first vowel whether they are right or wrong. For some reason they seem to get away with more than the rest of us. Bill Clinton, Britney Spears and Michael Jackson are forgiven. Similar to the saying, "Christians aren't perfect, just forgiven," can also be for the I first vowels. Somehow, right or wrong, people tend to follow those with an I first vowel and overlook their faults as if to put them on a pedestal.

I first vowel, Michelangelo, started his apprenticeship in the field of art at 12 years of age. Today he is regarded as one of the most famous artists ever born. Born in the 3rd month of March, on the 6th day, made him quite creative as well as those numbers adding up to a 9 attitude number. (3, 6, and 9 are the creative numbers.) It's no wonder he spent part of his youth and his entire adult life creating. It's the I in his name, however, that gave him natural artistic ability. The M influenced his work in sculpture, as it is a hard working, harsh letter. Marble starts with the letter M with which he worked most of his artistic career. To sculpt marble, one needs a hammer and chisel. The disciplined M in his name helped him to work tirelessly for many years on each masterpiece. The I as his first vowel, or heart's desire letter, led him to religious art work.

Bill O'Reilly of "The O'Reilly Factor" shows his humanitarianism by discussing world political affairs in his "fair and balanced" talk show. Bill's name sums up to an 8 power number, making him a little bit brutal, and the 2 L's give him the edge in communication matters; still, he is a humanitarian by his heart's desire letter "I." He invites people of all race and color, and does not seem to discriminate. When he verbally thrashes someone, it doesn't seem to matter what color, race, religion or political preference they are. This, brutal or not, makes him a humanitarian. Being color blind and sticking with the issues are idealistic qualities of an "I" first vowel.

Another Fox News regular is Dr. Isadore Rosenfeld. This famous Doctor has written numerous books and practiced medicine for many years. People tend to follow a person with an I first vowel. Not only is his first vowel an I, but the first letter of his name begins with I. So Dr. Isadore Rosenfeld wears his heart's desire letter up front for everyone to see. He comes across as the kind of person one can trust and count on. He no doubt works hard for the good of the whole and is probably taken advantage of often, as most 9 ruled individuals are. He has such a kind and caring face. Isadore sums up to an 8 power number, so the good Doctor is able to manage over material success more easily than most with this much 9 vibration.

Diane Sawyer, currently with ABC News, Primetime Thursday and co-anchor on Good Morning America, shows her humanitarianism through her work as well. The D in her name makes her systematic, organized and up for any task. Her first vowel, I, conjuncts A, giving her leadership qualities in her efforts to be as humanitarian as possible. Since the A flavors her "I" heart's desire letter, she is a more daring and bold humanitarian type.

Those born with I anywhere in their name tend to work hard for the good of the whole. I is the 9th letter of the alphabet and 9 rules completions. Those with an I in their name are completing a stage of learning in this lifetime. They are farther along than the rest of us in God's eyes. They are the ones donating their time to help a good cause. Often they are taken advantage of as they are so charitable. They will do their own job and everyone else's without complaining. They have a special mission on earth. They're put here to do God's work, sort of like Angels.

Some other famous names that begin with the letter "I" are: Ingrid Bergman, Indira Ghandi, Isaac Stern, Isaac Misrahi, Isabella Rossalini, Isaac Newton, Ivana Trump, Ira Gershwin, Irving Berlin, Ian Fleming, Ione Skye, Imogene Coca, Ice-T, Iggy Pop, Ice Cube and Isaac Hayes.

Quick Reference of "I" Names

Ian, 6- Artistic, having good taste. Pioneer and risk taker. Romantic and creative.

Ibrahim, 6- Artistic, having good taste. Friendly, but shy. Gentle, kind, a hard worker. Pioneer and risk taker. Excellent judge of character. Artistic, having good taste. Desires financial security.

Ice, 8- Gives practical gifts. Optimistic and outspoken. Original and creative.

Ichabod, 6- Artistic, having good taste. Self-expressive, cheerful. Excellent judge of character. Pioneer and risk taker. Friendly, but shy. Natural counselor and healer. Reliable, responsible.

Ida, 5- Generous, thoughtful. Domestic, hard working. Bright, adventuresome.

Idella, 7- Has spiritual undertones. Creative problem solver. A free spirit, very adaptable. Strong verbal skills. Frequent traveler. Not easily influenced.

Idelle, 11- Idealistic and humanitarian. Insightful, sensitive. Keenly perceptive. Strong verbal skills. Ups and downs financially. Loves adventure and excitement.

Iggy, 30- Communicates understanding. Scientific and philosophical. Stylish and refined. Needs a lot of freedom.

Ignacia, 8- Practical when giving. Creative opportunist. Romantic, sensual. Resolute and purposeful. Self-expressive, cheerful. Artistic, having good taste. Bold, courageous, a bit stubborn.

Ignacio, 4- Teaches kindness. Extremely intelligent. Original and unconventional. Resolute and purposeful. Great sense of humor. Artistic, having good taste. Natural counselor and healer.

Ignatia, 7- Has spiritual undertones. Scientific and philosophical. Original and unconventional. Not easily influenced. Dynamic, busy lifestyle. Artistic, having good taste. Bold, courageous, a bit stubborn.

Ignatius, 10- Works for group effort. Scientific and philosophical. Creative, opinionated. Independent, critical of self and others. Dynamic, busy lifestyle. Artistic, having good taste. Attractive and charming. Loving and devoted.

Ignatz, 5- Generous, thoughtful. Scientific and philosophical. Creative, opinionated. Bright, adventuresome. Dynamic, busy lifestyle. Uses common sense.

Igor, 4- Teaches kindness. A bit of a homebody. Natural counselor and healer. Gentle, kind, a hard worker.

Ike, 7- Has spiritual undertones. Strong desire to succeed. Not easily fooled.

Ilana, 10- Works for group effort. Strong verbal skills. Independent, critical of self and others. Original and unconventional. Bold, courageous, a bit stubborn.

Ilene, 9- Blessed in some ways. Communicates skillfully. Enjoys giving gifts. Creative and opinionated. Physical and passionate.

Ilenna, 10- Works for group effort. Strong verbal skills. Likes change and variety. Original and unconventional. Romantic, sensual. Independent, critical of self and others.

Iline, 4- Teaches kindness. Strong verbal skills. Artistic, having good taste. Original and unconventional. A free spirit, very adaptable.

Ilka, 6- Artistic, having good taste. Communicates well. Strong desire to succeed. Pioneer and risk taker.

Illene, 30- Communicates understanding. Ups and downs financially. Frequent traveler. A free spirit, very adaptable. Original and unconventional. Loves adventure and excitement.

Illona, 9- Blessed in some ways. Slow to make decisions. Frequent traveler. Natural counselor and healer. Original and unconventional. Independent, critical of self and others.

Ilona, 6- Artistic, having good taste. Strong verbal skills. Natural counselor and healer. Original and unconventional. Pioneer and risk taker.

Ilsa, 5- Generous, thoughtful. Communicates skillfully. Charming and devoted. Bright, adventuresome.

Ilse, 9- Blessed in some ways. Strong verbal skills. Charming and devoted. A free spirit, very adaptable.

Ima, 5- Generous, thoughtful. Domestic, hard working. Bright, adventuresome.

Imer, 9- Blessed in some ways. Diligent, generous with time. A free spirit, very adaptable. Gentle, kind, very helpful.

Imogene, 5- Generous, thoughtful. Domestic, hard working. Natural counselor and healer. Scientific and philosophical. A free spirit, very adaptable. Original and unconventional. Physical and passionate.

Immanuel, 7- Has spiritual undertones. Must have faith. Systematic, organized. Not easily influenced. Original and unconventional. Attractive and charming. A free spirit, very adaptable. Strong verbal skills.

Ina, 6- Artistic, having good taste. Creative and romantic. Pioneer and risk taker.

Inday, 8- Practical when giving. Romantic, sensual. Reliable, responsible. Resolute and purposeful. Needs a lot of freedom.

India, 10- Works for group effort. Friendly, likes people. Systematic, organized. Artistic, having good taste. Independent, critical of self and others.

Indiana, 7- Has spiritual undertones. Original and unconventional. Reliable, responsible. Blessed in some ways. Not easily influenced. Romantic, sensual. Bold, courageous, a bit stubborn.

Indigo, 4- Teaches kindness. Practical creativity. Reliable, responsible. Artistic, having good taste. Scientific and philosophical. Natural counselor and healer.

Indira, 10- Works for group effort. Friendly, likes people. A natural authority. Artistic, having good taste. Gentle, kind, a hard worker. Independent, critical of self and others.

Indra, 10- Works for group effort. Original and unconventional. Reliable, responsible. Gentle, kind, a hard worker. Independent, critical of self and others.

Indria, 10- (Same as Indira)

Indy, 7- Has spiritual undertones. Original and unconventional. Reliable, responsible. Needs a lot of freedom.

Ines, 20- Emotional and considerate. Socially active. A free spirit, very adaptable. Charming and devoted.

Inessa, 22- Idealistic and humanitarian. Perceptive, intuitive. Enjoys giving gifts. Charming and devoted. Impulsive and extreme. Independent, critical of self and others.

Inez, 9- Blessed in some ways. Original and unconventional. A free spirit, very adaptable. Uses common sense.

Inga, 22- Idealistic and humanitarian. Intuitive and creative. Thinks on a large scale. Independent, critical of self and others.

Inge, 8- Gives practical gifts. Romantic, sensual. Scientific and philosophical. A free spirit, very adaptable.

Ingemar, 4- Teaches kindness. Original and unconventional. Scientific and philosophical. A free spirit, very adaptable. Desires financial security. Independent, critical of self and others. Gentle, kind, a hard worker.

Inglebert, 11- Idealistic and humanitarian. Intuitive and creative. Scientific and philosophical. Strong verbal skills. A free spirit, very adaptable. Friendly, but shy. Loves adventure and excitement. Gentle, kind, a hard worker. Dynamic, busy lifestyle.

Ingram, 8- Gives practical gifts. Romantic, sensual. Scientific and philosophical. Intense inner power. Resolute and purposeful. Systematic, organized.

Ingraham, 8- Gives practical gifts. Romantic, sensual. Scientific and philosophical. Gentle, kind, a hard worker. Resolute and purposeful. Excellent judge of character. Bold, courageous, a bit stubborn. Systematic, organized.

Ingred, 3- Communicates understanding. Creative, opinionated. Scientific and philosophical. Gentle, kind, a hard worker. A free spirit, very adaptable. Reliable, responsible.

Ingrid, 7- Has spiritual undertones. Original and unconventional. Scientific and philosophical. Gentle, kind, a hard worker. Artistic, having good taste. Reliable, responsible.

Inness, 8- Gives practical gifts. Creative, original. Romantic, sensual. A free spirit, very adaptable. Charming and devoted. Impulsive and extreme.

Innis, 11- Idealistic and humanitarian. Perceptive, opinionated. Romantic, sensual. Artistic, having good taste. Charming and devoted.

Iola, 10- Works for group effort. Natural counselor and healer. Strong verbal skills. Independent, critical of self and others.

Iona, 3- Communicates understanding. Creates group harmony. Creative, opinionated. Pioneer and risk taker.

Ione, 7- Has spiritual undertones. Natural counselor and healer. Original and unconventional. A free spirit, very adaptable.

Ira, 10- Works for group effort. Gentle, kind, a hard worker. Independent, critical of self and others.

Ireland, 9- Blessed in some ways. Diligent, helpful. A free spirit, very adaptable. Communicates skillfully. Respectful, kind. Original and unconventional. Reliable, responsible.

Irena, 11- Idealistic and humanitarian. Gentle, kind, a hard worker. Physical and passionate. Original and unconventional. Independent, critical of self and others.

Irene, 6- Artistic, having good taste. Helpful, generous with time. A step ahead of others. Creative and opinionated. Loves adventure and excitement.

Irina, 6- Artistic, having good taste. Helpful, generous with time. Artistic, having good taste. Creative and opinionated. Pioneer and risk taker.

Iris, 10- Works for group effort. Gentle, kind, a hard worker. Blessed in some ways. Charming and devoted.

Irma, 5- Generous, thoughtful. Intense inner power. Systematic, organized. Bright, adventuresome.

Irv, 22- Idealistic and humanitarian. Gentle, kind, a hard worker. Intuitive and inspired.

Irvin, 9- Blessed in some ways. Kind hearted, helpful. Intuitive and inspired. Artistic, having good taste. Original and unconventional.

Irving, 7- Has spiritual undertones. Spiritually motivated. Intuitive and inspired. Blessed in some ways. Original and unconventional. Scientific and philosophical.

Irwin, 10- Works for group effort. Gentle, kind, a hard worker. Likes to meet new people. Artistic, having good taste. Original and unconventional.

Isaac, 6- Artistic, having good taste. Charming and devoted. Pioneer and risk taker. Bold, courageous, a bit stubborn. Self-expressive, cheerful.

Isabel, 3- Communicates understanding. Very charismatic. Aims to please. Friendly, but shy. A free spirit, very adaptable. Strong verbal skills.

Isabella, 7- Has spiritual undertones. Charming and devoted. Not easily influenced. Friendly, but shy. A free spirit, very adaptable. Strong verbal skills. Frequent traveler. Bold, courageous, a bit stubborn.

Isabelle, 11- Idealistic and humanitarian. Very charismatic. Intuitive, perceptive. Friendly, but shy. A free spirit, very adaptable. Strong verbal skills. Frequent traveler. Loves adventure and excitement.

Isadora, 4- Teaches kindness. Charming and devoted. Resolute and purposeful. Reliable, responsible. Natural counselor and healer. Gentle, kind, a hard worker. Bold, courageous, a bit stubborn.

Isadore, 8- Gives practical gifts. Passionate and loving. Resolute and purposeful. Reliable, responsible. Natural counselor and healer. Gentle, kind, a hard worker. A free spirit, very adaptable.

Isaiah, 11- Idealistic and humanitarian. Charming and devoted. Intuitive, perceptive. Artistic, having good taste. Bold, courageous, a bit stubborn. Self-reliant, successful.

Isham, 5- Generous, thoughtful. Charming and devoted. Excellent judge of character. Bright, adventuresome. Domestic, hard working.

Ishaq, 9- Blessed in some ways. Charming and devoted. Self-reliant, successful. Helpful, sincere. Attracts wealth.

Ishmael, 4- Teaches kindness. Able to access quickly. Self-reliant, successful. Domestic, hard working. Resolute and purposeful. A free spirit, very adaptable. Strong verbal skills.

Isidore, 7- Has spiritual undertones. Stylish and refined. Artistic, having good taste. Reliable, responsible. Natural counselor and healer. Gentle, kind, a hard worker. A free spirit, very adaptable.

Isis, 20- Emotional and considerate. Charming and devoted. Artistic, having good taste. Impulsive and extreme.

Ismael, 5- Generous, thoughtful. Passionate and loving. Domestic, hard working. Bright, adventuresome. A free spirit, very adaptable. Strong verbal skills.

Ismail, 9- Blessed in some ways. Charming and devoted. Domestic, hard working. Helpful, sincere. Artistic, having good taste. Strong verbal skills.

Isman, 20- Emotional and considerate. Charming and devoted. Domestic, hard working. Reads people easily. Original and unconventional.

Isolde, 10- Works for group effort. Very charismatic. Natural counselor and healer. Strong verbal skills. Reliable, responsible. A free spirit, very adaptable.

Israel, 10- Works for group effort. Very charismatic. Gentle, kind, a hard worker. Independent, critical of self and others. A free spirit, very adaptable. Strong verbal skills.

Iva, 5- Generous, thoughtful. Eccentric or unpredictable. Bright, adventuresome.

Ivah, 22- Idealistic and humanitarian. Great potential for accomplishment. Resolute and purposeful. Self-reliant, successful.

Ivan, 10- Works for group effort. Intuitive and inspired. Independent, critical of self and others. Original and unconventional.

Ivana, 20- Emotional and considerate. Tactful and refined. Reads people easily. Original and unconventional. Bold, courageous, a bit stubborn.

Ivane, 6- Artistic, having good taste. Intuitive and inspired. Pioneer and risk taker. Original and unconventional. A free spirit, very adaptable.

Ivar, 5- Generous, thoughtful. Eccentric or unpredictable. Bright, adventuresome. Gentle, kind, a hard worker.

Iven, 5- Generous, thoughtful. Eccentric or unpredictable. Physical and passionate. Original and unconventional.

Ives, 10- Works for group effort. Intuitive and inspired. Likes change and variety. Charming and devoted.

Ivy, 20- Emotional and considerate. Intuitive and inspired. Needs a lot of freedom.

Izak, 20- Emotional and considerate. Uses common sense. Reads people easily. Strong desire to succeed.

> "It really was no miracle. What happened was just this: The wind began to switch—the house to pitch and suddenly the hinges started to unhitch. Just then, the witch—to satisfy an itch—went flying on her broomstick thumbing for ... a ... hitch."
>
> ~Excerpted from "The Wizard of Oz"
> Used with permission

J

IF A NAME BEGINS WITH J, has more than one J, or ends with a J, this person is clever, talented, honest, sincere, and tries hard to please everyone.

The letter J is the 10th letter of the alphabet. Since $1 + 0 = 1$, the 10th letter is similar to the first letter, A, which is ruled by the number 1 vibration. So J is co-ruled by 1. In fact, if a person has a J and an A in their name, like Jack or Janice, then the 1 vibration is even more evident in their personality than say a Joe or a Jill. It's as if they have a double dose of the first vibration with two 1-ruled letters in the beginning of their name.

Although mathematically the zero in the 10th letter adds up to nothing, in numerology, the zero means "assistance from God." The influence of a zero can mean everything happening all at once (all hell breaking loose), or nothing happening at all (hearing crickets). Consequently, the J named person seems to either have a lot going on; or nothing much going on at all! "A," ruled by 1, means beginnings; the J ruled by 10 means beginnings with assistance from God. So these individuals often receive assistance from God at just the right moment. God tends not to be very far away from the J ruled.

Speaking of God, in the bible there are so many J names. Jehovah, Jesus, Joseph, John, James, Judas, Joel, Job, Jacob, Joshah, Jeremiah, Jesse, Jonah, Jonathan, Johanan, Joah and Joanna, are only some of the J names found in the bible. The bible also refers to cities where important biblical events took place that began with the letter J, such as Jerusalem, Judah, Jordan and Jericho.

Those whose names begin with J often choose to be single. J shares the need to be independent along with the letters A and S. It's no wonder Jesus Christ chose to stay single with 3 letters in his name ruled by the independent number 1. Jesus also had a freedom-loving E letter for his first vowel. E first vowels like to change the existing order of things. His first two letters added up to a hidden 6, the "counselor and healer." Also 6 is magnetic, which explains why so many were drawn to him. With both an intensity number 1 in his name and the assistance of God, he began the Christian movement as we know it today. Jesus ushered in the age of Pisces, the fish, which rules Christianity. Even today the fish symbolizes Christian faith. J names are leaders; they're bold and courageous, similar to the letter "A." It's also worth mentioning that his name summed up to an 11 power number. 11 is one of the master numbers. Many referred to him as "Master." His accomplishments were great for such a short time on earth. He definitely was and still is a master teacher.

J ruled individuals want to improve the lives of others. They are clever, bright as a penny, and as a rule very talented however, they sometimes need a little push in the motivation department. Sometimes they suffer from "procrastinitus." Some J names need "assistance from God" to help motivate them off the recliner.

As mentioned earlier, it's an all or nothing type of letter. Most of us know someone with a name beginning with J who doesn't seem to have much going on in their life—or too much going on all at once. Even months of the year that begin with J, for example: January, June and July, are all or nothing months for some businesses and many people.

Although Jodie Foster's birth name is Alicia, J and A are both ruled by the number 1, giving her that independent, bold and courageous personality. Both her names have influenced her. Alicia has two letters ruled by the number 3, L and C. The intensity 3 in her birth name gives her the ability to master the art of communication. In fact, it's been said she speaks flawless French. With the name Jodie, her heart's desire letter is the loving, nurturing letter "O." She's magnetic and has to have someone to love. Yet the independent J urges her to be independent. The duty bound O in Jodie makes her self-sacrificing and responsible. Her paychecks at an early age put food on the table for her and her family. She sacrificed her childhood to take care of her family. Her ability to memorize script at an early age landed her first in commercials, then in movies. The O and D are businesslike. The I helps to bless her in some ways. The J and E make her crave independence and freedom. She needs to be on her own, yet she has to be responsible for others to make herself happy. What a dilemma. Jodie adds up to a 7 power number, which is why she looks so good on the silver screen. The J and O add up to a hidden 7, so if she doesn't like someone they know it. She either likes a person or not—there's no gray area with her. She can act, but pretending is a different story for a 7 power number.

What about the nickname Jack for John? The late great President John F. Kennedy's nickname while growing up was Jack. Both names numerological-ally fit his personality. The C in Jack is a youthful letter, sort of Gemini-like. In fact his astrological sign was Gemini. The K can be a bit high-strung and sickly. History shows he was a sickly child. Jack has a power number 7. With the 1 ruled J and A this name is very intelligent. John has a power number 20, so reflected in his years in the presidency as partnership, assistance from God. 20 is sensitive, dynamic and social, just as he was.

Another independent J name who received assistance from God was Joan of Arc. At the young age of 16 she led an army of men to free her beloved country, France. It was thought she was guided by angels or spirits. She had a hidden 7 in the beginning of her name which is the number for faith. Unfortunately her name added up to a power number 13 which, as we all know, can be unlucky. That "cursed" number may have been her downfall.

J names want to please others. They are so clever and talented. Many are amazingly keen with electronics and machinery. They often surprise others with their talents and abilities. Although they are here to learn independence, it's possible to be happy in a relationship with the J named as long as they're not smothered with too much togetherness. All 1 vibration letters must learn to stand on their own two feet and not lean on others too much. If they are trying to be independent, then they are on the right path. Encourage their independence and they'll come back to you, smiling, with those new wireless head phones they just invented.

Some other famous J names are: John Travolta, Julia Roberts, Jim Carey, Jane Fonda, James Earl Jones, Jennifer Lopez, Jessica Simpson, Johnny Depp, Jamie Lee Curtis, James Taylor, Justin Timberlake, Jennifer Aniston, John Mayer, Jerry Seinfeld, Jason Alexander, Julia Louis-Dreyfus, Jackie Chan, Jessica

Lange, Jackson Browne, Jesse James, Jimi Hendrix, Janet Jackson, Jessica Walter, John Stamos, Jennifer Garner, Jack Nicholson, Jessica Biel and Jacqueline Bouvier-Kennedy.

Quick Reference of "J" Names

Jacinda, 6- Quick to service. Pioneer and risk taker. Self-expressive, cheerful. Blessed in some ways. Original and unconventional. Reliable, responsible. Bold, courageous, a bit stubborn.

Jacinta, 22- Improves the lives of others. Ambitious leader, great vision. Inspiring, creative. Blessed in some ways. Original and unconventional. Dynamic, busy lifestyle. Bold, courageous, a bit stubborn.

Jack, 7- For truth and justice. Not easily influenced. Optimistic, outspoken. Strong desire to succeed.

Jackee, 8- Accepts responsibility. Resolute and purposeful. Self-expressive, cheerful. Has a powerful presence. A free spirit, very adaptable. Loves adventure and excitement.

Jackie, 3- Cheerful and sincere. Aims to please. Youthful, outspoken. Enthusiastic, quick-witted. Blessed in some ways. A free spirit, very adaptable.

Jackson, 10- Extremely talented. Independent, critical of self and others. Optimistic, outspoken. Strong desire to succeed. Charismatic leader. Magnetic personality. Original and romantic.

Jacob, 4- Honest and reliable. Natural teaching ability. Self-expressive, cheerful. Natural counselor and healer. Friendly, but shy.

Jacqueline, 7- For truth and justice. Not easily influenced. Sees the irony in situations. Attracts wealth. Attractive and charming. A free spirit, very adaptable. Strong verbal skills. Blessed in some ways. Original and unconventional. Loves adventure and excitement.

Jacques, 22- Improves the lives of others. Ambitious leader, great vision. Self-expressive, cheerful. Attracts wealth. Youthful, appealing. A free spirit, very adaptable. Impulsive and extreme.

Jacqui, 7- For truth and justice. Not easily influenced. Sees the irony in situations. Attracts wealth. Attractive and charming. Blessed in some ways.

Jade, 11- Improves the lives of others. Intuitive, perceptive. Reliable, responsible. A free spirit, very adaptable.

Jag, 9- Generous and helpful. Hardworking, sincere. Scientific and philosophical.

Jagger, 30- Cheerful and sincere. Aims to please. Scientific and philosophical. Extremely intelligent. A free spirit, very adaptable. Gentle, kind, a hard worker.

Jaime, 20- Wants to please everyone. Reads people easily. Emotional, considerate. Domestic, hard working. A free spirit, very adaptable.

Jaimi, 6- Quick to service. Pioneer and risk taker. Blessed in some ways. Domestic, hard working. Artistic, having good taste.

Jairo, 8- Accepts responsibility. Resolute and purposeful. Generous in a practical way. Intense inner power. Natural counselor and healer.

Jakeem, 9- Generous and helpful. Hardworking, sincere. Sees the big picture. A free spirit, very adaptable. Loves adventure and excitement. Domestic and practical.

Jakob, 3- Cheerful and sincere. Aims to please. Strong desire to succeed. Natural counselor and healer. Friendly, but shy.

Jalil, 8- Accepts responsibility. Resolute and purposeful. Communicates skillfully. Blessed in some ways. Frequent traveler.

Jamal, 10- Extremely talented. Independent, critical of self and others. Systematic, organized. Bold, courageous, a bit stubborn. Strong verbal skills.

Jamar, 7- For truth and justice. Not easily influenced. Systematic, organized. Not easily fooled. Gentle, kind, a hard worker.

James, 3- Cheerful and sincere. Aims to please. Systematic, organized. A free spirit, very adaptable. Charming and devoted.

Jami, 6- Quick to service. Pioneer and risk taker. Domestic and hard working. Blessed in some ways.

Jamie, 20- Wants to please everyone. Reads people easily. Domestic and hard working. Blessed in some ways. A free spirit, very adaptable.

Jamil, 9- Generous and helpful. Hardworking, sincere. Domestic and hard working. Blessed in some ways. Strong verbal skills.

Jan, 7- For truth and justice. Not easily influenced. Original and unconventional.

Janae, 4- Honest and reliable. Natural teaching ability. Unconventional, opinionated. Independent, critical of self and others. A free spirit, very adaptable.

Jane, 3- Cheerful and sincere. Aims to please. Romantic, sensual. Loves adventure and excitement.

Janel, 6- Quick to service. Pioneer and risk taker. Puts the needs of others first. A step ahead of others. Communicates skillfully.

Janessa, 6- Quick to service. Pioneer and risk taker. Original and unconventional. A step ahead of others. Charming and devoted. Intense and extreme. Bold, courageous, a bit stubborn.

Janet, 5- Has a clever mind. Bright, adventuresome. Creative, opinionated. Physical and passionate. Dynamic, busy lifestyle.

Janette, 3- Cheerful and sincere. Aims to please. Original and unconventional. A free spirit, very adaptable. Dynamic, busy lifestyle. Sensitive and easily hurt. Loves adventure and excitement.

Janeva, 8- Accepts responsibility. Resolute and purposeful. Romantic, sensual. A free spirit, very adaptable. Intuitive and inspired. Bold, courageous, a bit stubborn.

Janice, 6- Quick to service. Pioneer and risk taker. Creative, opinionated. Artistic, having good taste. Self-expressive, cheerful. A free spirit, very adaptable.

Janie, 3- Cheerful and sincere. Aims to please. Original and unconventional. Blessed in some ways. Physical and passionate.

Janine, 8- Accepts responsibility. Resolute and purposeful. Original and unconventional. Blessed in some ways. Romantic and sensual. A free spirit, very adaptable.

Jared, 20- Wants to please everyone. Reads people easily. Gentle, kind, a hard worker. A free spirit, very adaptable. Reliable, responsible.

Jarell, 22- Improves the lives of others. Ambitious leader, great vision. Diligent, hard working. A free spirit, very adaptable. Strong verbal skills. Frequent traveler.

Jarrell, 4- Hardworking and reliable. Natural teaching ability. Diligent, hard working. Tendency to lose items. A free spirit, very adaptable. Strong verbal skills. Frequent traveler.

Jarvis, 7- For truth and justice. Not easily influenced. Gentle, kind, a hard worker. Intuitive and inspired. Blessed in some ways. Charming and devoted.

Jasmin, 3- Cheerful and sincere. Aims to please. Charming and devoted. Domestic and hard working. Blessed in some ways. Original and unconventional.

Jasmina, 22- Improves the lives of others. Ambitious leader, great vision. Charming and devoted. Domestic and hard working. Blessed in some ways. Original and unconventional. Bold, courageous, a bit stubborn.

Jasmine, 8- Accepts responsibility. Resolute and purposeful. Passionate and loving. Domestic and hard working. Blessed in some ways. Original and unconventional. A free spirit, very adaptable.

Jason, 5- Has a clever mind. Bright, adventuresome. Very charismatic. Natural counselor and healer. Original and unconventional.

Jasper, 6- Quick to service. Pioneer and risk taker. Charming and devoted. Intelligent and knowledgeable. A free spirit, very adaptable. Gentle, kind, a hard worker.

Javier, 11- Improves the lives of others. Intuitive, perceptive. Intuitive and inspired. Blessed in some ways. A free spirit, very adaptable. Gentle, kind, a hard worker.

Javon, 8- Accepts responsibility. Resolute and purposeful. Intuitive and inspired. Natural counselor and healer. Original and unconventional.

Javonne, 9- Generous and helpful. Hardworking, sincere. Intuitive and inspired. Natural counselor and healer. Original and unconventional. Romantic, sensual. A free spirit, very adaptable.

Jay, 9- Generous and helpful. Hardworking, sincere. Needs a lot of freedom.

Jayme, 9- Generous and helpful. Hardworking, sincere. Dislikes restrictions. Domestic, hard working. Loves adventure and excitement.

Jayne, 10- Extremely talented. Independent, critical of self and others. Needs a lot of freedom. Original and unconventional. Loves adventure and excitement.

Jax, 10- Extremely talented. Independent, critical of self and others. Artistic, sensual and perceptive.

Jazztine, 3- Cheerful and sincere. Aims to please. Uses common sense. Impatient and stubborn. Dynamic, busy lifestyle. Blessed in some ways. Original and unconventional. A free spirit, very adaptable.

Jean, 3- Cheerful and sincere. Aims to please. Pioneer and risk taker. Original and unconventional.

Jeane, 8- Accepts responsibility. Original and creative. Resolute and purposeful. Opinionated and unconventional. Physical and passionate.

Jeanette, 8- Accepts responsibility. Original and creative. Resolute and purposeful. Creative and unconventional. Physical and passionate. Dynamic, busy lifestyle. Sensitive and easily hurt. A free spirit, very adaptable.

Jeanne, 22- Improves the lives of others. Has big plans and ideas. Ambitious leader, great vision. Unconventional and original. Romantic, sensual. Needs change and variety.

Jeannine, 9- Generous and helpful. Enjoys giving gifts. Hardworking and sincere. Original and unconventional. Romantic, sensual. Blessed in some ways. Creative, opinionated. Tendency to overindulge.

Jeb, 8- Accepts responsibility. Original and creative. Friendly, but shy.

Jed, 10- Extremely talented. Likes change and variety. Workaholic, shrewd and determined.

Jedediah, 10- Extremely talented. Likes change and variety. Systematic, organized. Loves adventure and excitement. Down-to-earth, faithful. Blessed in some ways. Independent, critical of self and others. Great judge of character.

Jedidiah, 5- Has a clever mind. Physical and passionate. Reliable, responsible. Blessed in some ways. Down-to-earth, faithful. Artistic, having good taste. Independent, critical of self and others. Great judge of character.

Jeff, 9- Generous and helpful. Enjoys giving gifts. Self-sacrificing, loving. Easy going nature.

Jefferson, 8- Accepts responsibility. Original and creative. Self-sacrificing, loving. Likes competition. Physical and passionate. Gentle, kind, a hard worker. Charming and devoted. Natural counselor and healer. Original and unconventional.

Jeffrey, 3- Cheerful and sincere. A free spirit, very adaptable. Self-sacrificing, loving. Great with plants, kids and animals. Gentle, kind, a hard worker. Loves adventure and excitement. Dislikes limitations.

Jelani, 6- Quick to service. A step ahead of others. Strong verbal skills. Independent, critical of self and others. Original and unconventional. Blessed in some ways.

Jem, 10- Extremely talented. Likes variety and change. Systematic, organized.

Jemima, 6- Quick to service. A step ahead of others. Domestic, hard working. Blessed in some ways. Systematic, organized. Independent, critical of self and others.

Jemimah, 5- Has a clever mind. Physical and passionate. Domestic, hard working. Blessed in some ways. Systematic, organized. Independent, critical of self and others. Great judge of character.

Jen, 11- Improves the lives of others. Keenly perceptive. Creative, opinionated.

Jeneesa, 5- Has a clever mind. A free spirit, very adaptable. Original and unconventional. Loves adventure and excitement. Physical and passionate. Charming and devoted. Independent, critical of self and others.

Jeni, 20- Wants to please everyone. A free spirit, very adaptable. Original and unconventional. Blessed in some ways.

Jenna, 8- Accepts responsibility. Original and creative. Opinionated and unconventional. Romantic, sensual. Independent, critical of self and others.

Jennie, 30- Cheerful and sincere. A free spirit, very adaptable. Original and unconventional. Romantic, sensual. Blessed in some ways. Loves adventure and excitement.

Jennifer, 9- Generous and helpful. A true humanitarian. Original and unconventional. Romantic, sensual. Blessed in some ways. Self-sacrificing, loving. Loves adventure and excitement. Gentle, kind, a hard worker.

Jenny, 5- Has a clever mind. Physical and passionate. Original and unconventional. Creative, opinionated. Needs a lot of freedom.

Jeong-hee, 6- Quick to service. A step ahead of others. Natural counselor and healer. Original and unconventional. Scientific and philosophical. Great judge of character. Tendency to overindulge. Loves adventure and excitement.

Jeraldine, 6- Quick to service. A step ahead of others. Intense inner power. Independent, critical of self and others. Strong verbal skills. Reliable, responsible. Blessed in some ways. Original and unconventional. Loves adventure and excitement.

Jeralyn, 4- Honest and reliable. Accesses quickly. Gentle, kind, a hard worker. Independent, critical of self and others. Strong verbal skills. Dislikes limitations. Original and unconventional.

Jerelyn, 8- Accepts responsibility. Physical and passionate. Intense inner power. Loves adventure and excitement. Strong verbal skills. Dislikes limitations. Original and unconventional.

Jeremiah, 6- Quick to service. A step ahead of others. Intense inner power. Loves adventure and excitement. Systematic, organized. Blessed in some ways. Independent, critical of self and others. Great judge of character.

Jeremy, 4- Honest and reliable. Accesses quickly. Healthy, strong. Loves adventure and excitement. Systematic, organized. Dislikes limitations.

Jeri, 6- Quick to service. A step ahead of others. Gentle, kind, a hard worker. Artistic, having good taste.

Jerilyn, 3- Cheerful and sincere. A free spirit, very adaptable. Kind and considerate. Blessed in some ways. Strong verbal skills. Dislikes limitations. Original and unconventional.

Jerina, 30- Cheerful and sincere. Likes change and variety. Intense inner power. Artistic, having good taste. Romantic and opinionated. Independent, self-motivated.

Jermaine, 3- Cheerful and sincere. A free spirit, very adaptable. Gentle, kind, a hard worker. Systematic, organized. Independent, critical of self and others. Blessed in some ways. Original and unconventional. Loves adventure and excitement.

Jermyn, 6- Quick to service. A step ahead of others. Gentle, kind, a hard worker. Systematic, organized. Dislikes limitations. Original and unconventional.

Jerold, 10- Extremely talented. Likes change and variety. Gentle, kind, a hard worker. Natural counselor and healer. Strong verbal skills. Reliable, responsible.

Jerome, 30- Cheerful and sincere. A free spirit, very adaptable. Gentle, kind, a hard worker. Natural counselor and healer. Systematic, organized. Loves adventure and excitement.

Jerrell, 8- Accepts responsibility. Original and creative. Intense inner power. Diligent, helpful. Loves adventure and excitement. Strong verbal skills. Financial ups and downs.

Jerri, 6- Quick to service. A step ahead of others. Gentle, kind, a hard worker. Diligent, helpful. Blessed in some ways.

Jerrick, 11- Improves the lives of others. Keenly perceptive. Gentle, kind, a hard worker. Tendency to lose items. Blessed in some ways. Self-expressive, cheerful. Strong desire to succeed.

Jerrie, 11- Improves the lives of others. Keenly perceptive. Gentle, kind, a hard worker. Tendency to lose items. Blessed in some ways. Loves adventure and excitement.

Jerrold, 10- Extremely talented. Likes change and variety. Gentle, kind, a hard worker. Diligent, helpful. Natural counselor and healer. Strong verbal skills. Reliable, responsible.

Jerry, 4- Honest and reliable. Accesses quickly. Gentle, kind, a hard worker. Tendency to lose items. Dislikes limitations.

Jervis, 11- Improves the lives of others. Keenly perceptive. Gentle, kind, a hard worker. Intuitive and inspired. Blessed in some ways. Charming and devoted.

Jess, 8- Accepts responsibility. Original and creative. Very charismatic. Intense and extreme.

Jessa, 9- Generous and helpful. Enjoys giving gifts. Charming and devoted. Intense and extreme. Independent, critical of self and others.

Jesse, 4- Honest and reliable. Accesses quickly. Charming and devoted. Intense and extreme. Loves adventure and excitement.

Jessenia, 10- Extremely talented. Likes change and variety. Needs to be independent. Intense and extreme. Loves adventure and excitement. Original and unconventional. Blessed in some ways. Critical of self and others.

Jessica, 3- Cheerful and sincere. A free spirit, very adaptable. Charming and devoted. Intense and extreme. Blessed in some ways. Self-expressive, cheerful. Independent, critical of self and others.

Jessie, 22- Improves the lives of others. Keenly perceptive. Very charismatic. Intense and extreme. Blessed in some ways. Loves adventure and excitement.

Jessyca, 10- Extremely talented. Likes change and variety. Needs to be independent. Intense and extreme. Dislikes limitations. Self-expressive, cheerful. Critical of self and others.

Jesus, 11- Improves the lives of others. Intuitive, perceptive. Charming and devoted. Creative and inspiring. Intense and extreme.

Jethro, 4- Honest and reliable. Accesses quickly. Dynamic, busy lifestyle. Great judge of character. Gentle, kind, a hard worker. Natural counselor and healer.

Jevon, 3- Cheerful and sincere. A free spirit, very adaptable. Intuitive and inspired. Natural counselor and healer. Original and unconventional.

Jewel, 10- Extremely talented. Needs change and variety. Likes to meet new people. Loves adventure and excitement. Communicates skillfully.

Jezebel, 11- Improves the lives of others. Keenly perceptive. Able to achieve greatness. Physical and passionate. Good business partner. A free spirit, very adaptable. Strong verbal skills.

Jhamal, 9- Generous and helpful. Great judge of character. Independent, critical of self and others. Domestic, hard working. Bold, courageous, a bit stubborn. Strong verbal skills.

Jill, 7- Scientific aptitude. Blessed in some ways. Communicates skillfully. Slow to make decisions.

Jillian, 4- Sincere and reliable. Natural teacher. Strong verbal skills. Slow to make decisions. Artistic, having good taste. Independent, critical of self and others. Original and unconventional.

Jim, 5- Has a clever mind. Blessed in some ways. Systematic, organized.

Jimbo, 22- Improves the lives of others. Idealistic, humanitarian. Domestic, hard working. Friendly, but shy. Natural counselor and healer.

Jimi, 5- Has a clever mind. Blessed in some ways. Creative entrepreneur. Artistic, having good taste.

Jimmy, 7- For truth and justice. Spiritually motivated. Domestic, hard working. Desires financial security. Needs a lot of freedom.

Jina, 7- For truth and justice. Spiritually motivated. Original and unconventional. Independent, critical of self and others.

Jo, 7- For truth and justice. Natural counselor and healer. Must have faith to be happy.

Joachim, 5- Has a clever mind. Versatile in service. Independent, critical of self and others. Self-expressive, cheerful. Great judge of character. Blessed in some ways. Domestic, hard working.

Joan, 4- Sincere and reliable. Nurturing. loving. Natural teaching ability. Creative and opinionated.

Joann, 9- Generous and helpful. Creates group harmony. Hardworking, sincere. Creative and romantic. Unassuming, naive.

Joanna, 10- Extremely talented. Ambitious and innovative. Independent, critical of self and others. Original and unconventional. Creative, opinionated. Bold, courageous, a bit stubborn.

Joanne, 5- Has a clever mind. Versatile in service. Bold, adventuresome. Original and unconventional. Creative, opinionated. Physical and passionate.

Job, 9- Generous and helpful. Creates group harmony. Friendly, but shy.

Joby, 7- For truth and justice. Natural counselor and healer. Friendly, but shy. Needs a lot of freedom.

Jocelyn, 3- Cheerful and sincere. Has creative solutions. Self-expressive, cheerful. A free spirit, very adaptable. Strong verbal skills. Dislikes limitations. Original and unconventional.

Jodi, 20- Wants to please everyone. Natural counselor and healer. Reliable, responsible. Blessed in some ways.

Jodie, 7- For truth and justice. Open to opportunities. Domestic, responsible. Blessed in some ways. Loves adventure and excitement.

Jodina, 8- Accepts responsibility. Competitive in business. Systematic, organized. Blessed in some ways. Romantic, sensual. Resolute and purposeful.

Jody, 9- Generous and helpful. Creates group harmony. Reliable, responsible. Needs a lot of freedom.

Joe, 3- Cheerful and sincere. Natural counselor and healer. A free spirit, very adaptable.

Joel, 6- Quick to service. Assumes responsibility. A free spirit, very adaptable. Strong verbal skills.

Joella, 10- Extremely talented. Ambitious, innovative. A free spirit, very adaptable. Strong verbal skills. Financial ups and downs. Independent, critical of self and others.

Joelle, 5- Has a clever mind. Natural counselor and healer. A free spirit, very adaptable. Strong verbal skills. Financial ups and downs. Physical and passionate.

Joely, 22- Improves the lives of others. Respects rules. Likes to entertain. Frequent traveler. Needs a lot of freedom.

Joey, 10- Extremely talented. Ambitious, innovative. A free spirit, very adaptable. Dislikes limitations.

Johan, 3- Cheerful and sincere. Natural counselor and healer. Great judge of character. Independent, critical of self and others. Original and unconventional.

Johann, 8- Accepts responsibility. Competitive in business. Self-reliant, successful. Resolute and purposeful. Original and unconventional. Romantic, sensual.

Johanna, 9- Generous and helpful. Creates group harmony. Great judge of character. Independent, critical of self and others. Original and unconventional. Romantic, sensual. Bold, courageous, a bit stubborn.

Johannes, 5- Has a clever mind. Versatile in service. Great judge of character. Independent, critical of self and others. Original, unconventional. Creative, opinionated. Physical, passionate. Charming and devoted.

John, 20- Wants to please everyone. Natural counselor and healer. Great judge of character. Original and unconventional.

Johnny, 5- Has a clever mind. Versatile in service. Great judge of character. Original and unconventional. Creative and opinionated. Needs a lot of freedom.

Jolie, 6- Quick to service. Nurturing, loving. Strong verbal skills. Blessed in some ways. A free spirit, very adaptable.

Jomana, 9- Generous and helpful. Creates group harmony. Domestic, hard working. Independent, critical of self and others. Creative, original. Helpful, sincere.

Jomei, 7- For truth and justice. Open to opportunities. Domestic, hard working. A free spirit, very adaptable. Blessed in some ways.

Jon, 3- Cheerful and sincere. Natural counselor and healer. Romantic, opinionated.

Jonah, 3- Cheerful and sincere. Natural counselor and healer. Romantic, opinionated. Independent, critical of self and others. Great judge of character.

Jonas, 5- Has a clever mind. Versatile in service. Original and unconventional. Independent, critical of self and others. Charming and devoted.

Jonathan, 11- Improves the lives of others. Creates group harmony. Original and unconventional. Intuitive, perceptive. Dynamic, busy lifestyle. Great judge of character. Bold, courageous, a bit stubborn. Romantic, sensual.

Jonathon, 7- Clever and talented. Open to opportunities. Original and unconventional. Not easily influenced. Dynamic, busy lifestyle. Great judge of character. Natural counselor and healer. Romantic, sensual.

Jonette, 8- Accepts responsibility. Competitive in business. Original, opinionated. Physical and passionate. Dynamic, busy lifestyle. Natural mediator. A free spirit, very adaptable.

Jordan, 8- Accepts responsibility. Competitive in business. Intense inner power. Reliable, responsible. Independent, critical of self and others. Original and unconventional.

Jordana, 9- Generous and helpful. Creates group harmony. Gentle, kind, a hard worker. Reliable, responsible. Independent, critical of self and others. Original and unconventional. Bold, courageous, a bit stubborn.

Jordy, 9- Generous and helpful. Creates group harmony. Gentle, kind, a hard worker. Reliable, responsible. Needs a lot of freedom.

Jorge, 10- Extremely talented. Ambitious, innovative. Diligent, hard working. Scientific and philosophical. A free spirit, very adaptable.

Jose, 4- Honest and reliable. Natural counselor and healer. Charming and devoted. A free spirit, very adaptable.

Joseph, 10- Extremely talented. Ambitious, innovative. Charming and devoted. A free spirit, very adaptable. Intelligent and knowledgeable. Great judge of character.

Josephine, 11- Improves the lives of others. Natural counselor and healer. Very charismatic. A free spirit, very adaptable. Intelligent and knowledgeable. Great judge of character. Blessed in some ways. Original and unconventional. Loves adventure and excitement.

Joshua, 20- Wants to please everyone. Natural counselor and healer. Charming and devoted. Great judge of character. Creative, intuitive. Independent, critical of self and others.

Josiah, 8- Accepts responsibility. Competitive in business. Loving and devoted. Blessed in some ways. Independent, critical of self and others. Great judge of character.

Josie, 22- Improves the lives of others. Creates group harmony. Very charismatic. Blessed in some ways. A free spirit, very adaptable.

Jova, 3- Cheerful and sincere. Natural counselor and healer. Intuitive and inspired. Independent, critical of self and others.

Joy, 5- Has a clever mind. Natural counselor and healer. Needs a lot of freedom.

Joyce, 22- Improves the lives of others. Creates group harmony. Needs a lot of freedom. Self-expressive, cheerful. Loves adventure and excitement.

Joyita, 8- Accepts responsibility. Competitive in business. Needs a lot of freedom. Blessed in some ways. Dynamic, busy lifestyle. Independent, critical of self and others.

Juan, 10- Extremely talented. Optimistic, outgoing. Independent, critical of self and others. Original and unconventional.

Juana, 11- Improves the lives of others. Creative and inspiring. Independent, critical of self and others. Original and unconventional. Intuitive, perceptive.

Juanita, 22- Improves the lives of others. Creative and inspiring. Independent, critical of self and others. Original and unconventional. Blessed in some ways. Dynamic, busy lifestyle. Bold, courageous, a bit stubborn.

Juanito, 9- Generous and helpful. Attractive and charming. Independent, critical of self and others. Original and unconventional. Blessed in some ways. Dynamic, busy lifestyle. Natural counselor and healer.

Jud, 8- Accepts responsibility. Usually very lucky. Down to earth, practical.

Judah, 8- Accepts responsibility. Usually very lucky. Down to earth, practical. Resolute and purposeful. Excellent judge of character.

Jude, 4- Honest and reliable. Quickly sizes up situations. Systematic, organized. A free spirit, very adaptable.

Judi, 8- Accepts responsibility. Usually very lucky. Down to earth, practical. Blessed in some ways.

Judith, 9- Generous and helpful. Attractive and charming. Reliable, responsible. Blessed in some ways. Dynamic, busy lifestyle. Great judge of character.

Judy, 6- Quick to service. Attractive and charming. Reliable, responsible. Needs a lot of freedom.

Juelz, 20- Wants to please everyone. Attractive and charming. Physical and passionate. Communicates skillfully. An excellent mediator.

Jules, 4- Honest and reliable. Quickly sizes up situations. Strong verbal skills. A free spirit, very adaptable. Intense and extreme.

Juli, 7- For truth and justice. Stylish and refined. Communicates skillfully. Needs alone time.

Julia, 8- Accepts responsibility. Attractive and charming. Doesn't mince words. Blessed in some ways. Independent, critical of self and others.

Julian, 22- Improves the lives of others. Creative and inspiring. Strong verbal skills. Idealistic, humanitarian. Independent, critical of self and others. Original and unconventional.

Julie, 3- Cheerful and sincere. Attractive and charming. Communicates skillfully. Blessed in some ways. A free spirit, very adaptable.

Juliet, 5- Has a clever mind. Fun, flirtatious. Strong verbal skills. Generous, thoughtful. A free spirit, very adaptable. Dynamic, busy lifestyle.

Julieta, 6- Quick to service. Attractive and charming. Strong verbal skills. Blessed in some ways. A free spirit, very adaptable. Dynamic, busy lifestyle. Independent, critical of self and others.

Juliette, 30- Cheerful and sincere. Youthful, appealing. Strong verbal skills. Blessed in some ways. A free spirit, very adaptable. Dynamic, busy lifestyle. Sensitive, easily hurt. Loves adventure and excitement.

Julio, 22- Improves the lives of others. Creative and inspiring. Strong verbal skills. Blessed in some ways. Natural counselor and healer.

Julius, 20-Wants to please everyone. Attractive and charming. Strong verbal skills. Blessed in some ways. Creative, intuitive. Intense and extreme.

Jun, 9- Generous and helpful. Attractive and charming. Original and unconventional.

Juna, 10- Extremely talented. Attractive and charming. Original and unconventional. Independent, critical of self and others.

June, 5- Has a clever mind. Great social skills. Creative and opinionated. A free spirit, very adaptable.

Junie, 5- Has a clever mind. Great social skills. Creative and opinionated. Blessed in some ways. A free spirit, very adaptable.

Juno, 6- Quick to service. Attractive and charming. Original and unconventional. Natural counselor and healer.

Justin, 3- Cheerful and sincere. Youthful, appealing. Intense and extreme. Dynamic, busy lifestyle. Blessed in some ways. Original and unconventional.

Justina, 22- Improves the lives of others. Creative and inspiring. Intense and extreme. Dynamic, busy lifestyle. Blessed in some ways. Original and unconventional. Independent, critical of self and others.

Justine, 8- Accepts responsibility. Attractive and charming. Intense and extreme. Dynamic, busy lifestyle. Blessed in some ways. Original and unconventional. A free spirit, very adaptable.

Justis, 8- Accepts responsibility. Attractive and charming. Intense and extreme. Dynamic, busy lifestyle. Blessed in some ways. Passionate and loving.

Jynx, 10- Extremely talented. Needs a lot of freedom. Creative, original. Artistic, perceptive and sensual.

> "We thank you very sweetly
> For doing it so neatly.
> You've killed her so completely
> that we thank you very sweetly."
> ~*Excerpted from "The Wizard of Oz"*
> *Used with permission*

K

IF A NAME BEGINS with K, has more than one K, or ends with a K, this person is highly creative, sensitive, perceptive and intuitive with a strong desire to succeed.

The letter K is the 11th letter of the alphabet. 11 is one of the "master" numbers, 22 is the other one. We have only 2 master numbers in numerology. When a person is born with a letter K anywhere in their name, they are meant to accomplish something worthwhile this lifetime. Those whose names begin with K are special. Maybe we should call them "Special K." We can learn from them. K is the lightening bolt of letters. In astrology, the 11th house is ruled by Aquarius. This is the sign of genius and inspiration. As so the 11th letter K person seems driven toward their goals and aspirations. Occasionally we have the dreamer type, which is very spiritual and idealistic, but never seems to accomplish much of anything. The average K personality can be quite forceful as well as multifaceted. At the very least, they are different. Some are high-strung and exhibit nervous energy. Kirk's will have a double dose of this energy and could be even more driven to succeed in their chosen field. This letter seems in its element when with friends, groups, organizations and governmental positions. Some careers tend to fall into the field of electricity and modern technology. These individuals are prone to flashes of inspiration and are quite ingenious and creative.

In numerology we condense numbers down to one digit. Sometimes we add the 11; as 1+1=2, so this number is co-ruled by the number 2. As a rule, we never condense 11 down to 2; however, in the beginning of the adding of a name, if there is an 11 we count it as a 2 and keep adding all the letters until the name condenses down to 1 digit, unless it condenses down to an 11 or 22. At any rate, we cannot rule out this "2" energy. Similar to the 2 vibration, the 11 is emotional and partnership oriented. Most K's prefer to be in a partnership, romantic or business; unless their name is Jack or Kasey, with two independent 1 ruled letters in the beginning of their names. The average Katie or Kevin make wonderful partners. They will be focused on their goals and similar to the 11, or two 1's—which means beginning and beginning, the typical K named person can handle 2 beginnings—the career and family quite well.

Although this letter is extremely social or partnership oriented, it would seem they would put on weight more easily. Often socializing involves food and drink and calories galore. The K's social siblings, B and T often struggle with the extra pounds. But, unless the K name has escapist letters in it, often they are a little on the lean side. Perhaps it's because they often run on nervous energy. This is why a good night's sleep and plenty of exercise will keep our special K's happy and healthy. K's 11 is really double 1's, so exercise is important to the K ruled. 1's tend to have a bully in their head, imagine with double 1's, it's a double dose of this bully in the head. Exercise helps the K named get out of their head, otherwise they tend to beat themselves up twice as much as our A, J or S friends do. Their brain seems to get a continual workout, but more often than not, their bodies need a strong push. Exercise can help de-fuse much of the nervous energy this letter seems to have.

One famous K named person is Kelly Rippa of "Live with Regis and Kelly." She exhibits her strong desire to succeed by holding down many jobs. Not only does she co-host with Regis, but she also worked for 12 years on the popular daytime soap, "All My Children." She also stars on the primetime sitcom, "Hope and Faith" as well as the occasional shampoo commercial and movie; all while being an active wife and mother of three. Whew! Good thing her name starts with a K or she might not be able to handle all that! Her ability to make others laugh can be attributed to the double L's in her name. Also the L's give her the gift of gab as they are ruled by the number 3 which rules communication and transportation. She no doubt makes many short trips around town with her busy schedule. With a power number 20, and 2 L's in her name, it's no wonder she is so busy. Interestingly enough, she's a Libra which is ruled by the partnership oriented number 2. K is co-ruled by 2; it's social as well as partnership oriented, just like a Libra.

Singer, songwriter, and guitarist Kenny Loggins achieved fame by writing such popular songs as "House at Pooh Corner" and "Celebrate Me Home." His cheerful, sensitive style in the late 70's made him the King of movie sound tracks with hit songs in "Caddy Shack," "Footloose," and "Top Gun." This famous K named person was especially creative with an E first vowel and 2 N's, giving him an intensity 5 and power number 6. Kenny is a freedom loving name. Not only all that 5 vibration urging him to be free, but the Y at the end of his name makes him dislike restrictions. His 6 power number helps him on the business aspect of his musical career. 6 power numbers like to be their own boss. It is ultimately the K in the beginning of his name that opened doors with friends, groups and organizations. This letter is sensitive, unusual and finely tuned.

Another musically talented individual with the same name is Kenny G. Wilson, better known as "Kenny G." This musician is slightly controversial, not uncommon with a 5 intensity number. He's known as the musician jazz listeners love to hate, annoying jazz purists with his "smooth jazz" and "crossover jazz" style. He's a phenomenally successful instrumentalist whose recordings made the pop charts in the 80's and 90's. Kenny puts a lot of emotion in his solos. His music reflects the sensitive emotional side of his K first letter. Both Kenny's exhibit their musical talents through socially acceptable modes of expression. Both performers are sensitive, emotional and personal in their delivery. This letter leaves an impression that doesn't go away. Furthermore, with a 6 power number, both Kenny's tend to have that `magnetic` quality about them.

Notice the list of K names is shorter than most. This letter is for those who must accomplish something worthwhile. K names are unusual, uncommon and only meant for those with a master lesson to achieve excellence during their short time on earth. Those born with this letter are unique and have a special mission in life. They are our "special K's."

More famous people with K first names are: Karl Straus, Keifer Sutherland, Kate Beckinsale, Kelsey Grammer, Kermit the frog, Kate Hudson, Kim Basinger, Kevin Bacon, Keira Knightley, Keanu Reeves, Katharine Hepburn, Kirstie Alley, Kevin Spacey, Kobe Bryant, Kurt Russell, Kelly Clarkson, Kirk Douglas, Kris Kristofferson, Kevin Costner, Kathleen Quinlan, Kenny Rogers, Kanye West and Kirstin Dunst.

Quick Reference of "K" Names

Kacey, 9- Sees the big picture. Hard working and sincere. Self-expressive, cheerful. Loves adventure and excitement. Needs a lot of freedom.

Kacie, 20- Sensitive and diplomatic. Reads people easily. Self-expressive, cheerful. Blessed in some ways. A free spirit, very adaptable.

Kadeem, 3- Enthusiastic and quick witted. Aims to please. Reliable, responsible. A free spirit, very adaptable. Loves adventure and excitement. Domestic, hard working.

Kahlil, 8- Has a powerful presence. Resolute and purposeful. Great judge of character. Good verbal skills. Blessed in some ways. Frequent traveler.

Kai, 3- Enthusiastic and quick witted. Aims to please. Blessed in some ways.

Kalee, 7- Multifaceted and disciplined. Not easily influenced. Frequent traveler. A free spirit, very adaptable. Loves adventure and excitement.

Kaleena, 22- Strong desire to succeed. Ambitious leader, great vision. Communicates skillfully. A free spirit, very adaptable. Physical and passionate. Original and unconventional. Bold, courageous, a bit stubborn.

Kalei, 20- Sensitive and diplomatic. Reads people easily. Communicates skillfully. A free spirit, very adaptable. Blessed in some ways.

Kalil, 9- Sees the big picture. Hard working and sincere. Strong verbal skills. Blessed in some ways. Frequent traveler.

Kalina, 3- Enthusiastic and quick witted. Aims to please. Communicates skillfully. Blessed in some ways. Original and unconventional. Bold, courageous, a bit stubborn.

Kalinda, 7- Multifaceted and disciplined. Not easily influenced. Frequent traveler. Blessed in some ways. Original and unconventional. Reliable, responsible. Bold, courageous, a bit stubborn.

Kalli, 9- Empathetic, sees the big picture. Hard working and sincere. Strong verbal skills. Frequent traveler. Blessed in some ways.

Kallie, 5- Energetic, forceful. Bright, adventuresome. Communicates skillfully. Frequent traveler. Blessed in some ways. A free spirit, very adaptable.

Kalynn, 5- Energetic, forceful. Bright, adventuresome. Communicates skillfully. Needs a lot of freedom. Original and unconventional. Romantic, sensual.

Kam, 7- Multifaceted and disciplined. Not easily influenced. Domestic, hard working.

Kamal, 11- Strong desire to succeed. Intuitive, perceptive. Domestic, hard working. Bold, courageous, a bit stubborn. Good verbal skills.

Kameko, 20-Sensitive and diplomatic. Reads people easily. Domestic, hard working. A free spirit, very adaptable. Forceful at times. Natural counselor and healer.

Kane, 4- Practical imagination. Natural teaching ability. Original and unconventional. A free spirit, very adaptable.

Kareem, 8- Has a powerful presence. Resolute and purposeful. Intense inner power. A free spirit, very adaptable. Loves adventure and excitement. Systematic, organized.

Karen, 22- Strong desire to succeed. Ambitious leader, great vision. Gentle, kind, a hard worker. A free spirit, very adaptable. Creative and opinionated.

Kari, 3- Enthusiastic and quick witted. Aims to please. Sympathetic, kind. Blessed in some ways.

Karim, 7- Multifaceted and disciplined. Not easily influenced. Gentle, kind, a hard worker. Blessed in some ways. Systematic, organized.

Karin, 8- Has a powerful presence. Resolute and purposeful. Intense inner power. Blessed in some ways. Original and unconventional.

Karina, 9- Sees the big picture. Hard working and sincere. Sympathetic, kind. Artistic, having good taste. Original and unconventional. Bold, courageous, a bit stubborn.

Karis, 22- Strong desire to succeed. Ambitious leader, great vision. Gentle, kind, a hard worker. Blessed in some ways. Charming and devoted.

Karissa, 6- Creatively inspired. Pioneer and risk taker. Gentle, kind, a hard worker. Blessed in some ways. Charming and devoted. Intense and extreme. Bold, courageous, a bit stubborn.

Karl, 6- Creatively inspired. Pioneer and risk taker. Gentle, kind, a hard worker. Communicates skillfully.

Karla, 7- Multifaceted and disciplined. Not easily influenced. Gentle, kind, a hard worker. Strong verbal skills. Bold, courageous, a bit stubborn.

Karmen, 8- Has a powerful presence. Resolute and purposeful. Intense inner power. Systematic, organized. A free spirit, very adaptable. Original and unconventional.

Karol, 3- Enthusiastic and quick witted. Aims to please. Gentle, kind, hard worker. Natural counselor and healer. Communicates skillfully.

Karolina, 9- Sees the big picture. Hard working, sincere. Intense inner power. Natural counselor and healer. Strong verbal skills. Blessed in some ways. Original and unconventional. Bold, courageous, a bit stubborn.

Karoline, 4- Practical imagination. Natural teaching ability. Gentle, kind, a hard worker. Nurturing, loving. Strong verbal skills. Blessed in some ways. Original and unconventional. A free spirit, very adaptable.

Karolyn, 6- Creatively inspired. Pioneer and risk taker. Gentle, kind, a hard worker. Natural counselor and healer. Strong verbal skills. Needs a lot of freedom. Original and unconventional.

Karyn, 8- Has a powerful presence. Resolute and purposeful. Intense inner power. Needs a lot of freedom. Original and unconventional.

Kasmira, 9- Sees the big picture. Hard working, sincere. Loving and devoted. Domestic, hard working. Blessed in some ways. Intense inner power. Bold, courageous, a bit stubborn.

Kaspar, 3- Enthusiastic and quick witted. Aims to please. Attractive and charming. Level headed. Bold, courageous, a bit stubborn. Gentle, kind, a hard worker.

Kassidy, 7- Multifaceted and disciplined. Not easily influenced. Charming and devoted. Impulsive and extreme. Blessed in some ways. Reliable, responsible. Needs a lot of freedom.

Kata, 6- Creatively inspired. Pioneer and risk taker. Dynamic, busy lifestyle. Independent, self-motivated.

Kate, 10- Exercise very beneficial. Independent, critical of self and others. Energetic, highly charged. A free spirit, very adaptable.

Katerina, 7- Multifaceted and disciplined. Not easily influenced. Dynamic, busy lifestyle. A free spirit, very adaptable. Gentle, kind, a hard worker. Artistic, having good taste. Original, unconventional. Bold, courageous, a bit stubborn.

Katharine, 6- Creatively inspired. Pioneer and risk taker. Dynamic, busy lifestyle. Self-reliant, successful. Bold, courageous, a bit stubborn. Diligent, helpful. Artistic, having good taste. Original and unconventional. Physical and passionate.

Katherine, 10- Exercise very beneficial. Independent, critical of self and others. Energetic, highly charged. Great judge of character. A free spirit, very adaptable. Gentle, kind, a hard worker. Blessed in some ways. Original and unconventional. Loves adventure and excitement.

Kathie, 9- Sees the big picture. Hard working and helpful. Dynamic, busy lifestyle. Original and creative. Artistic, having good taste. Physical and passionate.

Kathleen, 4- Practical imagination. Natural teaching ability. Dynamic, busy lifestyle. Great judge of character. Good verbal skills. A free spirit, very adaptable. Loves adventure and excitement. Original and unconventional.

Kathlene, 4- (Same as Kathleen.)

Kathryn, 7- Multifaceted and disciplined. Not easily influenced. Dynamic, busy lifestyle. Self-reliant, successful. Gentle, kind, a hard worker. Needs a lot of freedom. Original and unconventional.

Kathy, 20- Sensitive and diplomatic. Reads people easily. Energetic, highly charged. Great judge of character. Needs a lot of freedom.

Katrina, 11- Strong desire to succeed. Intuitive, perceptive. Energetic, highly charged. Intense inner power. Artistic, having good taste. Original and unconventional. Bold, courageous, a bit stubborn.

Kay, 10- Exercise very beneficial. Independent, critical of self and others. Needs a lot of freedom.

Kaycee, 5- Energetic, forceful. Bright, adventuresome. Dislikes restrictions. Self-expressive, cheerful. Physical and passionate. A free spirit, very adaptable.

Kayla, 5- Energetic, forceful. Bright, adventuresome. Needs a lot of freedom. Communicates skillfully. Bold, courageous, a bit stubborn.

Kaylynn, 30- Enthusiastic and quick witted. Aims to please. Needs a lot of freedom. Strong verbal skills. Highly perceptive. Original and unconventional. Romantic, sensual.

Kayne, 20- Sensitive and diplomatic. Reads people easily. Needs a lot of freedom. Original and unconventional. Loves adventure and excitement.

Kazuki, 7- Multifaceted and disciplined. Not easily influenced. Excellent mediator. Attractive and charming. A bit high strung. Blessed in some ways.

Keane, 9- Sees the big picture. Enjoys giving gifts. Hard working, sincere. Original and unconventional. Physical and passionate.

Keanu, 7- Multifaceted and disciplined. Perceptive, not easily fooled. Romantic, sensual. Attractive and charming.

Keaton, 3- Enthusiastic and quick witted. A free spirit, very adaptable. Independent, critical of self and others. Dynamic, busy lifestyle. Natural counselor and healer. Original and unconventional.

Keefe, 5- Energetic, forceful. Physical and passionate. Loves adventure and excitement. Self-sacrificing, loving. Enjoys meeting new people.

Keegan, 7- Multifaceted and disciplined. Not easily fooled. Loves adventure and excitement. Scientific and philosophical. Independent, critical of self and others. Original and unconventional.

Keeley, 9- Sees the big picture. Enjoys giving gifts. Loves adventure and excitement. Communicates skillfully. Physical and passionate. Needs a lot of freedom.

Keely, 22- Strong desire to succeed. Has big plans and ideas. Loves adventure and excitement. Strong verbal skills. Dislikes limitations.

Keenan, 5- Energetic, forceful. Physical and passionate. Enjoys meeting new people. Original and unconventional. Independent, critical of self and others. Creative and opinionated.

Keifer, 9- Sees the big picture. Enjoys giving gifts. Blessed in some ways. Self-sacrificing, loving. Loves adventure and excitement. Gentle, kind, a hard worker.

Keir, 7- Multifaceted and disciplined. Not easily fooled. Blessed in some ways. Gentle, kind, a hard worker.

Keira, 8- Has a powerful presence. Original and creative. Artistic, having good taste. Intense inner power. Resolute and purposeful.

Keisha, 8- Has a powerful presence. Original and creative. Blessed in some ways. Charming and devoted. Great judge of character. Independent, critical of self and others.

Keith, 8- Has a powerful presence. Original and creative. Blessed in some ways. Dynamic, busy lifestyle. Great judge of character.

Kel, 10- Exercise very beneficial. Likes change and variety. Strong verbal skills.

Kelby, 10- Exercise very beneficial. Likes change and variety. Strong verbal skills. Friendly, but shy. Dislikes limitations.

Keli, 10- Exercise very beneficial. Likes change and variety. Frequent traveler. Blessed in some ways.

Keller, 9- Sees the big picture. Enjoys giving gifts. Strong verbal skills. Frequent traveler. Loves adventure and excitement. Gentle, kind, a hard worker.

Kelly, 20- Sensitive and diplomatic. Social and entertaining. Communicates skillfully. Travels frequently. Needs a lot of freedom.

Kelli, 22- Strong desire to succeed. Has big plans and ideas. Communicates skillfully. Travels frequently. Blessed in some ways.

Kellie, 9- Sees the big picture. Enjoys giving gifts. Strong verbal skills. Frequent traveler. Blessed in some ways. Loves adventure and excitement.

Kelsey, 5- Energetic, forceful. Physical and passionate. Communicates skillfully. Charming and devoted. Loves adventure and excitement. Needs a lot of freedom.

Kelsy, 9- Sees the big picture. Enjoys giving gifts. Strong verbal skills. Charming and devoted. Needs a lot of freedom.

Kelvin, 10- Exercise very beneficial. Likes change and variety. Strong verbal skills. Intuitive and inspired. Blessed in some ways. Original and unconventional.

Ken, 3- Enthusiastic and quick witted. A free spirit, very adaptable. Romantic, opinionated.

Kendall, 5- Energetic, forceful. Physical and passionate. Creative, opinionated. Reliable, responsible. Bright, adventuresome. Communicates skillfully. Frequent traveler.

Kendra, 8- Has a powerful presence. Original and creative. Romantic, opinionated. Systematic, organized. Intense inner power. Resolute and purposeful.

Kendrick, 3- Enthusiastic and quick witted. A free spirit, very adaptable. Original and unconventional. Reliable, responsible. Gentle, kind, a hard worker. Blessed in some ways. Self-expressive, cheerful. A bit forceful at times.

Kenisha, 4- Practical imagination. Accesses quickly. Creative and original. Blessed in some ways. Charming and devoted. Great judge of character. Natural teaching abilities.

Kenji, 22- Strong desire to succeed. Has big plans and ideas. Romantic, opinionated. Wants to please everyone. Idealistic and humanitarian.

Kenley, 9- Sees the big picture. Enjoys giving gifts. Original and unconventional. Communicates skillfully. Physical and passionate. Needs a lot of freedom.

Kennedy, 6- Creatively inspired. A step ahead of others. Original and unconventional. Romantic, opinionated. Likes change and variety. Natural authority. Needs a lot of freedom.

Kenneth, 5- Energetic, forceful. A free spirit, very adaptable. Creative and opinionated. Romantic, sensual. Loves adventure and excitement. Dynamic, busy lifestyle. Great judge of character.

Kenney, 11- Strong desire to succeed. Physical and passionate. Original and unconventional. Creative, opinionated. Likes change and variety. Needs a lot of freedom.

Kenny, 6- Creatively inspired. A step ahead of others. Opinionated, original. Romantic, sensual. Needs a lot of freedom.

Kenric, 6- Creatively inspired. A step ahead of others. Original and unconventional. Gentle, kind, a hard worker. Blessed in some ways. Self-expressive, cheerful.

Kent, 5- Energetic, forceful. Physical and passionate. Original and unconventional. Dynamic, busy lifestyle.

Kenton, 7- Multifaceted and disciplined. Perceptive, not easily fooled. Original and unconventional. Dynamic, busy lifestyle. Natural counselor and healer. Romantic, sensual.

Kenway, 7- Multifaceted and disciplined. Perceptive, not easily fooled. Original and unconventional. Likes to meet new people. Independent, critical of self and others. Needs a lot of freedom.

Kenyon, 30- Enthusiastic and quick witted. A free spirit, very adaptable. Original and unconventional. Dislikes limitations. Natural counselor and healer. Romantic, sensual.

Kerby, 7- Multifaceted and disciplined. Perceptive, not easily fooled. Gentle, kind, a hard worker. Friendly, but shy. Dislikes limitations.

Kermit, 4- Practical imagination. Accesses quickly. Gentle, kind, a hard worker. Systematic, organized. Blessed in some ways. Dynamic, busy lifestyle.

Keri, 7- Multifaceted and disciplined. Perceptive, not easily fooled. Gentle, kind, a hard worker. Blessed in some ways.

Kern, 3- Enthusiastic and quick witted. A free spirit, very adaptable. Sympathetic, kind. Original and unconventional.

Kerri, 7- Multifaceted and disciplined. Perceptive, not easily fooled. Gentle, kind, a hard worker. Tendency to lose items. Blessed in some ways.

Kerrie, 3- Enthusiastic and quick witted. A free spirit, very adaptable. Gentle, kind, a hard worker. Tendency to lose items. Blessed in some ways. Loves adventure and excitement.

Kerry, 5- Energetic, forceful. Perceptive, socially adept. Gentle, kind, a hard worker. Tendency to lose items. Needs a lot of freedom.

Kerwin, 8- Has a powerful presence. Original and creative. Intense inner power. Likes to meet new people. Blessed in some ways. Romantic, sensual.

Kesha, 8- Has a powerful presence. Original and creative. Charming and devoted. Great judge of character. Resolute and purposeful.

Ketti, 20- Perceptive and diplomatic. Social and entertaining. Dynamic, busy lifestyle. Sensitive and easily hurt. Blessed in some ways.

Ketura, 22- Strong desire to succeed. Has big plans and ideas. Energetic, highly charged. Attractive and charming. Gentle, kind, a hard worker. Independent, critical of self and others.

Ketzia, 9- Sees the big picture. Enjoys giving gifts. Dynamic, busy lifestyle. Uses common sense. Blessed in some ways. Independent, critical of self and others.

Keven, 3- Enthusiastic and quick witted. A free spirit, very adaptable. Intuitive and inspired. Likes to entertain. Romantic and sensual.

Kevin, 7- Multifaceted and disciplined. Not easily fooled. Intuitive and inspired. Blessed in some ways. Original and unconventional.

Keyla, 9- Sees the big picture. Enjoys giving gifts. Needs a lot of freedom. Strong verbal skills. Independent, critical of self and others.

Keyton, 9- Sees the big picture. Enjoys giving gifts. Needs a lot of freedom. Dynamic, busy lifestyle. Natural counselor and healer. Romantic, opinionated.

Kezi, 6- Creatively inspired. A step ahead of others. Uses common sense. Blessed in some ways.

Khadeem, 11- Strong desire to succeed. Great judge of character. Intuitive and perceptive. Reliable, responsible. A free spirit, very adaptable. Loves adventure and excitement. Systematic, organized.

Khamis, 7- Multifaceted and disciplined. Great judge of character. Not easily influenced. Domestic, hard working. Blessed in some ways. Charming and devoted.

Kidae, 3- Enthusiastic and quick witted. Blessed in some ways. Domestic, hard working. Aims to please. A free spirit, very adaptable.

Kieran, 4- Practical imagination. Devoted to family. Accesses quickly. Gentle, kind, a hard worker. Independent, critical of self and others. Original and unconventional.

Kieron, 9- Sees the big picture. Blessed in some ways. A free spirit, very adaptable. Gentle, kind, a hard worker. Natural counselor and healer. Original and unconventional.

Kiesha, 8- (Same as Keisha.)

Kiki, 22- Strong desire to succeed. Blessed in some ways. A bit forceful at times. Idealistic and humanitarian.

Kiko, 10- Exercise very beneficial. Respectful, kind. A bit forceful at times. Natural counselor and healer.

Kile, 10- Exercise very beneficial. Respectful, kind. Travels frequently. A free spirit, very adaptable.

Killian, 5- Energetic, forceful. Generous and thoughtful. Great verbal skills. Frequent traveler. Artistic, having good taste. Independent, critical of self and others. Original and unconventional.

Kim, 6- Creatively inspired. Artistic, having good taste. Domestic, hard working.

Kimba, 9- Sees the big picture. Blessed in some ways. Domestic, hard working. Friendly, but shy. Independent, critical of self and others.

Kimbal, 3- Enthusiastic and quick witted. Blessed in some ways. Domestic, hard working. Friendly, but shy. Independent, critical of self and others. Communicates skillfully.

Kimball, 6- Creatively inspired. Artistic, having good taste. Domestic, hard working. Friendly, but shy. Independent, critical of self and others. Great verbal skills. Frequent traveler.

Kimberlee, 8- Has a powerful presence. Blessed in some ways. Domestic, hard working. Friendly, but shy. Physical and passionate. Gentle, kind, humanitarian. Great verbal skills. Loves adventure and excitement. A free spirit, very adaptable.

Kimberly, 5- Energetic, forceful. Generous, thoughtful. Domestic, hard working. Friendly, but shy. A free spirit, very adaptable. Gentle, kind, humanitarian. Communicates skillfully. Dislikes limitations.

Kimi, 6- Creatively inspired. Blessed in some ways. Domestic, hard working. Artistic, having good taste.

Kimiko, 5- Energetic, forceful. Generous, thoughtful. Domestic, hard working. Artistic, having good taste. Strong desire to succeed. Natural counselor and healer.

Kimiyo, 10- Exercise very beneficial. Blessed in some ways. Domestic, hard working. Artistic, having good taste. Needs a lot of freedom. Natural counselor and healer.

Kimmi, 10- Exercise very beneficial. Respectful, kind. Domestic, hard working. Desires financial security. Artistic, having good taste.

Kimmy, 8- Has a powerful presence. Blessed in some ways. Domestic, hard working. Desires financial security. Needs a lot of freedom.

Kincaid, 6- Creatively inspired. Blessed in some ways. Original and unconventional. Self-expressive, cheerful. Independent, critical of self and others. Artistic, having good taste. Reliable, responsible.

Kindra, 30- Enthusiastic and quick witted. Understanding, kind. Original and unconventional. Reliable, responsible. Gentle, kind, a hard worker. Independent, critical of self and others.

Kine`, 3- Enthusiastic and quick witted. Blessed in some ways. Romantic, opinionated. A free spirit, very adaptable.

King, 5- Energetic, forceful. Generous, thoughtful. Creative, romantic. Scientific and philosophical.

Kingsley, 3- Enthusiastic and quick witted. Blessed in some ways. Original and unconventional. Scientific and philosophical. Charming and devoted. Strong verbal skills. A free spirit, very adaptable. Dislikes limitations.

Kingston, 10- Exercise very beneficial. Respectful, kind. Romantic, original. Scientific and philosophical. Charming and devoted. Dynamic, busy lifestyle. Natural counselor and healer. Creative and opinionated.

Kino, 22- Strong desire to succeed. Idealistic, humanitarian. Intuitive and creative. Natural counselor and healer.

Kinsey, 11- Strong desire to succeed. Idealistic, humanitarian. Original and unconventional. Charming and devoted. Loves adventure and excitement. Needs a lot of freedom.

Kion, 22- (Same as Kino)

Kip, 9- Sees the big picture. Blessed in some ways. Level headed, secretive.

Kirby, 11- Strong desire to succeed. Idealistic, humanitarian. Gentle, kind, a hard worker. Friendly, but shy. Needs a lot of freedom.

Kirill, 8- Has a powerful presence. Blessed in some ways. Intense inner power. Artistic, having good taste. Great verbal skills. Many financial ups and downs.

Kirk, 22- Strong desire to succeed. Idealistic, humanitarian. Gentle, kind, a hard worker. A bit forceful at times.

Kirsten, 6- Creatively inspired. Artistic, having good taste. Gentle, kind, a hard worker. Charming and devoted. Dynamic, busy lifestyle. A free spirit, very adaptable. Original and unconventional.

Kirstin, 10- Exercise very beneficial. Respectful, kind. Diligent, hard working. Charming and devoted. Dynamic, busy lifestyle. Artistic, having good taste.

Kirstie, 10- Exercise very beneficial. Respectful, kind. Diligent, hard working. Charming and devoted. Dynamic, busy lifestyle. Artistic, having good taste. A free spirit, very adaptable.

Kirsty, 30- Enthusiastic and quick witted. Blessed in some ways. Gentle, kind, a hard worker. Charming and devoted. Dynamic, busy lifestyle. Needs a lot of freedom.

Kisha, 3- Enthusiastic and quick witted. Blessed in some ways. Charming and devoted. Great judge of character. Independent, critical of self and others.

Kit, 4- Practical imagination. Blessed in some ways. Dynamic, busy lifestyle.

Kitty, 22- Strong desire to succeed. Idealistic, humanitarian. Dynamic, busy lifestyle. Sensitive and easily hurt. Needs a lot of freedom.

Kizzy, 7- Multifaceted and disciplined. Blessed in some ways. Uses common sense. Impatient and stubborn. Needs a lot of freedom.

Knox, 10- Exercise very beneficial. Original and unconventional. Natural counselor and healer. Artistic, sensual, perceptive.

Knute, 8- Has a powerful presence. Creative, original. Attractive and charming. Dynamic, busy lifestyle. A free spirit, very adaptable.

Kobe, 6- Creatively inspired. Magnetic personality. Friendly, but shy. Physical and passionate.

Koko, 7- Multifaceted and disciplined. Respects rules. Nervous, high strung. Musically inclined.

Konrad, 9- Sees the big picture. Natural counselor and healer. Original and unconventional. Gentle, kind, a hard worker. Independent, critical of self and others. Reliable, responsible.

Kori, 8- Has a powerful presence. Competitive in business. Gentle, kind, a hard worker. Blessed in some ways.

Kory, 6- Creatively inspired. Magnetic personality. Gentle, kind, a hard worker. Needs a lot of freedom.

Krishna, 8- Has a powerful presence. Intense inner power. Blessed in some ways. Charming and devoted. Great judge of character. Original and unconventional. Independent, critical of self and others.

Kriss, 22- Strong desire to succeed. Gentle, kind, a hard worker. Blessed in some ways. Charming and devoted. Intense and extreme.

Kristiana, 3- Enthusiastic and quick witted. Gentle, kind, a hard worker. Blessed in some ways. Charming and devoted. Dynamic, busy lifestyle. Artistic, having good taste. Independent, critical of self and others. Original and unconventional. Bold, courageous, a bit stubborn.

Kristin, 10- Exercise very beneficial. Diligent, hard working. Blessed in some ways. Charming and devoted. Dynamic, busy lifestyle. Artistic, having good taste. Original and unconventional.

Kristina, 11- Strong desire to succeed. Gentle, kind, a hard worker. Idealistic, humanitarian. Charming and devoted. Dynamic, busy lifestyle. Artistic, having good taste. Original and unconventional. Independent, critical of self and others.

Kristine, 6- Creatively inspired. Kind hearted, helpful. Blessed in some ways. Completely devoted. Dynamic, busy lifestyle. Artistic, having good taste. Original and unconventional. A free spirit, very adaptable.

Kristoffer, 10- Exercise very beneficial. Diligent, hard working. Blessed in some ways. Charming and devoted. Dynamic, busy lifestyle. Assumes responsibility easily. Strong family ties. Nurturing, protective. Physical, passionate. Tendency to lose items.

Krysta, 22- Strong desire to succeed. Gentle, kind, a hard worker. Needs a lot of freedom. Charming and devoted. Dynamic, busy lifestyle. Independent, critical of self and others.

Kultida, 6- Creatively inspired. Attractive and charming. Excellent verbal skills. Dynamic, busy lifestyle. Blessed in some ways. Reliable, responsible. Independent, critical of self and others.

Kumiko, 8- Has a powerful presence. Usually very lucky. Domestic, hard working. Artistic, having good taste. A bit forceful at times. Natural counselor and healer.

Kurt, 7- Multifaceted and disciplined. Attractive and charming. Gentle, kind, a hard worker. Dynamic, busy lifestyle.

Kwame, 8- Has a powerful presence. Likes to meet new people. Resolute and purposeful. Domestic, hard working. A free spirit, very adaptable.

Kwang-soo, 6- Creatively inspired. Likes to meet new people. Independent, critical of self and others. Original and unconventional. Scientific and philosophical. Charming and devoted. Natural counselor and healer. Has musical abilities.

Kyasha, 20- Sensitive and diplomatic. Needs a lot of freedom. Independent, critical of self and others. Charming and devoted. Great judge of character. Bold, courageous, a bit stubborn.

Kye, 5- Energetic, forceful. Needs a lot of freedom. Loves adventure and excitement.

Kyla, 4- Practical imagination. Finds shortcuts. Good verbal skills. Independent, critical of self and others.

Kylah, 3- Enthusiastic and quick witted. Needs a lot of freedom. Good verbal skills. Independent, critical of self and others. Great judge of character.

Kyle, 8- Has a powerful presence. Strong intuition. Good verbal skills. Physical and passionate.

Kylie, 8- Has a powerful presence. Strong intuition. Good verbal skills. Blessed in some ways. Physical and passionate.

Kym, 4- Practical imagination. Finds shortcuts. Domestic, hard working.

Kynan, 20- Sensitive and diplomatic. Needs a lot of freedom. Original and unconventional. Independent, critical of self and others. Romantic, sensual.

Kyne, 10- Exercise very beneficial. Needs a lot of freedom. Original and unconventional. Loves adventure and excitement.

Kyra, 10- Exercise very beneficial. Needs a lot of freedom. Gentle, kind, a hard worker. Independent, critical of self and others.

Kyurios, 10- Exercise very beneficial. Needs a lot of freedom. Attractive and charming. Gentle, kind, a hard worker. Blessed in some ways. Natural counselor and healer. Impulsive and extreme.

> "Oh, I'd give anything to get out of Oz altogether—but which is the way back to Kansas? I can't go the way I came."
> ~*Excerpted from "The Wizard of Oz"*
> *Used with permission*

L

IF A NAME BEGINS with L, has more than one L, or ends with an L, this person is lucky, good natured in disposition, travels and moves frequently, and is slow to make decisions.

The letter L is the 12th letter in the alphabet. 1+2=3, so the 12th letter has a 3 vibrational influence. This same vibration also rules the letters C and U. The 1 rules beginnings and the 2 rules partnerships, together they equal 3 which rules balance. So quite often the L ruled individual is learning to be in a partnership and must learn to be in balance with it. When the L person is emotionally stressed, they tend to be accident prone. They can be thrown off balance quite easily. It's important for the L ruled to maintain balance in all areas of life.

Persons with double L's in their names, for example, Bill or Kelly, tend to be good conversationalists. They seem to possess a high degree of creative self-expression and sociability. Kelly Ripa of "Live with Regis and Kelly" and Bill O'Reilly of "The O'Reilly Factor," have found themselves quite at home on talk shows. L's like to communicate almost as much as C's. The L's know how to make others feel at home. They are a welcome addition to any social situation.

The L can soften any name with A as their first vowel. Although Laura is an ambitious name with 2 A's in it, the L gives Laura a sense of humor, coupled with the U, she is easy going and youthful no matter how ambitious she is. Larry can be intimidating with the double R's. Double R's sometimes enjoy bullying others around, but with an L in the beginning of his name, he most likely will be a showman about it, acting as if on stage to get a laugh. L's, similar to C's, will be the first to crack a joke when things get a little quiet. They are warm, friendly, social and tend to express an air of openness.

Similar to the letters C and U, this 3 ruled letter is quite resilient and bounces back from illness better than the other letters. It has a strong constitution and won't stay down. Lance Armstrong, national and world champion cyclist, two time Olympian, renowned humanitarian, role model and cancer survivor is a good example of the power of the L. Lance, 7 time winner of the Tour De France, has two 3-ruled letters in his first name. 3 is the communicator and gifted in the area of writing. Lance has written 2 books so far. Cancer left him scarred physically and emotionally, but he now maintains it was an unexpected gift; a viewpoint shared by many cancer survivors. Getting cancer was "…the best thing that ever happened to me," Lance said, in relation to the direction this disease forced him to face. This is the optimistic, cheerfulness of the letter L. Lance Armstrong made the most stunning comeback ever in the history of sports. His chances of recovery were far less than 50/50 when he began an aggressive form of chemotherapy. He began riding and training only 5 months after his diagnosis. His strength and courage must in part be credited to his name summing up to an 8 power number. 8 is the survivor of numbers. He gives a lot of credit to his mother for the support she gave him; his mother's name also begins with the letter

L. Her name is Linda. Lance no doubt inherited his cheerful, optimistic attitude from his first letter L named mother.

Actor Leonardo Di Caprio knows how to bring reality on an emotional level to his roles. He has touched the hearts of millions all over the world, especially in the blockbuster movie, "Titanic." Leonardo's power number is 3, the same number that rules the letter L. It's no wonder he became successful during his adolescence as the number 3 rules adolescence along with the 3rd astrological sign Gemini. He has two O's in his name which give him a magnetic quality. Later the O's will lend toward a nurturing ability. No doubt he will want children some day as he has a lot of love to give out. He is a free spirit with an E first vowel, but just like his father, George, his E conjuncts the duty bound O vowel. Although he loves freedom and adventure, he is also service oriented and cannot help but to work very hard in any field he chooses. This is what he inherited from his father.

Another youthful famous person whose name starts with the letter L is Liv Tyler. Although she is no longer an adolescent, she appears very young on screen. Her first name sums up to a 7 power number. This number performs well in front of a camera. While still a teenager, a friend talked her into modeling—her career skyrocketed. A few years later she decided to try acting—she took to it like a fish takes to water, even without acting lessons. Of course she is blessed with an I first vowel. The 7 and 9 influence gives her an ethereal quality, which was beneficial for her role in "The Lord of the Ring" films. She also inherited the V from her famous father, Steven Tyler, rock band member of Aerosmith. V is an international letter ruled by the master number 22. Those with a V anywhere in their name tend to be tenacious about reaching goals. Still, she seems so easy going and easy to talk to. This letter L in the beginning of her name gives her a cheerful, optimist's youthful appearance. She tenacious about reaching her goals, but she's as smooth as whipped cream about it.

L is for lucky! The Lewis and Clark expedition had an L in each name. This dangerous expedition started May 1804 in St. Louis, Missouri and ended 2 years later back in St. Louis. The group traveled by foot and horseback and boat across the vast wilderness of the North West United States to the Pacific Ocean. Interestingly enough, despite the scorching and freezing weather, swift river currents, rugged mountain trails, dangerous animals, Indian tribes, hunger and exhaustion the group didn't quarrel and they had no serious casualties during the entire expedition! This lucky, cheerful, optimistic letter L seems to have played an important role in this expedition. No other expedition has the claim to fame this one does for everyone getting along so well in spite of their adversities. Never underestimate the power of the letter L!

L is a lovely letter to have anywhere in a name. The L influence is one of cheerfulness, creativity, social ability and excellent communication skills. It's a warm, go-with-the-flow letter that is forever youthful and happy, no matter the age the person.

Those in love with an L named person could be blessed depending on which way they look at it. This letter has a difficult time making up their mind for some reason. So, be patient, hang in there, and eventually he or she will notice you.

Some more famous L people are: Lucille O'ball, Laurence Olivier, Lee Majors, Lionel Richey, Leif Erickson, Louie Armstrong, Leanne Rhymes, Linda Blair, Liam Neeson, Laura Dern, Lea Thompson, Lisa Presley, Laurence Fishburne, Lana Turner, Laura Linney, Lucy Liu, Lauren Hutton, Linda Hamilton, Lenny Kravitz, Lee Remick, Levi Strauss, Leon Spinks, Leonard Nimoy, Larry Hagman, Liberace, LaToya Jackson, Lil Romeo, Lauren Bacall, Lou Ferrigno, Lawrence Welk, Little Richard, Luke Perry, Lyle Lovett and Larry King.

Quick Reference of "L" Names

Lachlan, 6- Easy going attitude. Pioneer and risk taker. A sense of humor. Great judge of character. Slow to make decisions. Bold, courageous, a bit stubborn. Creative and original.

Laila, 8- Recuperates quickly. Resolute and purposeful. Blessed in many ways. Slow to make decisions. Bold, courageous, a bit stubborn.

Laine, 5- Moves and travels often. Bright, adventuresome. Blessed in many ways. Original and unconventional. A free spirit, very adaptable.

Laird, 8- Recuperates quickly. Resolute and purposeful. Artistic, having good taste. Gentle, kind, a hard worker. Problem solver and natural authority.

Lakeesha, 8- Recuperates quickly. Resolute and purposeful. Desire to succeed. Physical and passionate. Loves adventure and excitement. Charming and devoted. Self-reliant, successful. Bold, courageous, a bit stubborn.

Lakeisha, 30- Slow to make decisions. Aims to please. Strong desire to succeed. A free spirit, very adaptable. Blessed in some ways. Charming and devoted. Great judge of character. Bold, courageous, a bit stubborn.

Lakisha, 7- Intellectually sound. Not easily fooled. Strong desire to succeed. Blessed in some ways. Charming and devoted. Great judge of character. Bold, courageous, a bit stubborn.

Lalaine, 9- Benefits from meditation. Helpful, sincere. Communicates skillfully. Bold, courageous, a bit stubborn. Blessed in some ways. Original and unconventional. A free spirit, very adaptable.

Lamar, 9- Benefits from meditation. Helpful, sincere. Domestic, hard working. Bold, courageous, a bit stubborn. Gentle, kind, diligent.

LaMarr, 9- Benefits from meditation. Helpful, sincere. Domestic, hard working. Bold, courageous, a bit stubborn. Gentle, kind, diligent. Could be forgetful.

Lambert, 8- Recuperates quickly. Resolute and purposeful. Domestic, hard working. Friendly, but shy. A free spirit, very adaptable. Gentle, kind, diligent. Dynamic, busy lifestyle.

Lamont, 3- Slow to make decisions. Aims to please. Domestic, hard working. Natural counselor and healer. Original and unconventional. Dynamic, busy lifestyle.

Lana, 10- Strong verbal skills. Independent, critical of self and others. Original and unconventional. Bold, courageous, a bit stubborn.

Lance, 8- Recuperates quickly. Resolute and purposeful. Creative, romantic. Self-expressive, cheerful. A free spirit, very adaptable.

Lancelot, 10- Strong verbal skills. Independent, critical of self and others. Creative, romantic. Self-expressive, cheerful. A free spirit, very adaptable. Frequent traveler. A natural counselor and healer. Dynamic, busy lifestyle.

Lander, 9- Benefits from meditation. Helpful, sincere. Creative, opinionated. Reliable, responsible. A free spirit, very adaptable. Gentle, kind, a hard worker.

Landon, 6- Easy going attitude. Pioneer and risk taker. Creative, opinionated. Reliable, responsible. Natural counselor and healer. Romantic, sensual.

Lane, 5- Moves and travels frequently. Bright, adventuresome. Romantic, sensual. A free spirit, very adaptable.

Lanette, 5- Moves and travels frequently. Bright, adventuresome. Creative, opinionated. A free spirit, very adaptable. Dynamic, busy lifestyle. Sensitive and easily hurt. Physical and passionate.

Lang, 7- Intellectually sound. Not easily influenced. Original and unconventional. Has willpower and determination.

Langdon, 4- Domestically creative. Natural teaching ability. Creative, original. Scientific and philosophical. Reliable, responsible. Nurturing, loving. Romantic, opinionated.

Langford, 5- Moves and travels frequently. Bright, adventuresome. Original and unconventional. Scientific and philosophical. Self-sacrificing, loving. Natural counselor and healer. Gentle, kind, a hard worker. Reliable, responsible.

Langley, 4- Domestically creative. Natural teaching ability. Original and unconventional. Scientific and philosophical. Frequent traveler. Loves adventure and excitement. Needs a lot of freedom.

Langston, 30- Slow to make decisions. Aims to please. Original and unconventional. Scientific and philosophical. Charming and devoted. Dynamic, busy lifestyle. Natural counselor and healer. Romantic, sensual.

Lani, 9- Benefits from meditation. Helpful, sincere. Original and unconventional. Blessed in some ways.

Lara, 5- Moves and travels frequently. Bright, adventuresome. Gentle, kind, a hard worker. Bold, courageous, a bit stubborn.

Laraine, 6- Easy going attitude. Pioneer and risk taker. Diligent, hard working. Bold, courageous, a bit stubborn. Blessed in some ways. Original and unconventional. A free spirit, very adaptable.

Larissa, 7- Intellectually sound. Not easily influenced. Gentle, kind, a hard worker. Blessed in some ways. Charming and devoted. Impulsive and extreme. Bold, courageous, a bit stubborn.

Lark, 6- Easy going attitude. Pioneer and risk taker. Diligent, hard working. Desires to succeed.

LaRoux, 10- Strong verbal skills. Independent, critical of self and others. Gentle, kind, a hard worker. Natural counselor and healer. Attractive and charming. Artistic, sensual, perceptive.

Larry, 11- Travels frequently. Intuitive, perceptive. Gentle, kind, a hard worker. Tendency to lose items. Needs a lot of freedom.

Lars, 5- Moves and travels often. Bright, adventuresome. Intense inner power. Charming and devoted.

Larz, 3- Slow to make decisions. Aims to please. Gentle, kind, a hard worker. Uses common sense.

Larson, 7- Intellectually sound. Not easily influenced. Intense inner power. Charming and devoted. Natural counselor and healer. Original and unconventional.

Lassie, 20- Honest and sincere. Reads people easily. Charming and devoted. Impulsive and extreme. Blessed in some ways. A free spirit, very adaptable.

Latania, 22- Travels frequently. Ambitious leader, great leader. Dynamic, busy lifestyle. Bold, courageous, a bit stubborn. Original and unconventional. Blessed in some ways. Pioneer and risk taker.

Latanya, 20- Honest and sincere. Independent, critical of self and others. Energetic, highly charged. Bold, courageous, a bit stubborn. Original and unconventional. Needs a lot of freedom. Pioneer and risk taker.

Lateefah, 4- Domestically creative. Natural teaching ability. Dynamic, busy lifestyle. A free spirit, very adaptable. Loves adventure and excitement. Self-sacrificing, loving. Bold, courageous, a bit stubborn. Great judge of character.

Latham, 10- Strong verbal skills. Independent, critical of self and others. Energetic, highly charged. Great judge of character. Bold, courageous, a bit stubborn. Domestic, hard working.

Lathrop, 9- Benefits from meditation. Helpful, sincere. Dynamic, busy lifestyle. Great judge of character. Gentle, kind, hard worker. Natural counselor and healer. Intelligent and knowledgeable.

Latimer, 6- Easy going attitude. Natural teaching ability. Dynamic, busy lifestyle. Blessed in some ways. Domestic, hard working. A free spirit, very adaptable. Tendency to lose items.

Latoya, 20- Honest and sincere. Reads people easily. Energetic, highly charged. Natural counselor and healer. Needs a lot of freedom. Bold, courageous, a bit stubborn.

Launce, 20- Honest and sincere. Reads people easily. Socially charming. Original and unconventional. Self-expressive, cheerful. A free spirit, very adaptable.

Launcelot, 4- Domestically creative. Natural teaching ability. Attractive and charming. Original and unconventional. Self-expressive, cheerful. A free spirit, very adaptable. Frequent traveler. Natural counselor and healer. Dynamic, busy lifestyle.

Laura, 8- Recuperates quickly. Resolute and purposeful. Attractive and charming. Intense inner power. Bold, courageous, a bit stubborn.

Laureen, 4- Domestically creative. Natural teaching ability. Attractive and charming. Gentle, kind, a hard worker. A free spirit, very adaptable. Loves adventure and excitement. Original and unconventional.

Laurel, 6- Easy going attitude. Natural teaching ability. Youthful and appealing. Gentle, kind, a hard worker. A free spirit, very adaptable. Frequent traveler.

Lauren, 8- Recuperates quickly. Resolute and purposeful. Attractive and charming. Intense inner power. A free spirit, very adaptable. Original and unconventional.

Laurence, 7- Intellectually sound. Not easily influenced. Attractive and charming. Gentle, kind, a hard worker. A free spirit, very adaptable. Original and unconventional. Self-expressive, cheerful. Loves adventure and excitement.

Laurent, 10- Strong verbal skills. Independent, critical of self and others. Attractive and charming. Gentle, kind, a hard worker. A free spirit, very adaptable. Original and unconventional. Dynamic, busy lifestyle.

Lauretta, 8- Recuperates quickly. Resolute and purposeful. Attractive and charming. Intense inner power. A free spirit, very adaptable. Dynamic, busy lifestyle. Sensitive and easily hurt. Bold, courageous, a bit stubborn.

Laurette, 30- Slow to make decisions. Aims to please. Youthful and appealing. Gentle, kind, a hard worker. A free spirit, very adaptable. Dynamic, busy lifestyle. Sensitive and easily hurt. Loves adventure and excitement.

Laurie, 30- Slow to make decisions. Aims to please. Youthful and appealing. Gentle, kind, a hard worker. Blessed in some ways. A free spirit, very adaptable.

LaVerne, 5- Moves and travels often. Bright, adventuresome. Intuitive and inspired. A free spirit, very adaptable. Gentle, kind, a hard worker. Original and unconventional. Tendency to overindulge.

Laverne, 5- (Same as LaVerne.)

Lavinia, 5- Moves and travels often. Bright, adventuresome. Intuitive and inspired. Blessed in some ways. Romantic and sensual. Artistic, having good taste. Independent, critical of self and others.

Lawford, 7- Intellectually sound. Not easily influenced. Likes to meet new people. Self-sacrificing, loving. Natural counselor and healer. Gentle, kind, a hard worker. Reliable, responsible.

Lawrence, 9- Benefits from meditation. Helpful, sincere. Likes to meet new people. Gentle, kind, a hard worker. A free spirit, very adaptable. Original and unconventional. Self-expressive, cheerful. Loves adventure and excitement.

Lawson, 3- Slow to make decisions. Aims to please. Likes to meet new people. Charming and devoted. Natural counselor and healer. Original and unconventional.

Lawton, 22- Travels frequently. Ambitious leader, great vision. Likes to meet new people. Dynamic, busy lifestyle. Natural counselor and healer. Original and unconventional.

Layla, 6- Easy going attitude. Pioneer and risk taker. Needs a lot of freedom. Frequent traveler. Bold, courageous, a bit stubborn.

Laylah, 5- Moves and travels often. Bright, adventuresome. Needs a lot of freedom. Frequent traveler. Bold, courageous, a bit stubborn. Great judge of character.

Lazarus, 8- Recuperates quickly. Resolute and purposeful. Uses common sense. Bold, courageous, a bit stubborn. Gentle, kind, a hard worker. Attractive and charming. Intense and extreme.

Lea, 9- Benefits from meditation. Enjoys giving gifts. Helpful and sincere.

Leah, 8- Recuperates quickly. Original and creative. Resolute and purposeful. Great judge of character.

Leander, 5- Moves and travels often. Physical and passionate. Bright, adventuresome. Original and unconventional. Reliable, responsible. Likes change and variety. Gentle, kind, a hard worker.

Leann, 10- Strong verbal skills. Likes change and variety. Independent, critical of self and others. Original and unconventional. Romantic, sensual.

Leanna, 20- Honest and sincere. Social and entertaining. Reads people easily. Original and unconventional. Romantic, sensual. Bold, courageous, a bit stubborn.

Leanne, 6- Easy going attitude. A step ahead of others. Pioneer and risk taker. Original and unconventional. Romantic, sensual. A free spirit, adaptable to change.

Lee, 4- Domestically creative. Accesses quickly. Loves adventure and excitement.

Leif, 5- Moves and travels often. Physical and passionate. Generous, thoughtful. Self-sacrificing, loving.

Leigh, 5- Moves and travels often. Physical and passionate. Generous, thoughtful. Scientific and philosophical. Great judge of character.

Leighton, 9- Benefits from meditation. Enjoys giving gifts. Blessed in some ways. Scientific and philosophical. Great judge of character. Dynamic, busy lifestyle. Natural counselor and healer. Original and unconventional.

Leila, 3- Slow to make decisions. A free spirit, very adaptable. Blessed in some ways. Frequent traveler. Independent, critical of self and others.

Leilani, 8- Recuperates quickly. Original and creative. Blessed in some ways. Frequent traveler. Resolute and purposeful. Romantic, sensual. Artistic, having good taste.

Lekisha, 11- Travels frequently. Has big plans and ideas. Strong desire to succeed. Blessed in some ways. Charming and devoted. Great judge of character. Independent, critical of self and others.

Lela, 3- Slow to make decisions. A free spirit, very adaptable. Frequent traveler. Independent, critical of self and others.

Leland, 3- Slow to make decisions. A free spirit, very adaptable. Frequent traveler. Aims to please. Original and unconventional. Reliable, responsible.

Lena, 5- Moves and travels often. Physical and passionate. Original and unconventional. Independent, critical of self and others.

Lenora, 11- Travels frequently. Keenly perceptive. Creative, romantic. Natural counselor and healer. Gentle, kind, a hard worker. Independent, critical of self and others.

Lenore, 6- Easy going attitude. A step ahead of others. Romantic, sensual. Natural counselor and healer. Gentle, kind, a hard worker. Loves adventure and excitement.

Lennie, 5- Moves and travels often. Physical and passionate. Original and unconventional. Creative, opinionated. Blessed in some ways. A free spirit, very adaptable.

Lenny, 7- Intellectually sound. Not easily fooled. Original and unconventional. Romantic, sensual. Needs a lot of freedom.

Leo, 5- Moves and travels often. Physical and passionate. Natural counselor and healer.

Leon, 10- Strong verbal skills. Likes change and variety. Self-sacrificing, devoted. Romantic, opinionated.

Leona, 20- Honest and sincere. Social and entertaining. Natural counselor and healer. Original and unconventional. Independent, critical of self and others.

Leonard, 6- Easy going attitude. A step ahead of others. Nurturing, loving. Original and unconventional. Independent, critical of self and others. Gentle, kind, a hard worker. Reliable, responsible.

Leonardo, 30- Slow to make decisions. A free spirit, very adaptable. Natural counselor and healer. Original and unconventional. Independent, critical of self and others. Gentle, kind, a hard worker. Reliable, responsible. Good parental skills.

Leonides, 11- Travels frequently. Keenly perceptive. Creates group harmony. Creative, opinionated. Blessed in some ways. Natural authority. Physical and passionate. Charming and devoted.

Leonora, 8- Recuperates quickly. Original and creative. Natural counselor and healer. Creative, opinionated. Good parental skills. Gentle, kind, a hard worker. Independent, critical of self and others.

Leonore, 3- Slow to make decisions. A free spirit, very adaptable. Natural counselor and healer. Original and unconventional. Good parental skills. Gentle, kind, a hard worker. Tendency to overindulge.

Leontyne, 11- Travels frequently. Keenly perceptive. Creates group harmony. Romantic, opinionated. Dynamic, busy lifestyle. Dislikes limitations. Romantic, sensual. Loves adventure and excitement.

Leony, 8- Recuperates quickly. Original and creative. Competitive in business. Romantic, sensual. Dislikes limitations.

Leopold, 7- Intellectually sound. Not easily fooled. Natural counselor and healer. Intelligent and knowledgeable. May have musical abilities. Slow to make decisions. Reliable, responsible.

Leroy, 30- Slow to make decisions. A free spirit, very adaptable. Gentle, kind, a hard worker. Natural counselor and healer. Needs a lot of freedom.

Les, 9- Benefits from meditation. Enjoys giving gifts. Charming and devoted.

Lesley, 6- Easy going attitude. A step ahead of others. Devoted and loving. Frequent traveler. Loves adventure and excitement. Needs a lot of freedom.

Lesli, 3- Slow to make decisions. A free spirit, very adaptable. Charming and devoted. Blessed in some ways.

Leslie, 8- Recuperates quickly. Original and creative. Passionate and loving. Slow to make decisions. Blessed in some ways. Loves adventure and excitement.

Lester, 7- Intellectually sound. Not easily fooled. Charming and devoted. Dynamic, busy lifestyle. Tendency to overindulge. Gentle, kind, a hard worker.

Leticia, 5- Moves and travels often. Physical and passionate. Dynamic, busy lifestyle. Blessed in some ways. Self-expressive, cheerful. Artistic, having good taste. Independent, critical of self and others.

Lettie, 8- Recuperates quickly. Original and creative. Dynamic, busy lifestyle. Sensitive and easily hurt. Blessed in some ways. Loves adventure and excitement.

Letty, 10- Strong verbal skills. Likes change and variety. Dynamic, busy lifestyle. Sensitive and easily hurt. Needs a lot of freedom.

Levi, 3- Slow to make decisions. A free spirit, very adaptable. Intuitive and inspired. Blessed in some ways.

Levy, 10- Strong verbal skills. Likes change and variety. Intuitive and inspired. Dislikes limitations.

Lew, 4- Domestically creative. Accesses quickly. Likes to meet new people.

Lewis, 5- Moves and travels often. Physical and passionate. Likes to meet new people. Blessed in some ways. Charming and devoted.

Lexie, 10- Strong verbal skills. Likes change and variety. Artistic, sensual, perceptive. Blessed in some ways. Tendency to overindulge.

Li, 3- Slow to make decisions. Blessed in some ways. Inspiring and creative.

Lia, 4- Domestically creative. Blessed in some ways. Independent, critical of self and others.

Liam, 8- Recuperates quickly. Blessed in some ways. Independent, critical of self and others. Domestic, hard working.

Liana, 10- Strong verbal skills. Respectful and kind. Independent, critical of self and others. Original and unconventional. Bold, courageous, a bit stubborn.

Lianne, 10- Strong verbal skills. Respectful and kind. Independent, critical of self and others. Original and unconventional. Romantic, sensual. A free spirit, very adaptable.

Libbie, 30- Slow to make decisions. Blessed in some ways. Affectionate, social. Emotional and sensitive. Artistic, having good taste. A free spirit, very adaptable.

Libby, 5- Moves and travels often. Generous and thoughtful. Friendly, but shy. Emotional, sensitive. Needs a lot of freedom.

Lida, 8- Recuperates quickly. Blessed in some ways. Reliable, responsible. Independent, critical of self and others.

Liddy, 9- Benefits from meditation. Idealistic and humanitarian. Reliable, responsible. Down-to-earth, faithful. Needs a lot of freedom.

Liene, 9- Benefits from meditation. Idealistic and humanitarian. A free spirit, very adaptable. Original and unconventional. Enjoys giving gifts.

Lil, 6- Easy going attitude. Artistic, having good taste. Communicates skillfully.

Lila, 7- Intellectually sound. Stylish and refined. Great verbal skills. Independent, critical of self and others.

Lilac, 10- Strong verbal skills. Respectful and kind. Slow to make decisions. Independent, critical of self and others. Self-expressive, cheerful.

Lilith, 7- Intellectually sound. Stylish and refined. Communicates skillfully. Artistic, having good taste. Dynamic, busy lifestyle. Great judge of character.

Lillian, 6- Easy going attitude. Artistic, having good taste. Slow to make decisions. Communicates skillfully. Artistic, having good taste. Independent, critical of self and others. Original and unconventional.

Lillie, 5- Moves and travels often. Generous and thoughtful. Slow to make decisions. Great verbal skills. Artistic, having good taste. A free spirit, very adaptable.

Lilly, 7- Intellectually sound. Stylish and refined. Slow to make decisions. Communicates skillfully. Needs a lot of freedom.

Lily, 22- Travels frequently. Blessed in some ways. Great verbal skills. Needs a lot of freedom.

Lincoln, 7- Intellectually sound. Stylish and refined. Original and unconventional. Self-expressive, cheerful. Natural counselor and healer. Frequent traveler. Romantic, sensual.

Lind, 3- Slow to make decisions. Blessed in some ways. Original and unconventional. Reliable, responsible.

Linda, 22- Travels frequently. Respectful and kind. Original and unconventional. Reliable, responsible. Independent, critical of self and others.

Linder, 8- Recuperates quickly. Blessed in some ways. Romantic, sensual. Reliable, responsible. A free spirit, very adaptable. Gentle, kind, a hard worker.

Lindie, 8- Recuperates quickly. Blessed in some ways. Romantic, sensual. Reliable, responsible. Artistic, having good taste. A free spirit, very adaptable.

Lindell, 5- Moves and travels often. Generous and thoughtful. Original and unconventional. Reliable, responsible. A free spirit, very adaptable. Communicates skillfully. Slow to make decisions.

Lindley, 9- Benefits from meditation. Idealistic, humanitarian. Original and unconventional. Reliable, responsible. Frequent traveler. A free spirit, very adaptable. Dislikes restrictions.

Lindsay, 30- Slow to make decisions. Blessed in some ways. Creative, romantic. Reliable, responsible. Charming and devoted. Aims to please. Needs a lot of freedom.

Lindsey, 7- Intellectually sound. Stylish and refined. Original and unconventional. Reliable, responsible. Charming and devoted. A free spirit, very adaptable. Dislikes limitations.

Lindy, 10- Strong verbal skills. Respectful and kind. Original and unconventional. Reliable, responsible. Needs a lot of freedom.

Linette, 4- Domestically creative. Blessed in some ways. Original and unconventional. A free spirit, very adaptable. Dynamic, busy lifestyle. Sensitive and easily hurt. Tendency to overindulge.

Link, 10- Frequent traveler. A gentle leader. Original and unconventional. Desires to be successful.

Linley, 5- Moves and travels often. Generous and thoughtful. Original and unconventional. Frequent traveler. A free spirit, very adaptable. Dislikes limitations.

Linne, 9- Benefits from meditation. Idealistic, humanitarian. Original and unconventional. Opinionated and creative. Physical and passionate.

Linsey, 30- Slow to make decisions. Blessed in some ways. Creative and romantic. Charming and devoted. A free spirit, very adaptable. Dislikes limitations.

Linus, 3- Slow to make decisions. Blessed in some ways. Creative and romantic. Attractive and lucky. Charming and devoted.

Lionel, 4- Domestically creative. Blessed in some ways. Natural counselor and healer. Original and unconventional. A free spirit, very adaptable. Frequent traveler.

Lisa, 5- Moves and travels often. Generous and thoughtful. Charming and devoted. Independent, critical of self and others.

Lisette, 9- Benefits from meditation. Idealistic, humanitarian. Angelic leanings. A free spirit, very adaptable. Dynamic, busy lifestyle. Sensitive and easily hurt. Tendency to overindulge.

Lisle, 3- Slow to make decisions. Blessed in some ways. Charming and devoted. Frequent traveler. A free spirit, very adaptable.

Lissa, 6- Easy going attitude. Artistic, having good taste. Charming and devoted. Impulsive and extreme. Independent, critical of self and others.

Litton, 9- Benefits from meditation. Idealistic, humanitarian. Dynamic, busy lifestyle. Sensitive and easily hurt. Natural counselor and healer. Original and unconventional.

Liu, 6- Easy going attitude. Artistic, having good taste. Attractive and charming.

Liv, 7- Intellectually sound. Stylish and refined. Intuitive and inspired.

Livia, 8- Recuperates quickly. Blessed in some ways. Intuitive and inspired. Artistic, having good taste. Independent, critical of self and others.

Livya, 6- Easy going attitude. Artistic, having good taste. Intuitive and inspired. Needs a lot of freedom. Independent, critical of self and others.

Liz, 20- Honest and sincere. Emotional and considerate. Tendency to look at the bright side.

Liza, 3- Slow to make decisions. Blessed in some ways. Uses common sense. Independent, critical of self and others.

Llewellyn, 3- Slow to make decisions. Frequent traveler. A free spirit, very adaptable. Likes to meet new people. Tendency to overindulge. Great verbal skills. Inspiring, very creative. Dislikes limitations. Original and unconventional.

Lloyd, 5- Moves and travels often. Communicates skillfully. Natural counselor and healer. Needs a lot of freedom. Reliable, responsible.

Loelia, 9- Benefits from meditation. Artistic, creative. A free spirit, very adaptable. Frequent traveler. Blessed in some ways. Independent, critical of self and others.

Logan, 22- Travels frequently. Creates group harmony. Scientific and philosophical. Ambitious leader, great vision. Original and unconventional.

Lois, 10- Strong verbal skills. Self-sacrificing, devoted. Blessed in some ways. Charming and devoted.

Lokelani, 7- Intellectually sound. Open to opportunities. Desire to succeed. A free spirit, very adaptable. Frequent traveler. Not easily influenced. Original and unconventional. Blessed in some ways.

Lola, 4- Domestically creative. Assumes responsibility. Communicates skillfully. Natural teaching ability.

Lolita, 6- Easy going attitude. Magnetic personality. Great verbal skills. Blessed in some ways. Dynamic, busy lifestyle. Independent, critical of self and others.

Lombard, 11- Travels frequently. Creates group harmony. Domestic, hard working. Friendly, but shy. Independent, critical of self and others. Gentle, kind, diligent. Reliable, responsible.

Lon, 5- Moves and travels often. Natural counselor and healer. Original and unconventional.

Lona, 6- Easy going attitude. Magnetic personality. Creative, opinionated. Self-motivated, independent.

Lonnie, 6- Easy going attitude. Magnetic personality. Creative, opinionated. Romantic, sensual. Blessed in some ways. A free spirit, very adaptable.

Lonny, 8- Recuperates quickly. Competitive in business. Original and unconventional. Romantic, sensual. Needs a lot of freedom.

Lora, 10- Strong verbal skills. Self-sacrificing, devoted. Diligent, helpful. Independent, critical of self and others.

Loraine, 11- Travels frequently. Creates group harmony. Gentle, kind, a hard worker. Intuitive, perceptive. Blessed in some ways. Original and unconventional. A free spirit, very adaptable.

Loralie, 9- Benefits from meditation. Artistically creative. Idealistic, humanitarian. Independent, critical of self and others. Frequent traveler. Blessed in some ways. A free spirit, very adaptable.

Lorelei, 4- Domestically creative. Assumes responsibility. Gentle, kind, a hard worker. Accesses quickly. Frequent traveler. Tendency to overindulge. Blessed in some ways.

Loren, 10- Strong verbal skills. Self-sacrificing, devoted. Diligent, helpful. Likes variety and change. Original and unconventional.

Lorena, 11- Travels frequently. Creates group harmony. Gentle, kind, a hard worker. Keenly perceptive. Original and unconventional. Self-motivated, independent.

Lorenzo, 6- Easy going attitude. Magnetic personality. Gentle, kind, a hard worker. A step ahead of others. Original and unconventional. Uses common sense. Nurturing, loving.

Loretta, 10- Strong verbal skills. Self-sacrificing, devoted. Diligent, helpful. Likes change and variety. Dynamic, busy lifestyle. Sensitive and easily hurt. Independent, critical of self and others.

L'Oretta, 10- (Same as Loretta.)

Lorette, 5- Moves and travels often. Natural counselor and healer. Intense inner power. A free spirit, very adaptable. Dynamic, busy lifestyle. Sensitive and easily hurt. Tendency to overindulge.

Lori, 9- Benefits from meditation. Artistic and creative. Gentle, kind, a hard worker. Blessed in some ways.

Lorie, 5- Moves and travels often. Natural counselor and healer. Intense inner power. Good deed doer. A free spirit, very adaptable.

Lorimer, 9- Benefits from meditation. Artistic and creative. Gentle, kind, a hard worker. Blessed in some ways. Systematic, organized. A free spirit, very adaptable. Tendency to lose items.

Lorin, 5- Moves and travels often. Natural counselor and healer. Intense inner power. Good deed doer. Original and unconventional.

Loring, 3- Slow to make decisions. Has creative solutions. Gentle, kind, a hard worker. Blessed in some ways. Original and unconventional. Scientific, philosophical.

Loris, 10- Strong verbal skills. Self-sacrificing, devoted. Diligent, hard working. Respectful, kind. Charming and devoted.

Lorna, 6- Easy going attitude. Magnetic personality. Self-sacrificing and duty bound. Original and unconventional. Independent, critical of self and others.

Lorne, 10- Strong verbal skills. Self-sacrificing, devoted. Diligent, hard working. Creative, opinionated. Physical and passionate.

Lorraine, 11- Travels frequently. Creates group harmony. Gentle, kind, a hard worker. Tendency to lose items. Independent, critical of self and others. Blessed in some ways. Original and unconventional. A free spirit, very adaptable.

Lorrie, 5- Moves and travels often. Natural counselor and healer. Intense inner power. Tendency to lose items. Blessed in some ways. A free spirit, very adaptable.

Lorry, 7- Intellectually sound. Open to opportunities. Gentle, kind, a hard worker. Tendency to lose items. Needs a lot of freedom.

Lot, 11- Travels frequently. Creates group harmony. Dynamic, busy lifestyle.

Lottie, 9- Benefits from meditation. Artistic and creative. Dynamic, busy lifestyle. Needs to slow down. Artistic, having good taste. A free spirit, very adaptable.

Lothario, 8- Recuperates quickly. Competitive in business. Dynamic, busy lifestyle. Great judge of character. Independent, critical of self and others. Gentle, kind, a hard worker. Blessed in some ways. Nurturing, loving.

Lou, 3- Slow to make decisions. Has creative solutions. Attractive and charming.

Louella, 6- Easy going attitude. Magnetic personality. Attractive and charming. A free spirit, very adaptable. Strong verbal skills. Ups and downs financially. Independent and self-motivated.

Louie, 8- Recuperates quickly. Competitive in business. Attractive and charming. Blessed in some ways. A free spirit, very adaptable.

Louis, 22- Travels frequently. Creates group harmony. Creative and inspiring. Blessed in some ways. Charming and devoted.

Louisa, 5- Moves and travels often. Natural counselor and healer. Fun, attractive. Generous, thoughtful. Charming and devoted. Bright, adventuresome.

Louise, 9- Benefits from meditation. Artistic and creative. Easy going manner. Blessed in some ways. Charming and devoted. A free spirit, very adaptable.

Lourdes, 4- Domestically creative. Assumes responsibility. Gracious, well mannered. Gentle, kind, a hard worker. Reliable, responsible. A free spirit, very adaptable. Charming and devoted.

Love, 9- Benefits from meditation. Artistic and creative. Intuitive and inspired. A free spirit, very adaptable.

Lowell, 7- Intellectually sound. Open to opportunities. Likes to meet new people. A free spirit, very adaptable. Frequent traveler. Many ups and downs financially.

Loyal, 20- Honest and sincere. Natural counselor and healer. Needs a lot of freedom. Reads people easily. Communicates skillfully.

L'Toya, 10- Strong verbal skills. Dynamic, busy lifestyle. Natural counselor and healer. Needs a lot of freedom. Independent, critical of self and others.

Lu, 6- Easy going attitude. Attractive and charming. Self-sacrificing and devoted.

Luana, 4- Domestically creative. Gracious, well mannered. Independent, critical of self and others. Original and unconventional. Bold, courageous, a bit stubborn.

Luanne, 22- Travels frequently. Gracious, well mannered. Independent, critical of self and others. Original and unconventional. Romantic, sensual. A free spirit, very adaptable.

Lucas, 11- Travels frequently. Creative and inspiring. Cheerful, lighthearted. Independent, critical of self and others. Charming and devoted. A bit forceful.

Luci, 9- Benefits from meditation. Easy going manner. Self-expressive, cheerful. Blessed in some ways.

Lucia, 10- Strong verbal skills. Attractive and charming. Optimistic, outspoken. Blessed in some ways. Independent, critical of self and others.

Lucian, 6- Easy going attitude. Lovely, attractive. Cheerful, optimistic. Artistic, having good taste. Independent, self-motivated. Creative and opinionated.

Luciana, 7- Intellectually sound. Stylish and refined. Self-expressive, cheerful. Blessed in some ways. Independent, critical of self and others. Original and unconventional. Bold, courageous, a bit stubborn.

Lucio, 6- Easy going attitude. Lovely and attractive. Self-expressive, cheerful. Artistic, having good taste. Natural counselor and healer.

Lucille, 11- Travels frequently. Creative and inspiring. Cheerful, lighthearted. Blessed in some ways. Frequent traveler. Many ups and downs financially. A free spirit, very adaptable.

Lucinda, 10- Strong verbal skills. Attractive and charming. Self-expressive, cheerful. Blessed in some ways. Original and unconventional. Reliable, responsible. Independent, critical of self and others.

Lucius, 22- Travels frequently. Creative and inspiring. Optimistic, outspoken. Blessed in some ways. Difficulty making decisions. Many mood swings.

Lucretia, 8- Recuperates quickly. Attractive and charming. Self-expressive, cheerful. Gentle, kind, a hard worker. A free spirit, very adaptable. Dynamic, busy lifestyle. Blessed in some ways. Independent, critical of self and others.

Lucy, 7- Intellectually sound. Stylish and refined. Self-expressive, cheerful. Needs a lot of freedom.

Ludlow, 6- Easy going attitude. Lovely and attractive. Systematic, organized. Frequent traveler. Natural counselor and healer. Likes to meet new people.

Ludovick, 7- Intellectually sound. Stylish and refined. Reliable, responsible. Natural counselor and healer. Intuitive and inspired. Blessed in some ways. Self-expressive, cheerful. Desire to succeed.

Ludvig, 30- Slow to make decisions. Youthful, appealing. Reliable, responsible. Intuitive and inspired. Blessed in some ways. Scientific and philosophical.

Ludwig, 4- Domestically creative. Gracious, well mannered. Systematic, organized. Likes to meet new people. Blessed in some ways. Scientific and philosophical.

Luella, 9- Benefits from meditation. Attractive and charming. A free spirit, very adaptable. Frequent traveler. Many ups and downs financially. Independent, critical of self and others.

Luigi, 4- Domestically creative. Gracious, well mannered. Blessed in some ways. Scientific and philosophical. Artistic, having good taste.

Luis, 7- Intellectually sound. Stylish and refined. Blessed in some ways. Impulsive and extreme.

Luke, 4- Domestically creative. Gracious, well mannered. Strong desire to succeed. A free spirit, very adaptable.

Lulu, 3- Slow to make decisions. Youthful, appealing. Great verbal skills. Ups and downs financially.

Luna, 3- Slow to make decisions. Youthful, appealing. Romantic, original. Aims to please.

Lundy, 22- Travels frequently. Gracious, well mannered. Original and unconventional. Reliable, responsible. Needs a lot of freedom.

Lunette, 7- Intellectually sound. Stylish and refined. Original and unconventional. A free spirit, very adaptable. Dynamic, busy lifestyle. Sensitive and easily hurt. Likes change and variety.

Lupe, 9- Benefits from meditation. Attractive and charming. Intelligent and knowledgeable. A free spirit, very adaptable.

Lupita, 7- Intellectually sound. Stylish and refined. Level headed, knowledgeable. Blessed in some ways. Dynamic, busy lifestyle. Not easily fooled.

Luther, 30- Slow to make decisions. Attractive and charming. Dynamic, busy lifestyle. Great judge of character. A free spirit, very adaptable. Gentle, kind, a hard worker.

Lydia, 6- Easy going attitude. Needs a lot of freedom. Reliable, responsible. Blessed in some ways. Independent, critical of self and others.

Lyell, 3- Slow to make decisions. Freedom loving. A free spirit, very adaptable. Frequent traveler. Many ups and downs financially.

Lyle, 9- Benefits from meditation. Dislikes limitations. Many ups and downs financially. A free spirit, very adaptable.

Lyman, 20- Honest and sincere. Perceptive, psychic. Domestic, hard working. Independent, critical of self and others. Original and unconventional.

Lyn, 6- Easy going attitude. Needs a lot of freedom. Creative, original.

Lynda, 20- Honest and sincere. Perceptive, psychic. Original and unconventional. Reliable, responsible. Independent, critical of self and others.

Lyndon, 30- Slow to make decisions. Freedom loving. Creative, original. Reliable, responsible. Natural counselor and healer. Romantic, sensual.

Lynette, 11- Travels frequently. A truth seeker. Original and unconventional. A free spirit, very adaptable. Dynamic, busy lifestyle. Sensitive and easily hurt. Tendency to overindulge.

Lynn, 20- Honest and sincere. Needs a lot of freedom. Original and unconventional. Romantic, sensual.

Lynne, 7- Intellectually sound. Stylish and refined. Original and unconventional. Romantic, sensual. A free spirit, very adaptable.

Lyon, 3- Slow to make decisions. Freedom loving. Natural counselor and healer. Original and unconventional.

Lyssa, 4- Domestically creative. Needs a lot of freedom. Charming and devoted. Many mood swings. Independent, critical of self and others.

> "Oh, very good, but very mysterious. He lives in the Emerald City, and that's a long journey from here. Did you bring your broomstick with you?"
> ~Excerpted from "The Wizard of Oz"
> Used with permission

M

IF A NAME BEGINS WITH M, has more than one M, or ends with an M, this person is domestic, hardworking, energetic, and has a strong physical constitution.

The letter M is the 13th letter of the alphabet. 1+3=4, so the 13th letter of the alphabet has the same vibrational influence as the number 4. 1 rules beginnings, 3 rules balance, and 4 rules work and family. So the person whose name begins with M is often beginning to balance work and family. They've been blessed with an extra strong physical constitution to handle this lifetime's demands.

The 13th letter is a "karmic debt" letter. Most of us grew up hearing that the number 13 was an unlucky number. The curse of this 13th letter M is that we often learn lessons the hard way in some area of our life. Actually, the reason it's unlucky is because it adds up to a 4. A square has 4 sides and in astrology, "squares" means difficulty. Those with this letter anywhere in their name must work very hard to accomplish their task at hand. Obstacles seem to get in the way and challenges must be overcome time and again. M is for Messy! Some with this letter in their name will give in to laziness or negativity. Some may easily give up on their goals. The M's key to success is to focus on one thing at a time, as opposed to wasting time scattering their energies over many different projects. The lesson of the M is simply to work hard and stay on task. That's why Moms work so hard and have so much to do. If Mommy didn't have so many M's in her name, she probably wouldn't have so many messes to clean up!

Those with M as the first letter of their name and A as the first vowel can be quite ambitious. If they don't accomplish much by the end of the day, they will beat themselves up over it. M's, similar to D's are list keepers. Most top executives keep a list of tasks to accomplish for the day. A successful M will learn to write a list every day. The 4 vibration rings through the letter M, coloring it with work and family; so M is very domestic. Cooking and cleaning come easily with this letter. Similar to the letter D, M doesn't mind doing the chores most of us hate doing. If the M person gives in to alcohol, it's to escape the bully in their head. They are their own worst critic! Also, similar to D and V, those with this letter will often say they don't want to argue, but end up arguing anyway. An hour after they've said they don't want to argue, they are still arguing.

Speaking of domestic, Martha Stewart is a prime example of the domestic type. This Domestic Goddess is best known as an entrepreneur. The intensity 1, from the 2 A's in her name, makes her quite a pioneer woman. With a hidden 5 in the beginning of her name, she loves adventure, coupled with the 2 A's, she is bold and daring too. Many entrepreneurs have at least one A in their name. She heads her own magazine and television show. Martha makes cooking, gardening, cleaning, organizing, and re-finishing furniture not only look easy, but fun too! Still, that unlucky 13th ruled letter has gotten her into some difficult situations. The 2004 jury of the "inside trading" scandal found her guilty of obstructing justice. As mentioned before, M is for messy. The combination of her two A's and power number 7 sometimes make it difficult for her to get along with others. Similar to Simon Cowell, she can't pretend to like someone she doesn't like with a power number 7. On the other hand, with two 1 ruled letters and a 2 ruled letter T in her name, she is a baby in some areas of her life. Her name is made up of very young and very old numbers. The very center of her name is a hard working, gentle, kind R, coupled with a very social and sensitive T. The outer part of her name has enough strength to carry her to any goal she undertakes. The material lessons of the H in her name plus the M first letter have caused her to learn lessons the hard way. H's and L's usually have many ups and downs financially. Many of the letters in her name are harsh, except the vulnerable and sensitive T in the middle. Her name is built like a Sherman tank on the outside, but vulnerable on the inside. Only those close to her really know her because she doesn't let very many people in.

Madonna is another famous ambitious M person with her 2 children and busy career schedule. Born a Leo, she desires to create children of her body and mind as well. She has 3 intensity numbers in her name, 1, 4 and 5. The 1 makes her bold and courageous, and also a pioneer, the 4 makes her hard working and domestic and the 5 makes her sort of wild. Many rock stars and strippers have an intensity 5 in their names. She does seem a bit intense, but it's her power number 8 that makes her the "material girl." With all this intensity, will she ever burn out? Probably not, she has a strong constitution with the M and D in her name. Notice the O in the middle of her name? Deep down in the middle of her is a nurturer. When she is done raising her children, she will most likely manage over groups of people who follow her. Her name is methodical, disciplined and service oriented. With the 8 power number, same as Lance Armstrong, she's a survivor and in complete control.

The late Martin Luther King was a civil rights leader who worked to bring about equal rights for black people. He was a Baptist minister who preached "nonviolent resistance." The intensity 9, from the R and I in his name made him a humanitarian. He liked people of all race and color. This trait helped him with his "I have a dream …" speech which rang out his futuristic vision of people not being "judged by the color of their skin, but by the content of their character." With a 30 power number, he was able to help others through communicating, counseling and advice, with the assistance from God. Although the M in his name made him systematic, disciplined and organized, it's ruled by that unlucky 4 vibration which may be why he did not live long enough to see his dream come true as on April 4, 1968 he died from a violent act.

The most important lesson for the M named person is to finish one task at a time to completion. This might be the single most important piece of advice for anyone with an M in their name. This will be how they will be able to achieve happiness. Achieving their goals will make them happy, to complete each task one at a time, will help them reach their goals. Then they'll be a happy camper.

Similar to D's, the typical M person doesn't feel comfortable being unfaithful. This letter also likes to be financially secure; the sound of rustling dollars soothes their nerves somehow. So as a rule, names that begin with M can be counted on to pay the bills on time and handle chores without complaining. All in all, those of us looking for some stability in our lives can turn to the M. They'll be right there, paying the bills and taking care of life's little burdens so we don't have to.

Some other famous people whose names start with M are; Mae West, Mary Tyler Moore, Macauley Calkin, Matthew Broderick, Madeleine Stowe, Mel Gibson, Maia Morgenstern, Mikhail Baryshnikov, Margot Kidder, Michael Douglas, Meg Ryan, Michael Keaton, Meryl Streep, Michael Jackson, Morgan Freeman, Michelle Pfeiffer, Michael J. Fox, Muhammad Ali, Mel Brooks, Morgan Fairchild, Mike Myers, Mary-Kate

Olsen, Matt Damon, Margaret O'Brien, Mariah Carey, Mark Twain, Marlon Brando, Martin Sheen, Michael Caine, Martin Short, Mick Jagger and Maya Angelou.

Quick Reference of "M" Names

Mabel, 6- Creative entrepreneur. Pioneer and risk taker. Friendly, but shy. A free spirit, very adaptable. Strong verbal skills.

Mac, 8- Patient, tolerant. Resolute and purposeful. Self-expressive, cheerful.

Macauley, 9- Works hard, devoted. Helpful, sincere. Self-expressive, cheerful. Bold, courageous, a bit stubborn. Attractive and charming. Strong verbal skills. A free spirit, very adaptable. Dislikes restrictions.

Machiko, 6- Creative entrepreneur. Pioneer and risk taker. Self-expressive, cheerful. Great judge of character. Blessed in some ways. Strong desire to succeed. Natural counselor and healer.

Mack, 10- Steadfast and determined. Independent, critical of self and others. Self-expressive, cheerful. Strong desire to succeed.

Mackenzie, 6- Creative entrepreneur. Pioneer and risk taker. Self-expressive, cheerful. Strong desire to succeed. A free spirit, very adaptable. Original and unconventional. Uses common sense. Blessed in some ways. Loves adventure and excitement.

Macy, 6- Creative entrepreneur. Pioneer and risk taker. Self-expressive, cheerful. Needs a lot of freedom.

Maddock, 6- Creative entrepreneur. Pioneer and risk taker. Domestic, hardworking. Workaholic, determined. Natural counselor and healer. Self-expressive, cheerful. Strong desire to succeed.

Maddox, 7- Must have faith. Not easily influenced. Reliable, responsible. Workaholic, determined. Natural counselor and healer. Artistic, sensual, perceptive.

Madeleine, 5- Entertains at home. Bright, adventuresome. Reliable, responsible. A free spirit, very adaptable. Strong verbal skills. Likes change and variety. Blessed in some ways. Original and unconventional. Physical and passionate.

Madeline, 9- Works hard, devoted. Helpful, sincere. Reliable, responsible. A free spirit, very adaptable. Strong verbal skills. Blessed in some ways. Original and unconventional. Loves adventure and excitement.

Madelyn, 11- Insightful, sensitive. Independent, self-motivated. Domestic, hardworking. A free spirit, very adaptable. Strong verbal skills. Dislikes limitations. Original and unconventional.

Madge, 3- Family communicator. Aims to please. Serious, yet fun-loving. Scientific and philosophical. A free spirit, very adaptable.

Madison, 30- Family communicator. Aims to please. Serious, yet fun-loving. Blessed in some ways. Charming and devoted. Natural counselor and healer. Original and unconventional.

Madonna, 8- Patient, tolerant. Resolute and purposeful. Domestic, hardworking. Natural counselor and healer. Original and unconventional. Romantic, sensual. Bold, courageous, a bit stubborn.

Mae, 10- Steadfast and determined. Independent, critical of self and others. A free spirit, very adaptable.

Maelyne, 30- Family communicator. Aims to please. A free spirit, very adaptable. Strong verbal skills. Dislikes limitations. Original and unconventional. Tendency to overindulge.

Magdelaine, 8- Patient, tolerant. Resolute and purposeful. Willpower and determination. Problem solver. A free spirit, very adaptable. Strong verbal skills. Not easily influenced. Artistic, having good taste. Creative, opinionated. Physical and passionate.

Maggie, 6- Creative entrepreneur. Pioneer and risk taker. Scientific and philosophical. Level headed. Blessed in some ways. A free spirit, very adaptable.

Magnolia, 9- Works hard, devoted. Helpful, sincere. Gracious, well mannered. Original and unconventional. Natural counselor and healer. Strong verbal skills. Blessed in some ways. Bold, courageous, a bit stubborn.

Magnus, 3- Family communicator. Aims to please. Gracious, well mannered. Original and unconventional. Very lucky. Charming and devoted.

Maguire, 11- Insightful, sensitive. Independent, self-motivated. Scientific and philosophical. Attractive and charming. Blessed in some ways. Gentle, kind, very diligent. A free spirit, very adaptable.

Mahalia, 9- Works hard, devoted. Helpful, sincere. Great judge of character. Critical of self and others. Strong verbal skills. Blessed in some ways. Pioneer and risk taker.

Mahina, 10- Steadfast and determined. Independent, critical of self and others. Great judge of character. Blessed in some ways. Original and unconventional. Bold, courageous, a bit stubborn.

Mai, 5- Entertains at home. Bright, adventuresome. Blessed in some ways.

Maia, 6- Creative entrepreneur. Pioneer and risk taker. Artistic, having good taste. Independent, a bit stubborn.

Maisie, 11- Insightful, sensitive. Independent, self-motivated. Blessed in some ways. Charming and devoted. Artistic, having good taste. A free spirit, very adaptable.

Maja, 7- Must have faith. Not easily influenced. Very clever and talented. Bold, courageous, a bit stubborn.

Major, 3- Family communicator. Aims to please. Very clever and talented. Natural counselor and healer. Gentle, kind, very diligent.

Makaila, 3- Family communicator. Aims to please. Strong desire to succeed. Critical of self and others. Blessed in some ways. Slow to make decisions. Not easily influenced.

Makayla, 10- Steadfast and determined. Independent, critical of self and others. Strong desire to succeed. Bright, adventuresome. Needs a lot of freedom. Communicates skillfully. Pioneer and risk taker.

Mala, 9- Works hard, devoted. Helpful, sincere. Strong verbal skills. Bold, courageous, a bit stubborn.

Malachai, 30- Family communicator. Aims to please. Great verbal skills. Independent, a bit stubborn. Self-expressive, cheerful. Great judge of character. Pioneer and risk taker. Blessed in some ways.

Malachi, 11- Insightful, sensitive. Independent, self-motivated. Communicates skillfully. Bold, courageous, a bit stubborn. Self-expressive, cheerful. Great judge of character. Blessed in some ways.

Malcolm, 6- Creative entrepreneur. Pioneer and risk taker. Strong verbal skills. Optimistic, outspoken. Nurturing, loving. Frequent traveler. Desires financial security.

Mali, 8- Patient, tolerant. Resolute and purposeful. Great verbal skills. Blessed in some ways.

Malina, 5- Entertains at home. Bright, adventuresome. Travels frequently. Blessed in some ways. Original and unconventional. Bold, courageous, a bit stubborn.

Malinda, 9- Works hard, devoted. Helpful, sincere. Communicates skillfully. Blessed in some ways. Original and unconventional. Reliable, responsible. Pioneer and risk taker.

Malorie, 10- Steadfast and determined. Independent, critical of self and others. Strong verbal skills. Natural counselor and healer. Gentle, kind, very diligent. Blessed in some ways. A free spirit, very adaptable.

Malory, 30- Family communicator. Aims to please. Great verbal skills. Natural counselor and healer. Gentle, kind, very diligent. Needs a lot of freedom.

Mallory, 6- Creative entrepreneur. Pioneer and risk taker. Travels frequently. Communicates skillfully. Natural counselor and healer. Gentle, kind, diligent. Needs a lot of freedom.

Malven, 22- A workaholic, focused. Ambitious leader, great vision. Travels frequently. Intuitive and inspired. A free spirit, very adaptable. Original and unconventional.

Malvina, 9- Works hard, devoted. Helpful, sincere. Strong verbal skills. Intuitive and inspired. Blessed in some ways. Original and unconventional. Pioneer and risk taker.

Mamie, 5- Entertains at home. Bright, adventuresome. Domestic, hard working. Artistic, having good taste. Physical and passionate.

Mamood, 7- Must have faith. Not easily influenced. Desires financial security. Natural counselor and healer. Strong parental skills. Reliable, responsible.

Manda, 6- Creative entrepreneur. Pioneer and risk taker. Original and unconventional. Reliable, responsible. Bold, courageous, a bit stubborn.

Mandel, 22- A workaholic, focused. Ambitious leader, great vision. Romantic, opinionated. Domestic, hardworking. A free spirit, very adaptable. Strong verbal skills.

Mandie, 10- Steadfast and determined. Independent, critical of self and others. Original and unconventional. Reliable, responsible. Blessed in some ways. A free spirit, very adaptable.

Mandy, 3- Family communicator. Aims to please. Romantic, creative. Reliable, responsible. Needs a lot of freedom.

Manfred, 7- Must have faith. Not easily influenced. Original and unconventional. Self-sacrificing, loving. Gentle, kind, very diligent. A free spirit, very adaptable. Reliable, responsible.

Manning, 9- Works hard, devoted. Helpful, sincere. Creative, opinionated. Romantic, sensual. Blessed in some ways. Creative, opinionated. Scientific and philosophical.

Manny, 22- A workaholic, focused. Ambitious leader, great vision. Original and opinionated. Romantic, sensual. Needs a lot of freedom.

Manrique, 8- Patient, tolerant. Resolute and purposeful. Creative and original. Gentle, kind, very helpful. Blessed in some ways. Influential, a natural leader. Attractive and charming. A free spirit, very adaptable.

Mansoor, 5- Entertains at home. Bright, adventuresome. Original and unconventional. Charming and devoted. Natural counselor and healer. Enjoys working. Gentle, kind, very diligent.

Manuel, 3- Family communicator. Aims to please. Creative, original. Attractive and charming. Physical and passionate. Slow to make decisions.

Manuela, 22- A workaholic, focused. Ambitious leader, great vision. Original and unconventional. Attractive and charming. A free spirit, very adaptable. Strong verbal skills. Bold, courageous, a bit stubborn.

Mara, 6- Creative entrepreneur. Pioneer and risk taker. Duty bound, self-sacrificing. Bold, courageous, a bit stubborn.

Marbin, 30- Family communicator. Aims to please. Sympathetic, kind. Friendly, but shy. Blessed in some ways. Original and unconventional.

Marc, 8- Patient, tolerant. Resolute and purposeful. Intense inner power. Self-expressive, cheerful.

Marcel, 7- Must have faith. Not easily influenced. Gentle, kind, very diligent. Self-expressive, cheerful. A free spirit, very adaptable. Strong verbal skills.

Marcela, 8- Patient, tolerant. Resolute and purposeful. Intense inner power. Self-expressive, cheerful. A free spirit, very adaptable. Strong verbal skills. Bold, courageous, a bit stubborn.

Marcella, 11- Insightful, sensitive. Independent, self-motivated. Gentle, kind, very diligent. Self-expressive, cheerful. A free spirit, very adaptable. Strong verbal skills. Ups and downs financially. Bold, courageous, a bit stubborn.

Marcelle, 6- Creative entrepreneur. Pioneer and risk taker. Duty bound, self-sacrificing. Self-expressive, cheerful. A free spirit, very adaptable. Strong verbal skills. Ups and downs financially. Loves adventure and excitement.

Marcelo, 4- Strong physical constitution. Resolute, purposeful. Gentle, kind, very diligent. Self-expressive, cheerful. Physical, passionate. Strong verbal skills. Natural counselor and healer.

Marci, 8- Patient, tolerant. Resolute and purposeful. Intense inner power. Self-expressive, cheerful. Blessed in some ways.

Marcia, 9- Works hard, devoted. Helpful, sincere. Humanitarian, idealistic. Self-expressive, cheerful. Blessed in some ways. Bold, courageous, a bit stubborn.

Marcie, 4- Strong physical constitution. Natural teaching ability. Gentle, kind, very diligent. Self-expressive, cheerful. Blessed in some ways. A free spirit, very adaptable.

Marco, 5- Entertains at home. Bright, adventuresome. Good deed doer. Self-expressive, cheerful. Natural counselor and healer.

Marcos, 6- Creative entrepreneur. Pioneer and risk taker. Duty bound, self-sacrificing. Self-expressive, cheerful. Natural counselor and healer. Charming and devoted.

Marcus, 3- Family communicator. Aims to please. Sympathetic, kind. Self-expressive, cheerful. Attractive and charming. Very devoted.

Marcy, 6- Creative entrepreneur. Pioneer and risk taker. Duty bound, self-sacrificing. Cheerful, great sense of humor. Needs a lot of freedom.

Margaret, 11- Insightful, sensitive. Independent, self-motivated. Gentle, kind, very diligent. Scientific and philosophical. Bold, courageous, a bit stubborn. Could be forgetful. A free spirit, very adaptable. Dynamic, busy lifestyle.

Margarita, 7- Must have faith. Not easily influenced. Diligent, helpful. Extremely intelligent. Resolute and purposeful. Tendency to lose items. Blessed in some ways. Dynamic, busy lifestyle. Independent, critical of self and others.

Margarite, 11- Insightful, sensitive. Independent, self-motivated. Gentle, kind, very diligent. Scientific and philosophical. Bold, courageous, a bit stubborn. Could be forgetful. Blessed in some ways. Dynamic, busy lifestyle. A free spirit, very adaptable.

Margarito, 3- Family communicator. Aims to please. Sympathetic, kind. Has willpower and determination. Bold, courageous, a bit stubborn. Diligent, helpful. Blessed in some ways. Dynamic, busy lifestyle. Natural counselor and healer.

Margaux, 4- Strong physical constitution. Natural teaching ability. Gentle, kind, a hard worker. Scientific and philosophical. Bold, courageous, a bit stubborn. Attractive and charming. Artistic, sensual, perceptive.

Marge, 8- Patient, tolerant. Resolute and purposeful. Intense inner power. Scientific and philosophical. A free spirit, very adaptable.

Margery, 6- Creative entrepreneur. Pioneer and risk taker. Duty bound, self-sacrificing. Scientific and philosophical. A step ahead of others. Tendency to lose items. Needs a lot of freedom.

Margo, 9- Works hard, devoted. Helpful, sincere. Humanitarian, idealistic. Scientific and philosophical. Natural counselor and healer.

Margot, 11- Insightful, sensitive. Independent, self-motivated. Gentle, kind, very diligent. Scientific and philosophical. Natural counselor and healer. Dynamic, busy lifestyle.

Mari, 5- Entertains at home. Bright, adventuresome. Good deed doer. Blessed in some ways.

Maria, 6- Creative entrepreneur. Pioneer and risk taker. Duty bound, self-sacrificing. Artistic, having good taste. Bold, courageous, a bit stubborn.

Mariah, 5- Entertains at home. Bright, adventuresome. Good deed doer. Blessed in some ways. Bold, courageous, a bit stubborn. Great judge of character.

Mariam, 10- Steadfast and determined. Independent, critical of self and others. Gentle, kind, very diligent. Blessed in some ways. Bold, courageous, a bit stubborn. Desires financial security.

Marian, 11- Insightful, sensitive. Independent, self-motivated. Gentle, kind, very diligent. Blessed in some ways. Bold, courageous, a bit stubborn. Original and unconventional.

Mariana, 30- Family communicator. Aims to please. Sympathetic, kind. Blessed in some ways. Bold, courageous, a bit stubborn. Original and unconventional. Pioneer and risk taker.

Marianne, 3- Family communicator. Aims to please. Sympathetic, kind. Blessed in some ways. Bold, courageous, a bit stubborn. Original and unconventional. Creative and opinionated. Physical and passionate.

Mariano, 8- Patient, tolerant. Resolute and purposeful. Intense inner power. Blessed in some ways. Bold, courageous, a bit stubborn. Original and unconventional. Natural counselor and healer.

Maricar, 9- Works hard, devoted. Helpful, sincere. Humanitarian, idealistic. Blessed in some ways. Self-expressive, cheerful. Bold, courageous, a bit stubborn. Tendency to lose items.

Maricella, 11- Insightful, sensitive. Independent, self-motivated. Gentle, kind, very diligent. Blessed in some ways. Self-expressive, cheerful. A free spirit, very adaptable. Great verbal skills. Ups and downs financially. Bold, courageous, a bit stubborn.

Marie, 10- Steadfast and determined. Independent, critical of self and others. Gentle, kind, very diligent. Blessed in some ways. A free spirit, very adaptable.

Mariela, 5- Entertains at home. Bright, adventuresome. Good deed doer. Blessed in some ways. A free spirit, very adaptable. Strong verbal skills. Bold, courageous, a bit stubborn.

Marietta, 6- Creative entrepreneur. Pioneer and risk taker. Duty bound, self-sacrificing . Artistic, having good taste. A free spirit, very adaptable. Dynamic, busy lifestyle. Sensitive and easily hurt. Bold, courageous, a bit stubborn.

Mariette, 10- Steadfast and determined. Independent, critical of self and others. Gentle, kind, very diligent. Blessed in some ways. A free spirit, very adaptable. Dynamic, busy lifestyle. Sensitive and easily hurt. Loves adventure and excitement.

Marili, 8- Patient, tolerant. Resolute and purposeful. Intense inner power. Blessed in some ways. Strong verbal skills. Artistic, having good taste.

Marilu, 11- Insightful, sensitive. Independent, self-motivated. Gentle, kind, very diligent. Blessed in some ways. Strong verbal skills. Attractive and charming.

Mariluz, 10- Steadfast and determined. Independent, critical of self and others. Gentle, kind, very diligent. Blessed in some ways. Strong verbal skills. Attractive and charming. Uses common sense.

Marilyn, 11- Insightful, sensitive. Independent, self-motivated. Gentle, kind, very diligent. Blessed in some ways. Strong verbal skills. Needs a lot of freedom. Original and unconventional.

Marina, 11- Insightful, sensitive. Independent, self-motivated. Gentle, kind, very diligent. Blessed in some ways. Original and unconventional. Bold, courageous, a bit stubborn.

Marini, 10- Steadfast and determined. Independent, critical of self and others. Gentle, kind, very diligent. Blessed in some ways. Original and unconventional. Artistic, having good taste.

Mario, 11- Insightful, sensitive. Independent, self-motivated. Gentle, kind, very diligent. Blessed in some ways. Natural counselor and healer.

Marion, 7- Must have faith. Not easily influenced. Gentle, kind, very diligent. Blessed in some ways. Natural counselor and healer. Original and unconventional.

Marisol, 6- Creative entrepreneur. Pioneer and risk taker. Duty bound, self-sacrificing. Artistic, having good taste. Charming and devoted. Natural counselor and healer. Strong verbal skills.

Marissa, 8- Patient, tolerant. Resolute and purposeful. Intense inner power. Blessed in some ways. Charming and devoted. Impulsive and extreme. Bold, courageous, a bit stubborn.

Maritza, 7- Must have faith. Not easily fooled. Gentle, kind, a hard worker. Artistic, having good taste. Dynamic, busy lifestyle. Great judge of character. Independent, critical of self and others.

Marjo, 3- Family communicator. Pioneer and risk taker. Sympathetic, kind. Clever and talented. Natural counselor and healer.

Marjorie, 8- Patient, tolerant. Resolute and purposeful. Intense inner power. Very clever and talented. Natural counselor and healer. Tendency to lose items. Blessed in some ways. A free spirit, very adaptable.

Mark, 7- Must have faith. Not easily influenced. Gentle, kind, a hard worker. Strong desire to succeed.

Marla, 9- Works hard, devoted. Helpful, sincere. Humanitarian, idealistic. Strong verbal skills. Bold, courageous, a bit stubborn.

Marleen, 5- Entertains at home. Bright, adventuresome. Good deed doer. Communicates skillfully. A free spirit, very adaptable. Physical and passionate. Original and unconventional.

Marlene, 5- (Same as Marleen.)

Marley, 11- Insightful, sensitive. Independent, self-motivated. Gentle, kind, a hard worker. Great verbal skills. A free spirit, very adaptable. Dislikes limitations.

Marlo, 5- Entertains at home. Pioneer and risk taker. Good deed doer. Strong verbal skills. Natural counselor and healer.

Marlow, 10- Steadfast and determined. Independent, critical of self and others. Gentle, kind, a hard worker. Strong verbal skills. Natural counselor and healer. Likes to meet new people.

Marly, 6- Creative entrepreneur. Pioneer and risk taker. Duty bound, self-sacrificing. Strong verbal skills. Needs a lot of freedom.

Marney, 4- Strong physical constitution. Natural teaching ability. Gentle, kind, very diligent. Original and unconventional. A free spirit, very adaptable. Dislikes limitations.

Marni, 10- Steadfast and determined. Independent, critical of self and others. Gentle, kind, very diligent. Original and unconventional. Blessed in some ways.

Marnie, 6- Creative entrepreneur. Pioneer and risk taker. Duty bound, self-sacrificing. Original and unconventional. Blessed in some ways. A free spirit, very adaptable.

Marquita, 10- Steadfast and determined. Independent, critical of self and others. Gentle, kind, a hard worker. Influential, a natural leader. Attractive and charming. Blessed in some ways. Dynamic, busy lifestyle. Bold, courageous, a bit stubborn.

Marsh, 5- Entertains at home. Bright, adventuresome. Good deed doer. Charming and devoted. Great judge of character.

Marsha, 6- Creative entrepreneur. Pioneer and risk taker. Duty bound, self-sacrificing. Charming and devoted. Great judge of character. Bold, courageous, a bit stubborn.

Marshall, 30- Family communicator. Aims to please. Sympathetic, kind. Charming and devoted. Great judge of character. Bold, courageous, a bit stubborn. Strong verbal skills. Financial ups and downs.

Marsi, 6- Creative entrepreneur. Pioneer and risk taker. Duty bound, self-sacrificing. Charming and devoted. Artistic, having good taste.

Mart, 7- Must have faith. Not easily influenced. Gentle, kind, very diligent. Dynamic, busy lifestyle.

Marta, 8- Patient, tolerant. Resolute and purposeful. Intense inner power. Dynamic, busy lifestyle. Bold, courageous, a bit stubborn.

Martha, 7- Must have faith. Not easily influenced. Gentle, kind, very diligent. Dynamic, busy lifestyle. Great judge of character. Bold, courageous, a bit stubborn.

Marthe, 11- Insightful, sensitive. Independent, self-motivated. Gentle, kind, very diligent. Dynamic, busy lifestyle. Great judge of character. A free spirit, very adaptable.

Marti, 7- Must have faith. Not easily influenced. Gentle, kind, very diligent. Dynamic, busy lifestyle. Blessed in some ways.

Martie, 30- Family communicator. Aims to please. Sympathetic, kind. Dynamic, busy lifestyle. Blessed in some ways. A free spirit, very adaptable.

Martin, 30- Family communicator. Aims to please. Sympathetic, kind. Dynamic, busy lifestyle. Blessed in some ways. Original and unconventional.

Martina, 4- Strong physical constitution. Natural teaching ability. Gentle, kind, very diligent. Dynamic, busy lifestyle. Blessed in some ways. Original and unconventional. Bold, courageous, a bit stubborn.

Martine, 8- Patient, tolerant. Resolute and purposeful. Intense inner power. Dynamic, busy lifestyle. Blessed in some ways. Original and unconventional. A free spirit, very adaptable.

Marten, 8- Patient, tolerant. Resolute and purposeful. Intense inner power. Dynamic, busy lifestyle. A free spirit, very adaptable. Original and unconventional.

Marty, 5- Entertains at home. Bright, adventuresome. Good deed doer. Dynamic, busy lifestyle. Needs a lot of freedom.

Martyne, 6- Creative entrepreneur. Pioneer and risk taker. Duty bound, self-sacrificing. Dynamic, busy lifestyle. Needs a lot of freedom. Original and unconventional. A free spirit, very adaptable.

Marv, 9- Works hard, devoted. Helpful, sincere. Humanitarian, idealistic. Intuitive and inspired.

Marvel, 8- Patient, tolerant. Resolute and purposeful. Intense inner power. Intuitive and inspired. A free spirit, very adaptable. Communicates skillfully.

Marvin, 5- Entertains at home. Bright, adventuresome. Good deed doer. Intuitive and inspired. Blessed in some ways. Original and unconventional.

Marwa, 20- Domestically social. Reads people easily. Gentle, kind, very diligent. Likes to meet new people. Bold, courageous, a bit stubborn.

Mary, 3- Family communicator. Aims to please. Sympathetic, kind. Needs a lot of freedom.

Maryam, 8- Patient, tolerant. Resolute and purposeful. Intense inner power. Needs a lot of freedom. Bold, courageous, a bit stubborn. Desires financial security.

Maryann, 5- Entertains at home. Bright, adventuresome. Good deed doer. Needs a lot of freedom. Bold, courageous, a bit stubborn. Original and unconventional. Romantic, sensual.

Marye, 8- Patient, tolerant. Resolute and purposeful. Intense inner power. Needs a lot of freedom. Physical and passionate.

Marylou, 6- Creative entrepreneur. Pioneer and risk taker. Duty bound, self-sacrificing. Dislikes limitations. Strong verbal skills. Natural counselor and healer. Attractive and charming.

Marylyn, 9- Works hard, devoted. Helpful and sincere. Should practice tolerance. Needs a lot of freedom. Strong verbal skills. Highly perceptive. Creative, opinionated.

Mashka, 8- Patient, tolerant. Resolute and purposeful. Passionate and loving. Great judge of character. Strong desire to succeed. Bold, courageous, a bit stubborn.

Masika, 9- Works hard, devoted. Helpful, sincere. Charming and devoted. Blessed in some ways. Strong desire to succeed. Bold, courageous, a bit stubborn.

Mason, 8- Patient, tolerant. Resolute and purposeful. Passionate and loving. Natural counselor and healer. Original and unconventional.

Mateo, 9- Works hard, devoted. Helpful and sincere. Dynamic, busy lifestyle. A free spirit, very adaptable. Natural counselor and healer.

Mathew, 7- Must have faith. Not easily influenced. Dynamic, busy lifestyle. Great judge of character. A free spirit, very adaptable. Likes to meet new people.

Mathilda, 5- Entertains at home. Bright, adventuresome. Energetic, highly charged. Great judge of character. Blessed in some ways. Strong verbal skills. Reliable, responsible. Bold, courageous, a bit stubborn.

Matilda, 6- Creative entrepreneur. Pioneer and risk taker. Dynamic, busy lifestyle. Blessed in some ways. Strong verbal skills. Reliable, responsible. Bold, courageous, a bit stubborn.

Matis, 8- Patient, tolerant. Resolute and purposeful. Energetic, highly charged. Blessed in some ways. Charming and devoted.

Matt, 9- Works hard, devoted. Helpful and sincere. Dynamic, busy lifestyle. Sensitive and easily hurt.

Matthew, 9- Works hard, devoted. Helpful and sincere. Dynamic, busy lifestyle. Sensitive and easily hurt. Great judge of character. A free spirit, very adaptable. Likes to meet new people.

Matti, 9- Works hard, devoted. Helpful and sincere. Dynamic, busy lifestyle. Sensitive and easily hurt. Blessed in some ways.

Mattie, 5- Entertains at home. Bright, adventuresome. Energetic, highly charged. Sensitive and easily hurt. Blessed in some ways. A free spirit, very adaptable.

Maud, 3- Family communicator. Aims to please. Youthful, attractive. Domestic, responsible.

Maude, 8- Patient, tolerant. Resolute and purposeful. Attractive and charming. Domestic, responsible. A free spirit, very adaptable.

Maura, 9- Works hard, devoted. Helpful, sincere. Attractive and charming. Gentle, kind, very diligent. Bold, courageous, a bit stubborn.

Maureen, 5- Entertains at home. Bright, adventuresome. Youthful, attractive. Gentle, kind, very diligent. A free spirit, very adaptable. Tendency to overindulge. Original and unconventional.

Maurice, 7- Must have faith. Not easily influenced. Attractive and charming. Gentle, kind, very diligent. Blessed in some ways. Self-expressive, cheerful. A free spirit, very adaptable.

Mauricio, 8- Patient, tolerant. Resolute and purposeful. Attractive and charming. Gentle, kind, a hard worker. Blessed in some ways. Cheerful, optimistic. Artistic, having good taste. Natural counselor and healer.

Maurey, 11- Insightful, sensitive. Independent, self-motivated. Attractive and charming. Gentle, kind, very diligent. A free spirit, very adaptable. Dislikes limitations.

Maury, 6- Creative entrepreneur. Pioneer and risk taker. Attractive and charming. Gentle, kind, very diligent. Dislikes limitations.

Mavis, 10- Steadfast and determined. Independent, critical of self and others. Intuitive and inspired. Blessed in some ways. Charming and devoted.

Max, 11- Insightful, sensitive. Independent, self-motivated. Artistic, sensual, perceptive.

Maximillian, 9- Works hard, devoted. Helpful, sincere. Artistic, sensual, perceptive. Blessed in some ways. Desires financial security. Artistic, having good taste. Strong verbal skills. Financial ups and downs. Idealistic, humanitarian. Bold, courageous, a bit stubborn. Original and unconventional.

Maxine, 30- Family communicator. Aims to please. Artistic, sensual, perceptive. Blessed in some ways. Original and unconventional. A free spirit, very adaptable.

Maxwell, 9- Works hard, devoted. Helpful, sincere. Artistic, sensual, perceptive. Likes to meet new people. A free spirit, very adaptable. Strong verbal skills. Financial ups and downs.

May, 3- Family communicator. Aims to please. Needs a lot of freedom.

Maya, 4- Strong physical constitution. Natural teaching ability. Needs a lot of freedom. Bold, courageous, a bit stubborn.

Mayeen, 9- Works hard, devoted. Helpful, sincere. Dislikes limitations. A free spirit, very adaptable. Tendency to overindulge. Original and unconventional.

Mayer, 8- Patient, tolerant. Resolute and purposeful. Needs a lot of freedom. Loves adventure and excitement. Gentle, kind, very diligent.

Mayfield, 3- Family communicator. Aims to please. Needs a lot of freedom. Self-sacrificing, loving. Blessed in some ways. Loves adventure and excitement. Strong verbal skills. Reliable, responsible.

Maynard, 4- Strong physical constitution. Natural teaching ability. Dislikes restrictions. Original and unconventional. Bold, courageous, a bit stubborn. Gentle, kind, very diligent. Reliable, responsible.

Mayra, 22- A workaholic, focused. Ambitious leader, great vision. Dislikes restrictions. Gentle, kind, very diligent. Bold, courageous, a bit stubborn.

Mead, 5- Entertains at home. Physical and passionate. Independent, critical of self and others. Reliable, responsible.

Mec, 3- Family communicator. A free spirit, very adaptable. Cheerful, optimistic.

Mecauley, 4- Strong physical constitution. Accesses quickly. Self-expressive, cheerful. Independent, critical of self and others. Attractive and charming. Strong verbal skills. Loves adventure and excitement. Dislikes limitations.

Meg, 7- Must have faith. Not easily fooled. Scientific and philosophical.

Megan, 22- A workaholic, focused. Has big plans and ideas. Scientific and philosophical. Independent, self-motivated. Creative, opinionated.

Meghan, 30- Family communicator. A free spirit, very adaptable. Scientific and philosophical. Great judge of character. Independent, critical of self and others. Original and unconventional.

Melanie, 9- Works hard, devoted. A true humanitarian. Great verbal skills. Independent, critical of self and others. Original and unconventional. Blessed in some ways. Loves adventure and excitement.

Melba, 6- Creative entrepreneur. A step ahead of others. Communicates skillfully. Friendly, but shy. Independent, critical of self and others.

Melbourne, 6- Creative entrepreneur. A step ahead of others. Communicates skillfully. Friendly, but shy. Natural counselor and healer. Attractive and charming. Gentle, kind, very diligent. Original and unconventional. Loves adventure and excitement.

Melina, 9- Works hard, devoted. A true humanitarian. Strong verbal skills. Blessed in some ways. Original and unconventional. Independent, critical of self and others.

Melinda, 4- Strong physical constitution. Accesses quickly. Travels frequently. Blessed in some ways. Original and unconventional. Reliable, responsible. Independent, critical of self and others.

Melissa, 6- Creative entrepreneur. A step ahead of others. Communicates skillfully. Blessed in some ways. Charming and devoted. Impulsive and extreme. Independent, critical of self and others.

Melodie, 9- Works hard, devoted. A true humanitarian. Great verbal skills. Natural counselor and healer. Reliable, responsible. Blessed in some ways. Loves adventure and excitement.

Melody, 11- Insightful, sensitive. Keenly perceptive. Travels frequently. Natural counselor and healer. Reliable, responsible. Dislikes limitations.

Melvin, 30- Family communicator. A free spirit, very adaptable. Communicates skillfully. Intuitive and inspired. Blessed in some ways. Original and unconventional.

Mendel, 8- Patient, tolerant. Original and creative. Opinionated and unconventional. Reliable, responsible. Physical and passionate. Great verbal skills.

Mercedes, 9- Works hard, devoted. A true humanitarian. Gentle, kind, very diligent. Self-expressive, cheerful. Tendency to overindulge. Reliable, responsible. Loves adventure and excitement. Charming and devoted.

Mercer, 8- Patient, tolerant. Original and creative. Intense inner power. Cheerful, optimistic. Physical and passionate. Needs to practice tolerance.

Mercy, 10- Steadfast and determined. Likes change and variety. Diligent, hardworking. Self-expressive, cheerful. Dislikes limitations.

Meredith, 10- Steadfast and determined. Likes change and variety. Diligent, hardworking. Loves adventure and excitement. Reliable, responsible. Blessed in some ways. Dynamic, busy lifestyle. Great judge of character.

Merelis, 9- Works hard, devoted. A true humanitarian. Gentle, kind, very diligent. Loves adventure and excitement. Strong verbal skills. Blessed in some ways. Charming and devoted.

Merle, 8- Patient, tolerant. Original and creative. Intense inner power. Strong verbal skills. Loves adventure and excitement.

Merlin, 8- Patient, tolerant. Original and creative. Intense inner power. Strong verbal skills. Blessed in some ways. Original and unconventional.

Merrick, 5- Entertains at home. Physical and passionate. Good deed doer. Tendency to lose items. Blessed in some ways. Self-expressive, cheerful. Strong desire to succeed.

Merrie, 5- Entertains at home. Physical and passionate. Good deed doer. Tendency to lose items. Blessed in some ways. A free spirit, very adaptable.

Merrill, 6- Creative entrepreneur. A step ahead of others. Duty bound, self-sacrificing. Tendency to lose items. Blessed in some ways. Strong verbal skills. Financial ups and downs.

Merritt, 4- Strong physical constitution. Accesses quickly. Gentle, kind, a hard worker. Tendency to lose items. Blessed in some ways. Dynamic, busy lifestyle. Sensitive and easily hurt.

Merry, 7- Must have faith. A free spirit, very adaptable. Gentle, kind, very diligent. Tendency to lose items. Dislikes limitations.

Merton, 4- Strong physical constitution. Accesses quickly. Gentle, kind, a hard worker. Dynamic, busy lifestyle. Natural counselor and healer. Original and opinionated.

Merv, 22- A workaholic, focused. Has big plans and ideas. Gentle, kind, very diligent. Intuitive and inspired.

Mervin, 9- Works hard, devoted. A true humanitarian. Gentle, kind, very diligent. Intuitive and inspired. Blessed in some ways. Original and unconventional.

Mervyn, 7- Must have faith. Not easily fooled. A truth seeker. Intuitive and inspired. Needs a lot of freedom. Original and unconventional.

Meryl, 10- Steadfast and determined. Likes change and variety. Gentle, kind, a hard worker. Dislikes limitations. Strong verbal skills.

Meyer, 30- Family communicator. A free spirit, very adaptable. Dislikes limitations. Loves adventure and excitement. Gentle, kind, a hard worker.

Mia, 5- Entertains at home. Generous, thoughtful. Bright, adventuresome.

Mic, 7- Must have faith. Blessed in some ways. Self-expressive, cheerful.

Micaela, 8- Patient, tolerant. Gives practical gifts. Optimistic, outspoken. Independent, self-motivated. Physical and passionate. Strong verbal skills. Resolute and purposeful.

Micah, 7- Must have faith. Blessed in some ways. Sees the irony in situations. Independent, critical of self and others.

Michael, 6- Creative entrepreneur. Artistic, having good taste. Self-expressive, cheerful. Great judge of character. Independent, critical of self and others. A free spirit, very adaptable. Strong verbal skills.

Michaela, 7- Must have faith. Blessed in some ways. Self-expressive, cheerful. Great judge of character. Independent, critical of self and others. A free spirit, very adaptable. Strong verbal skills. Not easily influenced.

Michel, 5- Entertains at home. Generous, thoughtful. Optimistic, outspoken. Great judge of character. A free spirit, very adaptable. Strong verbal skills.

Michele, 10- Steadfast and determined. Respectful, kind. Self-expressive, cheerful. Great judge of character. A free spirit, very adaptable. Strong verbal skills. Loves adventure and excitement.

Michelle, 4- Strong physical constitution. Teaches kindness. Self-expressive, cheerful. Great judge of character. A free spirit, very adaptable. Strong verbal skills. Loves adventure and excitement. Ups and downs financially.

Mick, 9- Works hard, devoted. Blessed in some ways. Self-expressive, cheerful. Strong desire to succeed.

Mickey, 30- Family communicator. Blessed in some ways. Cheerful, lighthearted. Strong desire to succeed. A free spirit, very adaptable. Dislikes limitations.

Micky, 7- Must have faith. Artistic, having good taste. Self-expressive, cheerful. Strong desire to succeed. Dislikes limitations.

Midori, 5- Entertains at home. Generous, thoughtful. Reliable, responsible. Natural counselor and healer. Gentle, kind, very diligent. Artistic, having good taste.

Miguel, 4- Strong physical constitution. Teaches kindness. Scientific and philosophical. Attractive and charming. A free spirit, very adaptable. Strong verbal skills.

Mika, 7- Must have faith. Artistic, having good taste. Strong desire to succeed. Independent, critical of self and others.

Mike, 20- Domestically social. Emotional, considerate. Diplomatic, tactful. A free spirit, very adaptable.

Mikey, 9- Works hard, devoted. Blessed in some ways. Sees the big picture. A free spirit, very adaptable. Dislikes limitations.

Mikhail, 9- Works hard, devoted. Blessed in some ways. Sees the big picture. Great judge of character. Independent, critical of self and others. Artistic, having good taste. Excellent verbal skills.

Mikko, 5- Entertains at home. Generous, thoughtful. Strong desire to succeed. A bit forceful at times. Natural counselor and healer.

Mildred, 11- Insightful, sensitive. Blessed in some ways. Strong verbal skills. Domestic, responsible. Gentle, kind, a hard worker. A free spirit, very adaptable. Down-to-earth, faithful.

Miles, 22- A workaholic, focused. Blessed in some ways. Strong verbal skills. A free spirit, very adaptable. Charming and devoted.

Milford, 5- Entertains at home. Generous, thoughtful. Strong verbal skills. Self-sacrificing, loving. Natural counselor and healer. Gentle, kind, very diligent. Reliable, responsible.

Millard, 6- Creative entrepreneur. Artistic, having good taste. Travels frequently. Ups and downs financially. Independent, self-motivated. Gentle, kind, a hard worker. Natural problem solver.

Millicent, 7- Must have faith. Needs alone time. Communicates skillfully. Ups and downs financially. Artistic, having good taste. Self-expressive, cheerful. A free spirit, very adaptable. Original and unconventional. Dynamic, busy lifestyle.

Millie, 6- Creative entrepreneur. Artistic, having good taste. Great verbal skills. Ups and downs financially. Blessed in some ways. A free spirit, very adaptable.

Milo, 22- A workaholic, focused. Blessed in some ways. Strong verbal skills. Natural counselor and healer.

Milt, 9- Works hard, devoted. Idealistic, humanitarian. Communicates skillfully. Dynamic, busy lifestyle.

Milton, 11- Insightful, sensitive. Blessed in some ways. Travels frequently. Dynamic, busy lifestyle. Natural counselor and healer. Original and unconventional.

Mimi, 8- Patient, tolerant. Blessed in some ways. Desires financial security. Artistic, having good taste.

Mina, 10- Steadfast and determined. Respectful, kind. Original and unconventional. Independent, critical of self and others.

Minerva, 10- Steadfast and determined. Respectful, kind. Romantic, opinionated. A free spirit, very adaptable. Gentle, kind, very diligent. Intuitive and inspired. Independent, critical of self and others.

Minette, 5- Entertains at home. Generous, thoughtful. Original and unconventional. A free spirit, very adaptable. Dynamic, busy lifestyle. Sensitive and easily hurt. Loves adventure and excitement.

Minna, 6- Creative entrepreneur. Artistic, having good taste. Original and opinionated. Sensual and romantic. Independent, self-motivated.

Minnie, 10- Steadfast and determined. Respectful, kind. Original and unconventional. Romantic, sensual. Artistic, having good taste. A free spirit, very adaptable.

Minoo, 30- Family communicator. Blessed in some ways. Creative, original. Natural counselor and healer. Has musical talent.

Mi-ok, 3- Family communicator. Blessed in some ways. Natural counselor and healer. Strong desire to succeed.

Mira, 5- Entertains at home. Generous, thoughtful. Intense inner power. Bright, adventuresome.

Mirabel, 6- Creative entrepreneur. Artistic, having good taste. Gentle, kind, a hard worker. Pioneer and risk taker. Friendly, but shy. A free spirit, very adaptable. Strong verbal skills.

Miranda, 6- Creative entrepreneur. Artistic, having good taste. Gentle, kind, a hard worker. Independent, critical of self and others. Original and unconventional. Reliable, responsible. Bold, courageous, a bit stubborn.

Miriam, 9- Works hard, devoted. Blessed in some ways. Idealistic, humanitarian. Artistic, having good taste. Helpful, sincere. Desires financial security.

Misael, 5- Entertains at home. Generous, thoughtful. Charming and devoted. Bright, adventuresome. A free spirit, very adaptable. Strong verbal skills.

Missy, 22- A workaholic, focused. Blessed in some ways. Very charismatic. Impulsive and extreme. Needs a lot of freedom.

Mistique, 5- Entertains at home. Generous, thoughtful. Charming and devoted. Dynamic, busy lifestyle. Artistic, having good taste. Attracts wealth. Very lucky. A free spirit, very adaptable.

Misty, 5- Entertains at home. Generous, thoughtful. Charming and devoted. Dynamic, busy lifestyle. Needs a lot of freedom.

Mitch, 8- Patient, tolerant. Blessed in some ways. Dynamic, busy lifestyle. Self-expressive, cheerful. Great judge of character.

Mitchell, 10- Steadfast and determined. Respectful, kind. Dynamic, busy lifestyle. Self-expressive, cheerful. Great judge of character. A free spirit, very adaptable. Strong verbal skills. Financial ups and downs.

Mitzi, 5- Entertains at home. Generous, thoughtful. Dynamic, busy lifestyle. Uses common sense. Artistic, having good taste.

Moe, 6- Creative entrepreneur. Natural counselor and healer. A free spirit, very adaptable.

Mohammad, 5- Entertains at home. Enjoys working. Great judge of character. Independent, self-motivated. Domestic, hard working. Systematic, organized. Bold, courageous, a bit stubborn. Practical, conservative.

Mohammed, 9- Works hard, devoted. Natural counselor and healer. Great judge of character. Independent, self-motivated. Domestic, hard working. Systematic, organized. A free spirit, very adaptable. Practical, conservative.

Moira, 11- Insightful, sensitive. Creates group harmony. Blessed in some ways. Gentle, kind, a hard worker. Independent, critical of self and others.

Moises, 8- Patient, tolerant. Competitive in business. Blessed in some ways. Charming and devoted. A free spirit, very adaptable. Many mood swings.

Mollie, 30- Family communicator. Natural counselor and healer. Strong verbal skills. Financial ups and downs. Blessed in some ways. A free spirit, very adaptable.

Molly, 5- Entertains at home. Enjoys working. Communicates skillfully. Financial ups and downs. Needs a lot of freedom.

Mona, 7- Must have faith. Open to opportunities. Creative and original. Independent, critical of self and others.

Monett, 6- Creative entrepreneur. Magnetic personality. Romantic, sensual. A free spirit, very adaptable. Dynamic, busy lifestyle. Sensitive and easily hurt.

Monetta, 7- Must have faith. Open to opportunities. Original and unconventional. A free spirit, very adaptable. Dynamic, busy lifestyle. Sensitive and easily hurt. Independent, critical of self and others.

Monica, 10- Steadfast and determined. Self-sacrificing, devoted. Creative and original. Blessed in some ways. Self-expressive, cheerful. Independent, critical of self and others.

Monika, 6- Creative entrepreneur. Magnetic personality. Original and unconventional. Artistic, having good taste. Strong desire to succeed. Independent, critical of self and others.

Monique, 4- Strong physical constitution. Assumes responsibility. Original and unconventional. Blessed in some ways. Attracts wealth. Very lucky. A free spirit, very adaptable.

Monroe, 8- Patient, tolerant. Competitive in business. Creative and original. Gentle, kind, a hard worker. May have musical abilities. Physical and passionate.

Monte, 22- A workaholic, focused. Creates group harmony. Original and unconventional. Dynamic, busy lifestyle. A free spirit, very adaptable.

Montgomery, 10- Steadfast and determined. Natural counselor and healer. Creative, original. Dynamic, busy lifestyle. Intelligent opportunist. Creates group harmony. Domestically organized. A free spirit, very adaptable. Gentle, kind, a hard worker. Dislikes limitations.

Monty, 6- Creative entrepreneur. Magnetic personality. Original and unconventional. Dynamic, busy lifestyle. Needs a lot of freedom.

Mora, 20- Domestically social. Natural counselor and healer. Gentle, kind, very diligent. Independent, critical of self and others.

Moreen, 7- Must have faith. Open to opportunities. Gentle, kind, a hard worker. A free spirit, very adaptable. Physical and passionate. Original and unconventional.

Morene, 7- (Same as Moreen.)

Morgan, 5- Entertains at home. Enjoys working. Intense inner power. Scientific and philosophical. Bright, adventuresome. Romantic, sensual.

Morley, 7- Must have faith. Open to opportunities. Gentle, kind, a hard worker. Great verbal skills. A free spirit, very adaptable. Dislikes limitations.

Morticia, 7- Must have faith. Open to opportunities. Gentle, kind, a hard worker. Dynamic, busy lifestyle. Blessed in some ways. Self-expressive, cheerful. Artistic, having good taste. Not easily influenced.

Morris, 11- Insightful, sensitive. Creates group harmony. Gentle, kind, very diligent. Tendency to lose items. Blessed in some ways. Charming and devoted.

Mort, 3- Family communicator. Nurturing, loving. Gentle, kind, a hard worker. Dynamic, busy lifestyle.

Mortie, 8- Patient, tolerant. Competitive in business. Intense inner power. Dynamic, busy lifestyle. Blessed in some ways. A free spirit, very adaptable.

Mortimer, 3- Family communicator. Natural counselor and healer. Gentle, kind, very diligent. Dynamic, busy lifestyle. Blessed in some ways. Desires financial security. A free spirit, very adaptable. Tendency to lose items.

Morton, 5- Entertains at home. Enjoys working. Gentle, kind, very diligent. Dynamic, busy lifestyle. Magnetic personality. Romantic, opinionated.

Morty, 10- Steadfast and determined. Self-sacrificing, devoted. Gentle, kind, very diligent. Dynamic, busy lifestyle. Needs a lot of freedom.

Moses, 8- Patient, tolerant. Competitive in business. Charming and devoted. A free spirit, very adaptable. Intense and extreme.

Moshe, 6- Creative entrepreneur. Magnetic personality. Charming and devoted. Great judge of character. A free spirit, very adaptable.

Mu Lan, 7- Must have faith. Stylish and refined. Communicates skillfully. Not easily influenced. Original and unconventional.

Muriel, 6- Creative entrepreneur. Attractive and charming. Gentle, kind, a hard worker. Blessed in some ways. A free spirit, very adaptable. Strong verbal skills.

Murray, 6- Creative entrepreneur. Attractive and charming. Gentle, kind, a hard worker. Intense inner power. Independent, self-motivated. Needs a lot of freedom.

Mustafa, 9- Works hard, devoted. Gracious, well mannered. Charming and devoted. Dynamic, busy lifestyle. Independent, critical of self and others. Self-sacrificing, loving. Bold, courageous, a bit stubborn.

Mutie, 5- Entertains at home. Attractive and charming. Dynamic, busy lifestyle. Blessed in some ways. A free spirit, very adaptable.

Myer, 7- Must have faith. Refined and stylish. Loves adventure and excitement. Gentle, kind, a hard worker.

Myra, 3- Family communicator. Needs a lot of freedom. Gentle, kind, a hard worker. Aims to please.

Myrna, 8- Patient, tolerant. Strong intuition. Intense inner power. Original and unconventional. Independent, critical of self and others.

Myron, 4- Strong physical constitution. Finds shortcuts. Gentle, kind, very diligent. Natural counselor and healer. Original and unconventional.

Myrtle, 30- Family communicator. Needs a lot of freedom. Gentle, kind, a hard worker. Dynamic, busy lifestyle. Strong verbal skills. Loves adventure and excitement.

Mystique, 3- Family communicator. Needs a lot of freedom. Charming and devoted. Dynamic, busy lifestyle. Blessed in some ways. Attracts wealth. Youthful, attractive. Loves adventure and excitement.

Myung-hee, 8- Patient, tolerant. Strong intuition. Attractive and charming. Original and unconventional. Scientific and philosophical. Great judge of character. Loves adventure and excitement. Needs change.

> "My! People come and go so quickly here!
>
> Follow the Yellow Brick Road. Follow the Yellow Brick Road?"
>
> ~Excerpted from "The Wizard of Oz"
> Used with permission

N

IF A NAME BEGINS WITH N, has more than one N, or ends with an N, this person is romantic, creative, tends to have many love affairs, and is opinionated and unconventional.

The letter N is the 14th letter of the alphabet. 1+4=5, so the 14th letter has the same vibrational influence as the number 5. The 1 rules beginnings, 4 rules work and family, and 5 rules change. So the N person is beginning work and family and dealing with change. It's difficult to be free when responsible for work and family, but the N person must buckle down to the obligations of work and family while having the desire to be free. The higher evolved N person will somehow manage to meet these obligations and attain freedom as well. The lesser evolved will have difficulty handling their obligations and may give in to tendencies of escapism.

An N anywhere in a person's name will make them more romantic and sensual. N people usually have many love affairs and often keep a diary. N names are very sentimental and will want to hang on to the mementos of a relationship long after it's over. Although this letter's influence tends to fall in and out of love quickly, when N is in the right relationship, it proves to be the model of happiness. The N is similar to the astrological signs Leo and Aquarius. They are as freedom oriented and unconventional as an Aquarian, yet romantic, creative and subtle as a Leo. Both of these signs are fixed and stubborn, and so is this number 5 ruled letter N.

N named people are original and unusual as we often see role reversal with this letter. Men stay at home with the kids and women are the head of the household. Often this personality finds itself in careers geared for the opposite sex. N's are ahead of their time, similar to letters E and W. They like to experiment; they'll wear a shirt inside out, they'll put peanut butter on lettuce and call it a sandwich; the strange and unusual is their wavelength. The Aquarian side of the N makes some secretly enjoy shocking others, however, most N names are a social delight. They seem to fit into any crowd, high, low or in the middle. This letter loves meeting new people almost as much as W's. They are often forward looking and interested in the latest fads and gadgets.

This letter is also very opinionated! Double N commentator and guest speaker on many talk shows, Dennis Miller, demonstrates his opinion on a regular basis. Pick a topic and he has an opinion. Don't try to change it, the N influence will put on their hat and leave with the same opinion as before. It's a very fixed and stubborn letter.

5 ruled letters E, N and W are in danger of falling victim to drug and alcohol abuse. They tend to overindulge in sensual pleasures, such as food, sex and other forms of escapism. Similar to E, N wants to experience all 5 senses: taste, smell, feel, sound and vision. Life's an adventure with so much to experience! Also similar to the letter E, the letter N's biggest fear is boredom. Similar to E and W, N needs to adopt the

attitude, "moderation in everything" or they'll over do it in some area. Ask Jenny Craig, she has 2 N's in her name she knows all about overindulgence.

The typical N person is adaptable and willing to go along with the changes life demands of them. Nicole Kidman adapted quickly to single life after being married for many years to the famous Tom Cruise. With 2 hidden 8's in her name, she will let us know why their marriage ended when she's ready, not before. She's in control, although it's not obvious, since her 8's are hidden. It's to no surprise that she is finally acting in movies based on comedy. With a C and an L in her name, she's a natural at it. Not only are those two letters good with comedy, but also communication. The film, "The Interpreter" showed us her abilities in the communication department. Last but not least, with a power number 4, she's professional. With a power number 4 she really studies her roles as she doesn't want to be made a fool.

Another interesting N person is Noah, of Noah's Ark. His name adds up to a 20 power number. 20 means partnership and assistance from God. Interestingly enough he received assistance from God when pairing up all the animals, male and female. Also his children had partners. All the pairs sailed off to insure our future! It's also worth noting that he had a parental O first vowel. This is the most nurturing and duty bound of all the vowels. Those with names that begin with N, or have an N anywhere, love adventure and excitement. How excited Noah must have been to go on that adventure! God knew what he was doing when he chose a man named Noah for the Ark project.

Nancy Reagan, First Lady and wife of the late Ronald Reagan also exemplifies her name. With 2 N's in her name, no wonder President Reagan wrote so many love letters to her. Double N's are very romantic. Her name also adds up to a power number 3 which is a natural in the area of communication and writing. With a 3 power number she was cheerful and easy going, just perfect for a man with so much on his mind. She's been able to communicate easily about her husband through books and shares the love letters from her famous Presidential husband freely. She's proud of the love they shared. It's the power number 3 that keeps her smiling, although it couldn't have been easy to deal with the President's Alzheimer's disease. Still, Nancy has a hidden 6 at the beginning of her name, so she is very nurturing and loving. Most people don't realize this because it's hidden. Only those who really know Nancy understand that she has a lot of love to give out.

We have at least 3 famous men whose names are Neil. Neil Armstrong, astronaut; Neil Diamond, singer/songwriter; and Neil Simon, playwright. The name Neil adds up to a 22 power number. 22 is one of the master numbers. Of all the power numbers, 22 seeks world-wide success; it's the "master builder." Each Neil in his own right has become an international success. Also, all of them share the romantic personality of the N. Neil Diamond wrote and sang romantic songs; Neil Simon wrote romantic plays; and while others gazed romantically at the moon, Astronaut Neil Armstrong actually walked on it!

As mentioned before, N is romantic. Even that great big ape, King Kong, has two N's in his name. Who'd have thought a giant gorilla could have love interests? Without the N's he'd have been a bore. Even the sound of N seems warm and loving somehow. The shape of this letter looks as though it's ready to take off. It's ready, it's a ready letter. It likes its freedom and it likes its romance. It's the first letter in the word "New" and just like a 5 ruled letter, N looks forward to experiencing all 5 senses with adventure and excitement. This letter hates being stuck in a routine for too long. So keep it fresh and new; our N friends will supply the romance—and they'll keep coming back, as usual, wearing all the latest fads.

Some other famous N names are: Nolan Ryan, Nicole Brown Simpson, Nicholas Cage, Nancy Travis, Neve Campbell, Nelly, Nick Nolte, Natalie Portman, Nat King Cole, Norah Jones, Nicholas Copernicus, Nostradamus, Noel Coward, Norman Vincent Peale, Neil Young, Nia Long, Nell Carter, Nick Lachey, Norman Rockwell, Newt Gingrich, and Natalie Wood.

Quick Reference of "N" Names

Naavah, 20- Socially active. Reads people easily. Bold, courageous, a bit stubborn. Intuitive and inspired. Pioneer and risk taker. Great judge of character.

Nader, 6- Puts needs of others first. Pioneer and risk taker. Reliable, responsible. A free spirit, very adaptable. Gentle, kind, hard worker.

Nadia, 20- Socially active. Reads people easily. Practical, conservative. Blessed in some ways. Bold, courageous, a bit stubborn.

Nadine, 11- Intuitive and creative. Intuitive, perceptive. Reliable, responsible. Blessed in some ways. Romantic, sensual. A free spirit, very adaptable.

Nadya, 9- Unassuming, naive. Helpful, sincere. Reliable, responsible. Needs a lot of freedom. Pioneer and risk taker.

Naeil, 5- Romantically inclined. Bright, adventuresome. A free spirit, very adaptable. Blessed in some ways. Strong verbal skills.

Naida, 20- (Same as Nadia.)

Namaste, 10- Initiates change. Independent, critical of self and others. Domestic, hard working. Bold, courageous, a bit stubborn. Charming and devoted. Dynamic, busy lifestyle. A free spirit, very adaptable.

Namid, 5- Romantically inclined. Bright, adventuresome. Domestic, hard working. Blessed in some ways. Reliable, responsible.

Nan, 11- Intuitive and creative. Intuitive, perceptive. Romantic, sensual.

Nance, 10- Initiates change. Independent, critical of self and others. Romantic, sensual. Self-expressive, cheerful. A free spirit, very adaptable.

Nanci, 5- Romantically inclined. Bright, adventuresome. Romantic, sensual. Self-expressive, cheerful. Blessed in some ways.

Nancy, 3- Young at heart. Aims to please. Romantic, sensual. Self-expressive, cheerful. Needs a lot of freedom.

Nanette, 7- Enjoys the mysteries of life. Not easily influenced. Romantic, sensual. A free spirit, very adaptable. Dynamic, busy lifestyle. Sensitive and easily hurt. Loves adventure and excitement.

Nani, 20- Socially active. Reads people easily. Romantic, sensual. Blessed in some ways.

Naoma, 8- Realistic with money. Resolute and purposeful. Natural counselor and healer. Domestic, hard working. Bold, courageous, a bit stubborn.

Naomi, 7- Enjoys the mysteries of life. Not easily influenced. Natural counselor and healer. Domestic, hard working. Blessed in some ways.

Naser, 3- Young at heart. Aims to please. Charming and devoted. Physical and passionate. Gentle, kind, a hard worker.

Nashia, 7- Enjoys the mysteries of life. Not easily influenced. Charming and devoted. Great judge of character. Blessed in some ways. Bold, courageous, a bit stubborn.

Nat, 8- Realistic with money. Resolute and purposeful. Energetic, highly charged.

Natacha, 3- Young at heart. Aims to please. Dynamic, busy lifestyle. Pioneer and risk taker. Cheerful, self-expressive. Great judge of character. Bold, courageous, a bit stubborn.

Natalie, 8- Realistic with money. Resolute and purposeful. Energetic, highly charged. Bold, courageous, a bit stubborn. Strong verbal skills. Blessed in some ways. A free spirit, very adaptable.

Natalya, 20- Socially active. Reads people easily. Dynamic, busy lifestyle. Bold, courageous, a bit stubborn. Strong verbal skills. Needs a lot of freedom. Pioneer and risk taker.

Natane, 10- Initiates change. Independent, critical of self and others. Dynamic, busy lifestyle. Bold, courageous, a bit stubborn. Original and opinionated. Physical and passionate.

Natasha, 10- Initiates change. Independent, critical of self and others. Dynamic, busy lifestyle. Bold, courageous, a bit stubborn. Charming and devoted. Great judge of character. Pioneer and risk taker.

Nate, 4- Original, but practical. Natural teaching ability. Dynamic, busy lifestyle. A free spirit, very adaptable.

Nathan, 22- Intuitive and creative. Ambitious leader, great vision. Dynamic, busy lifestyle. Great judge of character. Bold, courageous, a bit stubborn. Romantic, sensual.

Nathaniel, 3- Young at heart. Aims to please. Dynamic, busy lifestyle. Great judge of character. Bold, courageous, a bit stubborn. Romantic, sensual. Blessed in some ways. A free spirit, very adaptable. Strong verbal skills.

Neal, 5- Romantically inclined. Perceptive, socially adept. Bright, adventuresome. Strong verbal skills.

Neale, 10- Initiates change. Likes change and variety. Independent, critical of self and others. Strong verbal skills. Physical and passionate.

Ned, 5- Romantically inclined. Perceptive, socially adept. Domestic, responsible.

Neil, 22- Intuitive and creative. Has big plans and ideas. Blessed in some ways. Great verbal skills.

Nelcy, 5- Romantically inclined. Perceptive, socially adept. Communicates skillfully. Self-expressive, cheerful. Needs a lot of freedom.

Nell, 7- Enjoys the mysteries of life. Not easily fooled. Strong verbal skills. Slow to make decisions.

Nellie, 30- Young at heart. A free spirit, very adaptable. Great verbal skills. Travels frequently. Blessed in some ways. Loves adventure and excitement.

Nelly, 5- Romantically inclined. Perceptive, socially adept. Communicates skillfully. Slow to make decisions. Dislikes limitations.

Nelson, 7- Enjoys the mysteries of life. Not easily fooled. Travels frequently. Charming and devoted. Natural counselor and healer. Romantic, sensual.

Nelva, 9- Unassuming, naive. Enjoys giving gifts. Strong verbal skills. Intuitive and inspired. Helpful, sincere.

Nemo, 20- Socially active. Sound business aptitude. Domestic, hard working. Natural counselor and healer.

Neo, 7- Enjoys the mysteries of life. Not easily fooled. Open to opportunities.

Neon, 3- Young at heart. A free spirit, very adaptable. Natural counselor and healer. Romantic, sensual.

Nerina, 7- Enjoys the mysteries of life. Not easily fooled. Gentle, kind, a hard worker. Blessed in some ways. Romantic, sensual. Independent, critical of self and others.

Nerine, 11- Intuitive and creative. Keenly perceptive. Gentle, kind, a hard worker. Blessed in some ways. Romantic, sensual. Loves adventure and excitement.

Nerissa, 4- Original, but practical. Accesses quickly. Hard working, diligent. Blessed in some ways. Charming and devoted. Impulsive and extreme. Independent, critical of self and others.

Nero, 7- Enjoys the mysteries of life. Not easily fooled. Gentle, kind, a hard worker. Natural counselor and healer. (associated with Roman ruler - negative)

Netta, 6- Puts needs of others first. A step ahead of others. Dynamic, busy lifestyle. Sensitive and easily hurt. Independent, self-motivated.

Neve, 10- Initiates change. Likes change and variety. Intuitive and inspired. Tendency to overindulge.

Nevil, 8- Realistic with money. Original and creative. Intuitive and inspired. Blessed in some ways. Strong verbal skills.

Neville, 7- Enjoys the mysteries of life. Not easily fooled. Intuitive and inspired. Blessed in some ways. Strong verbal skills. Slow to make decisions. Physical and passionate.

Nevin, 10- Initiates change. Likes change and variety. Efficient, goal oriented. Blessed in some ways. Romantic, sensual.

Nevis, 6- Puts needs of others first. A step ahead of others. Intuitive and inspired. Artistic, having good taste. Charming and devoted.

Newman, 7- Enjoys the mysteries of life. Not easily fooled. Likes to meet new people. Domestic, hard working. Independent, critical of self and others. Romantic, sensual.

Newt, 8- Realistic with money. Original and creative. Likes to meet new people. Dynamic, busy lifestyle.

Newton, 10- Initiates change. Likes change and variety. Has charisma and charm. Dynamic, busy lifestyle. Natural counselor and healer. Romantic, sensual.

Nia, 6- Puts needs of others first. Artistic, having good taste. Pioneer and risk taker.

Nic, 8- Realistic with money. Gives practical gifts. Optimistic, outspoken.

Nichol, 7- Enjoys the mysteries of life. Needs alone time. Self-expressive, cheerful. Great judge of character. Natural counselor and healer. Strong verbal skills.

Nicholas, 9- Unassuming, naive. Blessed in some ways. Self-expressive, cheerful. Great judge of character. Natural counselor and healer. Strong verbal skills. Helpful, sincere. Charming and devoted.

Nichole, 3- Young at heart. Considerate, understanding. Youthful, outspoken. Great judge of character. Natural counselor and healer. Strong verbal skills. A free spirit, very adaptable.

Nick, 10- Initiates change. Respectful, kind. Self-expressive, cheerful. Strong desire to succeed.

Nicky, 8- Realistic with money. Gives practical gifts. Self-expressive, cheerful. Strong desire to succeed. Needs a lot of freedom.

Nico, 5- Romantically inclined. Generous, thoughtful. Cheerful, lighthearted. Natural counselor and healer.

Nicodemus, 4- Original, but practical. Blessed in some ways. Optimistic, outspoken. Natural counselor and healer. Reliable, responsible. A free spirit, very adaptable. Domestic, hard working. Attractive and charming. Very devoted.

Nicola, 9- Unassuming, naive. Blessed in some ways. Self-expressive, cheerful. Natural counselor and healer. Strong verbal skills. Independent, critical of self and others.

Nicolas, 10- Initiates change. Respectful, kind. Self-expressive, cheerful. Natural counselor and healer. Strong verbal skills. Independent, critical of self and others. Charming and devoted.

Nicole, 4- Original, but practical. Blessed in some ways. Optimistic, outspoken. Natural counselor and healer. Strong verbal skills. A free spirit, very adaptable.

Nicolette, 4- Original, but practical. Blessed in some ways. Optimistic, outspoken. Natural counselor and healer. Strong verbal skills. A free spirit, very adaptable. Dynamic, busy lifestyle. Sensitive and easily hurt. Loves adventure and excitement.

Nicolle, 7- Enjoys the mysteries of life. Needs alone time. Self-expressive, cheerful. Natural counselor and healer. Communicates skillfully. Ups and downs financially. A free spirit, very adaptable.

Nigel, 11- Intuitive and creative. Emotional, considerate. Scientific and philosophical. A free spirit, very adaptable. Strong verbal skills.

Nika, 8- Realistic with money. Gives practical gifts. Has a powerful presence. Resolute and purposeful.

Niki, 10- Initiates change. Respectful, kind. Strong desire to succeed. Artistic, having good taste.

Nikita, 10- Initiates change. Respectful, kind. Strong desire to succeed. Artistic, having good taste. Dynamic, busy lifestyle. Independent, critical of self and others.

Nikki, 30- Young at heart. Considerate, understanding. Strong desire to succeed. A bit forceful. Artistic, having good taste.

Nikky, 7- Enjoys the mysteries of life. Needs alone time. Multifaceted and disciplined. A bit forceful. Needs a lot of freedom.

Nila, 9- Unassuming, naive. Blessed in some ways. Great verbal skills. Helpful, sincere.

Niles, 5- Romantically inclined. Generous, thoughtful. Communicates skillfully. A free spirit, very adaptable. Charming and devoted.

Nina, 20- Socially active. Emotional, considerate. Romantic, sensual. Reads people easily.

Niro, 11- Intuitive and creative. Emotional and considerate. Gentle, kind, a hard worker. Natural counselor and healer.

Nita, 8- Realistic with money. Gives practical gifts. Dynamic, busy lifestyle. Resolute and purposeful.

Noah, 20- Socially active. Works well with others. Reads people easily. Great judge of character.

Noami, 7- (Same as Naomi.)

Noble, 3- Young at heart. Nurturing, loving. Friendly, but shy. Communicates skillfully. A free spirit, very adaptable.

Noel, 10- Initiates change. Self-sacrificing, devoted. A free spirit, very adaptable. Great verbal skills.

Noela, 20- Socially active. Works well with others. A free spirit, very adaptable. Strong verbal skills. Independent, critical of self and others.

Noelle, 9- Unassuming, naive. Artistic, creative. Physical and passionate. Frequent traveler. Ups and downs financially. Loves adventure and excitement.

Noemi, 11- Intuitive and creative. Creates group harmony. A free spirit, very adaptable. Domestic, hard working. Blessed in some ways.

Nola, 6- Puts needs of others first. Natural counselor and healer. Strong verbal skills. Pioneer and risk taker.

Nolan, 20- Socially active. Works well with others. Great verbal skills. Reads people easily. Romantic, sensual.

Noland, 6- Puts needs of others first. Magnetic personality. Strong verbal skills. Pioneer and risk taker. Romantic, sensual. Reliable, responsible.

Nomi, 6- Puts needs of others first. Magnetic personality. Domestic, hard working. Blessed in some ways.

Nona, 8- Realistic with money. Competitive in business. Romantic, sensual. Resolute and purposeful.

Nora, 3- Young at heart. Nurturing, loving. Gentle, kind, a hard worker. Aims to please.

Norah, 11- Intuitive and creative. Creates group harmony. Gentle, kind, a hard worker. Independent, ambitious. Great judge of character.

Norbert, 11- Intuitive and creative. Creates group harmony. Gentle, kind, a hard worker. Friendly, but shy. A free spirit, very adaptable. Tendency to lose items. Dynamic, busy lifestyle.

Noreen, 8- Realistic with money. Competitive in business. Intense inner power. A free spirit, very adaptable. Loves adventure and excitement. Romantic, sensual.

Norene, 8- (Same as Noreen.)

Nori, 11- Intuitive and creative. Creates group harmony. Gentle, kind, a hard worker. Blessed in some ways.

Noriko, 10- Initiates change. Self-sacrificing, devoted. Hardworking, diligent. Blessed in some ways. Strong desire to succeed. Natural counselor and healer.

Norine, 3- Young at heart. Nurturing, loving. Diligent, hardworking. Blessed in some ways. Romantic, sensual. A free spirit, very adaptable.

Norla, 6- Puts needs of others first. Magnetic personality. Sympathetic, kind. Strong verbal skills. Independent, critical of self and others.

Norlina, 11- Intuitive and creative. Creates group harmony. Gentle, kind, a hard worker. Strong verbal skills. Blessed in some ways. Romantic, sensual. Independent, self-motivated.

Norm, 6- Puts needs of others first. Magnetic personality. Sympathetic, kind. Domestic, hardworking.

Norma, 7- Enjoys the mysteries of life. Open to opportunities. Gentle, kind, a hard worker. Systematic, organized. Not easily influenced.

Norman, 30- Young at heart. Nurturing, loving. Diligent, hardworking. Systematic, organized. Aims to please. Romantic, sensual.

Normie, 11- Intuitive and creative. Creates group harmony. Gentle, kind, a hard worker. Systematic, organized. Blessed in some ways. A free spirit, very adaptable.

Norris, 3- Young at heart. Nurturing, loving. Diligent, hardworking. Tendency to lose items. Blessed in some ways. Charming and devoted.

Nort, 22- Intuitive and creative. Creates group harmony. Gentle, kind, a hard worker. Dynamic, busy lifestyle.

Northrop, 7- Enjoys the mysteries of life. Open to opportunities. Gentle, kind, a hard worker. Dynamic, busy lifestyle. Great judge of character. Tendency to lose items. Has musical talent. Intelligent and knowledgeable.

Norton, 6- Puts needs of others first. Magnetic personality. Sympathetic, kind. Dynamic, busy lifestyle. Natural counselor and healer. Romantic, sensual.

Norville, 8- Realistic with money. Competitive in business. Intense inner power. Intuitive and inspired. Blessed in some ways. Great verbal skills. Financial ups and downs. A free spirit, very adaptable.

Nova, 7- Enjoys the mysteries of life. Open to opportunities. Intuitive and inspired. Not easily influenced.

Nubia, 20- Socially active. Attractive and charming. Friendly, but shy. Blessed in some ways. Independent, critical of self and others.

Nubula, 8- Realistic with money. Attractive and charming. Friendly, but shy. Difficulty making decisions. Strong verbal skills. Independent, critical of self and others.

Nuri, 8- Realistic with money. Attractive and charming. Intense inner power. Blessed in some ways.

Nuriel, 7- Enjoys the mysteries of life. Has style and grace. Gentle, kind, a hard worker. Blessed in some ways. A free spirit, very adaptable. Strong verbal skills.

Nyla, 7- Enjoys the mysteries of life. Stylish and refined. Great verbal skills. Not easily influenced.

"If ever oh ever a Wiz there was
The Wizard of Oz
Is one because, because, because, because,
Because, because ...
Because of the wonderful things he does ..."
~Excerpted from "The Wizard of Oz"
Used with permission

O

IF A NAME BEGINS WITH O, is the first vowel, has more than one O, or ends with an O, this person is a natural counselor and healer, has strong religious convictions, has to have someone to love or nurture, and is very emotional.

The letter O is the 15th letter of the alphabet. 1+5=6, so the 15th letter has the same vibrational influence as the number 6. The 1 rules beginnings, 5 rules change, and 6 rules love. The O person is beginning to experience change and learning to love. Perhaps they are learning to love in a different way this lifetime. The types of love are manifold. Love encompasses all kinds of emotions and so does the O ruled person. Similar to the letter F, O is capable of jealousy and can be moody as well.

This love-ruled letter is magnetic. It's ruled by Venus, the planet of attraction. Joe and Lori may not be considered "good-looking," but people, and even animals, tend to be drawn to them somehow. When someone with an O, especially in the beginning or end of their name enters a room, people notice. Love is not intelligent; it's a feeling, an emotion. Sometimes it's blind, deaf, and dumb, but our O ruled friends are here to learn from the lessons of love. Some O's can be meddling and try to have their way in family quarrels. The O person needs to guard against feelings of jealousy and to feeling sorry for themselves or brooding for long periods of time. The O can really put a damper on the family dinner hour if upset while performing their duties of love. As the saying goes, "If Momma ain't happy, nobody is." That's because Momma has an O first vowel!

Many O types are found in religious settings. After all, "God is Love." God, Lord, and Love all have O as the first vowel. Even the word "morals" has an O first vowel. If a person has an O anywhere in their name, they will have more than the average dose of willpower and religious conviction. The typical O person will respect rules and regulations. Unfortunately, there is a down side to this letter. If not taught good moral values while young, they might not respect the rights and property of others when they become adults. Plenty of names in the news reflect the negative side of the O; the Scott Peterson double murder trial; Sharon Osborn allegedly broke into a star's dressing room and stole all their loot; Winona Ryder was caught on tape stealing clothes at Saks 5th Avenue; Tonya Harding hired a hit man to take out one of her competitors in the 1994 Winter Olympics. Unfortunately O's can be naughty this way.

The typical O is responsible for themselves and will take on the responsibilities of others willingly. Similar to the 6th letter, F, most of them are self-sacrificing and duty bound. The majority of O names make great parents, counselors and religious leaders. They are the natural counselors and healers, so they often attract patients to themselves. Since they often willingly burden themselves with service and duty, they may want to carefully choose their mate. The male with an O in his name seems to be attracted to the damsel in distress. The female with an O in her name is often attracted to a mama's boy, or someone whom she can coddle or dote over. Both seem to attract people who have counseling or nurturing needs, which sometimes ends up more of a burden than they bargained for.

The sense of smell is intensified with our O ruled friends. For some reason this letter tends to complain of odors more than the other letters. Similar to the letter F, some are allergic to perfumes or can feel sick if they have to endure unpleasant odors for long.

Those with an O anywhere in their name are often musically inclined. Which reminds me of a saying, "Music is love in search of a word." Unfortunately, most O's are too duty bound to pursue a musical career. Still some of the best in the music field have an O in their name: singers/song writers Josh Groban, Olivia Newton John, Norah Jones, Roberta Flack, Elton John, Joni Mitchell, Hootie and the Blowfish, Boz Scaggs, Bono, Rod Stewart, Beyonce Knowles, Johnny Cash, Bonnie Raite, Toby Keith, John Lennon, and Otis Rush are just a few that were able to make a career for themselves with music. Eccentric Ozzy Osborne, violinist YoYo Ma, and writer of musicals Oscar Hammerstein, also fit into this musical category.

O names make excellent gardeners, given their natural nurturing abilities. Children, pets and gardens are fortunate if an O person is taking care of them. O's have a way of making us feel taken care of when we're in their presence. We can count on the O. If the O person is unable to have children of their own, they'll often treat their pets as if they were children. They may put clothes, scarves, or sunglasses on them and take them everywhere. Same as "Mr. Bo Jangles," when they lose a pet, they may grieve for many years. If the O person doesn't have a pet or children they may manage over large groups of people. They are the natural parent and make wonderful bosses. The bible shows this example with O first-vowel Moses and Noah managing over large groups of people. Consequently, O types usually don't like anyone looking over their shoulder. They are responsible and duty bound, and resent when others don't recognize and respect their authority.

Oprah Winfrey has an empire of people she manages over quite well, plus millions of followers. Just like the O, she is emotional and not afraid to show it. She's human, real, and most people can relate to her. Oprah's a natural counselor and healer, counseling and healing complete strangers by the thousands over the air waves each week. Wearing her O up front in the beginning of her name makes her especially magnetic. The hidden 5 at the end of her name shows the enjoyment she receives while giving gifts to others. This same number helps her enjoy meeting new people, but it may keep her from getting married or tied down as the 5 likes to be free. The P in her name shows us that as much as she likes people, she still needs her privacy. The 4 power number helps keep her faithful as well as her moral, duty bound O. 2 hidden 4's at the beginning of her name, plus the 4 power number gives her the ability to go in and quickly access a situation. It's the human computer effect, she usually does her homework before taking on an assignment. The hidden 4's in her name also show she's had more hardships than most of us will ever know.

Orlando Bloom not only wears his O up front, but also at the end as he has 2 O's in his last name. The name Orlando adds up to a 7 power number which often performs well in the movie industry or in front of a camera. His two favorite cities are London and Los Angeles which both have the O and L in them. We often feel comfortable in cities that have the same letters as in our own names.

Another interesting and magnetic personality whose name starts with an O is Oliver North. O people are service-oriented and will work tirelessly to perform the task at hand. Oliver has a hidden 9 with the O and L adding up to 9, plus an I and an R in his name, which are both ruled by the number 9; and his name sums up to a power number 9, so people feel safe with him somehow. They ask him questions because they think he knows the answer. With all that 6 and 9 energy in his name, he's a go-with-the-flow type person, not uptight at all. He's a true humanitarian with that much 9 and the L gives him an above average ability to communicate.

O's live to love and love to give. They're service oriented and best placed among those who need them desperately. Their never too tired to demonstrate what love really is.

Some other famous "O" names are: Olympia Dukakis, Orsen Wells, Ozzy Nelson, Oscar Wilde, Ogden Nash, Ossie Davis, Olivia De Havilland, Oliver Hardy, O.J. Simpson, Oliver Wendell Holmes, Oleta Adams, Orville Wright, Otis Redding, Otto Premiger, and Omar Sharif.

Quick Reference of "O" Names

Oakley, 6- Magnetic personality. Pioneer and risk taker. Strong desire to succeed. Great verbal skills. A free spirit, very adaptable. Dislikes limitations.

Obadiah, 4- Assumes responsibility. Friendly, but shy. Natural teaching ability. Domestic, responsible. Blessed in some ways. Bold, courageous, a bit stubborn. Great judge of character.

Obayana, 5- Enjoys working. Sparkling, emotional outlook. Bright, adventuresome. Needs a lot of freedom. Bold, courageous, a bit stubborn. Original and unconventional. Pioneer and risk taker.

Oberon, 6- Magnetic personality. Friendly, but shy. A free spirit, very adaptable. Gentle, kind, a hard worker. Natural counselor and healer. Original and unconventional.

Octave, 3- Has creative solutions. Cheerful, lighthearted. Dynamic, busy lifestyle. Aims to please. Intuitive and inspired. A free spirit, very adaptable.

Octavia, 8- Competitive in business. Self-expressive, cheerful. Energetic, highly charged. Resolute and purposeful. Intuitive and inspired. Blessed in some ways. Bold, courageous, a bit stubborn.

Octavio, 4- Assumes responsibility. Self-expressive, cheerful. Dynamic, busy lifestyle. Natural teaching ability. Intuitive and inspired. Blessed in some ways. Natural counselor and healer.

Octavius, 11- Creates group harmony. Self-expressive, cheerful. Dynamic, busy lifestyle. Reads people easily. Intuitive and inspired. Blessed in some ways. Attractive and charming. Loving, devoted.

Odela, 10- Ambitious and innovative. Domestic, down-to-earth. Likes variety and change. Strong verbal skills. Independent, critical of self and others.

Odele, 5- Enjoys working. Reliable, responsible. A free spirit, very adaptable. Strong verbal skills. Physical and passionate.

Odelia, 10- Ambitious and innovative. Domestic, down-to-earth. Likes variety and change. Strong verbal skills. Blessed in some ways. Independent, critical of self and others.

Odell, 3- Has creative solutions. Reliable, responsible. A free spirit, very adaptable. Communicates skillfully. Slow to make decisions.

Odessa, 9- Artistic, creative. Reliable, responsible. A free spirit, very adaptable. Charming and devoted. Impulsive and extreme. Helpful, sincere.

Odetta, 20- Works well with others. Reliable, responsible. Social, entertaining. Dynamic, busy lifestyle. Sensitive and easily hurt. Reads people easily.

Odette, 6- Magnetic personality. Duty bound, self-sacrificing. A free spirit, very adaptable. Dynamic, busy lifestyle. Sensitive and easily hurt. Loves adventure and excitement.

Odin, 6- Magnetic personality. Duty bound, self-sacrificing. Blessed in some ways. Original and unconventional.

Ofelia, 30- Has creative solutions. Self-sacrificing, loving. A free spirit, very adaptable. Great verbal skills. Blessed in some ways. Independent, critical of self and others.

Ogden, 9- Artistic, creative. Scientific and philosophical. Reliable, responsible. A free spirit, very adaptable. Original and unconventional.

Ogilvie, 7- Open to opportunities. A thinker, determined. Blessed in some ways. Communicates skillfully. Intuitive and inspired. Artistic, having good taste. A free spirit, very adaptable.

Oglesby, 4- Assumes responsibility. Scientific and philosophical. Strong verbal skills. A free spirit, very adaptable. Charming and devoted. Friendly, but shy. Dislikes limitations.

Ojeda, 8- Competitive in business. Clever and talented. A free spirit, very adaptable. Reliable, responsible. Resolute and purposeful.

Ok-hee, 8- Competitive in business. Has a powerful presence. Great judge of character. A free spirit, very adaptable. Loves adventure and excitement.

Okilani, 8- Competitive in business. Has a powerful presence. Blessed in some ways. Great verbal skills. Independent, critical of self and others. Original and unconventional. Artistic, having good taste.

Oksana, 7- Open to opportunities. Strong desire to succeed. Charming and devoted. Independent, critical of self and others. Original and unconventional. Bold, courageous, a bit stubborn.

Ola, 10- Ambitious and innovative. Communicates skillfully. Bold, courageous, a bit stubborn.

Olaf, 7- Open to opportunities. Strong verbal skills. Bold, courageous, a bit stubborn. Self-sacrificing, loving.

Olavo, 20- Works well with others. Honest and sincere. Reads people easily. Has a strong imagination. Natural counselor and healer.

Oleg, 8- Competitive in business. Strong verbal skills. A free spirit, very adaptable. Scientific and philosophical

Olena, 20- Works well with others. Frequent traveler. Social and entertaining. Original and unconventional. Reads people easily.

Oleta, 8- Competitive in business. Great verbal skills. A free spirit, very adaptable. Dynamic, busy lifestyle. Resolute and purposeful.

Olga, 8- Competitive in business. Great verbal skills. Scientific and philosophical. Resolute and purposeful.

Olin, 5- Enjoys working. Communicates skillfully. Blessed in some ways. Original and unconventional.

Olisa, 20- Works well with others. Strong verbal skills. Blessed in some ways. Charming and devoted. Independent, critical of self and others.

Olive, 9- Artistic, creative. Frequent traveler. Artistic, having good taste. Tactful and refined. A free spirit, very adaptable.

Oliver, 9- Artistic, creative. Frequent traveler. Artistic, having good taste. Tactful and refined. A free spirit, very adaptable. Gentle, kind, a hard worker.

Olivia, 5- Enjoys working. Communicates skillfully. Blessed in some ways. Intuitive and inspired. Artistic, having good taste. Independent, critical of self and others.

Olivier, 9- Artistic, creative. Frequent traveler. Idealistic, humanitarian. Tactful and refined. Blessed in some ways. A free spirit, very adaptable. Gentle, kind, a hard worker.

Olivine, 5- Enjoys working. Communicates skillfully. Blessed in some ways. Intuitive and inspired. Artistic, having good taste. Original and unconventional. A free spirit, very adaptable.

Ollie, 8- Competitive in business. Great verbal skills. Ups and downs financially. Blessed in some ways. A free spirit, very adaptable.

Olney, 8- Competitive in business. Great verbal skills. Original and unconventional. A free spirit, very adaptable. Dislikes limitations.

Olympia, 10- Ambitious and innovative. Strong verbal skills. Needs a lot of freedom. Domestic, hard working. Level headed. Blessed in some ways. Independent, critical of self and others.

Omar, 20- Works well with others. Domestic, hard working. Reads people easily. Sensitive, emotional, kind.

Ona, 3- Has creative solutions. Original and unconventional. Aims to please.

Oona, 9- Artistic, creative. Natural counselor and healer. Original and unconventional. Helpful, sincere.

Opal, 8- Competitive in business. Intelligent, knowledgeable. Resolute and purposeful. Great verbal skills.

Opaline, 9- Artistic, creative. Level headed. Helpful, sincere. Strong verbal skills. Blessed in some ways. Original and unconventional. A free spirit, very adaptable.

Opra, 5- Enjoys working. Intelligent, knowledgeable. Gentle, kind, a hard worker. Bright, adventuresome.

Oprah, 4- Assumes responsibility. Intelligent, knowledgeable. Gentle, kind, a hard worker. Natural teaching ability. Great judge of character.

Ophelia, 3- Has creative solutions. Intelligent, knowledgeable. Great judge of character. A free spirit, very adaptable. Strong verbal skills. Blessed in some ways. Aims to please.

Opie, 9- Artistic, creative. Level headed. Blessed in some ways. A free spirit, very adaptable.

Oracio, 7- Open to opportunities. Diligent, helpful. Independent, self-motivated. Inspiring and creative. Blessed in some ways. Natural counselor and healer.

Oralie, 6- Magnetic personality. Gentle, kind, a hard worker. Pioneer and risk taker. Great verbal skills. Artistic, having good taste. A free spirit, very adaptable.

O-Ren, 7- Open to opportunities. Compassionate and understanding. Not easily fooled. Romantic and opinionated.

Oreste, 10- Ambitious and innovative. Diligent, helpful, kind. Likes change and variety. Charming and devoted. Dynamic, busy lifestyle. Physical and passionate.

Ori, 6- Magnetic personality. Duty bound, self-sacrificing. Artistic, having good taste.

Oriana, 4- Assumes responsibility. Gentle, kind, a hard worker. Blessed in some ways. Natural teaching ability. Original and unconventional. Bold, courageous, a bit stubborn.

Oribel, 7- Open to opportunities. Compassionate, understanding. Needs alone time. Friendly, but shy. A free spirit, very adaptable. Communicates skillfully.

Oriel, 5- Enjoys working. Good deed doer. Blessed in some ways. A free spirit, very adaptable. Great verbal skills.

Orino, 8- Competitive in business. Intense inner power. Blessed in some ways. Original and creative. Natural counselor and healer.

Orion, 8- (Same as Orino.)

Orlando, 7- Open to opportunities. Compassionate, understanding. Strong verbal skills. Not easily influenced. Original and unconventional. Reliable, responsible. Natural counselor and healer.

Ormond, 7- Open to opportunities. Compassionate, understanding. Domestic, hard working. May have musical abilities. Original and unconventional. Reliable, responsible.

Orpah, 4- (Same as Oprah.)

Orsen, 8- Competitive in business. Intense inner power. Charming and devoted. A free spirit, very adaptable. Original and unconventional.

Orson, 9- Artistic, creative. Gentle, kind, a hard worker. Charming and devoted. May have musical abilities. Original and unconventional.

Orval, 5- Enjoys working. Good deed doer. Intuitive and inspired. Bright, adventuresome. Strong verbal skills.

Orville, 3- Has creative solutions. Gentle, kind, a hard worker. Intuitive and inspired. Blessed in some ways. Strong verbal skills. Many ups and downs financially. A free spirit, very adaptable.

Os, 7- Open to opportunities. Charming and devoted. Very charismatic.

Osaka, 11- Creates group harmony. Charismatic and charming. Independent, critical of self and others. Strong desire to succeed. Bold, courageous, a bit stubborn.

Osborn, 11- Creates group harmony. Charismatic and charming. Friendly, but shy. Natural counselor and healer. Gentle, kind, a hard worker. Original and unconventional.

Osborne, 7- Open to opportunities. Charming and devoted. Friendly, but shy. May have musical abilities. Gentle, kind, a hard worker. Original and unconventional. A free spirit, very adaptable.

Osbourne, 10- Ambitious and innovative. Charming and devoted. Friendly, but shy. May have musical abilities. Attractive and lucky. Gentle, kind, a hard worker. Original and unconventional. A free spirit, very adaptable.

Oscar, 20- Works well with others. Socially refined. Self-expressive, cheerful. Independent, critical of self and others. Gentle, kind, a hard worker.

Osmond, 8- Competitive in business. Passionate and loving. Domestic, hard working. May have musical abilities. Original and unconventional. Reliable, responsible.

Osmund, 5- Enjoys working. Extremely charming. Responsible, duty bound. Youthful and appealing. Original and unconventional. Reliable, responsible.

Osvaldo, 7- Open to opportunities. Charming and devoted. Intuitive and inspired. Independent, critical of self and others. Strong verbal skills. Reliable, responsible. May have musical abilities.

Oswald, 20- Works well with others. Socially refined. Likes to meet new people. Reads people easily. Strong verbal skills. Reliable, responsible.

Othello, 6- Magnetic personality. Dynamic, busy lifestyle. Great judge of character. A free spirit, very adaptable. Great verbal skills. Frequent traveler. Natural counselor and healer.

Otis, 9- Artistic, creative. Dynamic, busy lifestyle. Blessed in some ways. Charming and devoted.

Otto, 7- Open to opportunities. Dynamic, busy lifestyle. Sensitive and easily hurt. Natural counselor and healer.

Owen, 3- Has creative solutions. Likes to meet new people. Physical and passionate. Original, opinionated.

Oxford, 10- Ambitious and innovative. Artistic, sensual, perceptive. Self-sacrificing, loving. Natural counselor and healer. Gentle, kind, a hard worker. Reliable, responsible.

Oz, 5- Enjoys working. Uses common sense. Creative and determined.

Ozzie, 9- Artistic, creative. Uses common sense. A great mediator. Blessed in some ways. A free spirit, very adaptable.

Ozzy, 10- Ambitious and innovative. Uses common sense. A great mediator. Needs a lot of freedom.

"I don't know. But some people without brains do an awful lot of talking, don't they?"

~Excerpted from "The Wizard of Oz"
Used with permission

P

IF A NAME BEGINS WITH P, has more than one P, or ends with a P, this person is level headed, intelligent, knowledgeable, and gives a commanding first impression.

The letter P is the 16th letter of the alphabet. 1+6=7, so the 16th letter has the same vibrational influence as the number 7. The 1 rules beginnings, 6 rules love, and 7 rules faith. The P person is beginning love in some aspect of their life, but the sum total is faith or religion, which requires solitude. So the P person desires love but also needs solitude for meditation. Since love can be demanding, the P needs to balance giving out love, and taking time to meditate or to be alone. This is the P's big challenge.

P names show common sense and seem level headed, but they can be impatient. P named people tend to be selfish with their time. The P is usually highly photogenic, similar to the G and Y names. That's because these letters are similar to the astrological Pisces the fish; which is ruled by Neptune. This same influence rules images or things that are "not real," as an image of a person is not the same as a real person. Neptune also rules the oceans and tides, so many influenced by the letter P prefer to live by water. As this letter is prone to escapism, the Neptunian influence can be so strong, some of them drink like a fish! So, the same amount of caution should be exercised in regard to drugs and alcohol as to their G and Y ruled siblings.

On the same note, when a break-up occurs, we often have difficulty remembering completely those ruled by P. They're a bit elusive, like a half remembered song. We can hum the melody, but the lyrics keep slipping away. The memory of them wants to evaporate somehow.

Those with a P anywhere in their name often prefer to work alone. Just stick them in a corner somewhere and they'll be happy. If a P person goes into acting or some type of stage life, they still want their privacy more than the other letters. Let's just say, P is for privacy! They might be emotional, but tend to have difficulty expressing their feelings. P's, similar to G and Y, sometimes have difficulty giving and receiving affection. This letter is extremely intelligent, and since love is not, the P often has difficulty understanding the emotion of love. P's can be stubborn and inflexible and insist upon being independent. This is another reason why it can be difficult for the P to maintain permanent relationships. The biggest downfall, however, is that this 7 ruled letter, similar to G and Y, can be egotistical. This letter is more enjoyable to be around when placing "faith" in a higher being. If the P doesn't humble itself to a higher source, it often has an inflated sense of self-importance. As the saying goes; some either worship God or think they are God. Those that bear this faith-based letter seem to be either one or the other.

Paul Newman, Paul McCartney, Paul Simon and Paul Anka not only share the same first name, but also share the interpretation. P is a 7 letter and the A is a 1, so there is a hidden 8 in the beginning of each of their names. This means they have lessons to learn having to do with material goods. They may be attracted to the subject of taxes, joint finances, sex, or other people's money. Often hidden 8's have a brush with death or lose a meaningful loved one unexpectedly. They secretly like being in control. When we add the hidden 8 to the U, which is a 3, it adds up to a hidden 11. All four of these men have a strong desire to succeed, even if it's not apparent on the outside. Then to the 11 we add the last letter L which is a 3 letter. This adds up to 14 which condenses down to a power number 5. All four of these famous men share the love of adventure and excitement. They are adaptable to change. They are natural entertainers. Most importantly, they really need their freedom with a power number 5. Yet at the front of their name, similar to a rising sign, is the private P. The first two letters are cerebral; these guys are extremely intelligent; however, the last two letters are ruled by the number 3, so they may be slow to make decisions. The number 3 ruled letters also tend to be lucky. They most likely managed to be in the right place at the right time at critical junctures in their lives. Last, but not least, the numbers 3, 5 and 8 bring ups and downs financially. So these men have no doubt ridden the financial roller coaster a time or two. Not every person named Paul is going to be famous, but there is potential, given the opportunity.

Phyllis Diller, with all those L's in her name is a natural comedian. L is ruled by the number 3 and along with number 5, gives a wonderful stage presence. Also her L's not only allow her to communicate well, but also to listen well. Still, she has 2 letters ruled by the number 7, so she really likes her privacy. Her name adds up to a power number 11, which is a master number. She has a very strong desire to succeed in life. The H in her name is the "Hercules" of letters. She is strong and with the P adds up to a hidden 6. She's a nurturer and prefers being her own boss. When we add the Y which is the 2nd 7 ruled letter, 7+8+7 it adds up to another master number; 22! Deep inside of her, hidden, is a desire to be successful on a global scale. We only have 2 master numbers; 11 and 22. Phyllis has both of them hidden in her name. Still the center of her name is an L which is ruled by 3, so she strives to communicate and be "out there," while all the 7's in her name want her to be alone. She must balance the desire to be alone with the need to be on stage. Ultimately, the H, which desires material wealth, most likely gives her the push she needs to get out there in the public eye, even though she really wants to be alone, she needs the money.

How about the name Peter, as in Peter Fonda, Peter Sellers, Peter Boyle or Peter Gallagher? First, 3 out of 5 letters are cerebral or intelligent, the P and 2 E's. The R at the end of their name is gentle, kind, and very hard working. The T in the middle of their names makes them dynamic, with a busy lifestyle. The first 3 letters add up to a hidden 5 and with a T in the middle, these guys like to entertain and keep very busy. Sometimes they need to be forced to slow down! With all that 5 energy, they love adventure and excitement. When we add the whole name it adds up to a power number 10. Power number 10's find themselves either extremely busy, or they personally have nothing going on at all. At times they are in great demand, inspired to counsel others with their assistance from God "0" in their 10 power number. At other times they are twiddling their thumbs.

It's possible to be happy in a relationship with a P name as long as we give them their space and time for privacy or solitude. Somehow it recharges their batteries and we're all the better for it. Besides, they're honest and can probably tell the boss what's wrong with his new marketing plan. Yes, they are that bold.

Some more famous "P" names are: Phil Donahue, Dr. Phil McGraw, Paris Hilton, Penny Marshall, Patrick Stewart, Patty Duke, Petula Clark, Pablo Picasso, Paloma Picasso, Patty Hearst, Paula Abdul, Peter Frampton, Phil Collins, Pat Sajack, Pamela Anderson, Pink, Pearl Bailey, Pat Boone, Pierre Cardin, Patrick Swayze, Pat Benatar, Prince, Perry Como, Paul Hogan, Patrick Henry, Paul Revere, Patricia Arquette and Patsy Cline.

Quick Reference of "P" Names

Pablo, 10- Strives for excellence. Independent, critical of self and others. Friendly, but shy. Strong verbal skills. Natural counselor and healer.

Paddy, 5- Maintains a high dream. Bright, adventuresome. Reliable, responsible. Down-to-earth, faithful. Needs a lot of freedom.

Padma, 7- Highly refined intellect. Not easily influenced. Reliable, responsible. Domestic, hard working. Bold, courageous, a bit stubborn.

Page, 20- Socially refined. Reads people easily. Scientific, philosophical. A free spirit, very adaptable.

Paige, 11- Knowledgeable in many areas. Intuitive, perceptive. Blessed in some ways. Scientific, philosophical. A free spirit, very adaptable.

Paine, 9- Gift for understanding others. Helpful, sincere. Blessed in some ways. Original and unconventional. A free spirit, very adaptable.

Paley, 5- Maintains a high dream. Bright, adventuresome. Communicates skillfully. A free spirit, very adaptable. Dislikes limitations.

Palmer, 11- Knowledgeable in many areas. Intuitive, perceptive. Strong verbal skills. Domestic, hard working. A free spirit, very adaptable. Gentle, kind, very helpful.

Paloma, 22- Knowledgeable in many areas. Ambitious leader, great vision. Strong verbal skills. Natural counselor and healer. Domestic, hard working. Bold, courageous, a bit stubborn.

Pam, 3- Optimistic in faith. Aims to please. Domestic, hard working.

Pamela, 3- Optimistic in faith. Aims to please. Domestic, hard working. A free spirit, very adaptable. Great verbal skills. Bold, courageous, a bit stubborn.

Pammy, 5- Maintains a high dream. Bright, adventuresome. Domestic, hard working. Systematic, organized. Needs a lot of freedom.

Pansy, 3- Optimistic in faith. Aims to please. Original and creative. Charming and devoted. Needs a lot of freedom.

Papa, 7- Highly refined intellect. Not easily influenced. Level headed. Bold, courageous, a bit stubborn.

Paris, 9- Gift for understanding others. Independent, self-motivated. Gentle, kind, a hard worker. Blessed in some ways. Charming and devoted.

Park, 10- Strives for excellence. Independent, critical of self and others. Gentle, kind, a hard worker. Strong desire to succeed.

Parker, 6- Needs harmony and beauty. Pioneer and risk taker. Duty bound, self-sacrificing. Strong desire to succeed. A free spirit, very adaptable. Tendency to lose items.

Parnel, 30- Optimistic in faith. Aims to please. Sympathetic, kind. Opinionated, creative. Physical and passionate. Strong verbal skills.

Parnell, 6- Needs harmony and beauty. Pioneer and risk taker. Duty bound, self-sacrificing. Original and unconventional. A free spirit, very adaptable. Communicates skillfully. Financial ups and downs.

Parrish, 8- Enjoys rivalry and challenge. Resolute and purposeful. Intense inner power. Compassionate, understanding. Blessed in some ways. Charming and devoted. Great judge of character.

Pascal, 7- Level headed. Not easily influenced. Charming and devoted. Self-expressive, cheerful. Bold, courageous, a bit stubborn. Communicates skillfully.

Pat, 10- Strives for excellence. Independent, critical of self and others. Takes the initiative.

Pate, 6- Needs harmony and beauty. Pioneer and risk taker. Dynamic, busy lifestyle. A free spirit, very adaptable.

Patience, 10- Strives for excellence. Independent, critical of self and others. Takes the initiative. Blessed in some ways. A free spirit, very adaptable. Original and unconventional. Self-expressive, cheerful. Loves adventure and excitement.

Patrice, 9- Gift for understanding others. Helpful, sincere. Generous to a fault. Gentle, kind, a hard worker. Blessed in some ways. Self-expressive, cheerful. A free spirit, very adaptable.

Patricia, 5- Maintains a high dream. Bright, adventuresome. Energetic, highly charged. Gentle, kind, a hard worker. Blessed in some ways. Self-expressive, cheerful. Artistic, having good taste. Bold, courageous, a bit stubborn.

Patrick, 6- Needs harmony and beauty. Pioneer and risk taker. Dynamic, busy lifestyle. Gentle, kind, a hard worker. Blessed in some ways. Self-expressive, cheerful. Strong desire to succeed.

Patsy, 9- Gift for understanding others. Helpful, sincere. Generous to a fault. Charming and devoted. Needs a lot of freedom.

Patti, 3- Optimistic in faith. Aims to please. Dynamic, busy lifestyle. Sensitive and easily hurt. Blessed in some ways.

Patton, 5- Maintains a high dream. Bright, adventuresome. Energetic, highly charged. Sensitive and easily hurt. Natural counselor and healer. Original and unconventional.

Patty, 10- Strives for excellence. Independent, critical of self and others. Takes the initiative. Sensitive and easily hurt. Needs a lot of freedom.

Paul, 5- Maintains a high dream. Bright, adventuresome. Attractive and charming. Strong verbal skills.

Paula, 6- Needs harmony and beauty. Independent, critical of self and others. Attractive and charming. Strong verbal skills. Bold, courageous, a bit stubborn.

Paulette, 10- Strives for excellence. Independent, critical of self and others. Youthful, appealing. Strong verbal skills. A free spirit, very adaptable. Dynamic, busy lifestyle. Sensitive and easily hurt. Loves adventure and excitement.

Paulina, 11- Knowledgeable in many areas. Intuitive, perceptive. Creative, inspiring. Strong verbal skills. Blessed in some ways. Original and unconventional. Bold, courageous, a bit stubborn.

Pauline, 6- Needs harmony and beauty. Pioneer and risk taker. Attractive and charming. Great verbal skills. Blessed in some ways. Original and unconventional. A free spirit, very adaptable.

Paulo, 20- Socially refined. Reads people easily. Attractive and charming. Communicates skillfully. A natural counselor and healer.

Paxon, 7- Level headed. Not easily influenced. Artistic, sensual, perceptive. Natural counselor and healer. Original and unconventional.

Paxton, 9- Gift for understanding others. Helpful, sincere. Artistic, sensual, perceptive. Dynamic, busy lifestyle. Natural counselor and healer. Original and unconventional.

Payne, 7- Level headed. Not easily influenced. Needs a lot of freedom. Original and unconventional. A free spirit, very adaptable.

Payton, 10- Strives for excellence. Independent, critical of self and others. Needs a lot of freedom. Dynamic, busy lifestyle. Natural counselor and healer. Original and unconventional.

Peace, 3- Optimistic in faith. A free spirit, very adaptable. Aims to please. Self-expressive, cheerful. Physical and passionate.

Pearce, 30- Optimistic in faith. A free spirit, very adaptable. Aims to please. Gentle, kind, a hard worker. Self-expressive, cheerful. Physical and passionate.

Pearl, 7- Level headed. Not easily fooled. Stylish and refined. Gentle, kind, a hard worker. Strong verbal skills.

Pearle, 30- Optimistic in faith. A free spirit, very adaptable. Aims to please. Gentle, kind, a hard worker. Communicates skillfully. Tendency to overindulge.

Pedro, 4- Bit of a homebody. Accesses quickly. Reliable, responsible. Gentle, kind, a hard worker. Natural counselor and healer.

Peg, 10- Strives for excellence. Likes change and variety. Scientific and philosophical.

Peggy, 6- Needs harmony and beauty. A step ahead of others. Scientific and philosophical. Needs solitude. Needs a lot of freedom.

Pembroke, 4- Bit of a homebody. Accesses quickly. Domestic, hardworking. Friendly, but shy. Gentle, kind, a hard worker. Natural counselor and healer. Strong desire to succeed. Loves adventure and excitement.

Penelope, 7- Level headed. Not easily fooled. Original and unconventional. Physical and passionate. Strong verbal skills. Natural counselor and healer. Intelligent, knowledgeable. Loves adventure and excitement.

Penley, 5- Maintains a high dream. Physical and passionate. Original and unconventional. Great verbal skills. Likes meeting new people. Needs a lot of freedom.

Penn, 22- Knowledgeable in many areas. Has big plans and ideas. Original and unconventional. Romantic, sensual.

Penny, 11- Knowledgeable in many areas. Keenly perceptive. Original and creative. Romantic, sensual. Needs a lot of freedom.

Penrod, 9- Gift for understanding others. Enjoys giving gifts. Romantic, opinionated. Gentle, kind, a hard worker. Natural counselor and healer. Reliable, responsible.

Peony, 30- Optimistic in faith. A free spirit, very adaptable. Natural counselor and healer. Original and unconventional. Dislikes limitations.

Pepita, 4- Bit of a homebody. Accesses quickly. Level headed. Blessed in some ways. Dynamic, busy lifestyle. Natural teaching ability.

Percival, 5- Maintains a high dream. Perceptive, socially adept. Intense inner power. Self-expressive, cheerful. Blessed in some ways. Intuitive and inspired. Bright, adventuresome. Great verbal skills.

Percy, 4- Bit of a homebody. Accesses quickly. Hardworking, kind, diligent. Self-expressive, cheerful. Dislikes limitations.

Peregrine, 7- Level headed. Not easily fooled. Spiritually motivated. A free spirit, very adaptable. Needs solitude. Tendency to lose items. Blessed in some ways. Original and unconventional. Loves adventure and excitement.

Peri, 30- Optimistic in faith. A free spirit, very adaptable. Sympathetic, kind. Blessed in some ways.

Perl, 6- Needs harmony and beauty. A step ahead of others. Gentle, kind, a hard worker. Strong verbal skills.

Perla, 7- Level headed. Not easily fooled. Spiritually motivated. Great verbal skills. Bold, courageous, a leader.

Perle, 11- Knowledgeable in many areas. Keenly perceptive. Gentle, kind, a hard worker. Travels frequently. Loves adventure and excitement.

Pernell, 10- Strives for excellence. Likes change and variety. Diligent, hardworking. Original and unconventional. Loves adventure and excitement. Strong verbal skills. Frequent traveler.

Perry, 10- Strives for excellence. Likes change and variety. Diligent, hardworking. Tendency to lose items. Needs a lot of freedom.

Pete, 10- Strives for excellence. Likes change and variety. Dynamic, busy lifestyle. Loves adventure and excitement.

Peter, 10- Strives for excellence. Likes change and variety. Dynamic, busy lifestyle. Loves adventure and excitement. Gentle, kind, a hard worker.

Petra, 6- Needs harmony and beauty. A step ahead of others. Dynamic, busy lifestyle. Gentle, kind, a hard worker. Independent, critical of self and others.

Petrina, 11- Knowledgeable in many areas. A free spirit, very adaptable. Dynamic, busy lifestyle. Gentle, kind, a hard worker. Blessed in some ways. Romantic, opinionated. Intuitive, perceptive.

Petula, 3- Optimistic in faith. A free spirit, very adaptable. Dynamic, busy lifestyle. Attractive and charming. Great verbal skills. Aims to please.

Petunia, 5- Maintains a high dream. Perceptive, socially adept. Dynamic, busy lifestyle. Attractive and charming. Original and unconventional. Blessed in some ways. Bright, adventuresome.

Peyton, 5- Maintains a high dream. Perceptive, socially adept. Needs a lot of freedom. Dynamic, busy lifestyle. Natural counselor and healer. Romantic, creative.

Phelan, 11- Knowledgeable in many areas. Self-reliant, successful. Keenly perceptive. Strong verbal skills. Independent, critical of self and others. Original and unconventional.

Phelia, 6- Needs harmony and beauty. Original, creative. A step ahead of others. Great verbal skills. Blessed in some ways. Independent, critical of self and others.

Phelps, 4- Bit of a homebody. Great judge of character. Accesses quickly. Frequent traveler. Level headed. Charming and devoted.

Phil, 9- Gift for understanding others. Relies on own judgment. Blessed in some ways. Great verbal skills.

Philbert, 9- Gift for understanding others. Relies on own judgment. Blessed in some ways. Great verbal skills. Friendly, but shy. A free spirit, very adaptable. Gentle, kind, a hard worker. Dynamic, busy lifestyle.

Philip, 7- Level headed. Great judge of character. Blessed in some ways. Communicates skillfully. Artistic, having good taste. Overly secretive, distant.

Philippa, 6- Needs harmony and beauty. Original, creative. Blessed in some ways. Strong verbal skills. Artistic, having good taste. Overly secretive, distant. Level headed. Not easily influenced.

Phillis, 4- Bit of a homebody. Great judge of character. Blessed in some ways. Great verbal skills. Frequent traveler. Artistic, having good taste. Charming and devoted.

Philo, 6- Needs harmony and beauty. Original, creative. Blessed in some ways. Frequent traveler. Natural counselor and healer.

Philomena, 3- Optimistic in faith. Makes and loses money easily. Blessed in some ways. Strong verbal skills. Natural counselor and healer. Domestic, hard working. A free spirit, very adaptable. Romantic, creative. Pioneer and risk taker.

Phineas, 9- Gift for understanding others. Relies on own judgment. Blessed in some ways. Romantic, opinionated. A free spirit, very adaptable. Not easily influenced. Charming and devoted.

Phoebe, 6- Needs harmony and beauty. Original, creative. Natural counselor and healer. A free spirit, very adaptable. Friendly, but shy. Tendency to overindulge.

Phoenix, 10- Strives for excellence. Great judge of character. Natural counselor and healer. A free spirit, very adaptable. Original and unconventional. Blessed in some ways. Artistic, sensual, perceptive.

Phylis, 8- Enjoys rivalry and challenge. Great judge of character. Needs a lot of freedom. Strong verbal skills. Blessed in some ways. Charming and devoted.

Phyllis, 11- Knowledgeable in many areas. Self-reliant, successful. Needs a lot of freedom. Communicates skillfully. Frequent traveler. Blessed in some ways. Charming and devoted.

Pia, 8- Enjoys rivalry and challenge. Blessed in some ways. Resolute and purposeful.

Pierce, 8- Enjoys rivalry and challenge. Blessed in some ways. A free spirit, very adaptable. Gentle, kind, a hard worker. Self-expressive, cheerful. Loves adventure and excitement.

Pilar, 11- Knowledgeable in many areas. Artistic, having good taste. Strong verbal skills. Independent, critical of self and others. Gentle, kind, a hard worker.

Piper, 10- Strives for excellence. Creative and artistic. Level headed. A free spirit, very adaptable. Gentle, kind, a hard worker.

Pita, 10- Strives for excellence. Creative and artistic. Dynamic, busy lifestyle. Independent, critical of self and others.

Pitney, 8- Enjoys rivalry and challenge. Blessed in some ways. Dynamic, busy lifestyle. Original and unconventional. A free spirit, very adaptable. Dislikes limitations.

Pius, 20- Socially refined. Blessed in some ways. Attractive and flirtatious. Charming and devoted.

Plato, 10- Strives for excellence. Communicates skillfully. Independent, critical of self and others. Dynamic, busy lifestyle. Natural counselor and healer.

Polly, 8- Enjoys rivalry and challenge. Competitive in business. Strong verbal skills. Ups and downs financially. Needs a lot of freedom.

Polo, 22- Knowledgeable in many areas. Natural counselor and healer. Strong verbal skills. Magnetic personality.

Pomeroy, 8- Enjoys rivalry and challenge. Competitive in business. Desires financial security. Loves adventure and excitement. Gentle, kind, a hard worker. Magnetic personality. Needs a lot of freedom.

Poncho, 8- Enjoys rivalry and challenge. Competitive in business. Original and unconventional. Self-expressive, cheerful. Great judge of character. Has musical abilities.

Poppy, 7- Level headed. Natural counselor and healer. Intelligent, knowledgeable. A bit secretive. Needs a lot of freedom.

Porsche, 3- Optimistic in faith. Nurturing, loving. Considerate, helpful. Charming and devoted. Self-expressive, cheerful. Great judge of character. A free spirit, very adaptable.

Porter, 3- Optimistic in faith. Nurturing, loving. Considerate, helpful. Dynamic, busy lifestyle. A free spirit, very adaptable. Tendency to lose items.

Portia, 7- Level headed. Natural counselor and healer. Gentle, kind, a hard worker. Dynamic, busy lifestyle. Blessed in some ways. Independent, critical of self and others,

Preciosa, 5- Maintains a high dream. Good deed doer. A free spirit, very adaptable. Self-expressive, cheerful. Blessed in some ways. Natural counselor and healer. Charming and devoted. Independent, critical of self and others.

Precious, 7- Level headed. Gentle, kind, a hard worker. Not easily fooled. Self-expressive, cheerful. Blessed in some ways. Natural counselor and healer. Youthful, appealing. Charming and devoted.

Prentice, 9- Gift for understanding others. Gentle, kind, a hard worker. A free spirit, very adaptable. Original and unconventional. Dynamic, busy lifestyle. Blessed in some ways. Self-expressive, cheerful. Loves adventure and excitement.

Prescott, 8- Enjoys rivalry and challenge. Intense inner power. Original, creative. Passionate and loving. Self-expressive, cheerful. Natural counselor and healer. Dynamic, busy lifestyle. Sensitive and easily hurt.

Presley, 10- Strives for excellence. Diligent, hard working. Likes change and variety. Charming and devoted. Strong verbal skills. Loves adventure and excitement. Dislikes limitations.

Preston, 8- Enjoys rivalry and challenge. Intense inner power. Original, creative. Passionate and loving. Dynamic, busy lifestyle. Natural counselor and healer. Original and unconventional.

Price, 6- Needs harmony and beauty. Duty bound, self-sacrificing. Artistic, having good taste. Self-expressive, cheerful. A free spirit, very adaptable.

Pricilla, 8- Enjoys rivalry and challenge. Intense inner power. Blessed in some ways. Self-expressive, cheerful. Artistic, having good taste. Communicates skillfully. Ups and downs financially. Resolute and purposeful.

Princess, 4- Bit of a homebody. Gentle, kind, a hard worker. Blessed in some ways. Original and unconventional. Self-expressive, cheerful. A free spirit, very adaptable. Charming and devoted. Impulsive and extreme.

Priscilla, 9- Gift for understanding others. Gentle, kind, a hard worker. Blessed in some ways. Charming and devoted. Self-expressive, cheerful. Artistic, having good taste. Strong verbal skills. Ups and downs financially. Helpful, sincere.

Proctor, 6- Needs harmony and beauty. Duty bound, self-sacrificing. Natural counselor and healer. Self-expressive and cheerful. Dynamic, busy lifestyle. May have musical abilities. Gentle, kind, a hard worker.

Pru, 10- Strives for excellence. Gentle, kind, a hard worker. Attractive and charming.

Prudence, 5- Maintains a high dream. Good deed doer. Youthful, appealing. Reliable, responsible. A free spirit, very adaptable. Original and unconventional. Self-expressive, cheerful. Physical and passionate.

Prudy, 30- Optimistic in faith. Sympathetic, kind. Attractive and charming. Reliable, responsible. Needs a lot of freedom.

Prunella, 9- Gift for understanding others. Gentle, kind, a hard worker. Attractive and charming. Original and unconventional. A free spirit, very adaptable. Great verbal skills. Frequent traveler. Helpful, sincere.

Pryce, 4- Bit of a homebody. Gentle, kind, a hard worker. Needs a lot of freedom. Self-expressive, cheerful. Loves adventure and excitement.

Pryor, 11- Knowledgeable in many areas. Gentle, kind, a hard worker. Needs a lot of freedom. Natural counselor and healer. Tendency to lose items.

Pulani, 10- Strives for excellence. Attractive and charming. Great verbal skills. Independent, critical of self and others. Original and unconventional. Blessed in some ways.

Punky, 6- Needs harmony and beauty. Creative, inspiring. Original and unconventional. Strong desire to succeed. Needs a lot of freedom.

Purcell, 6- Needs harmony and beauty. Creative, inspiring. Gentle, kind, a hard worker. Self-expressive, cheerful. A step ahead of others. Communicates skillfully. Frequent traveler.

Putnam, 22- Knowledgeable in many areas. Attractive and charming. Dynamic, busy lifestyle. Original and unconventional. Ambitious leader, great vision. Domestic, hard working.

> "Helping the little lady along, are you, my fine gentlemen? Well, stay away from her! Or I'll stuff a mattress with you! And you! I'll Use you for a bee-hive!"
> ~*Excerpted from "The Wizard of Oz"*
> *Used with permission*

Q

IF A NAME BEGINS WITH Q, has more than one Q, or ends with a Q, this person attracts money and wealth, has a natural authority, and has the ability to influence others.

The letter Q is the 17th letter of the alphabet. 1+7=8, so the 17th letter has the same vibrational influence as the number 8, similar to it's sibling letters, H and Z. It's more highly evolved than the H, but more youthful than the Z as the 3 ruled U tends to accompany this letter more often than not. The 1 rules beginnings, 7 rules religion, and 8 rules rewards. So in many ways the Q person is beginning to have faith which will bring rewards. Since Q is ruled by the number 8 vibration, which is Scorpio-like, there can be many changes beyond their control. This depends on the karmic lessons they have brought to themselves. Although they prefer to be in control, there must be a certain amount of prayer work and faith before the reward comes into play. Still, Q's have a natural authority. Others seem to respect Q automatically, because it is a rare letter, not often seen, and has that intimidating, unpredictable Scorpio-type energy.

Q anywhere in a person's name is seldom seen without the letter U immediately following. This can make the Q person a victim of gossip. U is a communication letter and Q is Scorpio-like with its stinger tail, so the world of media can be pretty cruel to anyone with the Qu combination in their name. This also makes the person with these letters in their name outspoken, if not brutally honest. Although some of the Q's are boring and compulsive talkers, most with the Qu are extremely impressive with a talent for oration. Similar to H and Z, this letter likes to delegate authority and be in control. This letter also, similar to it's alphabetical siblings H and Z, enjoys rivalry and competition.

Q plus U equal the master number 11, making "Queenie" a bit high strung and gives her a strong desire to be successful as she would have a hidden master number 11. Also 1+1=2, with the Q and U making a good partnership, since 2 rules partnerships. Rarely is Q seen without its partner U. Q names are rare in and of themselves, with Quincy or Quentin for a boy or Quinta or Questa for a girl. Even these familiar Q names are not at all common.

In the psychology of sales, we know that when a salesperson asks a question, they are in control. Whoever asks the most questions controls the conversation. This is why children seem to always be in control! The very word, "question" starts with a Q which is ruled by the controlling Scorpio-like 8. Next to a young, attractive and charming U, really, how can we get mad? This same thinking is how the Qu person moves ahead. The U likes to intellectualize, so they may need time to make decisions. Still, the Q person seems to be able to hold our interest and control the outcome, making them more sexy, attractive and charming than the others.

In fact, this combination is similar to that of the CH combination and may be compatible to those with a CH in their names. I know a young boy named Chris who gets along very well with a boy in his class named Quentin. They probably get along well because their personalities are similar in some ways. They are able to relate to one another because C and U are ruled by the same number 3 and H and Q are ruled by the same number 8. The beginning of their names are compatible.

Quentin Tarantino is a director, actor and writer. His most familiar films include "Pulp Fiction" and "Kill Bill." Interestingly enough, he's an Aries, which is the first sun sign of the Zodiac. His first name adds up to a 10 power number; 1+0=1, an Aries number. Also his nickname, "QT" adds up to a 10. The 1 rules beginnings, which is Aries-like. The 0 rules assistance from God, which means he personally receives assistance from God. The 0 is an all or nothing number. It seems everything is happening all at once, or nothing is happening at all. So this very famous director must take advantage of his extremely busy "all" while it's here, before he gets a lot of "nothing" going on, according to nameology. The Q is ruled by number 8 which is materialistic, so, chances are, he's smart about managing his money. The U is a very lucky letter, so he may have been able to cash in on some of that luck. Talk about luck, the numbers 3, 5 and 8 tend to be lucky. Also these numbers tend to be associated with ups and downs financially. He has all 3 of these numbers in his first name. Consequently, he may have many ups and downs his whole life in the area of finances. Quentin has an intensity 5 in his name with the E and 2 N's. During a television interview shortly after the first "Kill Bill" movie was released, he mentioned, "I wanted this movie to be entertaining ..." That would be the intensity 5 in his name. He's not afraid to take chances and be unusual in his delivery. Rock stars and strippers often have an intensity 5 in their names. His name says his personality is freedom loving, unconventional, charming, sexy and in control. What a combination!

Another famous Q name is Quincy Jones, Producer, Director, and Composer of music. He wrote television theme music for "Ironside," "Sanford and Son," and "The Bill Cosby Show." He also produced Michael Jackson's first solo album, "Off the Wall," then teamed up again to produce "Thriller." Q names always have a hidden master number 11 in them as the Q is an 8 and the U is a 3, which sums up to an 11. The pitfall of the 8 and the 3 is, once again, having ups and downs financially. This aspect of Quincy's name almost put him out of business, if it weren't for the lucky U bringing help in the form of a loan at a critical time in his life. The I right next to his U blesses him in the area of youth. He may have been lucky as a youth, or in working with young people. The I also gives him good taste as well as natural artistic ability, which he demonstrated time and again through his work with music. The Y at the end of his name makes him need a lot of freedom. Quincy adds up to an 8 power number, so he's a survivor. No matter what, he will survive to receive his rewards. The Scorpio-like 8 ruled letter Q sometimes gives the bearer a brush with death to help them know how truly fortunate they really are.

Quinn Cummings was a child star in the 70's. Because of the youthful U as a first vowel, Q people tend to have something to do with the young. In Quinn's case, she was a child actress. Now an adult with a young child herself, she is known to have invented the "Hip Hugger," a cling-like baby carrier. With her name adding up to a power number 30, she now works with writers to publish short stories on-line. The number 3 is the number for writers and 0 is assistance from God, so she must be a tremendous help to new writers with her wise and inspired counseling.

Some famous "Q" names: Queen Latifah, Quentin Tarentino, Quinn Cummings, Quincy Jones. Famous person with a Q in his name: Shaquille O'Neal, "Shaq."

Quick Reference of "Q" Names

Quartus, 9- Highly evolved. Easy going attitude. Helpful, sincere. Gentle, kind, a hard worker. Dynamic, busy lifestyle. Very lucky. Charming and devoted.

Queena, 9- Highly evolved. Easy going attitude. A free spirit, very adaptable. Physical and passionate. Original and unconventional. Independent, critical of self and others.

Queenie, 4- Constructive, helpful. Gracious, well mannered. A free spirit, very adaptable. Physical and passionate. Original and unconventional. Blessed in some ways. Loves adventure and excitement.

Quenby, 30- Direct and outspoken. Youthful, appealing. A free spirit, very adaptable. Original and unconventional. Friendly, but shy. Dislikes limitations.

Quenelle, 10- A strong leader. Attractive and charming. A free spirit, very adaptable. Original and unconventional. Physical and passionate. Strong verbal skills. Frequent traveler. Loves adventure and excitement.

Quenelles, 11- Potential to achieve greatness. Creative, inspiring. A free spirit, very adaptable. Original and unconventional. Physical and passionate. Strong verbal skills. Frequent traveler. Loves adventure and excitement. Charming and devoted.

Quennel, 7- Often misunderstood. Stylish and refined. Not easily fooled. Original and unconventional. Romantic, sensual. Likes change and variety. Great verbal skills.

Quent, 5- Sudden losses and gains. Fun, flirtatious. Physical and passionate. Original and unconventional. Dynamic, busy lifestyle.

Quentin, 10- A strong leader. Attractive and charming. A free spirit, very adaptable. Original and unconventional. Dynamic, busy lifestyle. Blessed in some ways. Romantic, sensual.

Quenton, 7- Often misunderstood. Stylish and refined. Not easily fooled. Original and unconventional. Dynamic, busy lifestyle. Natural counselor and healer. Romantic, sensual.

Questa, 20- Highly developed sense of tact. Social, charming. A free spirit, very adaptable. Many mood swings. Dynamic, busy lifestyle. Independent, critical of self and others.

Queta, 10- A strong leader. Attractive and charming. A free spirit, very adaptable. Dynamic, busy lifestyle. Independent, critical of self and others.

Quigley, 6- Ability to influence others. Idealistic in relationships. Artistic, having good taste. Scientific, philosophical. Great verbal skills. A free spirit, very adaptable. Dislikes limitations.

Quillion, 10- A strong leader. Attractive and charming. Blessed in some ways. Strong verbal skills. Frequent traveler. Artistic, having good taste. Natural counselor and healer. Original and unconventional.

Quinby, 7- Often misunderstood. Stylish and refined. Needs alone time. Original and unconventional. Friendly, but shy. Needs a lot of freedom.

Quincy, 8- A true survivor. Usually very lucky. Blessed in some ways. Original and unconventional. Self-expressive, cheerful. Needs a lot of freedom.

Quinn, 30- Direct and outspoken. Youthful, appealing. Considerate, understanding. Original and unconventional. Romantic, sensual.

Quinsy, 6- Ability to influence others. Idealistic in relationships. Artistic, having good taste. Original and unconventional. Many mood swings. Needs a lot of freedom.

Quint, 9- Highly evolved. Easy going attitude. Blessed in some ways. Original and unconventional. Dynamic, busy lifestyle.

Quinta, 10- A strong leader. Attractive and charming. Blessed in some ways. Original and unconventional. Dynamic, busy lifestyle. Independent, critical of self and others.

Quintana, 7- Often misunderstood. Stylish and refined. Needs alone time. Original and unconventional. Dynamic, busy lifestyle. Independent, critical of self and others. Romantic, sensual. Bold, courageous, a bit stubborn.

Quintin, 5- Sudden losses and gains. Fun, flirtatious. Generous, thoughtful. Original and unconventional. Dynamic, busy lifestyle. Artistic, having good taste. Romantic, sensual.

Quinton, 11- Potential to achieve greatness. Creative, inspiring. Blessed in some ways. Original and unconventional. Dynamic, busy lifestyle. Natural counselor and healer. Romantic, sensual.

Quirita, 5- Sudden losses and gains. Fun, flirtatious. Generous, thoughtful. Gentle, kind, a hard worker. Artistic, having good taste. Dynamic, busy lifestyle. Independent, critical of self and others.

> "Oh, you're the best friends anybody ever had! And it's funny, but I feel as if I've known you all the time. But I couldn't have, could I?"
> ~*Excerpted from "The Wizard of Oz"*
> *Used with permission*

R

IF A NAME BEGINS WITH R, has more than one R, or ends with an R, this person is kind, gentle, and works very hard for the good of the whole, but may need to practice tolerance.

The letter R is the 18th letter of the alphabet. 1+8=9, so the 18th letter has the same vibrational influence as the number 9. The 1 rules beginnings, 8 rules rewards and 9 rules completions. The person whose name begins with R is often beginning to receive rewards and completing a stage of learning in this lifetime. The 1 and 8 combination can produce a bit of a bully. Except for number 4, 1 and 8 are two of the harshest numbers. The number 9 is similar to the astrological sign Sagittarius which is ruled by the largest planet, Jupiter. Jupiter is more than twice as massive as all the other planets put together! So when a person with an R anywhere in their name enters a room, people somehow sense this bigness about them. The R ruled person can seem pretty large or intimidating, even unintentionally. They command respect, and usually get it. Similar to the I, they are blessed more than the rest. They often get away with being a little naughty because, even God sometimes looks the other way. Similar to Christians, they aren't perfect, just forgiven. Somehow, right or wrong, people will follow them and forgive or overlook their faults. R people are usually gentle, kind and hardworking. R's, similar to I's, are often placed upon a pedestal. They are at the end of their journey in some aspects of their development, and are given a little more lee way; okay, a lot more lee way. But who's going to argue with them when they've got God on their side?

The toughest task for the R ruled individual is to stay balanced and even tempered. Three 3's go into 9 making balance of utmost importance. They tend to over do things. If the R drinks, they'll over drink. Again, it's the Jupiter influence. Jupiter is the planet of abundance. The tendency of the R is to be overly optimistic or enthusiastic in almost everything; often making promises they can't keep. Still they have this intense inner power that enables them to work hard toward any goal. They'll do their job and everyone else's too. The R person is a humanitarian by nature and will work tirelessly for the good of the whole, without complaining and often without even a "Thank-you." Turning within for meditation or hypnosis can be a wonderful tool for any R ruled individual. Prayer also seems to help the R names. If they don't attempt to stay balanced by going within to meditate, they can become very critical and ill-tempered.

9 plus any number will condense down to the other number. For example: Raymond- R-9, A-1; when we add 9+1=10, which condenses down to 1, the 9 is colored by 1. So R is mutable. The letter R is a "go with the flow" letter which is easily influenced by the letter conjuncting, or next to it. 9 added to any number goes back into itself after condensing. This is why our R named friends are so diverse. R's can do almost anything the rest of the letters in their name allow them to do. They are heavily influenced by the letter next to it. Our alphabet only has two 9 ruled letters, unlike all the others having three. So these two

letters ruled by 9 are very special. Those completing a cycle of learning in this lifetime, usually have an R or I somewhere in their name.

If their name begins with Ri, as in Rick or Ir, as in Irene, they are especially blessed in some ways. Richey Rich, a cartoon character, is an example of the extremely blessed. This is because of the double 9, or intensity 9 in the beginning of his name. Intensity 9 names seem to have an artistic eye for beauty. People tend to look up to them or place them on a pedestal whether they are right or wrong. These types are especially idealistic, humanitarian and like to spread themselves out far and wide.

If their name begins with Ro, these names often, but not always, have a voice that carries. Some Robs and Roseannes don't need a megaphone to have a crowd hear them. This combination also makes for dynamic orators in the religious field. Robert Schuller, with his crystal cathedral is an excellent example of this type. The Ro names often make great singers as well. Usually they excel in providing a service of some kind and are more nurturing, as well as gifted counselors.

If their name begins with Ra, as in Ralph or Raquel, they will be more ambitious and independent. This combination is hard to beat. Actress, Raquel Welch is a bit more ambitious because of the Q, which is ruled by the materialistic 8. Also her name adds up to a power number 11 which encourages her desire for success. The Scorpio-like Q in her name conjuncting the attractive and charming U is responsible for her having so much sex appeal.

Talk about sex appeal, another sexy actress is Renee Zellweger. She seems to be a chameleon with the ability to change her looks and personality with every role. That would be the E's in her name. Renee has an intensity 5, causing her to prefer variety, change and adventure. She may secretly enjoy shocking or surprising others with all that 5 energy in her name. At the very least she's extremely adaptable.

Rex Harrison, an English actor who starred in "The Ghost and Mrs. Muir," and "My Fair Lady," and a variety of other productions also seems to like change. Rex adds up to a power number 20, so with him it's all or nothing with partnership and other people. It seems some of his greatest roles had to do with him and a partner, which would portray the power number 20: partnership and assistance from God.

Rudy Guilliani, former Mayer of New York City, has the attractive and charming U first vowel. The U gives him an above average ability to communicate. The D lends him toward being systematic and organized. The Y, well, he needs a lot of freedom. All together his name sums up to a 5 power number. 5 rules change; he made a lot of changes for the better in New York City. No city is really safe; New York City use to have a much higher crime rate before Rudy came along. Rudy changed all that. The R made him want to work for the good of the whole. He also proved to be gentle, kind and hardworking during the 911 ordeal. Although his term was up, he stayed on, working late into the nights to help everyone through the turmoil. He wouldn't leave his beloved city, New York, when it needed him most. This is typical of an R named person. They work for the whole, keeping the big picture in mind.

Those whose names begin with R, or have an R anywhere in their name, have a tendency to lose items or to be a little forgetful. They're not unlike the absent minded professor. If they lose something, they might look for days, ranting and raving, only to be embarrassed later when finding it exactly where they left it. R's are great at helping others; they see the big picture, often spreading themselves far and wide for the good of the whole. They could misplace their keys, or forget where they parked the car while out buying a present for you, but their heart is always in the right place.

Some other famous "R" names: Ralph Lauren, Rock Hudson, Robin Williams, Richard Gere, Richard Burton, Ron Howard, Rob Reiner, Rachel Hunter, Rod Stewart, Ralph Nader, Roberta Flack, Rob Thomas, Rosie O'Donnell, Roman Polanski, Rita Moreno, Rosa Parks, Richard Chamberlain, Rush

Limbaugh, Rob Lowe, R. Kelly, Rosemary Clooney, Richard Nixon, Rita Hayworth, Randolph W. Hearst, Rocky Marciano, Roy Rodgers, Robert Wagner, Russell Crow, Reba McEntire, Ray Charles, Rudolf Nureyev, Reese Witherspoon, Regis Philbin, Roger Moore, Robert Redford and Richard Dreyfuss.

Quick Reference of "R" Names

Rabi, 3- Sympathetic, kind. Aims to please. Friendly, but shy. Blessed in some ways.

Race, 9- Humanitarian, idealistic. Helpful, sincere. Self-expressive, cheerful. A free spirit, very adaptable.

Rachael, 30- Sympathetic, kind. Aims to please. Self-expressive, cheerful. Great judge of character. A free spirit, very adaptable. Strong verbal skills.

Rachel, 11- Strives to improve humanity. Intuitive, perceptive. Self-expressive, cheerful. Great judge of character. A free spirit, very adaptable. Communicates skillfully.

Rachelle, 10- Diligent, hard working. Independent, critical of self and others. Self-expressive, cheerful. Great judge of character. A free spirit, very adaptable. Communicates skillfully. Frequent traveler. Loves adventure and excitement.

Radcliff, 5- Good deed doer. Bright, adventuresome. Reliable, responsible. Optimistic, outspoken. Great verbal skills. Blessed in some ways. Self-sacrificing, loving. High moral standards.

Radcliffe, 10- Diligent, hard working. Independent, critical of self and others. Reliable, responsible. Self-expressive, cheerful. Strong verbal skills. Blessed in some ways. Self-sacrificing, loving. High moral standards. A free spirit, very adaptable.

Rae, 6- Duty bound, self-sacrificing. Pioneer and risk taker. A free spirit, very adaptable.

Rafael, 7- Spiritual, a truth seeker. Not easily influenced. Self-sacrificing, loving. Bold, courageous, a bit stubborn. A free spirit, very adaptable. Strong verbal skills.

Rafferty, 9- Humanitarian, idealistic. Helpful, sincere. Self-sacrificing, loving. High moral standards. A free spirit, very adaptable. Tendency to lose items. Dynamic, busy lifestyle. Dislikes limitations.

Rahim, 4- Strong and healthy. Natural teaching ability. Great judge of character. Blessed in some ways. Systematic, organized.

Rain, 6- Duty bound, self-sacrificing. Pioneer and risk taker. Artistic, having good taste. Creative and Opinionated.

Raina, 7- Spiritual, a truth seeker. Not easily influenced. Blessed in some ways. Original and unconventional. Bold, courageous, a bit stubborn.

Raini, 6- Duty bound, self-sacrificing. Pioneer and risk taker. Blessed in some ways. Original and unconventional. Idealistic and humanitarian.

Raisa, 3- Sympathetic, kind. Aims to please. Blessed in some ways. Charming and devoted. Bold, courageous, a bit stubborn.

Raizel, 8- Uses good judgment. Resolute and purposeful. Blessed in some ways. Uses common sense. A free spirit, very adaptable. Strong verbal skills.

Raleigh, 6- Duty bound, self-sacrificing. Pioneer and risk taker. Communicates skillfully. A free spirit, very adaptable. Blessed in some ways. Scientific and philosophical. Great judge of character.

Ralph, 10- Diligent, hard working. Independent, critical of self and others. Strong verbal skills. Intelligent and knowledgeable. Great judge of character.

Ralston, 9- Humanitarian, idealistic. Helpful, sincere. Strong verbal skills. Charming and devoted. Dynamic, busy lifestyle. Natural counselor and healer. Original and unconventional.

Rambert, 5- Good deed doer. Bright, adventuresome. Systematic, organized. Friendly, but shy. A free spirit, very adaptable. Tendency to lose items. Dynamic, busy lifestyle.

Rambo, 22- Strives to improve humanity. Ambitious leader, great vision. Systematic, organized. Friendly, but shy. Natural counselor and healer.

Ramon, 7- Spiritual, a truth seeker. Not easily influenced. Systematic, organized. Natural counselor and healer. Original and unconventional.

Ramona, 8- Uses good judgment. Resolute and purposeful. Systematic, organized. Natural counselor and healer. Original and unconventional. Bold, courageous, a bit stubborn.

Ramsey, 9- Humanitarian, idealistic. Helpful, sincere. Systematic, organized. Charming and devoted. A free spirit, very adaptable. Dislikes limitations.

Randall, 8- Uses good judgment. Resolute and purposeful. Creative, original. Reliable, responsible. Bold, courageous, a bit stubborn. Communicates skillfully. Travels frequently.

Randi, 10- Diligent, hard working. Independent, critical of self and others. Original and unconventional. Reliable, responsible. Blessed in some ways.

Randie, 6- Duty bound, self-sacrificing. Pioneer and risk taker. Creative, opinionated. Reliable, responsible. Blessed in some ways. A free spirit, very adaptable.

Randolf, 7- Spiritual, a truth seeker. Not easily influenced. Original and unconventional. Reliable, responsible. Natural counselor and healer. Strong verbal skills. Self-sacrificing, loving.

Randolph, 7- Spiritual, a truth seeker. Not easily influenced. Original and unconventional. Reliable, responsible. Natural counselor and healer. Strong verbal skills. Intelligent, knowledgeable. Great judge of character.

Randy, 8- Uses good judgment. Resolute and purposeful. Creative, original. Reliable, responsible. Needs a lot of freedom.

Ranger, 9- Humanitarian, idealistic. Helpful, sincere. Original and unconventional. Scientific, philosophical. A free spirit, very adaptable. Tendency to lose items.

Rani, 6- Duty bound, self-sacrificing. Pioneer and risk taker. Creative, opinionated. Artistic, having good taste.

Ranice, 5- Good deed doer. Bright, adventuresome. Romantic, opinionated. Blessed in some ways. Self-expressive cheerful. A free spirit, very adaptable.

Ranit, 8- Uses good judgment. Resolute and purposeful. Original and unconventional. Blessed in some ways. Dynamic, busy lifestyle.

Ranita, 9- Humanitarian, idealistic. Helpful, sincere. Original and unconventional. Blessed in some ways. Dynamic, busy lifestyle. Bold, courageous, a bit stubborn.

Raoul, 22- Strives to improve humanity. Ambitious leader, great vision. Natural counselor and healer. Attractive and charming. Strong verbal skills.

Raphael, 7- Spiritual, a truth seeker. Not easily influenced. Intelligent, knowledgeable. Great judge of character. Bold, courageous, a bit stubborn. A free spirit, very adaptable. Strong verbal skills.

Raphaela, 8- Uses good judgment. Resolute and purposeful. Intelligent, knowledgeable. Great judge of character. Bold, courageous, a bit stubborn. A free spirit, very adaptable. Strong verbal skills. Pioneer and risk taker.

Raquel, 11- Strives to improve humanity. Intuitive, perceptive. Attracts wealth. Attractive and charming. A free spirit, very adaptable. Strong verbal skills.

Rasha, 20- Sensitive, emotional. Reads people easily. Charming and devoted. Great judge of character. Independent, critical of self and others.

Rashaad, 7- Spiritual, a truth seeker. Not easily influenced. Charming and devoted. Great judge of character. Bold, courageous, a bit stubborn. Pioneer and risk taker. Reliable, responsible.

Rashi, 10- Diligent, hard working. Independent, critical of self and others. Charming and devoted. Great judge of character. Blessed in some ways.

Rashid, 5- Good deed doer. Bright, adventuresome. Charming and devoted. Great judge of character. Blessed in some ways. Reliable, responsible.

Rashida, 6- Duty bound, self-sacrificing. Pioneer and risk taker. Charming and devoted. Great judge of character. Blessed in some ways. Reliable, responsible. Bold, courageous, a bit stubborn.

Ravi, 5- Good deed doer. Bright, adventuresome. Intuitive and inspired. Blessed in some ways.

Rawling, 3- Sympathetic, kind. Aims to please. Likes to meet new people. Strong verbal skills. Blessed in some ways. Original and unconventional. Scientific and philosophical.

Ray, 8- Uses good judgment. Resolute and purposeful. Needs a lot of freedom.

Raye, 22- Strives to improve humanity. Ambitious leader, great vision. Needs a lot of freedom. Loves adventure and excitement.

Rayburn, 9- Humanitarian, idealistic. Helpful, sincere. Needs a lot of freedom. Friendly, but shy. Attractive and charming. Can be forgetful. Original and unconventional.

Raymond, 9- Humanitarian, idealistic. Helpful, sincere. Needs a lot of freedom. Systematic, organized. Natural counselor and healer. Original and unconventional. Reliable, responsible.

Rayna, 5- Good deed doer. Bright, adventuresome. Needs a lot of freedom. Romantic, opinionated. Bold, courageous, a bit stubborn.

Rayne, 9- Humanitarian, idealistic. Helpful, sincere. Stylish and refined. Creative and opinionated. Loves adventure and excitement.

Raynor, 10- Diligent, hard working. Independent, critical of self and others. Needs a lot of freedom. Original and unconventional. Natural counselor and healer. Tendency to lose items.

Read, 10- Diligent, hard working. Likes change and variety. Independent, critical of self and others. Reliable, responsible.

Reade, 6- Duty bound, self-sacrificing. A step ahead of others. Pioneer and risk taker. Reliable, responsible. Loves adventure and excitement.

Reagan, 10- Diligent, hard working. Likes change and variety. Independent, critical of self and others. Scientific and philosophical. Bold, courageous, a bit stubborn. Original and unconventional.

Reah, 5- Good deed doer. Physical and passionate. Resolute and purposeful. Great judge of character.

Reanna, 8- Uses good judgment. Original and creative. Resolute and purposeful. Original and unconventional. Romantic, sensual. Bold, courageous, a bit stubborn.

Reba, 8- Uses good judgment. Original and creative. Friendly, but shy. Resolute and purposeful.

Rebba, 10- Diligent, hard working. Likes change and variety. Friendly, but shy. Emotional, sensitive. Independent, critical of self and others.

Rebecca, 10- Diligent, hard working. Likes change and variety. Friendly, but shy. Likes change and variety. Self-expressive, cheerful. Outgoing, youthful outlook. Independent, critical of self and others.

Rebekah, 5- Good deed doer. Physical and passionate. Friendly, but shy. A free spirit, very adaptable. Strong desire to succeed. Bright, adventuresome. Great judge of character.

Red, 9- Humanitarian, idealistic. Enjoys giving gifts. Reliable, responsible.

Redd, 22- Strives to improve humanity. Has big plans and ideas. Reliable, responsible. Down-to-earth, faithful.

Redford, 7- Spiritual, a truth seeker. Not easily fooled. Reliable, responsible. Self-sacrificing, loving. Natural counselor and healer. May be forgetful. Reliable, responsible.

Redmond, 10- Diligent, hard working. Likes change and variety. Reliable, responsible. Systematic, organized. Natural counselor and healer. Original and unconventional. Down-to-earth, faithful.

Reece, 9- Humanitarian, idealistic. Enjoys giving gifts. A free spirit, adaptable to change. Self-expressive, cheerful. Loves adventure and excitement.

Reed, 5- Good deed doer. Physical and passionate. A free spirit, adaptable to change. Reliable, responsible.

Reena, 7- Spiritual, a truth seeker. Not easily fooled. Physical and passionate. Original and unconventional. Independent, critical of self and others.

Reeve, 10- Diligent, hard working. Likes change and variety. Physical and passionate. Intuitive and inspired. Loves adventure and excitement.

Regan, 9- Humanitarian, idealistic. Enjoys giving gifts. Scientific and philosophical. Independent, critical of self and others. Original and unconventional.

Reggie, 6- Duty bound, self-sacrificing. A step ahead of others. Has willpower and determination. Periodically needs solitude. Blessed in some ways. Loves adventure and excitement.

Regina, 9- Humanitarian, idealistic. Enjoys giving gifts. Scientific and philosophical. Blessed in some ways. Original and unconventional. Independent, critical of self and others.

Reginald, 7- Spiritual, a truth seeker. Not easily fooled. Scientific and philosophical. Blessed in some ways. Original and unconventional. Independent, critical of self and others. Strong verbal skills. Reliable, responsible.

Regis, 4- Strong and healthy. Accesses quickly. Has willpower and determination. Blessed in some ways. Charming and devoted.

Rei, 5- Good deed doer. Physical and passionate. Blessed in some ways.

Reid, 9- Humanitarian, idealistic. Enjoys giving gifts. Artistic, having good taste. Reliable, responsible.

Reiko, 4- Strong and healthy. Accesses quickly. Blessed in some ways. Strong desire to succeed. Natural counselor and healer.

Reina, 11- Strives to improve humanity. Keenly perceptive. Blessed in some ways. Original and unconventional. Independent, critical of self and others.

Remington, 7- Spiritual, a truth seeker. Not easily fooled. Systematic, organized. Blessed in some ways. Original and unconventional. Scientific and philosophical. Dynamic, busy lifestyle. Natural counselor and healer. Romantic, sensual.

Rena, 20- Sensitive, emotional. Social and entertaining. Original and unconventional. Reads people easily.

Renata, 5- Good deed doer. Physical and passionate. Creative and original. Bright, adventuresome. Dynamic, busy lifestyle. Bold, courageous, a bit stubborn.

Renato, 10- Diligent, hard working. Likes change and variety. Original and unconventional. Independent, critical of self and others. Dynamic, busy lifestyle. Natural counselor and healer.

Rene, 6- Duty bound, self-sacrificing. A step ahead of others. Creative and opinionated. Loves adventure and excitement.

Renee, 11- Strives to improve humanity. Keenly perceptive. Creative and opinionated. Physical and passionate. Loves adventure and excitement.

Reni, 10- Diligent, hard working. Likes change and variety. Original and unconventional. Blessed in some ways.

Renita, 4- Strong and healthy. Accesses quickly. Original and unconventional. Blessed in some ways. Dynamic, busy lifestyle. Independent, critical of self and others.

Renne, 11- Strives to improve humanity. Keenly perceptive. Original and unconventional. Romantic, sensual. A free spirit, very adaptable.

Rennie, 11- Strives to improve humanity. Keenly perceptive. Original and unconventional. Romantic, sensual. Blessed in some ways. Physical and passionate.

Reone, 30- Sympathetic, kind. A free spirit, very adaptable. Natural counselor and healer. Creative, opinionated. Physical and passionate.

Reseda, 7- Spiritual, a truth seeker. Not easily fooled. Charming and devoted. A free spirit, very adaptable. Reliable, responsible. Independent, critical of self and others.

Reuben, 11- Strives to improve humanity. Keenly perceptive. Attractive and charming. Friendly, but shy. Physical and passionate. Original and unconventional.

Reva, 10- Diligent, hard working. Likes change and variety. Intuitive and inspired. Independent, critical of self and others.

Rex, 20- Sensitive, emotional. Social and entertaining. Artistic, sensual, perceptive.

Rexana, 9- Humanitarian, idealistic. Enjoys giving gifts. Artistic, sensual, perceptive. Independent, critical of self and others. Original and unconventional. Bold, courageous, a bit stubborn.

Rexanne, 9- Humanitarian, idealistic. Enjoys giving gifts. Artistic, sensual, perceptive. Independent, critical of self and others. Original and unconventional. Creative, opinionated. A free spirit, adaptable to change.

Rexine, 3- Sympathetic, kind. A free spirit, very adaptable. Artistic, sensual, perceptive. Blessed in some ways. Original and unconventional. Physical and passionate.

Rey, 3- Sympathetic, kind. A free spirit, very adaptable. Dislikes limitations.

Reyla, 7- Spiritual, a truth seeker. Not easily fooled. Needs a lot of freedom. Communicates skillfully. Not easily fooled.

Reymundo, 7- Spiritual, a truth seeker. Not easily fooled. Needs a lot of freedom. Domestic, hard working. Attractive and charming. Original and unconventional. Reliable, responsible. Natural counselor and healer.

Reyna, 9- Idealistic, humanitarian. Enjoys giving gifts. Needs a lot of freedom. Original and unconventional. Helpful, sincere

Reynalda, 8- Uses good judgment. Original and creative. Dislikes limitations. Original and unconventional. Resolute and purposeful. Strong verbal skills. Reliable, responsible. Bold, courageous, a bit stubborn.

Reynard, 4- Strong and healthy. Accesses quickly. Dislikes limitations. Original and unconventional. Resolute and purposeful. Gentle, kind, a hard worker. Natural problem solver.

Rhett, 8- Uses good judgment. Great judge of character. Original and creative. Dynamic, busy lifestyle. Sensitive and easily hurt.

Rhoda, 10- Diligent, hard working. Self-reliant, successful. Natural counselor and healer. Reliable, responsible. Independent, critical of self and others.

Rhodes, 6- Duty bound, self-sacrificing. Creative in business. Magnetic personality. Reliable, responsible. A free spirit, very adaptable. Charming and devoted.

Rhodie, 5- Good deed doer. Makes and loses money easily. Natural counselor and healer. Reliable, responsible. Blessed in some ways. A free spirit, very adaptable.

Rhona, 11- Strives to improve humanity. Great judge of character. Creates group harmony. Original and unconventional. Intuitive, perceptive.

Rhonda, 6- Duty bound, self-sacrificing. Creative in business. Magnetic personality. Original and unconventional. Reliable, responsible. Independent, critical of self and others.

Ricardo, 5- Good deed doer. Generous, thoughtful. Optimistic, outspoken. Bright, adventuresome. Could be forgetful. Reliable, responsible. Natural counselor and healer.

Rich, 11- Strives to improve humanity. Blessed in some ways. Self-expressive, cheerful. Great judge of character.

Richard, 7- Spiritual, a truth seeker. Needs alone time. Self-expressive, cheerful. Great judge of character. Independent, critical of self and others. Could be forgetful. Reliable, responsible.

Richelle, 9- Humanitarian, idealistic. Blessed in some ways. Self-expressive, cheerful. Great judge of character. A free spirit, very adaptable. Strong verbal skills. Frequent traveler. Loves adventure and excitement.

Rick, 5- Good deed doer. Generous, thoughtful. Self-expressive, cheerful. Strong desire to succeed.

Ricky, 30- Sympathetic, kind. Considerate, understanding. Optimistic, outspoken. Strong desire to succeed. Needs a lot of freedom.

Rigo, 4- Strong and healthy. Blessed in some ways. Scientific and philosophical. Natural counselor and healer.

Riki, 11- Strives to improve humanity. Blessed in some ways. Strong desire to succeed. Artistic, having good taste.

Riley, 6- Duty bound self-sacrificing,. Artistic, having good taste. Communicates well. Likes change and variety. Needs a lot of freedom.

Rilla, 7- Spiritual, a truth seeker. Needs alone time. Great verbal skills. Frequent traveler. Not easily influenced.

Rina, 6- Duty bound, self-sacrificing. Artistic, having good taste. Original and unconventional. Pioneer and risk taker.

Rinaldo, 10- Diligent, hard working. Respectful, kind. Original and unconventional. Independent critical of self and others. Strong verbal skills. Reliable, responsible. Natural counselor and healer.

Riordan, 7- Spiritual, a truth seeker. Needs alone time. Natural counselor and healer. Could be forgetful. Reliable, responsible. Independent, critical of self and others. Original and unconventional.

Ripley, 4- Strong and healthy. Blessed in some ways. Intelligent, knowledgeable. Strong verbal skills. A free spirit, very adaptable. Dislikes limitations.

Risa, 20- Sensitive, emotional. Friendly, considerate. Charming and devoted. Reads people easily.

Rita, 3- Sympathetic, kind. Considerate, understanding. Dynamic, busy lifestyle. Aims to please.

Rito, 8- Uses good judgment. Gives practical gifts. Dynamic, busy lifestyle. Natural counselor and healer.

Riva, 5- Good deed doer. Generous, thoughtful. Intuitive and inspired. Bright, adventuresome.

Roan, 3- Sympathetic, kind. Nurturing, loving. Aims to please. Romantic and creative.

Roana, 22- Strives to improve humanity. Creates group harmony. Independent, self-motivated. Original and unconventional. Bold, courageous, a bit stubborn.

Roanna, 9- Humanitarian, idealistic. Natural counselor and healer. Helpful, sincere. Creative and opinionated. Romantic, sensual. Bold, courageous, a bit stubborn.

Roanne, 4- Strong and healthy. Assumes responsibility. Natural teaching ability. Original and unconventional. Romantic, sensual. A free spirit, very adaptable.

Roark, 9- Humanitarian, idealistic. Artistic, creative. Helpful, sincere. Could be forgetful. Strong desire to succeed.

Roarke, 5- Good deed doer. Enjoys working. Bright, adventuresome. Could be forgetful. Strong desire to succeed. A free spirit, very adaptable.

Rob, 8- Uses good judgment. Competitive in business. Enjoys luxury items.

Robbie, 6- Duty bound, self-sacrificing. Magnetic personality. Friendly, but shy. Emotional, sensitive. Blessed in some ways. A free spirit, very adaptable.

Robert, 6- Duty bound, self-sacrificing. Magnetic personality. Friendly, but shy. A free spirit, very adaptable. Could be forgetful. A free spirit, very adaptable. Dynamic, busy lifestyle.

Roberta, 7- Spiritual, a truth seeker. Open to opportunities. Gives moral support. A free spirit, very adaptable. Could be forgetful. A free spirit, very adaptable. Dynamic, busy lifestyle. Not easily influenced.

Robin, 4- Strong and healthy. Assumes responsibility. Friendly, but shy. Blessed in some ways. Original and unconventional.

Robyn, 11- Strives to improve humanity. Creates group harmony. Friendly, but shy. Needs a lot of freedom. Creative and original.

Rocco, 9- Humanitarian, idealistic. Artistic, creative. Self-expressive, cheerful. Outgoing, youthful outlook. Natural counselor and healer.

Rochella, 11- Strives to improve humanity. Creates group harmony. Self-expressive, cheerful. Great judge of character. A free spirit, very adaptable. Great verbal skills. Frequent traveler. Intuitive, perceptive.

Rochelle, 6- Duty bound, self-sacrificing. Magnetic personality. Optimistic, outspoken. Great judge of character. A free spirit, very adaptable. Strong verbal skills. Frequent traveler. Loves adventure and excitement.

Rochester, 3- Sympathetic, kind. Nurturing, loving. Self-expressive, cheerful. Great judge of character. A free spirit, very adaptable. Charming and devoted. Dynamic, busy lifestyle. Tendency to overindulge. Could be forgetful.

Rocio, 6- Duty bound, self-sacrificing. Magnetic personality. Self-expressive, cheerful. Blessed in some ways. Natural counselor and healer.

Rock, 20- Sensitive, emotional. Works well with others. Self-expressive, cheerful. Strong desire to succeed.

Rockley, 8- Uses good judgment. Competitive in business. Self-expressive, cheerful. Strong desire to succeed. Great verbal skills. A free spirit, very adaptable. Dislikes limitations.

Rockwell, 9- Humanitarian, idealistic. Artistic, creative. Optimistic, outspoken. Strong desire to succeed. Likes to meet new people. A free spirit, very adaptable. Great verbal skills. Frequent traveler.

Rod, 10- Diligent, hard working. Self-sacrificing, devoted. Domestic, practical.

Roderic, 9- Humanitarian, idealistic. Artistic, creative. Reliable, responsible. A free spirit, very adaptable. Could be forgetful. Blessed in some ways. Self-expressive, cheerful.

Roderick, 11- Strives to improve humanity. Creates group harmony. Reliable, responsible. A free spirit, very adaptable. Could be forgetful. Blessed in some ways. Self-expressive, cheerful. Strong desire to succeed.

Rodger, 4- Strong and healthy. Assumes responsibility. Reliable, responsible. Has willpower and determination. A free spirit, very adaptable. Gentle, kind, a hard worker.

Rodney, 9- Humanitarian, idealistic. Artistic, creative. Reliable, responsible. Opinionated, original. Physical and passionate. Needs a lot of freedom.

Rodrick, 6- Duty bound, self-sacrificing. Magnetic personality. Reliable, responsible. Could be forgetful. Blessed in some ways. Self-expressive, cheerful. Strong desire to succeed.

Roger, 9- Humanitarian, idealistic. Artistic, creative. Scientific and philosophical. A free spirit, very adaptable. Could be forgetful.

Rohana, 30- Sympathetic, kind. Nurturing, loving. Great judge of character. Independent, critical of self and others. Original and unconventional. Bold, courageous, a bit stubborn.

Rohelio, 10- Diligent, hard working. Self-sacrificing, devoted. Great judge of character. A free spirit, very adaptable. Strong verbal skills. Blessed in some ways. May have musical abilities.

Rohit, 7- Spiritual, a truth seeker. Open to opportunities. Great judge of character. Blessed in some ways. Dynamic, busy lifestyle.

Rola, 10- Diligent, hard working. Self-sacrificing, devoted. Great verbal skills. Independent, critical of self and others.

Roland, 10- Diligent, hard working. Self-sacrificing, devoted. Great verbal skills. Independent, critical of self and others. Creative and original. Domestic, responsible.

Rolanda, 11- Strives to improve humanity. Creates group harmony. Strong verbal skills. Independent, critical of self and others. Original and unconventional. Reliable, responsible. Bold, courageous, a bit stubborn.

Rolland, 4- Strong and healthy. Assumes responsibility. Strong verbal skills. Frequent traveler. Independent, critical of self and others. Original and unconventional. Reliable, responsible.

Rollo, 9- Humanitarian, idealistic. Artistic, creative. Strong verbal skills. Frequent traveler. Natural counselor and healer.

Rolls, 22- Strives to improve humanity. Creates group harmony. Strong verbal skills. Frequent traveler. Charming and devoted.

Rolf, 6- Duty bound, self-sacrificing. Magnetic personality. Strong verbal skills. Has musical abilities.

Rolph, 6- Duty bound, self-sacrificing. Magnetic personality. Strong verbal skills. Intelligent and knowledgeable. Great judge of character.

Roma, 8- Uses good judgment. Competitive in business. Domestic, responsible. Resolute and purposeful.

Romaine, 3- Sympathetic, kind. Nurturing, loving. Systematic, organized. Aims to please. Blessed in some ways. Romantic, creative. A free spirit, very adaptable.

Romala, 3- Sympathetic, kind. Nurturing, loving. Systematic, organized. Aims to please. Communicates skillfully. Bold, courageous, a bit stubborn.

Roman, 7- Spiritual, a truth seeker. Open to opportunities. Systematic, organized. Not easily influenced. Original and unconventional.

Romana, 8- Uses good judgment. Competitive in business. Domestic, responsible. Resolute and purposeful. Original and unconventional. Bold, courageous, a bit stubborn.

Romeo, 30- Sympathetic, kind. Nurturing, loving. Systematic, organized. A free spirit, very adaptable. Natural counselor and healer.

Romulus, 5- Good deed doer. Enjoys working. Creative entrepreneur. Attractive and charming. Strong verbal skills. Very lucky. Intense and extreme.

Ron, 20- Sensitive, emotional. Works well with others. Creative, romantic.

Rona, 3- Sympathetic, kind. Nurturing, loving. Creative, romantic. Independent, critical of self and others.

Ronald, 10- Diligent, hard working. Self-sacrificing, devoted. Opinionated, romantic. Independent, critical of self and others. Great verbal skills. Reliable, responsible.

Ronalda, 11- Strives to improve humanity. Creates group harmony. Original and unconventional. Intuitive, perceptive. Communicates skillfully. Reliable, responsible. Bold, courageous, a bit stubborn.

Ronan, 8- Uses good judgment. Competitive in business. Creative and original. Resolute and purposeful. Romantic, sensual.

Ronda, 7- Spiritual, a truth seeker. Natural counselor and healer. Original and unconventional. Independent, critical of self and others. Reliable, responsible. Not easily influenced.

Ronit, 4- Strong and healthy. Assumes responsibility. Original and unconventional. Blessed in some ways. Dynamic, busy lifestyle.

Ronnie, 10- Diligent, hard working. Self-sacrificing, devoted. Original and unconventional. Romantic, sensual. Blessed in some ways. A free spirit, very adaptable.

Ronny, 5- Good deed doer. Enjoys working. Original and unconventional. Romantic, sensual. Needs a lot of freedom.

Ronson, 5- Good deed doer. Enjoys working. Original and unconventional. Charming and devoted. Natural counselor and healer. Romantic, sensual.

Roper, 9- Humanitarian, idealistic. Artistic, creative. Intelligent and knowledgeable. A free spirit, very adaptable. Gentle, kind, a hard worker.

Rorie, 11- Strives to improve humanity. Creates group harmony. Gentle, kind, a hard worker. Blessed in some ways. A free spirit, very adaptable.

Rory, 4- Strong and healthy. Assumes responsibility. Gentle, kind, hardworking. Needs a lot of freedom.

Ros, 7- Spiritual, a truth seeker. Open to opportunities. Stylish and refined.

Rosa, 8- Uses good judgment. Competitive in business. Charming and devoted. Resolute and purposeful.

Rosabel, 9- Humanitarian, idealistic. Artistic, creative. Angelic leanings. Helpful and sincere. Friendly, but shy. A free spirit, very adaptable. Strong verbal skills.

Rosalee, 30- Sympathetic, kind. Nurturing, loving. Gift of gab. Aims to please. Strong verbal skills. A free spirit, very adaptable. Physical and passionate.

Rosaleen, 8- Uses good judgment. Competitive in business. Charming and devoted. Resolute and purposeful. Strong verbal skills. A free spirit, very adaptable. Physical and passionate. Original and unconventional.

Rosales, 8- Uses good judgment. Competitive in business. Charming and devoted. Resolute and purposeful. Strong verbal skills. A free spirit, very adaptable. Intense and extreme.

Rosalie, 7- Spiritual, a truth seeker. Open to opportunities. Stylish and refined. Not easily influenced. Strong verbal skills. Blessed in some ways. A free spirit, very adaptable.

Rosalind, 11- Strives to improve humanity. Creates group harmony. Charming and devoted. Intuitive, perceptive. Strong verbal skills. Blessed in some ways. Original and unconventional. Reliable, responsible.

Rosaline, 3- Sympathetic, kind. Nurturing, loving. Gift of gab. Aims to please. Strong verbal skills. Blessed in some ways. Original and unconventional. A free spirit, very adaptable.

Rosamond, 9- Humanitarian, idealistic. Artistic, creative. Angelic leanings. Helpful, sincere. Systematic, organized. Natural counselor and healer. Original and unconventional. Reliable, responsible.

Rosamund, 6- Duty bound, self-sacrificing. Magnetic personality. Completely devoted. Pioneer and risk taker. Systematic, organized. Attractive and charming. Creative, original. Reliable, responsible.

Rosana, 5- Good deed doer. Enjoys working. Charming and devoted. Independent, critical of self and others. Original and unconventional. Bold, courageous, a bit stubborn.

Rosanna, 10- Diligent, hard working. Self-sacrificing, devoted. Charming and devoted. Independent, critical of self and others. Original and unconventional. Romantic, sensual. Bold, courageous, a bit stubborn.

Rosario, 5- Good deed doer. Enjoys working. Charming and devoted. Independent, critical of self and others. Gentle, kind, a hard worker. Blessed in some ways. May have musical abilities.

Roscoe, 30- Sympathetic, kind. Nurturing, loving. Gift of gab. Self-expressive, cheerful. May have musical abilities. A free spirit, very adaptable.

Rose, 3- Sympathetic, kind. Nurturing, loving. Gift of gab. A free spirit, very adaptable.

Roseanna, 6- Duty bound, self-sacrificing. Magnetic personality. Charming and devoted. Physical and passionate. Resolute and purposeful. Creative and opinionated. Original and unconventional. Independent, self-motivated.

Roseanne, 10- Diligent, hard working. Self-sacrificing, devoted. Charming and devoted. A free spirit, very adaptable. Independent, critical of self and others. Original and unconventional. Romantic, sensual. Tendency to overindulge.

Rosel, 6- Duty bound, self-sacrificing. Magnetic personality. Charming and devoted. A free spirit, very adaptable. Strong verbal skills.

Roselani, 3- Sympathetic, kind. Nurturing, loving. Gift of gab. A free spirit, very adaptable. Strong verbal skills. Aims to please. Original and unconventional. Blessed in some ways.

Rosemarie, 4- Strong and healthy. Assumes responsibilities. Quickly sizes up situations. A free spirit, very adaptable. Systematic, organized. Pioneer and risk taker. May be forgetful. Blessed in some ways. Loves adventure and excitement.

Rosemary, 6- Duty bound, self-sacrificing. Magnetic personality. Charming and devoted. A free spirit, very adaptable. Systematic, organized. Pioneer and risk taker. May be forgetful. Dislikes limitations.

Rosie, 30- Sympathetic, kind. Nurturing, loving. Gift of gab. Blessed in some ways. A free spirit, very adaptable.

Rosita, 10- Diligent, hard working. Self-sacrificing, devoted. Charming and devoted. Blessed in some ways. Dynamic, busy lifestyle. Independent, critical of self and others.

Roslin, 6- Duty bound, self-sacrificing. Magnetic personality. Charming and devoted. Strong verbal skills. Blessed in some ways. Original and unconventional.

Roslyn, 4- Strong and healthy. Assumes responsibilities. Quickly sizes up situations. Strong verbal skills. Needs a lot of freedom. Original and unconventional.

Ross, 8- Uses good judgment. Competitive in business. Charming and devoted. Impulsive and extreme.

Rowena, 4- Strong and healthy. Assumes responsibilities. Likes to meet new people. A free spirit, very adaptable. Original and unconventional. Natural teaching abilities.

Rox, 3- Sympathetic, kind. Nurturing, loving. Artistic, sensual, perceptive.

Roxane, 5- Good deed doer. Enjoys working. Artistic, sensual, perceptive. Bright, adventuresome. Original and unconventional. A free spirit, very adaptable.

Roxanna, 6- Duty bound, self-sacrificing. Magnetic personality. Artistic, sensual, perceptive. Pioneer and risk taker. Original and unconventional. Creative, opinionated. Bold, courageous, a bit stubborn.

Roxanne, 10- Diligent, hard working. Self-sacrificing, devoted. Artistic, sensual, perceptive. Independent, critical of self and others. Original and unconventional. Creative, opinionated. A free spirit, very adaptable.

Roxette, 8- Uses good judgment. Competitive in business. Artistic, sensual, perceptive. A free spirit, very adaptable. Dynamic, busy lifestyle. Sensitive and easily hurt. Tendency to overindulge.

Roxie, 8- Uses good judgment. Competitive in business. Artistic, sensual, perceptive. Blessed in some ways. A free spirit, very adaptable.

Roxy, 10- Diligent, hard working. Self-sacrificing, devoted. Artistic, sensual, perceptive. Needs a lot of freedom.

Roy, 22- Strives to improve humanity. Creates group harmony. Needs a lot of freedom.

Royce, 30- Sympathetic, kind. Nurturing, loving. Needs a lot of freedom. Self-expressive, cheerful. Loves adventure and excitement.

Roz, 5- Good deed doer. Enjoys working. Uses common sense.

Rozalie, 5- Good deed doer. Enjoys working. Uses common sense. Bright, adventuresome. Strong verbal skills. Blessed in some ways. A free spirit, very adaptable.

Rozalinda, 10- Diligent, hard working. Self-sacrificing, devoted. Uses common sense. Independent, critical of self and others. Strong verbal skills. Blessed in some ways. Original and unconventional. Reliable, responsible. Bold, courageous, a bit stubborn.

Rozeanne, 8- Uses good judgment. Competitive in business. A great mediator. A free spirit, very adaptable. Resolute and purposeful. Original and unconventional. Romantic, sensual. Loves adventure and excitement.

Rube, 10- Diligent, hard working. Optimistic and outgoing. Anticipates next move. A free spirit, very adaptable.

Ruben, 6- Duty bound, self-sacrificing. Idealistic in relationships. Friendly, but shy. A free spirit, very adaptable. Original and unconventional.

Rubin, 10- Diligent, hard working. Optimistic and outgoing. Anticipates next move. Blessed in some ways. Creative and opinionated.

Rubentina, 5- Good deed doer. Fun, flirtatious. Friendly, but shy. Physical and passionate. Original and unconventional. Dynamic, busy lifestyle. Blessed in some ways. Romantic, sensual. Bright, adventuresome.

Ruby, 3- Sympathetic, kind. Youthful and appealing. Loyal and understanding. Needs a lot of freedom.

Rudolf, 4- Strong and healthy. Gracious, well mannered. Domestic, hardworking. Natural counselor and healer. Communicates skillfully. Self-sacrificing, loving.

Rudolph, 4- Strong and healthy. Gracious, well mannered. Domestic, hardworking. Natural counselor and healer. Communicates skillfully. Intelligent and knowledgeable. Great judge of character.

Rudy, 5- Good deed doer. Fun, flirtatious. Reliable, responsible. Needs a lot of freedom.

Ruel, 20- Sensitive, emotional. Attractive and charming. A free spirit, very adaptable. Strong verbal skills.

Rufina, 6- Duty bound, self-sacrificing. Idealistic in relationships. Magnetic, charming. Blessed in some ways. Original and unconventional. Independent, critical of self and others.

Rufus, 22- Strives to improve humanity. Creative and inspiring. Self-sacrificing, loving. Attractive and charming. Intense and Extreme.

Rumaldo, 30- Sympathetic, kind. Difficulty making decisions. Domestic, hard working. Pioneer and risk taker. Strong verbal skills. Down-to-earth, faithful. Natural counselor and healer.

Rumford, 5- Good deed doer. Fun, flirtatious. Systematic, organized. Self-sacrificing, loving. Natural counselor and healer. Tendency to lose items. Reliable, responsible.

Rupert, 8- Uses good judgment. Attractive and charming. Intelligent, knowledgeable. A free spirit, very adaptable. Tendency to lose items. Dynamic, busy lifestyle.

Rush, 3- Sympathetic, kind. Difficulty making decisions. Charming and devoted. Great judge of character.

Russ, 5- Good deed doer. Fun, flirtatious. Charming and devoted. Intense and extreme.

Russell, 7- Spiritual, a truth seeker. Stylish and refined. Charming and devoted. Intense and extreme. A free spirit, very adaptable. Strong verbal skills. Ups and downs financially.

Rust, 6- Duty bound, self-sacrificing. Idealistic in relationships. Charming and devoted. Dynamic, busy lifestyle.

Rusty, 22- Strives to improve humanity. Creative and inspiring. Charming and devoted. Dynamic, busy lifestyle. Needs a lot of freedom.

Ruta, 6- Duty bound, self-sacrificing. Idealistic in relationships. Dynamic, busy lifestyle. Independent, critical of self and others.

Ruth, 22- Strives to improve humanity. Creative and inspiring. Dynamic, busy lifestyle. Great judge of character.

Rutherford, 7- Spiritual, a truth seeker. Stylish and refined. Dynamic, busy lifestyle. Great judge of character. A free spirit, adaptable. Could be forgetful. High moral standards. Natural counselor and healer. Needs to practice tolerance. Reliable, responsible.

Rutley, 11- Strives to improve humanity. Attractive and charming. Dynamic, busy lifestyle. Strong verbal skills. A free spirit, very adaptable. Dislikes limitations.

Ry, 7- Spiritual, a truth seeker. Needs a lot of freedom. Influential.

Ryan, 22- Strives to improve humanity. Needs a lot of freedom. Independent, self-motivated. Original and creative.

Ryana, 5- Good deed doer. Needs a lot of freedom. Bright, adventuresome. Original and creative. Bold, courageous, a bit stubborn.

Ryann, 9- Humanitarian, idealistic. Needs a lot of freedom. Helpful, sincere. Original and opinionated. Romantic, sensual.

Ryanna, 10- Diligent, hard working. Needs a lot of freedom. Independent, critical of self and others. Original and unconventional. Romantic, sensual. Bold, courageous, a bit stubborn.

Ryder, 7- Spiritual, a truth seeker. Needs a lot of freedom. Reliable, responsible. Loves adventure and excitement. Gentle, kind, a hard worker.

> "Put 'em up! Put 'em ... up!
> Which one of you first? I'll fight
> you both together if you want! I'll fight
> you with one paw tied behind my back. I'll
> fight you standing on one foot."
> ~*Excerpted from "The Wizard of Oz"*
> *Used with permission*

S

IF A NAME BEGINS WITH S, has more than one S, or ends with an S, this person is charming, loving and devoted; however, they can be impulsive, extreme and exhibit mood swings.

The letter S is the 19th letter of the alphabet. 1+9=10, 1+0=1, so the 19th letter has the same vibrational influence as the number 1. The person whose name begins with S is often beginning a new stage of learning as well as completing a stage of learning in this lifetime. The 1 and 9 combination is very dynamic and charismatic. The energy of the 1 makes the S ruled person ambitious, competitive, energetic, confident and self-reliant. Similar to the letters A and J, they are perfectionists and their own worst critic, however, the 1 ruled S is more highly evolved than it's siblings A and J. Combining 1 with the 9 vibration gives them angelic "higher love" qualities. They are more broadminded and less prejudiced than most of the other letters. This rare combination can cause others to be jealous of them. They are capable of achievement and somehow blessed more than the rest of us. It just doesn't seem fair that the S person has so much going for them, and they are often good-looking too!

Before you start hating them, there is one flaw in their personality. With the 9 influence, the S person can have a balance problem. They need to take the time to carefully make the right choices. If they had a difficult childhood, it could be the reason they act in extreme ways. Remember the 9 won't be happy unless they can forgive others for past wrong doings. The inability to let go of the past creates many emotional ups and downs for this charming letter.

Simon Cowell, of "American Idol," a popular television show, not only gets away with being critical, but actually is in demand for it. S is ruled by the critical and independent number 1 vibration. It's natural and easy for him to criticize as his role on American Idol is to be one of the judges. It's not so much his talent to criticize that he's famous for, but for being 'real mean.' His nicknames are "Mr. Nasty" and "Judge Dread." Simon's name adds up to a power number 7 which can have a mean streak. Of all the numbers, 7 is capable of being the meanest. Power number 7's are truthseekers, which, consequently, is the quality that most people admire about Simon. Simon's not afraid to say what he feels to be truthful. The M in the center of his name is systematic and organized. He goes in and assesses the situation in a clinical, almost terminator fashion. His heart's desire letter, or first vowel, is an I. This influence helps him to get away with murder, if you will. People think he has all the answers and will follow him whether he's right or wrong with an I first vowel. The I first vowel also helps him to appreciate art. The O in his name makes him want to be his own boss. Although he can be mean, he can also be nurturing and healing. An O anywhere in a name will give the bearer a real need to give out love to children, pets, a garden or to manage over a group of people. There is a bit of nurturing and loving "parent" in Simon Cowell.

Hollywood's best known director, Steven Spielberg, fits his name well as Steven adds up to a 22 power number. 22 is a master number, the number for global enterprises. Those with this power number seem to have no limits. This well known producer, director and writer has directed films "Saving Private Ryan," "Schindler's List," "Jurassic Park," "Indiana Jones," "E.T.," and countless others. He is one of the wealthiest filmmakers in the world. Still his name begins with an S, which means he is charming and devoted. The T is ruled by the number 2 which is social and partnership oriented. The T is also dynamic and quite busy all the time. When we add these two letters together they sum up to a hidden 3. 3 is the writer and communicator. His hidden talent is the ability to communicate. Adding the 3 to his 5 ruled E adds up to a hidden 8. He is materialistically motivated. Also 3, 5 and 8 are the luckiest numbers to have for winning the lottery. He seems to ride the financial waves quite well, although he's no doubt had his pitfalls. Steven Spielberg has an intensity 5 in his name. Half of his name is ruled by letters that are ruled by the number 5 vibration. So taking chances are a part of his make up. He loves adventure and excitement. 5 rules change, so he's naturally prepared to make changes and is adaptable and adjustable to life's many ups and downs. Interestingly enough, V is the 22nd letter of the alphabet, giving validation to Steven's global mission in life. Not all Steven's are going to be this talented, however, the potential for greatness is there. This Steven has served his name well.

Sheryl Crow has a nice blend of letters in her first name. None of the numbers repeat themselves; in other words, she has no intensity numbers in her name. This means she doesn't have to repeat her lessons. Furthermore, Sheryl adds up to a 6 power number. Often those with a 6 anywhere in their name are musical as well as magnetic. She ends up getting the message across with an L at the end of her name. Communication is important and often her songs express her rather kicky, upbeat way of getting her point across. The S and H are sexually dynamic as well as her E first vowel. With all this at the beginning of her name, she leaves quite a lasting first impression.

Sean Connery and Sean P. Diddy Combs, share the same first name and celebrity status. Again we have a sexually attractive E first vowel. Both of these men are charming and devoted with an S in the beginning of their name. The name Sean adds up to a 3 power number. 3 is also the number for "temporary." Coupled with an intensity 5, which rules "change," explains why Sean Puff Daddy, P. Diddy, Diddy Combs keeps changing his name! Both men have a youthful outlook on life, no matter what their age. They each share the first two letters adding up to a hidden 6. This causes them to want to be their own boss, even if it isn't obvious. They are magnetic and have nurturing abilities. Both are natural counselors and healers. Add to the hidden 6 the 1 ruled A and we have a hidden 7 which likes the camera and could explain their ability to look so good on film. They are truth-seekers and value their privacy, although many may not see these qualities, as they are ruled by a hidden number. What better man to have played the sexy James Bond than Sean Connery with an intensity 5 in his first name. The intensity 5 is physical, passionate and loves adventure and excitement. Interesting that the name "James" also adds up to a 3 power number. He was perfect for the role, if only "temporary."

S people are often sexy and attractive. S is shaped like a snake; which in Chinese Astrology is symbolically defined as sexy, charming and seductive. S people are very much like that snake symbol. If you're in love with an S named person, then muster up your courage, because it takes a brave person to charm the S.

Some other famous S names are: Sammy Davis Jr., Sylvester Stallone, Sarah Ferguson, Suse Orman, Selma Hyatt, Sarah Jessica Parker, Sean Penn, Sandra Bullock, Sandra Dee, Steven Seagal, Shania Twain, Serena Williams, Samuel L. Jackson, Sting, Sandra Day O'Connor, Sidney Sheldon, Susan B. Anthony, Sally Field, Snoop Dog, Sidney Poitier, Sigmund Freud, Sela Ward, Scarlett Johansson, Samuel Goldwyn, Spiro Agnew, Sonny Bono, Sofia Loren, Shirley Temple, Spencer Tracy, Scott Carpenter, Steven Tyler, Spike Lee, Shirley Jones, Selma Blair, Shirley MacLaine, Stevie Nicks and Shia LeBeouf.

Quick Reference of "S" Names

Saba, 5- Extremely charming. Bright, adventuresome. Friendly, but shy. Bold, courageous, a bit stubborn.

Sabina, 10- Needs to be independent. Critical of self and others. Anticipates next move. Blessed in some ways. Original and unconventional. Bold, courageous, a bit stubborn.

Sabine, 5- Extremely charming. Bright, adventuresome. Friendly, but shy. Blessed in some ways. Original and unconventional. A free spirit, very adaptable.

Sabra, 5- Extremely charming. Bright, adventuresome. Friendly, but shy. Gentle, kind, a hard worker. Bold, courageous, a bit stubborn.

Sabrina, 10- Needs to be independent. Critical of self and others. Anticipates next move. Gentle, kind, a hard worker. Blessed in some ways. Original and unconventional. Bold, courageous, a bit stubborn.

Sacha, 5- Extremely charming. Bright, adventuresome. Self-expressive, cheerful. Great judge of character. Bold, courageous, a bit stubborn.

Sadelle, 22- A charismatic person. Ambitious leader, great vision. Reliable, responsible. A free spirit, very adaptable. Great verbal skills. Travels frequently. Physical and passionate.

Sadie, 20- Charming and devoted. Reads people easily. Reliable, responsible. Blessed in some ways. A free spirit, very adaptable.

Sadira, 7- An opportunist. Not easily influenced. Domestic, responsible. Blessed in some ways. Gentle, kind, a hard worker. Bold, courageous, a bit stubborn.

Sadye, 9- Angelic leanings. Helpful, sincere. Reliable, responsible. Needs a lot of freedom. Loves adventure and excitement.

Saeb, 9- Angelic leanings. Helpful, sincere. A free spirit, very adaptable. Friendly, but shy.

Sage, 5- Extremely charming. Bright, adventuresome. Scientific and philosophical. A free spirit, very adaptable.

Sahara, 3- Gift of gab. Aims to please. Great judge of character. Bold, courageous, a bit stubborn. Gentle, kind, a hard worker. Pioneer and risk taker.

Saira, 3- Gift of gab. Aims to please. Blessed in some ways. Gentle, kind, a hard worker. Bold, courageous, a bit stubborn.

Saki, 4- Quickly sizes up situations. Natural teaching ability. Strong desire to succeed. Blessed in some ways.

Sal, 5- Extremely charming. Bright, adventuresome. Communicates skillfully.

Salena, 7- An opportunist. Not easily influenced. Strong verbal skills. A free spirit, very adaptable. Creative and opinionated. Bold, courageous, a bit stubborn.

Sallie, 22- A charismatic person. Ambitious leader, great vision. Strong verbal skills. Frequent traveler. Blessed in some ways. A free spirit, very adaptable.

Sally, 6- Completely devoted. Pioneer and risk taker. Strong verbal skills. Frequent traveler. Needs a lot of freedom.

Salome, 20- Charming and devoted. Reads people easily. Strong verbal skills. Natural counselor and healer. Domestic and hard working. A free spirit, very adaptable.

Salvador, 11- A charismatic person. Intuitive, perceptive. Strong verbal skills. Intuitive and inspired. Bold, courageous, a bit stubborn. Reliable, responsible. Natural counselor and healer. Gentle, kind, a hard worker.

Salvatore, 5- Extremely charming. Bright, adventuresome. Strong verbal skills. Intuitive and inspired. Bold, courageous, a bit stubborn. Reliable, responsible. Natural counselor and healer. Gentle, kind, a hard worker. A free spirit, very adaptable.

Sam, 6- Completely devoted. Pioneer and risk taker. Systematic, organized.

Samantha, 5- Extremely charming. Bright, adventuresome. Domestic, hard working. Bold, courageous, a bit stubborn. Original and unconventional. Dynamic, busy lifestyle. Great judge of character. Pioneer and risk taker.

Samara, 8- Passionate and loving. Resolute and purposeful. Domestic, hard working. Bold, courageous, a bit stubborn. Gentle, kind, a hard worker. Pioneer and risk taker.

Sami, 6- Completely devoted. Pioneer and risk taker. Systematic, organized. Blessed in some ways.

Samina, 3- Gift of gab. Aims to please. Domestic, hard working. Blessed in some ways. Original and unconventional. Bold, courageous, a bit stubborn.

Samira, 7- An opportunist. Not easily influenced. Domestic, hard working. Blessed in some ways. Gentle, kind, a hard worker. Bold, courageous, a bit stubborn.

Sammie, 6- Completely devoted. Pioneer and risk taker. Systematic, organized. Desires financial security. Blessed in some ways. A free spirit, very adaptable.

Sammy, 8- Passionate and loving. Resolute and purposeful. Domestic, hard working. Desires financial security. Needs a lot of freedom.

Sampson, 7- An opportunist. Not easily influenced. Domestic, hard working. Intelligent and knowledgeable. Charming and devoted. Natural counselor and healer. Original and unconventional.

Samson, 6- Completely devoted. Pioneer and risk taker. Systematic, organized. Impulsive and extreme. Natural counselor and healer. Original and unconventional.

Samuel, 8- Passionate and loving. Resolute and purposeful. Domestic, hard working. Very lucky. A free spirit, very adaptable. Strong verbal skills.

Sancho, 6- Completely devoted. Pioneer and risk taker. Romantic, creative. Self-expressive, cheerful. Great judge of character. Natural counselor and healer.

Sandi, 20- Charming and devoted. Reads people easily. Original and unconventional. Reliable, responsible. Blessed in some ways.

Sandie, 7- An opportunist. Not easily influenced. Original and unconventional. Reliable, responsible. Blessed in some ways. A free spirit, very adaptable.

Sandra, 3- Gift of gab. Aims to please. Romantic, creative. Reliable, responsible. Gentle, kind, a hard worker. Bold, courageous, a bit stubborn.

Sandy, 9- Angelic leanings. Helpful, sincere. Original and unconventional. Reliable, responsible. Needs a lot of freedom.

Sanford, 5- Extremely charming. Bright, adventuresome. Original, opinionated. Self-sacrificing, loving. Natural counselor and healer. Gentle, kind, a hard worker. Reliable, responsible.

Santiago, 5- Extremely charming. Bright, adventuresome. Original and unconventional. Dynamic, busy lifestyle. Blessed in some ways. Bold, courageous, a bit stubborn. Scientific and philosophical. Natural counselor and healer.

Sapphire, 11- A charismatic person. Intuitive, perceptive. Intelligent and knowledgeable. Overly secretive, distant. Great judge of character. Blessed in some ways. Gentle, kind, a hard worker. A free spirit, very adaptable.

Sara, 3- Gift of gab. Aims to please. Gentle, kind, a hard worker. Independent, critical of self and others.

Sarah, 20- Charming and devoted. Reads people easily. Sensitive, emotional. Bold, courageous, a bit stubborn. Great judge of character.

Sargent, 30- Gift of gab. Aims to please. Gentle, kind, a hard worker. Stylish and refined. Physical and passionate. Original, opinionated. Dynamic, busy lifestyle.

Sari, 20- Charming and devoted. Reads people easily. Gentle, kind, a hard worker. Blessed in some ways.

Sarila, 6- Completely devoted. Pioneer and risk taker. Duty bound, self-sacrificing. Blessed in some ways. Strong verbal skills. Bold, courageous, a bit stubborn.

Sarita, 5- Extremely charming. Bright, adventuresome. Good deed doer. Blessed in some ways. Dynamic, busy lifestyle. Bold, courageous, a bit stubborn.

Sasha, 3- Gift of gab. Aims to please. Impulsive and extreme. Great judge of character. Bold, courageous, a bit stubborn.

Saul, 8- Passionate and loving. Resolute and purposeful. Attractive and charming. Strong verbal skills.

Savanah, 3- Gift of gab. Aims to please. Intuitive and inspired. Bold, courageous, a bit stubborn. Original and unconventional. Pioneer and risk taker. Great judge of character.

Savannah, 8- Passionate and loving. Resolute and purposeful. Intuitive and inspired. Bold, courageous, a bit stubborn. Original and unconventional. Romantic, sensual. Pioneer and risk taker. Great judge of character.

Saverio, 8- Passionate and loving. Resolute and purposeful. Intuitive and inspired. A free spirit, very adaptable. Gentle, kind, a hard worker. Blessed in some ways. Natural counselor and healer.

Scarlet, 6- Completely devoted. Optimistic, outspoken. Pioneer and risk taker. Gentle, kind, a hard worker. Strong verbal skills. A free spirit, very adaptable. Dynamic, busy lifestyle.

Scarlett, 8- Passionate and loving. Optimistic, outspoken. Resolute and purposeful. Intense inner power. Communicates skillfully. A free spirit, very adaptable. Dynamic, busy lifestyle. Sensitive and easily hurt.

Schuyler, 3- Gift of gab. Cheerful, lighthearted. Great judge of character. Attractive and charming. Needs a lot of freedom. Strong verbal skills. A free spirit, very adaptable. Gentle, kind, a hard worker.

Scot, 3- Gift of gab. Cheerful, lighthearted. Natural counselor and healer. Dynamic, busy lifestyle.

Scott, 5- Extremely charming. Optimistic, outspoken. Natural counselor and healer. Dynamic, busy lifestyle. Sensitive and easily hurt.

Scottie, 8- Passionate and loving. Optimistic, outspoken. Natural counselor and healer. Dynamic, busy lifestyle. Sensitive and easily hurt. Blessed in some ways. A free spirit, very adaptable.

Scotty, 3- Gift of gab. Cheerful, lighthearted. Natural counselor and healer. Dynamic, busy lifestyle. Sensitive and easily hurt. Needs a lot of freedom.

Seamus, 6- Completely devoted. A step ahead of others. Independent, critical of self and others. Domestic, hard working. Attractive and charming. Loving and devoted.

Sean, 3- Gift of gab. A free spirit, very adaptable. Aims to please. Romantic and creative.

Sebastian, 9- Angelic leanings. A true humanitarian. Friendly, but shy. Independent, critical of self and others. Impulsive and extreme. Dynamic, busy lifestyle. Artistic, having good taste. Bold, courageous, a bit stubborn. Original and unconventional.

Sedgewick, 5- Extremely charming. Physical and passionate. Reliable, responsible. Scientific and philosophical. A free spirit, adaptable to change. Likes to meet new people. Blessed in some ways. Optimistic, outspoken. Strong desire to succeed.

Sedgwick, 9- Angelic leanings. A true humanitarian. Reliable, responsible. Scientific and philosophical. Likes to meet new people. Blessed in some ways. Self-expressive, cheerful. Strong desire to succeed.

Seki, 8- Passionate and loving. Original and creative. Strong desire to succeed. Blessed in some ways.

Sela, 10- Needs to be independent. Likes change and variety. Great verbal skills. Critical of self and others.

Selby, 9- Angelic leanings. A true humanitarian. Strong verbal skills. Friendly, but shy. Dislikes limitations.

Seldon, 6- Completely devoted. A step ahead of others. Communicates well. Creative problem solver. Natural counselor and healer. Original and opinionated.

Selena, 20- Charming and devoted. Social and entertaining. Strong verbal skills. Physical and passionate. Original and unconventional. Reads people easily.

Selma, 5- Extremely charming. Physical and passionate. Strong verbal skills. Domestic, hard working. Bright, adventuresome.

Serena, 8- Passionate and loving. Original and creative. Gentle, kind, a hard worker. A free spirit, very adaptable. Opinionated and unconventional. Resolute and purposeful.

Serge, 9- Angelic leanings. A true humanitarian. Gentle, kind, a hard worker. Scientific and philosophical. Physical and passionate.

Setareh, 4- Quickly sizes up situations. Enjoys working. Dynamic, busy lifestyle. Independent, critical of self and others. Gentle, kind, a hard worker. A free spirit, very adaptable. Great judge of character.

Seth, 7- An opportunist. Not easily fooled. Dynamic, busy lifestyle. Great judge of character.

Seton, 10- Needs to be independent. Likes change and variety. Dynamic, busy lifestyle. Natural counselor and healer. Original and unconventional.

Sevag, 9- Angelic leanings. A true humanitarian. Intuitive and inspired. Helpful, sincere. Scientific and philosophical.

Seymour, 8- Passionate and loving. Original and creative. Dislikes limitations. Domestic, hard working. Natural counselor and healer. Attractive and charming. Intense inner power.

Shaina, 7- An opportunist. Perceptive, psychic. Not easily influenced. Blessed in some ways. Original and unconventional. Bold, courageous, a bit stubborn.

Shana, 7- An opportunist. Perceptive, psychic. Not easily influenced. Original and unconventional. Bold, courageous, a bit stubborn.

Shane, 20- Charming and devoted. Excellent mediator. Reads people easily. Romantic, sensual. A free spirit, very adaptable.

Shania, 7- (Same as Shaina.)

Shannon, 4- Quickly sizes up situations. Great judge of character. Natural teaching ability. Original and unconventional. Romantic, sensual. Natural counselor and healer. Creative, opinionated.

Sharai, 11- A charismatic person. Self-reliant, successful. Intuitive, perceptive. Gentle, kind, a hard worker. Bold, courageous, a bit stubborn. Blessed in some ways.

Shareen, 7- An opportunist. Perceptive, psychic. Not easily influenced. Gentle, kind, a hard worker. A free spirit, very adaptable. Physical and passionate. Creative and opinionated.

Shari, 10- Needs to be independent. Great judge of character. Critical of self and others. Gentle, kind, a hard worker. Blessed in some ways.

Sharletta, 5- Extremely charming. Very passionate. Bright, adventuresome. Gentle, kind, a hard worker. Strong verbal skills. A free spirit, very adaptable. Dynamic, busy lifestyle. Sensitive and easily hurt. Bold, courageous, a bit stubborn.

Sharon, 30- Gift of gab. Makes and loses money easily. Aims to please. Gentle, kind, a hard worker. Natural counselor and healer. Original and unconventional.

Sharyn, 4- Quickly sizes up situations. Great judge of character. Natural teaching ability. Gentle, kind, a hard worker. Needs a lot of freedom. Original and unconventional.

Shaun, 9- Angelic leanings. Enjoys helping others. Hardworking, sincere. Attractive and charming. Creative and original.

Shauna, 10- Needs to be independent. Great judge of character. Critical of self and others. Very lucky. Original and unconventional. Bold, courageous, a bit stubborn.

Shaunti, 11- A charismatic person. Self-reliant, successful. Independent, critical of self and others. Very lucky. Original and unconventional. Dynamic, busy lifestyle. Blessed in some ways.

Shawn, 20- Charming and devoted. Excellent mediator. Reads people easily. Works well with others. Romantic, opinionated.

Shawna, 3- Gift of gab. Makes and loses money easily. Aims to please. Likes to meet new people. Original and unconventional. Bold, courageous, a bit stubborn.

Shawnee, 30- Gift of gab. Makes and loses money easily. . Aims to please. Likes to meet new people. Original and unconventional. A free spirit, very adaptable. Tendency to overindulge.

Shawni, 11- A charismatic person. Self-reliant, successful. Intuitive, perceptive. Involved in major activities. Original and unconventional. Blessed in some ways.

Shawnti, 4- Quickly sizes up situations. Great judge of character. Natural teaching ability. Likes to meet new people. Original and unconventional. Dynamic, busy lifestyle. Blessed in some ways.

Shayna, 5- Extremely charming. Very passionate. Bright, adventuresome. Needs a lot of freedom. Original and unconventional. Bold, courageous, a bit stubborn.

Shea, 6- Completely devoted. Creative in business. Physical and passionate. Pioneer and risk taker.

Sheba, 8- Passionate and loving. Great judge of character. Original and creative. Friendly, but shy. Independent, critical of self and others.

Sheena, 7- An opportunist. Perceptive, psychic. Not easily fooled. Physical and passionate. Original and unconventional. Independent, critical of self and others.

Sheila, 9- Angelic leanings. Enjoys helping others. A free spirit, very adaptable. Blessed in some ways. Great verbal skills. Independent, critical of self and others.

Sheilah, 8- Passionate and loving. Great judge of character. Original and creative. Blessed in some ways. Strong verbal skills. Resolute and purposeful. Self-reliant, successful.

Shelby, 8- Passionate and loving. Great judge of character. Original and creative. Strong verbal skills. Friendly, but shy. Dislikes limitations.

Sheldon, 5- Extremely charming. Very passionate. A free spirit, very adaptable. Communicates skillfully. Reliable, responsible. Natural counselor and healer. Original and unconventional.

Shelly, 9- Angelic leanings. Enjoys helping others. A free spirit, very adaptable. Frequent traveler. Ups and downs financially. Dislikes limitations.

Shelley, 5- Extremely charming. Very passionate. A free spirit, very adaptable. Communicates skillfully. Many ups and downs financially. Tendency to overindulge. Dislikes limitations.

Shelton, 30- Gift of gab. Makes and loses money easily. A free spirit, very adaptable. Frequent traveler. Dynamic, busy lifestyle. Natural counselor and healer. Original and unconventional.

Sheri, 5- Extremely charming. Very passionate. A free spirit, very adaptable. Gentle, kind, a hard worker. Blessed in some ways.

Sherif, 11- A charismatic person. Great judge of character. A free spirit, very adaptable. Gentle, kind, a hard worker. Blessed in some ways. Self-sacrificing, loving.

Sherlock, 10- Needs to be independent. Great judge of character. Likes change and variety. Gentle, kind, a hard worker. Frequent traveler. Natural counselor and healer. Self-expressive, cheerful. Strong desire to succeed.

Sherman, 6- Completely devoted. Great judge of character. A step ahead of others. Gentle, kind, a hard worker. Systematic, organized. Independent, critical of self and others. Original and unconventional.

Sherri, 5- Extremely charming. Very passionate. A free spirit, very adaptable. Gentle, kind, a hard worker. Sometimes forgetful. Blessed in some ways.

Sherrill, 11- A charismatic person. Great judge of character. A free spirit, very adaptable. Gentle, kind, a hard worker. Sometimes forgetful. Blessed in some ways. Strong verbal skills. Travels frequently.

Sherry, 3- Gift of gab. Makes and loses money easily. A free spirit, very adaptable. Gentle, kind, a hard worker. Tendency to lose items. Dislikes limitations.

Sherwin, 6- Completely devoted. Creative in business. Physical and passionate. Gentle, kind, a hard worker. Likes to meet new people. Blessed in some ways. Original and opinionated.

Sheryl, 6- Completely devoted. Creative in business. A free spirit, very adaptable. Gentle, kind, a hard worker. Dislikes limitations. Strong verbal skills.

Shia, 10- Needs to be independent. Great judge of character. Blessed in some ways. Ambitious, critical of self and others.

Shifra, 7- An opportunist. Perceptive, psychic. Blessed in some ways. Devoted, loving. Gentle, kind, a hard worker. Not easily influenced.

Shilo, 9- Angelic leanings. Enjoys helping others. Blessed in some ways. Strong verbal skills. Natural counselor and healer.

Shipley, 4- Quickly sizes up situations. Great judge of character. Blessed in some ways. Intelligent and knowledgeable. Strong verbal skills. A free spirit, very adaptable. Dislikes limitations.

Shipuh, 9- Angelic leanings. Enjoys helping others. Blessed in some ways. Intelligent and knowledgeable. Attractive and charming. Self-reliant, successful.

Shirlee, 4- Quickly sizes up situations. Great judge of character. Blessed in some ways. Gentle, kind, a hard worker. Strong verbal skills. A free spirit, very adaptable. Likes change and variety.

Shirleen, 9- Angelic leanings. Enjoys helping others. Blessed in some ways. Gentle, kind, a hard worker. Strong verbal skills. A free spirit, very adaptable. Physical and passionate. Original and unconventional.

Shirlene, 9- (Same as Shirleen.)

Shirley, 6- Completely devoted. Creative in business. Artistic, having good taste. Gentle, kind, a hard worker. Strong verbal skills. A free spirit, very adaptable. Dislikes limitations.

Shizu, 11- A charismatic person. Self-reliant, successful. Blessed in some ways. A good mediator. Attractive and charming.

Sibil, 6- Completely devoted. Artistic, having good taste. Friendly, but shy. Blessed in some ways. Strong verbal skills.

Sibyl, 22- A charismatic person. Idealistic, humanitarian. Friendly, but shy. Needs a lot of freedom. Strong verbal skills.

Sid, 5- Extremely charming. Generous, thoughtful. Domestic, responsible.

Sidney, 4- Quickly sizes up situations. Blessed in some ways. Reliable, responsible. Original and unconventional. A free spirit, very adaptable. Dislikes limitations.

Siegfried, 10- Needs to be independent. Respectful, kind. Likes change and variety. Has willpower and determination. Self-sacrificing, loving. Gentle, kind, a hard worker. Artistic, having good taste. Physical and passionate. Natural authority.

Sigfried, 5- Extremely charming. Generous, thoughtful. Has willpower and determination. Self-sacrificing, loving. Gentle, kind, a hard worker. Artistic, having good taste. Physical and passionate. Natural authority.

Sigmund, 6- Completely devoted. Artistic, having good taste. Scientific and philosophical. Domestic, hard working. Very lucky. Original and unconventional. Reliable, responsible.

Silas, 6- Completely devoted. Artistic, having good taste. Strong verbal skills. Independent, critical of self and others. Many mood swings.

Silvano, 11- A charismatic person. Blessed in some ways. Frequent traveler. Intuitive and inspired. Independent, critical of self and others. Original and unconventional. Natural counselor and healer.

Silvester, 3- Gift of gab. Considerate, understanding. Communicates skillfully. Intuitive and inspired. Physical and passionate. Charming and devoted. Dynamic, busy lifestyle. Loves freedom and adventure. Gentle, kind, a hard worker.

Silvia, 9- Angelic leanings. Blessed in some ways. Strong verbal skills. Intuitive and inspired. Artistic, having good taste. Helpful, sincere.

Silvio, 5- Extremely charming. Generous, thoughtful. Communicates skillfully. Intuitive and inspired. Artistic, having good taste. Natural counselor and healer.

Sima, 6- Completely devoted. Artistic, having good taste. Domestic, hard working. Pioneer and risk taker.

Simon, 7- An opportunist. Needs alone time. Systematic, organized. Natural counselor and healer. Creative, opinionated.

Simone, 30- Gift of gab. Considerate, understanding. Domestic, hard working. Natural counselor and healer. Romantic, sensual. A free spirit, very adaptable.

Sinclair, 4- Quickly sizes up situations. Blessed in some ways. Original and unconventional. Self-expressive, cheerful. Communicates skillfully. Natural teaching ability. Artistic, having good taste. Gentle, kind, a hard worker.

Sisley, 8- Passionate and loving. Blessed in some ways. Charming and devoted. Strong verbal skills. Likes change and variety. Needs a lot of freedom.

Sissy, 10- Needs to be independent. Blessed in some ways. Charming and devoted. Impulsive and extreme. Needs a lot of freedom.

Skelly, 3- Gift of gab. Strong desire to succeed. A free spirit, very adaptable. Excellent verbal skills. Ups and downs financially. Dislikes limitations.

Skip, 10- Needs to be independent. Strong desire to succeed. Respectful, kind. Intelligent and knowledgeable.

Skipp, 8- Passionate and loving. Strong desire to succeed. Blessed in some ways. Intelligent and knowledgeable. Level headed.

Sky, 10- Needs to be independent. Strong desire to succeed. Needs a lot of freedom.

Skye, 6- Completely devoted. Strong desire to succeed. Needs a lot of freedom. A step ahead of others.

Skylar, 5- Extremely charming. Strong desire to succeed. Dislikes restrictions. Communicates skillfully. Bright, adventuresome. Gentle, kind, a hard worker.

Skyler, 9- Angelic leanings. Strong desire to succeed. Dislikes restrictions. Communicates skillfully. A free spirit, very adaptable. Gentle, kind, a hard worker.

Slade, 5- Extremely charming. Communicates skillfully. Bright, adventuresome. Reliable, responsible. A free spirit, very adaptable.

Sloan, 7- An opportunist. Strong verbal skills. Natural counselor and healer. Not easily influenced. Original and unconventional.

Sly, 11- A charismatic person. Communicates skillfully. Needs a lot of freedom.

Smedley, 11- A charismatic person. Domestic, hard working. Keenly perceptive. Reliable, responsible. Strong verbal skills. Physical and passionate. Needs a lot of freedom.

Sofia, 5- Extremely charming. Natural counselor and healer. Self-sacrificing, loving. Blessed in some ways. Independent, critical of self and others.

Sol, 10- Needs to be independent. Self-sacrificing, devoted. Strong verbal skills.

Solomon, 4- Quickly sizes up situations. Assumes responsibility. Strong verbal skills. Natural counselor and healer. Domestic, hard working. Has musical talent. Original and unconventional.

Sondra, 8- Passionate and loving. Competitive in business. Original and unconventional. Reliable, responsible. Gentle, kind, a hard worker. Resolute and purposeful.

Song, 10- Needs to be independent. Self-sacrificing, devoted. Creative and opinionated. Stylish and refined.

Sonia, 22- A charismatic person. Creates group harmony. Intuitive and creative. Blessed in some ways. Ambitious leader, great vision.

Sonja, 5- Extremely charming. Natural counselor and healer. Original and unconventional. Clever and talented. Bright, adventuresome.

Sonny, 6- Completely devoted. Magnetic personality. Creative, opinionated. Romantic, sensual. Needs a lot of freedom.

Sonya, 20- Charming and devoted. Works well with others. Original and unconventional. Needs a lot of freedom. Reads people easily.

Sophia, 5- Extremely charming. Natural counselor and healer. Intelligent and knowledgeable. Great judge of character. Blessed in some ways. Bright, adventuresome.

Sophie, 9- Angelic leanings. Artistic, creative. Level headed. Great judge of character. Blessed in some ways. A free spirit, very adaptable.

Sophey, 7- An opportunist. Natural counselor and healer. Stylish and refined. Great judge of character. Not easily fooled. Needs a lot of freedom.

Sophy, 11- A charismatic person. Creates group harmony. Intelligent and knowledgeable. Great judge of character. Needs a lot of freedom.

Spalding, 10- Needs to be independent. Intelligent and knowledgeable. Bold, courageous, a bit stubborn. Strong verbal skills. Reliable, responsible. Blessed in some ways. Original and unconventional. Scientific and philosophical.

Spangler, 11- A charismatic person. Highly refined intellect. Intuitive, perceptive. Original and unconventional. Scientific and philosophical. Strong verbal skills. A free spirit, very adaptable. Gentle, kind, a hard worker.

Spence, 8- Passionate and loving. Enjoys rivalry and challenge. A free spirit, very adaptable. Original and unconventional. Optimistic, outspoken. Likes change and variety.

Spencer, 8- Passionate and loving. Enjoys rivalry and challenge. A free spirit, very adaptable. Original and unconventional. Optimistic, outspoken. Likes change and variety. Gentle, kind, a hard worker.

Spike, 6- Completely devoted. Intelligent and knowledgeable. Blessed in some ways. Strong desire to succeed. A free spirit, very adaptable.

Spiro, 5- Extremely charming. Intelligent and knowledgeable. Blessed in some ways. Gentle, kind, a hard worker. Natural counselor and healer.

Spring, 11- A charismatic person. Highly refined intellect. Gentle, kind, a hard worker. Blessed in some ways. Creative and original. Scientific and philosophical.

Srila, 5- Extremely charming. Gentle, kind, a hard worker. Blessed in some ways. Strong verbal skills. Independent, critical of self and others.

Stacey, 10- Needs to be independent. Dynamic, busy lifestyle. Critical of self and others. Self-expressive, cheerful. A free spirit, very adaptable. Dislikes limitations.

Stacie, 3- Gift of gab. Dynamic, busy lifestyle. Aims to please. Optimistic, outspoken. Blessed in some ways. A free spirit, very adaptable.

Stacy, 5- Extremely charming. Energetic, highly charged. Bright, adventuresome. Self-expressive, cheerful. Needs a lot of freedom.

Stafford, 8- Passionate and loving. Dynamic, busy lifestyle. Resolute and purposeful. Self-sacrificing, loving. High moral standards. Natural counselor and healer. Gentle, kind, a hard worker. Reliable, responsible.

Stan, 9- Angelic leanings. Generous to a fault. Helpful, sincere. Original and unconventional.

Standish, 3- Gift of gab. Dynamic, busy lifestyle. Aims to please. Creative, opinionated. Reliable, responsible. Blessed in some ways. Impulsive and extreme. Great judge of character.

Stanford, 7- An opportunist. Dynamic, busy lifestyle. Not easily influenced. Original and unconventional. Self-sacrificing, loving. Natural counselor and healer. Gentle, kind, a hard worker. Reliable, responsible.

Stanislaus, 9- Angelic leanings. Generous to a fault. Helpful, sincere. Original and unconventional. Blessed in some ways. Charming and devoted. Strong verbal skills. Independent, critical of self and others. Attractive, flirtatious. Impulsive and extreme.

Stanley, 6- Completely devoted. Dynamic, busy lifestyle. Pioneer and risk taker. Romantic, opinionated. Strong verbal skills. A free spirit, very adaptable. Needs a lot of freedom.

Starr, 22- A charismatic person. Dynamic, busy lifestyle. Ambitious leader, great vision. Gentle, kind, a hard worker. Intense inner power.

Steadman, 5- Extremely charming. Energetic, highly charged. A free spirit, very adaptable. Bright, adventuresome. Reliable, responsible. Domestic, hard working. Bold, courageous, a bit stubborn. Romantic, opinionated.

Stefan, 20- Charming and devoted. Dynamic, busy lifestyle. Social, entertaining. Self-sacrificing, loving. Reads people easily. Creative, original.

Stefanie, 7- An opportunist. Perceptive, psychic. Not easily fooled. Self-sacrificing, loving. Independent, critical of self and others. Original and unconventional. Blessed in some ways. Likes change and variety.

Stella, 6- Completely devoted. Dynamic, busy lifestyle. A step ahead of others. Great verbal skills. Frequent traveler. Independent, critical of self and others.

Stephan, 11- A charismatic person. Dynamic, busy lifestyle. Keenly perceptive. Intelligent and knowledgeable. Great judge of character. Independent, critical of self and others. Original and creative.

Stephane, 7- An opportunist. Perceptive, psychic. Not easily fooled. Intelligent and knowledgeable. Great judge of character. Independent, critical of self and others. Original and unconventional. Physical and passionate.

Stephanie, 7- An opportunist. Perceptive, psychic. Not easily fooled. Intelligent and knowledgeable. Great judge of character. Independent, critical of self and others. Original and unconventional. Blessed in some ways. Physical and passionate.

Stephen, 6- Completely devoted. Dynamic, busy lifestyle. A step ahead of others. Intelligent and knowledgeable. Great judge of character. Physical and passionate. Original and unconventional.

Sterling, 5- Extremely charming. Energetic, highly charged. A free spirit, very adaptable. Gentle, kind, a hard worker. Strong verbal skills. Blessed in some ways. Creative, opinionated. Scientific and philosophical.

Steve, 8- Passionate and loving. Dynamic, busy lifestyle. Original, creative. Intuitive and inspired. Loves adventure and excitement.

Steven, 22- A charismatic person. An excellent mediator. Has big plans and ideas. Intuitive and inspired. Physical and passionate. Creative and opinionated.

Stevie, 8- Passionate and loving. Dynamic, busy lifestyle. A free spirit, very adaptable. Intuitive and inspired. Blessed in some ways. Loves adventure and excitement.

Stew, 4- Quickly sizes up situations. Dynamic, busy lifestyle. A free spirit, very adaptable. Likes to meet new people.

Stewart, 7- An opportunist. Perceptive, psychic. Not easily fooled. Likes to meet new people. Independent, critical of self and others. Gentle, kind, a hard worker. Sensitive and easily hurt.

Storm, 22- A charismatic person. An excellent mediator. Creates group harmony. Gentle, kind, a hard worker. Systematic, organized.

Stormy, 11- A charismatic person. An excellent mediator. Creates group harmony. Gentle, kind, a hard worker. Systematic, organized. Needs a lot of freedom.

Stu, 6- Completely devoted. Dynamic, busy lifestyle. Attractive and charming.

Stuart, 9- Angelic leanings. Dynamic, busy lifestyle. Attractive and charming. Helpful, sincere. Gentle, kind, a hard worker. Sensitive and easily hurt.

Sue, 9- Angelic leanings. Attractive and charming. A free spirit, very adaptable.

Suke, 11- A charismatic person. Creative and inspiring. Strong desire to succeed. A free spirit, very adaptable.

Suki, 6- Completely devoted. Idealistic in relationships. Strong desire to succeed. Blessed in some ways.

Sullivan, 11- A charismatic person. Creative and inspiring. Great verbal skills. Frequent traveler. Blessed in some ways. Intuitive and inspired. Intuitive, perceptive. Original and Romantic.

Summer, 8- Passionate and loving. Attractive and charming. Domestic, hardworking. Systematic, organized. A free spirit, very adaptable. Intense inner power.

Sunita, 3- Gift of gab. Youthful, appealing. Original and unconventional. Blessed in some ways. Dynamic, busy lifestyle. Aims to please.

Sunni, 5- Extremely charming. Attractive and charming. Original and unconventional. Romantic, sensual. Blessed in some ways.

Sunny, 3- Gift of gab. Youthful, appealing. Original and unconventional. Romantic, sensual. Needs a lot of freedom.

Susan, 11- A charismatic person. Attractive and charming. Impulsive and extreme. Intuitive, perceptive. Original and romantic.

Susana, 3- Gift of gab. Youthful, appealing. Impulsive and extreme. Aims to please. Original and creative. Bold, courageous, a bit stubborn.

Susanna, 8- Passionate and loving. Attractive and charming. Impulsive and extreme. Resolute and purposeful. Original and unconventional. Romantic, sensual. Bold, courageous, a bit stubborn.

Susannah, 7- An opportunist. Attractive and charming. Impulsive and extreme. Independent, critical of self and others. Original and unconventional. Romantic, sensual. Bold, courageous, a bit stubborn. Great judge of character.

Susanne, 3- Gift of gab. Youthful, appealing. Impulsive and extreme. Aims to please. Original and unconventional. Romantic, sensual. A free spirit, very adaptable.

Suse, 10- Needs to be independent. Optimistic, outgoing. Impulsive and extreme. A free spirit, very adaptable.

Susie, 10- Needs to be independent. Attractive and charming. Impulsive and extreme. Blessed in some ways. A free spirit, very adaptable.

Sutcliff, 6- Completely devoted. Idealistic in relationships. Dynamic, busy lifestyle. Self-expressive, cheerful. Strong verbal skills. Blessed in some ways. Self-sacrificing. Loving. High moral standards.

Suzann, 5- Extremely charming. Attractive and charming. Has high expectations. Independent, critical of self and others. Original and unconventional. Romantic, sensual.

Suzanna, 6- Completely devoted. Idealistic in relationships. Uses common sense. Independent, critical of self and others. Original and unconventional. Romantic, sensual. Bold, courageous, a bit stubborn.

Suzanne, 10- Needs to be independent. Optimistic, outgoing. Uses common sense. Independent, critical of self and others. Original and unconventional. Romantic, sensual. A free spirit, very adaptable.

Suzette, 8- Passionate and loving. Attractive and charming. Has great reflexes. A free spirit, very adaptable. Dynamic, busy lifestyle. Sensitive and easily hurt. Loves adventure and excitement.

Suzi, 3- Gift of gab. Youthful, appealing. Uses common sense. Blessed in some ways.

Suzie, 8- Passionate and loving. Attractive and charming. Has great reflexes. Blessed in some ways. A free spirit, very adaptable.

Suzy, 10- Needs to be independent. Attractive and charming. Uses common sense. Needs a lot of freedom.

Sven, 6- Completely devoted. Intuitive and inspired. A step ahead of others. Creative and opinionated.

Sweeney, 6- Completely devoted. Likes to meet new people. A step ahead of others. Tendency to overindulge. Original and unconventional. Physical and passionate. Needs a lot of freedom.

Swen, 7- An opportunist. Likes to meet new people. Not easily fooled. Romantic and sensual.

Sybil, 22- A charismatic person. Dislikes limitations. Friendly, but shy. Blessed in some ways. Great verbal skills.

Sybill, 7- An opportunist. Needs a lot of freedom. Friendly, but shy. Blessed in some ways. Great verbal skills. Frequent traveler.

Syd, 3- Gift of gab. Needs a lot of freedom. Domestic, responsible.

Sydney, 11- Charismatic person. Needs a lot of freedom. Reliable, responsible. Original and creative. Loves adventure and excitement. Highly perceptive.

Sylvester, 10- Needs to be independent. Dislikes limitations. Strong verbal skills. Intuitive and inspired. Loves adventure and excitement. Impulsive and extreme. Dynamic, busy lifestyle. A free spirit, very adaptable. Gentle, kind, a hard worker.

Sylvia, 7- An opportunist. Dislikes limitations. Strong verbal skills. Intuitive and inspired. Blessed in some ways. Not easily influenced.

Sylvie, 11- A charismatic person. Dislikes limitations. Strong verbal skills. Intuitive and inspired. Blessed in some ways. A free spirit, very adaptable.

> "... so she is! Well, bust my buttons! Why
> didn't you say that in the ... first place?
> That's a horse ... of a different color! Come on in!"
> ~Excerpted from "The Wizard of Oz"
> Used with permission

T

IF A NAME BEGINS WITH T, has more than one T, or ends with a T, this person is dynamic, social and has a very busy lifestyle. They need to force themselves to slow down and they can be overly sensitive.

The letter T is the 20th letter of the alphabet. 2+0=2, so the 20th letter has the same vibrational influence as the number 2; it's co-ruled by number 2. The person whose name begins with T is partnership oriented, and extremely protective of others. 2 rules partnership, 0 rules assistance from God, so invariably, the T ruled person is learning lessons in partnership and has times in their life when all or nothing is happening with partnerships, other people or social situations. Consequently, they are either very busy in their social life or with partners, or they have nothing going on at all. Of course, if it were up to them, they'd be constantly busy. This is what makes them so dynamic.

Similar to the number 2, the T ruled person seeks peace and harmony and avoids conflict whenever possible. If a T is anywhere in a person's name, they will automatically be more diplomatic and sensitive to the needs of others. They might be interested in psychic phenomena and numerology or other studies that allow them to have a better understanding of people. T named people are "people" people. Seldom do they enjoy being alone. If it were up to them, they'd always have a mate.

Those with a T anywhere in their name have a hustle-bustle kind of lifestyle. It's difficult for them to slow down as they like to add to their already busy schedule. They will be the first to volunteer when they already have a lot on their plate, and they usually manage to get it all done. T names sometimes need to force themselves to slow down! With all this dynamic energy and sensitivity, they can sometimes react too quickly and make the wrong decisions. Some of their wrong decisions are morally incorrect. This is what gives the reputation, "terrible two's" to the number 2 ruled letters. Similar to the 10th letter J, the 20th letter T has an assistance from God number 0, which can often pull them out of predicaments they get themselves into. Except for the T, God's assistance usually has something to do with partnerships or social situations. The typical T person is so charming and cuddly, one can't help but overlook their faults. You just have to love them. It's impossible to stay mad when they are being so cute.

Tom Hanks, Tom Cruise and Tom Jones have more than their first name in common. First of all, because their names start with a T, they each have a very dynamic and busy lifestyle. Also, they each are social and like to add to their already busy agendas. Because T is a 2 and the letter O is a 6, Toms have a hidden 8 in their name. 8 can be very sexy as it is similar to the sign Scorpio. This number is also materialistic, or let's just say, they like quality as opposed to quantity, or we could say; they like the finer things in life. An 8 anywhere in a name can give it's bearer an attitude of, "He who dies with the most toys wins!" Because the 8 is hidden, it's possible they are good at dabbling with stocks or other investments, but prefer to keep it to themselves.

As mentioned in the "O" section, an O anywhere in a name can lean toward musical abilities, as Tom Jones demonstrates. The T is similar to the letter B. Often these letters cling to ideas long after they have outlived their usefulness. In the case of Tom Jones, this quality is beneficial as it doesn't matter what he sings, his style never changes. He radiates sexuality with that hidden 8 and sings with a robust throaty voice that drives women wild. Still today, after over 30 years of performing, women throw their underwear at him while he's on stage.

Speaking of underwear, Tom Cruise's claim to fame was performing in the movie "Risky Business," where he played the part of a typical upscale teenager who worried about his grades and upsetting his parent's trust. He met a prostitute and ended up operating a business with her out of his parent's home while they were away. The sex and money fit in perfectly with Tom's hidden 8. Was it a coincidence Tom Cruise was cast so well in the movie "Top Gun?" The name of this movie has the same first two letters in it as Tom's first name. The movie "Top Gun" had death, ruled by 8, and airplanes, which are ruled by 3 as well. Tom adds up to a 3 power number; which among many things rules youthfulness or adolescence, and all forms of transportation (like airplanes), which helped Tom fit perfectly into both roles.

3 is a lucky power number as Tom Hanks found out. What started Tom Hank's career was that he couldn't get cast in a college play, but was invited by the director to go to Cleveland, which is where his career started. He's most known for playing conflicted regular guys in movies. 3 is the natural comedian and Tom Hanks generally plays characters that make us laugh, even when he's being serious. O first vowels like to be the boss. Power number 3 knows how to communicate, so it's no surprise that Tom Hanks is now directing films as well as acting in them.

Double T's in a name can create a whirlwind like the Tasmanian Devil of Looney Tunes. In a 2003 television interview with double-T Patty Duke, Patty mentioned that at one point she had to force herself to slowdown. At one time during her life she had too much going on and didn't know how to stop. She's an actress, mother, political activist for issues such as the ERA (equal rights amendment), Aids, and nuclear disarmament. T is the 20th letter, so it's an all or nothing letter; imagine 2 of them in a name, making a person busier than the Tasmanian Devil himself!

Tiger Woods is another dynamic, energetic T person. He's been golfing since he was old enough to walk. Tiger has a lot of 9's in his name which blesses him tremendously. He is quite a humanitarian according to his name, although "Tiger" adds up to a 5 power number, so he likes his freedom and loves adventure and excitement. The G in the middle of his name is what makes him look good on camera. So, no doubt we'll be seeing more of him in the film industry. He is already doing commercials and was recently cast in his first film.

Tina Turner also has been blessed with an I first vowel, however, her name adds up to an 8 power number, so she's sexy and a survivor. Although she loves people, the hidden 7 shows she needs her solitude as well. Dynamic as she is, Tina needs her solitude to commune with God. Also, with the I first vowel, she must forgive those who have hurt her in the past in order to be happy today.

T's make wonderful partners, but may be a little bewildered about parenthood at first. Unless they have some 6 ruled letters or numbers in their name. Similar to B names, they tend to become friends with their children later in life. As children, the T named can get their feelings hurt very easily and will need lots of hugs for healthy emotional development. Next to B's and K's, they are among the most affectionate of all the letters.

Similar to the letter B, T's wrote the book on partnership. If in love with a T, no need to look further. This is one of the best, most socially acceptable partners to be with. They'll protect you and stand by you no matter what. What more could anyone ask for in a partner?

Other famous T names are: Thomas Jefferson, Thomas Edison, Mother Teresa, Ted Danson, Theodore Roosevelt, Tony Danza, Tony Curtis, Tanya Tucker, Troy Donahue, Tyra Banks, Tara Reid, Tommy Lee, Tori Amos, Ted Williams, Tug McGraw, Tracey Ullman, Tommy Hilfiger, Ted Kennedy, Timothy Leary, Tony Bennett, Tyrone Power, Travis Twitt, Tracy Chapman, Tom Green and Truman Capote.

Quick Reference of "T" Names

Tabia, 6- Has business aptitude. Pioneer and risk taker. Friendly, but shy. Blessed in some ways. Bold, courageous, a bit stubborn.

Tabitha, 7- Perceptive, psychic. Not easily influenced. Friendly, but shy. Blessed in some ways. Sensitive and easily hurt. Great judge of character. Bold, courageous, a bit stubborn.

Taber, 10- Takes the initiative. Independent, critical of self and others. Anticipates next move. A free spirit, very adaptable. Gentle, kind, a hard worker.

Tabor, 20- Extremely social. Reads people easily. Friendly, but shy. Natural counselor and healer. Gentle, kind, a hard worker.

Tad, 7- Perceptive, psychic. Not easily influenced. Reliable, responsible.

Tae, 8- An excellent mediator. Resolute and purposeful. Physical and passionate.

Tahnee, 8- An excellent mediator. Resolute and purposeful. Great judge of character. Original and unconventional. Physical and passionate. Loves adventure and excitement.

Tai, 3- Always coming and going. Aims to please. Blessed in some ways.

Taima, 8- An excellent mediator. Resolute and purposeful. Blessed in some ways. Domestic, hard working. Bold, courageous, a bit stubborn.

Taj, 4- Busy family life. Natural teaching ability. Clever and talented.

Takara, 7- Perceptive, psychic. Not easily influenced. Strong desire to succeed. Bold, courageous, a bit stubborn. Gentle, kind, a hard worker. Pioneer and risk taker.

Tahlia, 6- Has business aptitude. Pioneer and risk taker. Great judge of character. Strong verbal skills. Blessed in some ways. Bold, courageous, a bit stubborn.

Talar, 7- Perceptive, psychic. Not easily influenced. Communicates skillfully. Not easily fooled. Gentle, kind, a hard worker.

Talia, 7- Perceptive, psychic. Not easily influenced. Communicates skillfully. Blessed in some ways. Bold, courageous, a bit stubborn.

Tallulah, 6- Has business aptitude. Pioneer and risk taker. Strong verbal skills. Ups and downs financially. Attractive and charming. Frequent traveler. Bold, courageous, a bit stubborn. Great judge of character.

Tally, 7- Perceptive, psychic. Not easily influenced. Strong verbal skills. Ups and downs financially. Needs a lot of freedom.

Talya, 5- Dynamic, busy lifestyle. Bright, adventuresome. Strong verbal skills. Needs a lot of freedom. Bold, courageous, a bit stubborn.

Tamar, 8- An excellent mediator. Resolute and purposeful. Patient, tolerant. Bold, courageous, a bit stubborn. Gentle, kind, a hard worker.

Tamara, 9- Generous to a fault. Helpful, sincere. Desires financial security. Bold, courageous, a bit stubborn. Gentle, kind, a hard worker. Pioneer and risk taker.

Tami, 7- Perceptive, psychic. Not easily influenced. Desires financial security. Blessed in some ways.

Tamica, 20- Needs to slow down. Reads people easily. Down-to-earth, practical. Blessed in some ways. Optimistic, outspoken. Independent, critical of self and others.

Tamilyn, 6- Has business aptitude. Pioneer and risk taker. Creative entrepreneur. Artistic, having good taste. Strong verbal skills. Needs a lot of freedom. Original and unconventional.

Tammi, 20- Extremely social. Reads people easily. Down-to-earth, practical. Domestic, hard working. Blessed in some ways.

Tammie, 7- Perceptive, psychic. Not easily influenced. Desires financial security. Domestic, hard working. Blessed in some ways. A free spirit, very adaptable.

Tammy, 8- An excellent mediator. Resolute and purposeful. Patient, tolerant. Domestic, hard working. Needs a lot of freedom.

Tani, 8- An excellent mediator. Resolute and purposeful. Romantic, sensual. Artistic, having good taste.

Tania, 9- Generous to a fault. Helpful, sincere. Creative and opinionated. Blessed in some ways. Pioneer and risk taker.

Tanisha, 9- Generous to a fault. Helpful, sincere. Creative and opinionated. Blessed in some ways. Charming and devoted. Great judge of character. Bold, courageous, a bit stubborn.

Tanja, 10- Takes the initiative. Independent, critical of self and others. Creative, opinionated. Clever and talented. Bold, courageous, a bit stubborn.

Tanner, 9- Generous to a fault. Helpful, sincere. Original and unconventional. Creative, opinionated. Physical and passionate. Gentle, kind, a hard worker.

Tanya, 7- Perceptive, psychic. Not easily influenced. Original and unconventional. Needs a lot of freedom. Bold, courageous, a bit stubborn.

Tara, 4- Busy family life. Natural teaching ability. Gentle, kind, a hard worker. Bold, courageous, a bit stubborn.

Taralyn, 10- Takes the initiative. Independent, critical of self and others. Gentle, kind, a hard worker. Bold, courageous, a bit stubborn. Strong verbal skills. Needs a lot of freedom. Creative and original.

Tarrah, 30- Always coming and going. Aims to please. Gentle, kind, a hard worker. May be forgetful. Bold, courageous, a bit stubborn. Great judge of character.

Taryn, 6- Has business aptitude. Aims to please. Gentle, kind, a hard worker. Needs a lot of freedom. Creative and original.

Tasha, 4- Busy family life. Natural teaching ability. Charming and devoted. Great judge of character. Bold, courageous, a bit stubborn.

Tashi, 3- Always coming and going. Aims to please. Charming and devoted. Great judge of character. Blessed in some ways.

Tate, 10- Takes the initiative. Independent, critical of self and others. Sensitive and easily hurt. A free spirit, very adaptable.

Tatiana, 3- Always coming and going. Aims to please. Sensitive and easily hurt. Blessed in some ways. Bold, courageous, a bit stubborn. Original and unconventional. Pioneer and risk taker.

Tatum, 3- Always coming and going. Aims to please. Sensitive and easily hurt. Attractive and charming. Domestic, hard working.

Tavis, 8- An excellent mediator. Resolute and purposeful. Intuitive and inspired. Blessed in some ways. Charming and devoted.

Tawnee, 5- Dynamic, busy lifestyle. Bright, adventuresome. Likes to meet new people. Original and unconventional. A free spirit, very adaptable. Physical and passionate.

Tawni, 22- A force of nature. Ambitious leader, great vision. Likes to meet new people. Original and romantic. Blessed in some ways.

Tawny, 20- Extremely social. Reads people easily. Likes to meet new people. Original and unconventional. Needs a lot of freedom.

Taylor, 10- Takes the initiative. Independent, critical of self and others. Needs a lot of freedom. Strong verbal skills. Natural counselor and healer. Gentle, kind, a hard worker.

Tayna, 7- Perceptive, psychic. Not easily influenced. Needs a lot of freedom. Original and unconventional. Bold, courageous, a bit stubborn.

Teah, 7- Perceptive, psychic. Not easily fooled. Resolute and purposeful. Great judge of character.

Ted, 11- A force of nature. Keenly perceptive. Domestic, responsible.

Teddy, 22- A force of nature. Has big plans and ideas. Reliable, responsible. Workaholic, determined. Needs a lot of freedom.

Teena, 9- Generous to a fault. A free spirit, very adaptable. Physical and passionate. Original and unconventional. Independent, critical of self and others.

Tempestt, 10- Takes the initiative. Likes change and variety. Domestic, hard working. Intelligent, knowledgeable. Loves adventure and excitement. Charming and devoted. Sensitive and easily hurt. Needs to slow down.

Templeton, 3- Always coming and going. A free spirit, very adaptable. Domestic, hard working. Intelligent, knowledgeable. Strong verbal skills. Loves adventure and excitement. Sensitive and easily hurt. Natural counselor and healer. Original and unconventional.

Tennyson, 9- Generous to a fault. A free spirit, very adaptable. Original and unconventional. Romantic, sensual. Needs a lot of freedom. Charming and devoted. Natural counselor and healer. Creative, opinionated.

Terence, 7- Perceptive, psychic. Not easily fooled. Gentle, kind, a hard worker. Physical and passionate. Original and unconventional. Self-expressive, cheerful. Loves adventure and excitement.

Teresa, 5- Dynamic, busy lifestyle. Perceptive, socially adept. Gentle, kind, a hard worker. Physical and passionate. Charming and devoted. Bright, adventuresome.

Teri, 7- Perceptive, psychic. Not easily fooled. Gentle, kind, a hard worker. Blessed in some ways.

Terrence, 7- Perceptive, psychic. Not easily fooled. Gentle, kind, a hard worker. Could be forgetful. Physical and passionate. Original and unconventional. Self-expressive, cheerful. Loves adventure and excitement.

Terri, 7- Perceptive, psychic. Not easily fooled. Gentle, kind, a hard worker. Could be forgetful. Blessed in some ways.

Terrill, 4- Busy family life. Accesses quickly. Diligent, hardworking. Could be forgetful. Blessed in some ways. Communicates skillfully. Frequent traveler.

Terry, 5- Dynamic, busy lifestyle. Perceptive, socially adept. Intense inner power. Could be forgetful. Needs a lot of freedom.

Tess, 9- Generous to a fault. A free spirit, very adaptable. Charming and devoted. Impulsive and extreme.

Tessa, 10- Takes the initiative. Likes change and variety. Charming and devoted. Impulsive and extreme. Independent, critical of self and others.

Tessie, 5- Dynamic, busy lifestyle. Perceptive, socially adept. Charming and devoted. Impulsive and extreme. Blessed in some ways. Physical and passionate.

Thad, 6- Has business aptitude. Creative in business. Pioneer and risk taker. Domestic, responsible.

Thaddea, 7- Perceptive, psychic. Great judge of character. Not easily influenced. Reliable, responsible. Workaholic, determined. A free spirit, very adaptable. Bold, courageous, a bit stubborn.

Thaddeus, 10- Takes the initiative. Sometimes a loner. Independent, critical of self and others. Reliable, responsible. Workaholic, determined. A free spirit, very adaptable. Attractive and charming. Very devoted.

Thalia, 6- Has business aptitude. Creative in business. Pioneer and risk taker. Strong verbal skills. Blessed in some ways. Bold, courageous, a bit stubborn.

Thao, 8- An excellent mediator. Enjoys competition. Resolute and purposeful. Natural counselor and healer.

Thatcher, 11- A force of nature. Self-reliant, successful. Independent, critical of self and others. Dynamic, busy lifestyle. Optimistic, outspoken. Great judge of character. A free spirit, very adaptable. Gentle, kind, a hard worker.

Thea, 7- Perceptive, psychic. Great judge of character. A free spirit, very adaptable. Not easily influenced.

Theda, 20- Extremely social. Excellent mediator. A free spirit, very adaptable. Practical, conservative. Reads people easily.

Thelma, 5- Dynamic, busy lifestyle. Very passionate. A free spirit, very adaptable. Strong verbal skills. Domestic, hard working. Bright, adventuresome.

Theo, 3- Always coming and going. Makes and loses money easily. A free spirit, very adaptable. Natural counselor and healer.

Theodora, 5- Dynamic, busy lifestyle. Very passionate. A free spirit, very adaptable. Natural counselor and healer. Reliable, responsible. Has musical talent. Gentle, kind, a hard worker. Independent, critical of self and others.

Theodore, 9- Generous to a fault. Great judge of character. A free spirit, very adaptable. Natural counselor and healer. Reliable, responsible. Has musical talent. Gentle, kind, a hard worker. Loves adventure and excitement.

Theresa, 4- Busy family life. Relies on own judgment. Accesses quickly. Gentle, kind, a hard worker. Loves adventure and excitement. Charming and devoted. Independent, critical of self and others.

Therese, 8- An excellent mediator. Great judge of character. Original and creative. Gentle, kind, a hard worker. Loves adventure and excitement. Charming and devoted. Physical and passionate.

Thia, 20- Extremely social. Excellent mediator. Blessed in some ways. Reads people easily.

Thomas, 22- A force of nature. Self-reliant, successful. Natural counselor and healer. Domestic, hard working. Ambitious leader, great vision. Charming and devoted.

Thor, 7- Perceptive, psychic. Great judge of character. Natural counselor and healer. Gentle, kind, a hard worker.

Thurman, 5- Dynamic, busy lifestyle. Very passionate. Attractive and charming. Gentle, kind, a hard worker. Systematic, organized. Bright, adventuresome. Creative, romantic.

Thurston, 9- Generous to a fault. Great judge of character. Attractive and charming. Gentle, kind, a hard worker. Charming and devoted. Sensitive and easily hurt. Natural counselor and healer. Original and unconventional.

Tia, 3- Always coming and going. Considerate, understanding. Aims to please, thoughtful.

Tiah, 20- Extremely social. Emotional, considerate. Reads people easily. An excellent mediator.

Tiana, 9- Generous to a fault. Blessed in some ways. Independent, critical of self and others. Original and unconventional. Bold, courageous, a bit stubborn.

Tiegh, 4- Busy family life. Blessed in some ways. A free spirit, very adaptable. Scientific and philosophical. Great judge of character.

Tifanie, 10- Takes the initiative. Respectful, kind. Self-sacrificing, loving. Independent, critical of self and others. Original and unconventional. Artistic, having good taste. A free spirit, very adaptable.

Tiff, 5- Dynamic, busy lifestyle. Generous, thoughtful. Self-sacrificing, loving. Has musical abilities.

Tiffany, 9- Generous to a fault. Blessed in some ways. Self-sacrificing, loving. Has musical abilities. Independent, critical of self and others. Original and unconventional. Needs a lot of freedom.

Tiffy, 30- Always coming and going. Considerate, understanding. Self-sacrificing, loving. Has musical abilities. Needs a lot of freedom.

Tilden, 10- Takes the initiative. Respectful, kind. Strong verbal skills. Natural authority. Physical and passionate. Original and unconventional.

Tillie, 4- Busy family life. Blessed in some ways. Communicates skillfully. Frequent traveler. Artistic, having good taste. A free spirit, very adaptable.

Tilly, 6- Has business aptitude. Artistic, having good taste. Communicates skillfully. Frequent traveler. Needs a lot of freedom.

Tim, 6- Has business aptitude. Artistic, having good taste. Domestic, hard working.

Timmy, 8- An excellent mediator. Blessed in some ways. Domestic, hard working. Systematic, organized. Needs a lot of freedom.

Timothy, 11- A force of nature. Intuitive, perceptive. Domestic, hard working. Natural counselor and healer. Sensitive and easily hurt. Great judge of character. Needs a lot of freedom.

Tina, 8- An excellent mediator. Blessed in some ways. Original and unconventional. Independent, critical of self and others.

Tiona, 5- Dynamic, busy lifestyle. Generous, thoughtful. Natural counselor and healer. Original and unconventional. Independent, critical of self and others.

Tipper, 3- Always coming and going. Considerate, understanding. Intelligent and knowledgeable. Stylish and refined. A free spirit, very adaptable. Gentle, kind, a hard worker.

Tippi, 7- Perceptive, psychic. Needs alone time. Intelligent and knowledgeable. Stylish and refined. Artistic, having good taste.

Tippie, 3- Always coming and going. Considerate, understanding. Intelligent and knowledgeable. Stylish and refined. Artistic, having good taste. A free spirit, very adaptable.

Titania, 11- A force of nature. Intuitive, perceptive. Sensitive and easily hurt. Reads people easily. Original and unconventional. Artistic, having good taste. Bold, courageous, a bit stubborn.

Titus, 8- An excellent mediator. Blessed in some ways. Dynamic, busy lifestyle. Attractive and charming. Loving and devoted.

Tobe, 6- Has business aptitude. Magnetic personality. Friendly, but shy. A free spirit, very adaptable.

Tobey, 22- A force of nature. Creates group harmony. Friendly, but shy. A free spirit, very adaptable. Dislikes limitations.

Tobi, 10- Takes the initiative. Self-sacrificing, devoted. Anticipates next move. Blessed in some ways.

Tobiah, 10- Takes the initiative. Self-sacrificing, devoted. Anticipates next move. Blessed in some ways. Independent, critical of self and others. Great judge of character.

Tobias, 3- Always coming and going. Nurturing, loving. Loyal and understanding. Blessed in some ways. Aims to please. Charming and devoted.

Tobin, 6- Has business aptitude. Magnetic personality. Friendly, but shy. Blessed in some ways. Original and unconventional.

Toby, 8- An excellent mediator. Competitive in business. Enjoys luxury items. Needs a lot of freedom.

Tod, 3- Always coming and going. Nurturing, loving. Domestic, responsible.

Todd, 7- Perceptive, psychic. Open to opportunities. Reliable, responsible. Workaholic, determined.

Tom, 3- Always coming and going. Nurturing, loving. Domestic, hard working.

Tomas, 5- Dynamic, busy lifestyle. Enjoys working. Systematic, organized. Independent, critical of self and others. Charming and devoted.

Tomiko, 11- A force of nature. Creates group harmony. Domestic, hard working. Blessed in some ways. Strong desire to succeed. May have musical abilities.

Tommy, 5- Dynamic, busy lifestyle. Enjoys working. Systematic, organized. Domestically social. Needs a lot of freedom.

Tomkin, 10- Takes the initiative. Self-sacrificing, devoted. Domestic, hard working. Strong desire to succeed. Blessed in some ways. Original and unconventional.

Toney, 7- Perceptive, psychic. Open to opportunities. Original and unconventional. A free spirit, very adaptable. Dislikes limitations.

Toni, 22- A force of nature. Creates group harmony. Original and unconventional. Blessed in some ways.

Tonia, 5- Dynamic, busy lifestyle. Enjoys working. Romantically inclined. Blessed in some ways. Independent, critical of self and others.

Tonisha, 5- Dynamic, busy lifestyle. Enjoys working. Romantically inclined. Blessed in some ways. Charming and devoted. Great judge of character. Bright, adventuresome.

Tony, 20- Extremely social. Works well with others. Original and unconventional. Needs a lot of freedom.

Tonya, 3- Always coming and going. Nurturing, loving. Young at heart. Needs a lot of freedom. Aims to please.

Topaz, 6- Has business aptitude. Magnetic personality. Intelligent and knowledgeable. Pioneer and risk taker. Uses common sense.

Tor, 8- An excellent mediator. Competitive in business. Gentle, kind, a hard worker.

Torey, 11- A force of nature. Creates group harmony. Intense inner power. Likes change and variety. Needs a lot of freedom.

Tori, 8- An excellent mediator. Competitive in business. Intense inner power. Blessed in some ways.

Torin, 4- Busy family life. Assumes responsibility. Gentle, kind, a hard worker. Blessed in some ways. Original and unconventional.

Tory, 6- Has business aptitude. Magnetic personality. Gentle, kind, a hard worker. Needs a lot of freedom.

Torrance, 4- Busy family life. Assumes responsibility. Gentle, kind, a hard worker. Could be forgetful. Independent, critical of self and others. Original and unconventional. Self-expressive, cheerful. A free spirit, very adaptable.

Toshiro, 5- Dynamic, busy lifestyle. Enjoys working. Charming and devoted. Great judge of character. Blessed in some ways. Gentle, kind, a hard worker. May have musical abilities.

Tova, 11- A force of nature. Creates group harmony. Intuitive and inspired. Reads people easily.

Tovah, 10- Takes the initiative. Self-sacrificing, devoted. Intuitive and inspired. Independent, critical of self and others. Great judge of character.

Trace, 20- Extremely social. Sensitive, emotional. Reads people easily. Self-expressive, cheerful. A free spirit, very adaptable.

Tracey, 9- Generous to a fault. Humanitarian, idealistic. Helpful, sincere. Optimistic, outspoken. A free spirit, very adaptable. Dislikes limitations.

Traci, 6- Has business aptitude. Duty bound, self-sacrificing. Pioneer and risk taker. Self-expressive, cheerful. Blessed in some ways.

Tracie, 11- A force of nature. Strives to improve humanity. Intuitive, perceptive. Self-expressive, cheerful. Blessed in some ways. A free spirit, very adaptable.

Tracy, 22- A force of nature. Strives to improve humanity. Ambitious leader, great vision. Self-expressive, cheerful. Needs a lot of freedom.

Travers, 4- Busy family life. Strong and healthy. Natural teaching ability. Intuitive and inspired. A free spirit, very adaptable. Could be forgetful. Charming and devoted.

Travis, 8- An excellent mediator. Uses good judgment. Resolute and purposeful. Intuitive and inspired. Blessed in some ways. Charming and devoted.

Trejo, 5- Dynamic, busy lifestyle. Intense inner power. A free spirit, very adaptable. Clever and talented. A natural counselor and healer.

Trent, 5- Dynamic, busy lifestyle. Intense inner power. Physical and passionate. Original and unconventional. Sensitive and easily hurt.

Trevor, 8- An excellent mediator. Uses good judgment. Original and creative. Intuitive and inspired. Natural counselor and healer. Tendency to lose items.

Trey, 5- Dynamic, busy lifestyle. Intense inner power. A free spirit, very adaptable. Dislikes limitations.

Trianna, 5- Dynamic, busy lifestyle. Intense inner power. Blessed in some ways. Bright, adventuresome. Original and unconventional. Romantic, sensual. Pioneer and risk taker.

Tricia, 6- Has business aptitude. Duty bound, self-sacrificing. Blessed in some ways. Self-expressive, cheerful. Artistic, having good taste. Pioneer and risk taker.

Trieu, 10- Takes the initiative. Diligent, hardworking. Blessed in some ways. Likes change and variety. Attractive and charming.

Trina, 8- An excellent mediator. Original and creative. Blessed in some ways. Romantic, sensual. Resolute and purposeful.

Trinity, 7- Perceptive, psychic. Spiritually motivated. Blessed in some ways. Original and unconventional. Artistic, having good taste. Dynamic, busy lifestyle. Needs a lot of freedom.

Trish, 11- A force of nature. Strives to improve humanity. Blessed in some ways. Charming and devoted. Great judge of character.

Tristan, 11- A force of nature. Strives to improve humanity. Blessed in some ways. Charming and devoted. Sensitive, easily hurt. Intuitive, perceptive. Original and unconventional.

Trixie, 4- Busy family life. Strong and healthy. Blessed in some ways. Artistic, sensual, perceptive. Idealistic and humanitarian. Accesses quickly.

Troy, 6- Has business aptitude. Duty bound, self-sacrificing. Natural counselor and healer. Needs a lot of freedom.

Trudie, 5- Dynamic, busy lifestyle. Intense inner power. Attractive and charming. Reliable, responsible. Blessed in some ways. A free spirit, very adaptable.

Trudy, 7- Perceptive, psychic . Spiritually motivated. Attractive and charming. Reliable, responsible. Needs a lot of freedom.

Truman, 6- Has business aptitude. Duty bound, self-sacrificing. Attractive and charming. Domestic, hard working. Pioneer and risk taker. Original and unconventional.

Tuck, 10- Takes the initiative. Attractive and charming. Optimistic, outspoken. Strong desire to succeed.

Tucker, 6- Has business aptitude. Idealistic in relationships. Self-expressive, cheerful. Strong desire to succeed. A step ahead of others. Gentle, kind, a hard worker.

Tuesday, 5- Dynamic, busy lifestyle. Attractive and charming. A free spirit, very adaptable. Many mood swings. Reliable, responsible. Independent, critical of self and others. Dislikes limitations.

Tulia, 9- Generous to a fault. Attractive and charming. Strong verbal skills. Blessed in some ways. Helpful, sincere.

Tullia, 3- Always coming and going. Youthful, appealing. Communicates skillfully. Ups and downs financially. Blessed in some ways. Aims to please.

Tully, 9- Generous to a fault. Attractive and charming. Strong verbal skills. Ups and downs financially. Needs a lot of freedom.

Ty, 9- Generous to a fault. Needs a lot of freedom. Very perceptive.

Tyla, 4- Busy family life. Needs a lot of freedom. Strong verbal skills. Natural teaching ability.

Tylena, 5- Dynamic, busy lifestyle. Dislikes limitations. Communicates skillfully. A free spirit, very adaptable. Romantic, sensual. Bright, adventuresome.

Tyler, 8- An excellent mediator. Dislikes limitations. Strong verbal skills. Original, creative. Gentle, kind, a hard worker.

Tyra, 10- Takes the initiative. Needs a lot of freedom. Gentle, kind, a hard worker. Independent, critical of self and others.

Tyrone, 7- Perceptive, psychic. Dislikes limitations. Spiritually motivated. Natural counselor and healer. Romantic, sensual. A free spirit, very adaptable.

Tyrus, 22- A force of nature. Needs a lot of freedom. Strives to improve humanity. Attractive and charming. Loving, devoted.

Tyson, 3- Always coming and going. Needs a lot of freedom. Charming and devoted. Natural counselor and healer. Original and unconventional.

"That's how the crickets crick all day
In the Merry Old Land of Oz!
We get up at twelve … And start to work at one
Take an hour for lunch … And then at two we're done
Jolly good fun!"
~*Excerpted from "The Wizard of Oz"*
Used with permission

U

If a name begins with U, U is the first vowel, has more than one U, or ends with a U, this person has many financial ups and downs, is attractive, charming and very lucky, but may have difficulty making decisions.

The letter U is the 21st letter of the alphabet. 2+1=3, so the 21st letter has the same vibrational influence as the number 3. 2 rules partnership, 1 rules beginnings and 3 rules balance. They must balance their ability to be in a partnership on the one hand, while striving to be independent on the other hand.

Similar to the number 3 ruled letters C and L, the U ruled individual likes to intellectualize their experiences. This makes it difficult for them to make up their mind. U names need to assess their situations more quickly and then be ready to make a commitment to those goals. Unfortunately selfishness or the inability to make up their mind causes many of their financial problems. What they lack in stability, they make up for in good looks and charm. The U ruled person can be quite glamorous and attractive. They easily fit into any social circle, whether high, low or in the middle. A person with this letter in their name could grace the cover of any glamour magazine. The 3 vibrational influence could win a best dressed contest, unless they were up against an E first vowel. If they didn't win, they would at least come in second place. The U's are bright and witty and a welcome addition to any social event.

The best qualities of the U ruled individual are their ability to bounce back from financial and physical setbacks, their creativity, strong communication skills and their luck at being in the right place at the right time. The U's charming, sunny, open-hearted manner is another one of their greatest attributes. The worst qualities of the U's are the abilities to be frivolous, superficial and overly dramatic about their situations. They may scatter their energies and give-in to escapist tendencies. Sometimes they can be very selfish. But, all in all, this letter is a positive one.

Ulysses S. Grant, 18th President of the United States, exemplified his U letter by having many financial ups and downs throughout his entire life. Similar to the letters L and C, U tends to be very lucky. Ulysses had a U and an L in his name so he was very lucky as he spent many years on the battle field without serious injury. His claim to fame was when he forced Robert E. Lee to surrender which ended the 4-year bloody Civil War. He became an overnight success and international hero. Even the Queen of England wanted to meet him. His two terms were best remembered for financial scandals among members of his party and his administration. He went bankrupt when he put his money into an investment firm that stole their investors' money. He turned to writing his memoirs to support his family. His books became a success, but unfortunately his health gave out and he never lived to see his books' profits. Still, the letter U is ruled by the number 3 which lends skill in the area of writing. His name also added up to a 3 power number. It's too bad he waited so long to write, or he may not have died bankrupt.

Most people with names that begin with U or have a U first vowel are attractive and charming, as is our beautiful actress Ursula Andreas. She is most remembered for her appearance as a Bond Girl in "Dr. No." Also she was once married to actor and director, John Derek, and remained friends until his death. This number 3 ruled letter U is a letter of communication, so it's to no surprise that Ursula, with two U's in her name speaks fluent English, French, Italian, German and Swiss-German! Her name adds up to a 20 power number, so it seems she is either very busy with partnerships and social situations, or has nothing going on at all romantically or socially. It's an all or nothing power number.

Another interesting U name is the ever popular Uma Thurman of the "Kill Bill" movies. Uma's an attractive and charming 6` tall model-turned-actress. Her father, Robert Thurman was the first westerner to become a Tibetan Buddhist monk. Uma was named for a Hindu Goddess. Her mother was a Swedish model. She is very easy going and has a cheerful attitude about life. This is one of the best traits of the U. They are pleasant to be around and "go with the flow." The M in the middle of Uma's name gives her domestic tendencies. She probably loves being at home and doesn't mind doing the household chores and errands. M is a 4 ruled letter and rules work and family. She no doubt loves the whole family scene. Her name adds up to an 8 power number, so she is a survivor and will achieve financial awards in this lifetime. Also the number 8 often is associated with death, so "Kill Bill" was a natural attraction for her. She's strong with an 8 power number, healthy and resilient with a U first letter, down-to-earth with an M in the middle, and a perfectionist with an A at the end of her name. No doubt we'll be seeing a great deal more of Uma in future films. She's talented, strong and easy on the eyes.

The United States of America, more commonly called U.S.A., is also a U name. Although many call the U.S.A. "America," technically it's the United States of America. U.S.A. is considered lucky by most other countries. Also U is a youthful letter and U.S.A is one of the youngest countries on the continent. One of U.S.A.'s most important resources is in the area of communication and transportation; which is a quality of the 3 ruled letter U. We have a difficult time making decisions, taking forever passing bills through our congress and intellectualizing the whole process, another common U trait. The U.S. has a Gemini rising, which is a youthful, adolescent personality. We are young, misunderstood, and think we know everything, rather similar to teenagers. Other countries who have been around longer probably find us irritating.

The letter U is one of the shortest name sections because not many names begin with the letter U. Still, a U anywhere in a name will give the bearer a more attractive and charming quality. They will have a natural ability to communicate socially with others. Most find the U names youthful, easy going and cheerful for the most part. Although this letter finds itself going through many ups and downs financially, it is one of the luckiest of letters in the alphabet to have in a name.

Interesting fact: Mount Rushmore, with its U first vowel, is noted that in its 14 years of construction there was never a serious accident. Never under estimate the luck of the U.

Famous names that begin with U are: Uma Thurman, Usher, Ursula Andreas and Ulysses S. Grant, Uri Geller and Upton Sinclair. Famous names with U first vowels: Humphrey Bogart, Julius Ceaser, Jules Verne, Dustin Hoffman, Rudolph Valentino, Julie Andrews, Audrey Hepburn, Julia Roberts, Lucille Ball, and Suzanne Somers.

Quick Reference of "U" Names

Udel, 6- Idealistic in relationships. Creative problem solver. A step ahead of others. Strong verbal skills.

Udele, 20- Social and charming. Practical, conservative. A free spirit, very adaptable. Strong verbal skills. Physical and passionate.

Udell, 9- Go with the flow. Reliable, responsible. A free spirit, very adaptable. Communicates skillfully. Ups and downs financially.

Udo, 4- Socially organized. Down-to-earth, faithful. Natural counselor and healer.

Ukiah, 5- Ups and downs financially. Strong desire to succeed. Blessed in some ways. Bright, adventuresome. Great judge of character.

Ula, 7- Has style and grace. Intellectually sound. Independent, critical of self and others.

Ulani, 3- Youthful, appealing. Slow to make decisions. Aims to please. Creative, romantic. Blessed in some ways.

Ullah, 9- Go with the flow. Great verbal skills. Ups and downs financially. Helpful, sincere. Great judge of character.

Ulna, 3- Youthful, appealing. Slow to make decisions. Original and romantic. Aims to please.

Ulric, 9- Go with the flow. Great verbal skills. Humanitarian, idealistic. Blessed in some ways. Self-expressive, cheerful.

Ulrick, 11- Creative and inspiring. Travels frequently. Gentle, kind, a hard worker. Artistic, having good taste. Self-expressive, cheerful. Sensitive and diplomatic.

Ulrich, 8- Usually very lucky. Strong verbal skills. Uses good judgment. Blessed in some ways. Self-expressive, cheerful. Great judge of character.

Ultima, 22- Creative and inspiring. Travels frequently. Dynamic, busy lifestyle. Blessed in some ways. Domestic, hard working. Ambitious leader, great vision.

Ultimo, 9- Go with the flow. Great verbal skills. Dynamic, busy lifestyle. Blessed in some ways. Domestic, hard working. Natural counselor and healer.

Ulysses, 3- Youthful, appealing. Slow to make decisions. Dislikes restrictions. Loving, devoted. Impulsive and extreme. A free spirit, very adaptable. Needs to be independent.

Uma, 8- Usually very lucky. Domestic, hard working. Resolute and purposeful.

Umeko, 20- Social and charming. Domestic, hard working. A free spirit, very adaptable. Strong desire to succeed. Natural counselor and healer.

Umi, 7- Has style and grace. Domestic, hard working. Blessed in some ways.

Una, 9- Go with the flow. Original and unconventional. Helpful, sincere.

Upton, 5- Ups and downs financially. Intelligent and knowledgeable. Dynamic, busy lifestyle. Natural counselor and healer. Romantic, opinionated.

Urania, 10- Optimistic and outgoing. Gentle, kind, a hard worker. Independent, critical of self and others. Original and unconventional. Blessed in some ways. Bold, courageous, a bit stubborn.

Urban, 20- Social and charming. Sensitive, emotional. Friendly, but shy. Independent, critical of self and others. Original and unconventional.

Urea, 9- Go with the flow. Humanitarian, idealistic. A free spirit, very adaptable. Independent, critical of self and others.

Uri, 3- Youthful, appealing. Sympathetic, kind. Friendly, considerate.

Uria, 22- Creative and inspiring. Strives to improve humanity. Blessed in some ways. Independent, critical of self and others.

Uriah, 30- Youthful, appealing. Sympathetic, kind. Friendly, considerate. Independent, critical of self and others. Great judge of character.

Urias, 5- Ups and downs financially. Good deed doer. Blessed in some ways. Independent, critical of self and others. Impulsive and extreme.

Uric, 6- Idealistic in relationships. Duty bound, self-sacrificing. Artistic, having good taste. Self-expressive, cheerful.

Uriel, 11- Creative and inspiring. Strives to improve humanity. Blessed in some ways. A free spirit, very adaptable. Strong verbal skills.

Ursala, 9- Go with the flow. Humanitarian, idealistic. Angelic leanings. Independent, critical of self and others. Strong verbal skills. Bold, courageous, a bit stubborn.

Ursei, 9- Go with the flow. Humanitarian, idealistic. Angelic leanings. A free spirit, very adaptable. Blessed in some ways.

Ursina, 10- Optimistic and outgoing. Diligent, hardworking. Charming and devoted. Blessed in some ways. Original and unconventional. Independent, critical of self and others.

Ursine, 5- Ups and downs financially. Good deed doer. Charming and devoted. Blessed in some ways. Original and unconventional. Physical and passionate.

Ursula, 20- Social and charming. Sensitive, emotional. Impulsive and extreme. Difficulty making decisions. Strong verbal skills. Reads people easily.

Ursuline, 11- Creative and inspiring. Strives to improve humanity. Very charismatic. Attractive, flirtatious, slightly scattered. Strong verbal skills. Blessed in some ways. Original, opinionated. Physical and passionate.

Usher, 8- Usually very lucky. Charming and devoted. Great judge of character. Physical and passionate. Gentle, kind, a hard worker.

Uziel, 10- Optimistic and outgoing. Uses common sense. Blessed in some ways. Likes change and variety. Strong verbal skills.

Uzoma, 22- Creative and inspiring. Uses common sense. Natural counselor and healer. Reliable, responsible. Ambitious leader, great vision.

> "The Witch's Dorothy? Well—that makes a difference. Just wait here—I'll announce you at once."
> ~*Excerpted from "The Wizard of Oz"*
> *Used with permission*

V

IF A NAME BEGINS WITH V, has more than one V, or ends with a V, this person is successful, sincere, loyal and dependable; however, they can also be overly possessive, unpredictable and eccentric.

The letter V is the 22nd letter of the alphabet. 22 is one of the "master numbers." We have only 2 master numbers, 11 and 22. The number 22 is often referred to as the "master builder." It is the most successful of all the numbers. This 22nd letter must serve the world in a practical way. 2+2 = 4, so the person with this letter in their name will experience lessons in partnership, twice over from the double 2's and the 4 vibrational influence will bring lessons in work and family. Partnership, partnership, work and family. This person will be quite a hard worker, down to earth and practical in most respects. This does not mean they will have two partners or two marriages. The double emphasis on partners means dealing with the outside world in a social way. In a big way! They will be Capricorn-like or goal oriented and possess the ability to manifest big plans and ideas. With a V anywhere in their name, they may feel pressured into accomplishing something worthwhile on a grand scale. The pressure comes from within, they will be harder on themselves than anyone else could ever be. V is for Victory! They should be efficient goal setters. At the very least, they will be as hard working as a 4 ruled letter.

The V produces inspiring and prophetic individuals; however, their imagination can be so strong, it sometimes interferes with their best judgment. Also the V can be too possessive in relationships with the opposite sex. On a positive note, similar to the letters D and M, this letter has the ability to be faithful. Somehow cheating on a partner goes against their grain. They are sincere, not flirtatious, and they tend to dislike flamboyant, superficial personalities. Those looking for a financially stable relationship can stop looking when in love with a V person. Anyone with a V in their name has the ability to accomplish great tasks. Most are domestic, down-to-earth and have a strong desire to be financially secure. Similar to D and M, the sound of rustling currency is soothing to their nerves.

Viggo Mortensen of "Lord of the Rings," who also had a part in the movie "Witness," fits his name quite well. The V is world-wide and so is Viggo. As a child he and his family traveled to other countries because of his father's work. He has a serious, yet sad look in his eyes. The I first vowel added to his first letter V sums up to a hidden 4, so he's had to endure some hardships. The I influences him into not being happy unless he's able to forgive others who have hurt him in his past. This serious sadness sort-of-look helped him in "The Lord of the Rings." His 7 ruled two G's in the middle of his name indicate the very center of his being. He is a very private, introspective person. As it turns out, besides being an actor, he is also an accomplished poet, photographer and painter. G is very stylish, but Viggo wears his style on the inside. He has an intensity number 7 which makes him a truth seeker. It also helps him to look good on camera. He is also a nurturer and healer with a 6 ruled O at the end of his name. His name also adds up to a power number 6. All this means he has to have someone to love. Viggo almost turned down the roll for "The Lord of the Rings" because he wanted to spend time with his 10 year old son. Fortunately his son was knowledgeable about the series and enthusiastically convinced his father to take the roll. The O and power number 6 make for a good parent; he's duty bound, nurturing, loving and caring. Also he is magnetic with that much love ruled 6 in his name.

Another well known actress, who is also a singer, is Vanessa Williams. The V added to her first vowel, A, sums up to a hidden 5. She loves adventure and excitement. She also has an intensity 1 in her name as she has 4 letters ruled by the number 1, two A's and two S's. She is a perfectionist and works very hard to maintain her high status. Vanessa was the first black Miss America. 1 is a leader, pioneer and risk taker. Vanessa is driven to accomplish great things with an intensity 1 in her name. She was born to pave the way for others. As it turns out, her name adds up to a 9 power number. She's a humanitarian and blessed in some ways. Often those with a 9 power number are blessed; others can be very jealous of this. So she most likely has to watch her back, especially with 2 S's in her name.

Val Kilmer also seems to have the perfect name for himself. He also has a hidden 5 in the beginning of his name as the 4 ruled V and the 1 ruled A add up to a 5. So he loves adventure and excitement. The hidden 5 may be the reason he is so adaptable in his films. He has the ability to play very diverse characters. Val was in block buster films "Top Gun," "Batman Forever," and "The Prince of Egypt." He has 3 letters in his first name so he is a communicator. Also, his name adds up to an 8 power number, so he's a survivor, enjoys the finer things in life, and is very sexy. The L at the end of his name makes it difficult for him to make decisions at times, however, once he's made his mind up, he sticks with it. The L also gives him strong verbal skills. The A first vowel makes him very critical of himself and others, so he most likely does his homework on each movie script. Last, but not least, the L gives him a cheerful, youthful and easy going attitude. With 3 letters in his name and an L at the end, he's probably a little "car happy." Also if he finds himself lucky, it's the L that should receive the credit. Next to C and U, L is one of the luckiest letters to have in a name.

V is similar to the letters D and M in that the person with this letter in their name is able to go into a situation, look around and quickly assess their surroundings. They don't want to look like a fool, so they will do their homework before deciding to take on a project. This letter is like "The Terminator"—not much gets past them, they notice everything! V people make excellent teachers and usually end up in some type of professional field. Also, as a rule, V names don't usually get along with superficial people. They can see right through them. Although the V is ruled by the same number that rules D and M, this letter is more highly evolved, it's worldly and prominent. Only those who are truly up to the task can wear it.

More famous people whose name begins with V are: Vincent Price, Valentino, Valerie Bertinelli, Venus Williams, Veronica Lake, Vladimir Horowitz, Valerie Harper, Vivian Leigh, Vincent Van Gogh, Vladimir Putin, Van Morrison, Vanna White, Victoria Principal, Vikki Carr, Voltaire and Vanessa Redgrave.

Quick Reference of "V" Names

Vaclav, 7- A brilliant mind. Not easily influenced. Self-expressive, cheerful. Communicates skillfully. Bold, courageous, a bit stubborn. Overly possessive.

Vadin, 5- Eccentric or unpredictable. Bright, adventuresome. Reliable, responsible. Blessed in some ways. Romantic, opinionated.

Val, 8- Efficient, wants to see results. Resolute and purposeful. Strong verbal skills.

Vala, 9- Has big plans and ideas. Helpful, sincere. Frequent traveler. Bold, courageous, a bit stubborn.

Valda, 4- Honest and sincere. Natural teaching abilities. Great verbal skills. Reliable, responsible. Bold, courageous, a bit stubborn.

Valdemar, 4- Honest and sincere. Natural teaching abilities. Great verbal skills. Reliable, responsible. A free spirit, very adaptable. Domestic, hard working. Bold, courageous, a bit stubborn. Diligent, helpful.

Vale, 4- Honest and sincere. Natural teaching abilities. Frequent traveler. A free spirit, very adaptable.

Valente, 7- A brilliant mind. Not easily influenced. Communicates skillfully. A free spirit, very adaptable. Original and unconventional. Dynamic, busy lifestyle. Physical and passionate.

Valentina, 8- Efficient, wants to see results. Resolute and purposeful. Strong verbal skills. A free spirit, very adaptable. Original and unconventional. Dynamic, busy lifestyle. Blessed in some ways. Romantic, sensual. Independent, critical of self and others.

Valentine, 3- Inspired and prophetic. Aims to please. Communicates skillfully. A free spirit, very adaptable. Original and unconventional. Dynamic, busy lifestyle. Blessed in some ways. Romantic, sensual. Tendency to overindulge.

Valerie, 9- Has big plans and ideas. Helpful, sincere. Frequent traveler. A free spirit, very adaptable. Gentle, kind, a hard worker. Blessed in some ways. Physical and passionate.

Valery, 11- Great potential. Intuitive, perceptive. Strong verbal skills. A free spirit, very adaptable. Gentle, kind, a hard worker. Dislikes limitations.

Valetta, 9- Has big plans and ideas. Helpful, sincere. Frequent traveler. A free spirit, very adaptable. Dynamic, busy lifestyle. Sensitive and easily hurt. Bold, courageous, a bit stubborn.

Valiant, 7- A brilliant mind. Not easily influenced. Strong verbal skills. Blessed in some ways. Bold, courageous, a bit stubborn. Original and unconventional. Dynamic, busy lifestyle.

Van, 10- Self-reliant, a natural leader. Independent, critical of self and others. Original and unconventional.

Vance, 9- Has big plans and ideas. Helpful, sincere. Romantic, opinionated. Self-expressive, cheerful. A free spirit, very adaptable.

Vanessa, 9- Has big plans and ideas. Helpful, sincere. Romantic, opinionated. A free spirit, very adaptable. Charming and devoted. Impulsive and extreme. Bold, courageous, a bit stubborn.

Vanna, 7- A brilliant mind. Not easily influenced. Original and unconventional. Romantic, sensual. Bold, courageous, a bit stubborn.

Vaughan, 11- Great potential. Intuitive, perceptive. Attractive and charming. Scientific and philosophical. Great judge of character. Bold, courageous, a bit stubborn. Original and unconventional.

Vaughn, 10- Self-reliant, a natural leader. Independent, critical of self and others. Attractive and charming. Scientific and philosophical. Great judge of character. Original and unconventional.

Veda, 5- Eccentric or unpredictable. Physical and passionate. Reliable, responsible. Bright, adventuresome.

Vega, 8- Efficient, wants to see results. Original and creative. Scientific and philosophical. Resolute and purposeful.

Vegas, 9- Has big plans and ideas. Enjoys giving gifts. Stylish and refined. Helpful, sincere. Charming and devoted.

Vela, 4- Honest and sincere. Accesses quickly. Great verbal skills. Natural teaching ability.

Velda, 8- Efficient, wants to see results. Original and creative. Strong verbal skills. Reliable, responsible. Resolute and purposeful.

Velma, 8- Efficient, wants to see results. Original and creative. Strong verbal skills. Domestic, hard working. Resolute and purposeful.

Velvet, 5- Eccentric or unpredictable. Physical and passionate. Great verbal skills. Overly possessive. Loves adventure and excitement. Dynamic, busy lifestyle.

Venus, 9- Has big plans and ideas. Enjoys giving gifts. Romantic, opinionated. Attractive and charming. Loving, devoted.

Vera, 10- Self-reliant, a natural leader. Likes change and variety. Diligent, hardworking. Independent, critical of self and others.

Vergil, 10- Self-reliant, a natural leader. Likes change and variety. Diligent, hardworking. Scientific, philosophical. Blessed in some ways. Communicates skillfully.

Verlyn, 6- Responsible and trustworthy. A step ahead of others. Duty bound, self-sacrificing. Strong verbal skills. Needs a lot of freedom. Romantic, opinionated.

Vern, 5- Eccentric or unpredictable. Physical and passionate. Gentle, kind, a hard worker. Original and unconventional.

Verna, 6- Responsible and trustworthy. A free spirit, very adaptable. Duty bound, self-sacrificing. Original and unconventional. Pioneer and risk taker.

Verne, 10- Self-reliant, a natural leader. Likes change and variety. Diligent, hardworking. Original and unconventional. Physical and passionate.

Vernita, 8- Efficient, wants to see results. Physical and passionate. Intense inner power. Original, creative. Blessed in some ways. Dynamic, busy lifestyle. Resolute and purposeful.

Vernon, 7- A brilliant mind. Not easily fooled. Gentle, kind, a hard worker. Creative, original. Natural counselor and healer. Romantic, sensual.

Veronica, 6- Responsible and trustworthy. A step ahead of others. Duty bound, self-sacrificing. Natural counselor and healer. Original and unconventional. Blessed in some ways. Self-expressive, cheerful. Independent, critical of self and others.

Veronique, 9- Has big plans and ideas. Enjoys giving gifts. Gentle, kind, a hard worker. Natural counselor and healer. Original and unconventional. Blessed in some ways. Attracts wealth. Attractive and charming. Tendency to overindulge.

Vespera, 5- Eccentric or unpredictable. Physical and passionate. Charming and devoted. Intelligent and knowledgeable. Loves adventure and excitement. Gentle, kind, a hard worker. Independent, critical of self and others.

Vi, 4- Honest and sincere. Teaches kindness. Hard working, organized.

Vic, 7- A brilliant mind. Needs alone time. Self-expressive, cheerful.

Vick, 9- Has big plans and ideas. Blessed in some ways. Self-expressive, cheerful. Strong desire to succeed.

Vicki, 9- Has big plans and ideas. Blessed in some ways. Self-expressive, cheerful. Strong desire to succeed. Blessed in some ways.

Vickie, 5- Eccentric or unpredictable. Blessed in some ways. Optimistic, outspoken. Strong desire to succeed. Blessed in some ways. A free spirit, very adaptable.

Vicky, 7- A brilliant mind. Needs alone time. Self-expressive, cheerful. Strong desire to succeed. Needs a lot of freedom.

Vichy, 4- Honest and sincere. Blessed in some ways. Self-expressive, cheerful. Great judge of character. Needs a lot of freedom.

Victor, 6- Responsible and trustworthy. Artistic, having good taste. Self-expressive, cheerful. Dynamic, busy lifestyle. Natural counselor and healer. Gentle, kind, a hard worker.

Victoria, 7- A brilliant mind. Needs alone time. Self-expressive, cheerful. Dynamic, busy lifestyle. Natural counselor and healer. Gentle, kind, a hard worker. Artistic, having good taste. Not easily influenced.

Vida, 9- Has big plans and ideas. Blessed in some ways. Reliable, responsible. Independent, critical of self and others.

Vidal, 3- Inspired and prophetic. Considerate, understanding. Optimistic, outspoken. Pioneer and risk taker. Frequent traveler.

Viggo, 6- Responsible and trustworthy. Artistic, having good taste. Scientific and philosophical. Extremely intelligent. Natural counselor and healer.

Viktor, 5- Eccentric or unpredictable. Blessed in some ways. Strong desire to succeed. Dynamic, busy lifestyle. Natural counselor and healer. Gentle, kind, a hard worker.

Vin, 9- Has big plans and ideas. Blessed in some ways. Original and unconventional.

Vince, 8- Efficient, wants to see results. Gives practical gifts. Romantic, sensual. Self-expressive, cheerful. Original and creative.

Vincent, 6- Responsible and trustworthy. Artistic, having good taste. Original and unconventional. Self-expressive, cheerful. A step ahead of others. Romantic, sensual. Dynamic, busy lifestyle.

Vincente, 11- Great potential. Intuitive, perceptive. Original and unconventional. Self-expressive, cheerful. A free spirit, very adaptable. Romantic, sensual. Dynamic, busy lifestyle. Loves adventure and excitement.

Vincenzo, 9- Has big plans and ideas. Blessed in some ways. Original and unconventional. Self-expressive, cheerful. A free spirit, very adaptable. Romantic, sensual. Uses common sense. Natural counselor and healer.

Vinnie, 10- Self-reliant, a natural leader. Respectful, kind. Creative, opinionated. Romantic, sensual. Artistic, having good taste. Likes variety and change.

Vinny, 30- Inspired and prophetic. Considerate, understanding. Original and unconventional. Romantic, sensual. Needs a lot of freedom.

Viola, 5- Eccentric or unpredictable. Generous, thoughtful. Natural counselor and healer. Strong verbal skills. Bright, adventuresome.

Violet, 11- Great potential. Intuitive, perceptive. Natural counselor and healer. Strong verbal skills. A free spirit, very adaptable. Dynamic, busy lifestyle.

Virg, 11- Great potential. Intuitive, perceptive. Gentle, kind, a hard worker. Scientific, and philosophical.

Virgie, 7- A brilliant mind. Blessed in some ways. Spiritually motivated. Stylish and refined. Artistic, having good taste. Not easily fooled.

Virgil, 5- Eccentric or unpredictable. Generous, thoughtful. Good deed doer. Scientific, and philosophical. Artistic, having good taste. Communicates skillfully.

Virgilio, 11- Great potential. Intuitive, perceptive. Gentle, kind, a hard worker. Scientific, philosophical. Artistic, having good taste. Strong verbal skills. Blessed in some ways. Natural counselor and healer.

Virginia, 8- Efficient, wants to see results. Gives practical gifts. Uses good judgment. Scientific, philosophical. Artistic, having good taste. Original, creative. Blessed in some ways. Resolute, purposeful.

Virgy, 9- Has big plans and ideas. Blessed in some ways. Gentle, kind, a hard worker. Scientific, and philosophical. Needs a lot of freedom.

Visolela, 5- Eccentric or unpredictable. Generous, thoughtful. Charming and devoted. Natural counselor and healer. Strong verbal skills. A free spirit, very adaptable. Frequent traveler. Bright, adventuresome.

Vita, 7- A brilliant mind. Needs alone time. Dynamic, busy lifestyle. Not easily influenced.

Vito, 3- Inspired and prophetic. Considerate, understanding. Dynamic, busy lifestyle. Natural counselor and healer.

Vittorio, 11- Great potential. Blessed in some ways. Dynamic, busy lifestyle. Sensitive and easily hurt. Natural counselor and healer. Gentle, kind, a hard worker. Artistic, having good taste. Musically talented.

Viv, 8- Efficient, wants to see results. Blessed in some ways. Has a strong imagination.

Vivian, 5- Eccentric or unpredictable. Generous, thoughtful. Has a strong imagination. Artistic, having good taste. Bright, adventuresome. Creative, opinionated.

Vivica, 30- Inspired and prophetic. Considerate, understanding. Has a strong imagination. Artistic, having good taste. Self-expressive, cheerful. Pioneer and risk taker.

Vivien, 9- Has big plans and ideas. Blessed in some ways. Has a strong imagination. Artistic, having good taste. A free spirit, very adaptable. Creative, opinionated.

Vivienne, 10- Self-reliant, a natural leader. Respectful, kind. Has a strong imagination. Artistic, having good taste. A free spirit, very adaptable. Original and unconventional. Romantic, sensual. Tendency to overindulge.

Vlad, 3- Inspired and prophetic. Great verbal skills. Aims to please. Domestic, responsible.

Vladamir, 8- Efficient, wants to see results. Strong verbal skills. Resolute and purposeful. Reliable, responsible. Bold, courageous, a bit stubborn. Desires financial security. Blessed in some ways. Gentle, kind, a hard worker.

Vladimir, 7- A brilliant mind. Communicates skillfully. Not easily influenced. Domestic, responsible. Artistic, having good taste. Desires financial security. Blessed in some ways. Gentle, kind, a hard worker.

Voleta, 3- Inspired and prophetic. Natural counselor and healer. Frequent traveler. A free spirit, very adaptable. Dynamic, busy lifestyle. Aims to please.

Volta, 7- A brilliant mind. Open to opportunities. Strong verbal skills. Dynamic, busy lifestyle. Independent, critical of self and others.

Von, 6- Responsible and trustworthy. Natural counselor and healer. Creative and original.

Vonn, 20- Tactful and refined. Natural counselor and healer. Original and unconventional. Romantic, sensual.

Vonnie, 7- A brilliant mind. Open to opportunities. Creative, opinionated. Romantic, sensual. Blessed in some ways. A free spirit, very adaptable.

Vonny, 9- Has big plans and ideas. Natural counselor and healer. Original and unconventional. Romantic, sensual. Needs a lot of freedom.

> "Going so soon? I wouldn't hear of it.
> Why, my little party's just beginning!"
> ~Excerpted from "The Wizard of Oz"
> Used with permission

W

IF A NAME BEGINS WITH W, has more than one W, or ends with a W, this person likes to meet new people, has charisma, can be superficial, is creative and needs change.

The letter W is the 23rd letter of the alphabet. 2+3=5, so the person with a W influence will experience partnership, balance and changing circumstances. They will be very social and adept in conversation and prefer variety and change. Since the W is influenced by the number 5, they love adventure and excitement. 5 rules entertainment, so you can count on the W person to keep you entertained.

Names that begin with W are able to express themselves quite well and seem to have a strong sense of purpose. Just the thought of travel and freedom to roam excites them. W is the last 5 ruled letter of the alphabet and so is more highly evolved than the E and N. Sometimes this influence can be quite opinionated and stubborn. If they remain patient and stay on target with their goals, they could achieve greatness.

As in the case of George "W." Bush, the emphasis being on the W in his name, as opposed to his father's name, indicates "change." In other words, with George W. Bush, there will be change. George W. Bush immediately set out to change the way things were done in office, and wanted the world to know he was not the same as his father, even though they shared the same name. When this president took office, the previous administration played a little joke by removing all the W's from the keyboards in the White House office. Still, that didn't stop the sweeping reforms from being made, because W means change!

The negative side of the W would be a tendency to cut corners or procrastinate. Some names with a W can be superficial; however, the average W person is a social delight, extremely bright, loves to meet new people, and is highly adaptable to change.

Winona Ryder, actress who starred in movies "Mr. Deeds," "Beetle Juice," "Dracula," and "Edward Scissorhands" is adaptable in each changing roll. The W and 2 N's give her an intensity 5. This influence is in part responsible for the diversity in her roles. She can't be stereotyped with all that 5 influence. Intensity 5 names are very romantic and love adventure and excitement. Also, just as their 5 ruled siblings, E and N, they must guard against overindulgence. 5 is the intensity number that enjoys surprising, or even shocking others. Winona likes to meet new people, as indicated by the W in the front of her name. With an I first vowel, others tend to follow her whether she's right or wrong. And similar to I first vowel Tina Turner, she won't be truly happy unless she forgives those in her past who have hurt her. She has a 4 power number; this number doesn't want to look like a fool, so no doubt she studies hard before she agrees to accepting a role. The 4 power number, or a 4 anywhere in a name, can bring a curse to a name. Only Winona knows where her curse is. She may desire children someday, with an O in her name; however, with all that freedom loving 5, it may take some adjustment at first. Children and freedom don't go together, at least at first, as children need so much love and care in their early years. If she did have children, she would be good at teaching them because of her 4 power number.

Back in 1879, Wyatt Earp was best known for his role in the famous gunfight at the O.K. Corral in Tombstone, Arizona. He was a peace officer who grew up in the American west. Interestingly enough, his name adds up to an 8 power number and the letters O and K also add up to an 8. As history tells us, three of Clayton's men were shot to death while Doc Holliday and Wyatt were trying to make an arrest. 8 is the number for death. Even though Wyatt liked meeting new people, with a Y as his first vowel, if he didn't like someone, they knew it. Y is the truth seeker and it can't "pretend" to like someone it doesn't like. The 8 power number enjoys rivalry and competition, and also rules death. Wyatt seemed to fit perfectly in his historical role at the O.K. Corral.

Another interesting W person is the late Walt Disney. His name adds up to a power number, "master number" 11. 11 power numbers have a strong desire to achieve something worthwhile. He liked meeting new people, with a W up front. He was critical of himself and others with an A first vowel. The L helped him to communicate well and the T gave him a very dynamic, social, busy lifestyle. What he achieved in the creation of Disneyland and cartoon characters like Mickey Mouse and Donald Duck will live on forever all over the world. 11 is the "lightening bolt" of great ideas, as Walt demonstrated to the world. It's been said, Walt frequently asked people what they thought of a new idea; if he received an overwhelming "No," he would get started immediately on making it work. This is the reversal or topsy-turvy way of the W's thinking. Walt's name added up to the inspired lightening bolt of power numbers. He truly was a genius.

Wayne Brady of the "Wayne Brady Show" also loves meeting new people. This famous person shows the versatility of the letter W, as some say he is a master of comedy. He seems to be a genius in the area of "improv." He has a power number 5 and an intensity 5, so along with the others, he must be careful of overindulgence. All that 5 gives him the ability to get out there and be on stage. He likes variety and most likely loves surprising or shocking others with so much 5 influence in his name. Acutely funny, without being offensive is his trademark to the world of comedy.

Austrian-born, Wolfgang Puck, famous Chef-restaurateur began training at 14 years of age. He developed his cooking skills at several three-star French restaurants. His creativity shows up in his name with the 6 ruled O and F and the 3 ruled L. Numbers 3, 6 and 9 are highly creative. These letters in the beginning of his name gave Wolfgang an early start in his career. The W and N give him the ability to be unusual; he likes change and variety. The end of his name, 2 G's, the A and N are all ruled by cerebral numbers. This man is extremely intelligent. His name adds up to a power number 4; he does his homework first before each presentation. Also 4 power numbers make excellent teachers. With the W in the beginning, he loves freedom and adventure, but he's smart about it.

If a name begins with Wa, they will be very intelligent, opinionated, stubborn, and critical of themselves and others. Also they'll be good at managing, owning and operating a business. If their name begins with We, they will be intelligent, they'll look and smell good, they'll be adventuresome and freedom-oriented. If their name begins with Wi, they will be humanitarian, more artistic and blessed in some ways. If their name begins with Wo, they will be self-sacrificing, responsible, they'd make an excellent counselor. If their name begins with Wu, they will be more charming and social and possess good communication skills.

This letter likes freedom, and similar to E and N, W's are romantic and love adventure. So as the saying goes: "Sit down, shut up, and hold on!" Because if you are in love with a W named person, you are in for the adventure of your life.

Some other famous people whose names start with W are: Whitney Houston, Walter Matthau, Winston Churchill, Warren Beatty, Woody Allen, Will Ferrell, Walter Cronkite, Wayne Newton, Willie Mays,

Wolfgang Amedeus Mozart, William Shakespeare, Will Smith, Walt Whitman, Whoppi Goldberg, W.C. Fields, Wilford Brimley and Willie Nelson.

Quick Reference of "W" Names

Wade, 6- Has charisma and charm. Pioneer and risk taker. Domestic, down-to-earth. A free spirit, very adaptable.

Wadell, 3- Expressive and outgoing. Aims to please. Reliable, responsible. A free spirit, very adaptable. Communicates skillfully. Frequent traveler.

Wadsworth, 5- Likes to meet new people. Bright, adventuresome. Domestic, responsible. Charming and devoted. Creative and determined. Natural counselor and healer. Gentle, kind, a hard worker. Dynamic, busy lifestyle. Great judge of character.

Wagner, 5- Likes to meet new people. Bright, adventuresome. Scientific and philosophical. Original and unconventional. Physical and passionate. Gentle, kind, a hard worker.

Wain, 20- Works well with others. Reads people easily. Blessed in some ways. Creative, opinionated.

Waine, 7- Strong sense of purpose. Not easily influenced. Blessed in some ways. Original and unconventional. A free spirit, very adaptable.

Waldemar, 5- Likes to meet new people. Bright, adventuresome. Great verbal skills. Reliable, responsible. A free spirit, very adaptable. Domestic, hard working. Bold, courageous, a bit stubborn. Diligent, helpful.

Waldimar, 9- Enjoys helping others. Hardworking, sincere. Frequent traveler. Reliable, responsible. Blessed in some ways. Domestic, down-to-earth. Bold, courageous, a bit stubborn. Diligent, helpful.

Walden, 5- Likes to meet new people. Bright, adventuresome. Great verbal skills. Reliable, responsible. Physical and passionate. Original and unconventional.

Waldo, 10- Implements original ideas. Independent, critical of self and others. Communicates skillfully. Domestic, responsible. Natural counselor and healer.

Walker, 7- Strong sense of purpose. Not easily influenced. Communicates skillfully. Strong desire to succeed. A free spirit, very adaptable. Gentle, kind, a hard worker.

Wallace, 3- Expressive and outgoing. Aims to please. Strong verbal skills. Frequent traveler. Bold, courageous, a bit stubborn. Self-expressive, cheerful. A free spirit, very adaptable.

Wallie, 8- Highly creative, needs change. Resolute and purposeful. Great verbal skills. Frequent traveler. Blessed in some ways. Physical and passionate.

Wallis, 22- Involved in major activities. Ambitious leader, great vision. Communicates skillfully. Travels frequently. Blessed in some ways. Charming and devoted.

Wally, 10- Implements original ideas. Independent, critical of self and others. Strong verbal skills. Frequent traveler. Needs a lot of freedom.

Walsh, 9- Enjoys helping others. Hardworking, sincere. Great verbal skills. Charming and devoted. Great judge of character.

Walt, 11- Involved in major activities. Intuitive, perceptive. Communicates skillfully. Dynamic, busy lifestyle.

Walter, 7- Strong sense of purpose. Not easily influenced. Communicates skillfully. Dynamic, busy lifestyle. A free spirit, very adaptable. Gentle, kind, a hard worker.

Wanda, 7- Strong sense of purpose. Not easily influenced. Original and unconventional. Reliable, responsible. Bold, courageous, a bit stubborn.

Wanetta, 3- Expressive and outgoing. Aims to please. Romantic and creative. A free spirit, very adaptable. Dynamic, busy lifestyle. Sensitive and easily hurt. Bold, courageous, a bit stubborn.

Ward, 10- Implements original ideas. Independent, critical of self and others. Gentle, kind, a hard worker. Domestic, down-to-earth.

Warner, 7- Strong sense of purpose. Not easily influenced. Gentle, kind, a hard worker. Original and unconventional. Physical and passionate. Tendency to lose items.

Warren, 7- Strong sense of purpose. Not easily influenced. Gentle, kind, a hard worker. Tendency to lose items. Physical and passionate. Creative and opinionated.

Wasfi, 22- Involved in major activities. Ambitious leader, great vision. Charming and devoted. Self-sacrificing, loving. Blessed in some ways.

Wassef, 10- Implements original ideas. Independent, critical of self and others. Charming and devoted. Impulsive and extreme. Loves adventure and excitement. Self-sacrificing, loving.

Wauneta, 22- Involved in major activities. Ambitious leader, great vision. Attractive and charming. Original and creative. Physical and passionate. Dynamic, busy lifestyle. Bold, courageous, a bit stubborn.

Waverly, 7- Strong sense of purpose. Not easily influenced. Intuitive and inspired. A free spirit, very adaptable. Gentle, kind, a hard worker. Strong verbal skills. Dislikes limitations.

Wayland, 3- Expressive and outgoing. Aims to please. Needs a lot of freedom. Communicates skillfully. Bold, courageous, a bit stubborn. Creative and opinionated. Domestic, responsible.

Wayne, 5- Likes to meet new people. Bright, adventuresome. Needs a lot of freedom. Creative and opinionated. Physical and passionate.

Webster, 11- Involved in major activities. Keenly perceptive. Friendly, but shy. Charming and devoted. Dynamic, busy lifestyle. Loves adventure and excitement. Gentle, kind, a hard worker.

Wendel, 9- Enjoys helping others. Generous humanitarian. Original and unconventional. Systematic, organized. Physical and passionate. Great verbal skills.

Wendell, 30- Expressive and outgoing. A free spirit, very adaptable. Romantic, sensual. Reliable, responsible. Tendency to overindulge. Great verbal skills. Frequent traveler.

Wendy, 8- Highly creative, needs change. Relies on own judgment. Original and romantic. Domestic, responsible. Dislikes limitations.

Wenona, 9- Enjoys helping others. Generous humanitarian. Original and unconventional. Natural counselor and healer. Romantic, sensual. Independent, self-motivated.

Wenonah, 8- Highly creative, needs change. Relies on own judgment. Original and unconventional. Natural counselor and healer. Romantic, sensual. Resolute and purposeful. Great judge of character.

Wenses, 22- Involved in major activities. Has big plans and ideas. Original and unconventional. Charming and devoted. Physical and passionate. Impulsive and extreme.

Werner, 11- Involved in major activities. Keenly perceptive. Gentle, kind, a hard worker. Romantic and sensual. Loves adventure and excitement. Tendency to lose items.

Wes, 11- Involved in major activities. Keenly perceptive. A charismatic person.

Wescott, 6- Has charisma and charm. A step ahead of others. Charming and devoted. Self-expressive, cheerful. Natural counselor and healer. Dynamic, busy lifestyle. Sensitive and easily hurt.

Wesley, 8- Highly creative, needs change. Relies on own judgment. Passionate and loving. Frequent traveler. Loves adventure and excitement. Dislikes limitations.

Wesly, 3- Expressive and outgoing. A free spirit, very adaptable. Charming and devoted. Communicates skillfully. Dislikes limitations.

Weston, 6- Has charisma and charm. A step ahead of others. Charming and devoted. Dynamic, busy lifestyle. Natural counselor and healer. Original and unconventional.

Wheaton, 11- Involved in major activities. Great judge of character. Keenly perceptive. Independent, self-motivated. Dynamic, busy lifestyle. Natural counselor and healer. Original and unconventional.

Whitley, 3- Expressive and outgoing. Great judge of character. Blessed in some ways. Dynamic, busy lifestyle. Communicates skillfully. A free spirit, very adaptable. Dislikes limitations.

Whitney, 5- Likes to meet new people. Relies on own judgment. Blessed in some ways. Dynamic, busy lifestyle. Original and unconventional. A free spirit, very adaptable. Dislikes limitations.

Wilbur, 4- Able to teach. Blessed in some ways. Strong verbal skills. Friendly, but shy. Attractive and charming. Gentle, kind, a hard worker.

Wilda, 22- Involved in major activities. Idealistic, humanitarian. Great verbal skills. Domestic, down-to-earth. Ambitious leader, great vision.

Wiley, 11- Involved in major activities. Blessed in some ways. Strong verbal skills. Physical and passionate. Needs a lot of freedom.

Wilford, 6- Has charisma and charm. Artistic, having good taste. Communicates skillfully. Self-sacrificing, loving. Natural counselor and healer. Gentle, kind, a hard worker. Systematic, organized.

Wilfred, 5- Likes to meet new people. Generous, thoughtful. Strong verbal skills. Self-sacrificing, devoted. Gentle, kind, a hard worker. A free spirit, very adaptable. Reliable, responsible.

Wilfreda, 6- Has charisma and charm. Artistic, having good taste. Communicates skillfully. Self-sacrificing, loving. Gentle, kind, a hard worker. A free spirit, very adaptable. Reliable, responsible. Pioneer, risk taker.

Wilhelmina, 7- Strong sense of purpose. Blessed in some ways. Strong verbal skills. Great judge of character. A free spirit, very adaptable. Frequent traveler. Domestic, hard worker. Artistic, having good taste. Original and unconventional. Not easily influenced.

Will, 20- Works well with others. Blessed in some ways. Strong verbal skills. Frequent traveler.

Willa, 3- Expressive and outgoing. Considerate, understanding. Communicates skillfully. Ups and downs financially. Pioneer and risk taker.

Willette, 7- Strong sense of purpose. Needs alone time. Great verbal skills. Frequent traveler. A free spirit, very adaptable. Dynamic, busy lifestyle. Sensitive and easily hurt. Physical and passionate.

William, 7- Strong sense of purpose. Needs alone time. Great verbal skills. Frequent traveler. Artistic, having good taste. Not easily influenced. Domestic, hard working.

Willie, 7- Strong sense of purpose. Needs alone time. Great verbal skills. Frequent traveler. Artistic, having good taste. A free spirit, very adaptable.

Willis, 30- Expressive and outgoing. Considerate, understanding. Strong verbal skills. Ups and downs financially. Artistic, having good taste. Charming and devoted.

Willow, 4- Able to teach. Blessed in some ways. Communicates skillfully. Ups and downs financially. Natural counselor and healer. Can be superficial.

Willy, 9- Enjoys helping others. Blessed in some ways. Strong verbal skills. Frequent traveler. Needs a lot of freedom.

Wilma, 22- Involved in major activities. Idealistic, humanitarian. Communicates skillfully. Domestic, hard working. Independent, self-motivated.

Wilona, 11- Involved in major activities. Blessed in some ways. Strong verbal skills. Natural counselor and healer. Original and unconventional. Intuitive, perceptive.

Wilson, 11- Involved in major activities. Blessed in some ways. Strong verbal skills. Charming and devoted. Natural counselor and healer. Original and unconventional.

Win, 10- Implements original ideas. Respectful, kind. Creative and opinionated.

Windy, 30- Expressive and outgoing. Considerate, understanding. Romantic, original. Reliable, responsible. Needs a lot of freedom.

Winfield, 10- Implements original ideas. Respectful, kind. Original and unconventional. Self-sacrificing, loving. Artistic, having good taste. A free spirit, very adaptable. Strong verbal skills. Reliable, responsible.

Winfred, 7- Strong sense of purpose. Needs alone time. Creative, opinionated. Self-sacrificing, loving. Gentle, kind, a hard worker. Physical and passionate. Reliable, responsible.

Winifred, 7- Strong sense of purpose. Needs alone time. Creative, opinionated. Artistic, having good taste. Self-sacrificing, loving. Gentle, kind, a hard worker. Physical and passionate. Reliable, responsible.

Wingate, 7- Strong sense of purpose. Needs alone time. Original and unconventional. Scientific and philosophical. Not easily influenced. Dynamic, busy lifestyle. A free spirit, very adaptable.

Winnie, 11- Involved in major activities. Blessed in some ways. Original and unconventional. Romantic, sensual. Artistic, having good taste. A free spirit, very adaptable.

Winny, 4- Able to teach. Blessed in some ways. Creative, original. Romantic, sensual. Needs a lot of freedom.

Winona, 4- Able to teach. Blessed in some ways. Original and unconventional. Natural counselor and healer. Romantic, sensual. Independent, critical of self and others.

Winslow, 7- Strong sense of purpose. Needs alone time. Original and unconventional. Charming and devoted. Strong verbal skills. Natural counselor and healer. Can be superficial.

Winston, 6- Has charisma and charm. Artistic, having good taste. Creative, opinionated. Charming and devoted. Dynamic, busy lifestyle. Natural counselor and healer. Romantic, sensual.

Winthrop, 6- Has charisma and charm. Artistic, having good taste. Creative, opinionated. Dynamic, busy lifestyle. Great judge of character. Gentle, kind, a hard worker. Natural counselor and healer. Intelligent, level headed.

Winton, 5- Likes to meet new people. Generous, thoughtful. Original and unconventional. Dynamic, busy lifestyle. Natural counselor and healer. Romantic, sensual.

Wladimir, 8- Highly creative, needs change. Communicates skillfully. Resolute and purposeful. Reliable, responsible. Blessed in some ways. Systematic, organized. Artistic, having good taste. Gentle, kind, a hard worker.

Wolf, 20- Works well with others. Natural counselor and healer. Strong verbal skills. Self-sacrificing, loving.

Wolfe, 7- Strong sense of purpose. Open to opportunities. Strong verbal skills. Self-sacrificing, loving. A free spirit, very adaptable.

Wolfgang, 4- Able to teach. Assumes responsibility. Great verbal skills. Self-sacrificing, loving. Scientific and philosophical. Resolute and purposeful. Original and unconventional. Extremely intelligent.

Wood, 3- Expressive and outgoing. Nurturing, loving. Natural counselor and healer. Reliable, responsible.

Woodie, 8- Highly creative, needs change. Competitive in business. Nurturing, loving. Reliable, responsible. Blessed in some ways. A free spirit, very adaptable.

Woodrow, 5- Likes to meet new people. Enjoys working. Natural counselor and healer. Domestic, responsible. Gentle, kind, a diligent. Very magnetic. Creative and determined.

Woods, 22- Involved in major activities. Creates group harmony. Natural counselor and healer. Down-to-earth, practical. Charming and devoted.

Woody, 10- Implements original ideas. Self-sacrificing, devoted. Nurturing, loving. Reliable, responsible. Needs a lot of freedom.

Wyatt, 8- Highly creative, needs change. Strong intuition, perceptive. Resolute and purposeful. Dynamic, busy lifestyle. Sensitive and easily hurt.

Wylie, 11- Involved in major activities. Dislikes limitations. Strong verbal skills. Blessed in some ways. A free spirit, very adaptable.

Wyllie, 5- Likes to meet new people. Dislikes limitations. Communicates skillfully. Ups and downs financially. Blessed in some ways. A free spirit, very adaptable.

Wyne, 22- Involved in major activities. Finds shortcuts. Romantic, sensual. A free spirit, very adaptable.

Wynn, 22- Involved in major activities. Finds shortcuts. Original, opinionated. Romantic, sensual.

Wynne, 9- Enjoys helping others. Keeps intelligent company. Opinionated, creative. Romantic, sensual. A free spirit, very adaptable.

Wynona, 11- Involved in major activities. Needs a lot of freedom. Original and unconventional. Natural counselor and healer. Romantic, sensual. Intuitive, perceptive.

Wyome, 9- Enjoys helping others. Highly creative. Natural counselor and healer. Domestic, hard working. A free spirit, very adaptable.

Wyomia, 5- Likes to meet new people. Needs a lot of freedom. Natural counselor and healer. Domestic, hard working. Blessed in some ways. Independent, critical of self and others.

*"What a nice little dog! And you, my dear.
What an unexpected pleasure! It's so kind
of you to visit me in my loneliness."*
~*Excerpted from "The Wizard of Oz"*
Used with permission

X

IF A NAME BEGINS WITH X, has more than one X, or ends with an X, this person is very artistic, sensual, responsive and perceptive. This is a more highly evolved 6 ruled letter of love with more mature lessons involved.

The letter X is the 24th letter of the alphabet. 2 + 4 = 6, so the person with an X in their name will experience partnership, work and family, which sum up to love. The X sounds ideal and complete; however, the X ruled person needs to guard against over indulgence in their sexual activities. They can also be as temperamental as the other 6 ruled letters. Furthermore, the X seems to have an addictive personality, as it is a more highly evolved magnetic letter.

X names are influenced by the number 6 vibration, so they need to love and nurture someone. Similar to their F and O siblings, they have a natural gift with gardens, flowers, pets and children. Also they seem to have natural parenting skills and are among the most responsible of letters, however, more evolved than its younger siblings.

Although the X person seems to be blessed with an abundance of artistic talent and creativity, they must guard against the temptation to acquire beautiful objects by morally improper means. Their other downfall is that they can be meddlesome, thinking they have to have their own way in a dissagreement. Similar to letters F and O, they can be jealous, moody, temperamental and too bossy, especially if they have an "O" elsewhere in their first name or a 6 power number. This being the case, they will be highly magnetic.

Also similar to the O vibration, X seems to have musical abilities. If they are able to spend time cultivating their abilities, they can be quite extraordinary. Unfortunately, because they are so duty-bound as the 6th vibration of love requires, they often put their musical talents aside to take care of loved ones. This letter is service oriented and often will work late hours to be sure there is food on the table.

Xavier Cugat, a conductor remembered for his highly-commercial approach to pop music, is a perfect example of an X type personality. He made his mark as one of the pioneers of Latin-American dance music. During his eight-decade career, Xavier helped to popularize the tango, the cha-cha, the mambo and the rhumba. Despite being criticized for his middle-of-the-road approach, Xavier remained committed to his commercial-minded sound. He later explained, "I would rather play 'Chiquita Banana' and have my swimming pool than play Bach and starve." This is the duty-bound part of the X. He did what it took to take care of his loved ones. On the surface, this letter seems exotic, but in reality, it's quite practical and business-like. X is also all about love as it is ruled by the 6th vibration which rules love. Even the word "sex" which has an X in it, is also referred to as "making love." Xavier's 4th wife was the beautiful Latin entertainer, Charo, who is still today the guest on many talk shows. He was known to have beautiful women consistently featured in his band.

Speaking of sex and beautiful women, the word sex is also magnetic because of the X in it. It's been said time and again, "Sex sells." This 6 ruled letter of love means business. It's one of the business type letters and seems to do well in the area of service. People are magnetically drawn to this letter, so it's not a bad idea to use it in advertising. The beer commercial, Dos Equis, which means two X's in Spanish seems to understand this when they use beautiful, sexy women in their commercials. It draws attention and people remember the message.

Although she's not real, Xena, Warrior Princess wears her X up front. She's sexy, magnetic and strong. Her name adds up to an 8 power number which is what gives her name Herculean strength. The intensity 5 in her name makes her a bit unique and unusual. With all that 5 and 8 energy, coupled with the magnetic X first letter one cannot help but think of sex when seeing her. She's a free spirit and loves variety and change. The A at the end of her name makes her independent, bold and courageous. She's a perfectionist and is good, with a bully in her head always pushing her to be the best she can be. Although she can be critical of herself with an A at the end of her name, she is good, but doesn't seem to know how good she really is—another quality of the A in her name.

The pop music performer, Sting, while still with the band "Police," wrote the song "Roxanne." This song really is all about a woman who exhibits the negative side of the X in her name. She is a "lady of the night" or, in other words, a prostitute. Often the X will lead to sexual overindulgences. As the song goes, "Roxanne, you don't have to put on the red light, you don't have to sell your body to the night, you don't have to wear that dress tonight, walk the streets for money, you don't care if it's wrong or if it's right." Sometimes the X seems to have no morals. This woman, Roxanne, must not have been taught good moral values when she was growing up, or else she wouldn't have behaved this way. This is the down side of the X—"not caring if it's wrong or right." She had an intensity 6 in her name with an O first vowel. R first names are quite bold and sometimes intimidating. All those 5 ruled letters at the end of her name also give way to an overindulgence in sex. So, Sting really had the right name for a song like this.

The person who was taught good moral values, who happens to bear an X in their name, will manage to uphold their ideals in marriage, work and family. They are the natural parents and employers. People tend to rely on them as they are most responsible and trustworthy. Similar to the O, there can be religious leanings. The typical X has a high regard for honesty and justice. The letter X is also as musical as the other 6 ruled letters. When learning the alphabet, most of us learned the word, "xylophone" which is a musical instrument as our first X word. Xylophones come in all shapes and sizes and colors. So do our X named friends, who are both rare and extraordinaire! It's a warm and colorful letter, exploding with the emotion of love!

Famous names that begin with X are; Xavier Cugat- Conductor, Xuxa- Brazilian actress, X.J. Kennedy- Writer and poet.

Quick Reference of "X" Names

Xandra, 8- Perceptive and responsive. Resolute and purposeful. Original and unconventional. Reliable, responsible. Gentle, kind, a hard worker. Bold, courageous, a bit stubborn.

Xanthe, 9- Nurturing and giving. Helpful, sincere. Original and unconventional. Dynamic, busy lifestyle. Great judge of character. A free spirit, very adaptable.

Xarah, 7- Learns quickly and easily. Not easily influenced. Gentle, kind, a hard worker. Bold, courageous, a bit stubborn. Great judge of character.

Xasha, 8- Perceptive and responsive. Resolute and purposeful. Charming and devoted. Great judge of character. Bold, courageous, a bit stubborn.

Xavier, 7- Learns quickly and easily. Self-motivated and independent. Intuitive and inspired. Blessed in some ways. A free spirit, very adaptable. Gentle, kind, a hard worker.

Xaviera, 8- Perceptive and responsive. Resolute and purposeful. Intuitive and inspired. Blessed in some ways. A free spirit, very adaptable. Gentle, kind, a hard worker. Bold, courageous, a bit stubborn.

Xena, 8- Perceptive and responsive. Original and creative. Romantic and sensual. Bold, courageous, a bit stubborn.

Xenia, 8- Perceptive and responsive. Original and creative. Romantic and sensual. Blessed in some ways. Resolute and purposeful.

Xenias, 9- Nurturing and giving. Generous, thoughtful. Opinionated, creative. Artistic, having good taste. Helpful, sincere. Charming and devoted.

Xenon, 9- Nurturing and giving. Generous, thoughtful. Original and unconventional. Natural counselor and healer. Creative, opinionated.

Xenos, 5- Sensual and loves excitement. Perceptive, socially adept. Original and unconventional. Natural counselor and healer. Charming and devoted.

Xerxes, 5- Sensual and loves excitement. Perceptive, socially adept. Gentle, kind, a hard worker. Prone to sexual indulgences. Loves adventure and excitement. Charming and devoted.

Xina, 3- Has an addictive personality. Blessed in some ways. Original and unconventional. Independent, critical of self and others.

Xiomara, 9- Nurturing and giving. Artistic, having good taste. Natural counselor and healer. Systematic, organized. Independent, critical of self and others. Gentle, kind, a hard worker. Pioneer and risk taker.

Xochitl, 10- Artistic, sensual, perceptive. Self-sacrificing, devoted. Optimistic, outspoken. Great judge of character. Blessed in some ways. Dynamic, busy lifestyle. Communicates skillfully.

Xuyen, 8- Perceptive and responsive. Attractive and charming. Dislikes limitations. Original and creative. Romantic, sensual.

Xylia, 8- Perceptive and responsive. Needs a lot of freedom. Communicates skillfully. Blessed in some ways. Resolute and purposeful.

Xylon, 9- Nurturing and giving. Needs a lot of freedom. Slow to make decisions. Natural counselor and healer. Romantic, original.

> "Oh, no, my dear—I'm—I'm a very good
> man. I'm just a very bad Wizard."
> ~Excerpted from "The Wizard of Oz"
> Used with permission

Y

IF A NAME BEGINS WITH Y, is the first vowel, has more than one Y, or ends with a Y, this person is honest, loves freedom, is a seeker of truth, and may be psychic or have excellent intuition.

The letter Y is the 25th letter of the alphabet. 2+5=7, so the person with a Y influence will experience partnership, change, and will need to have faith in order to be happy. They will be partnership oriented, but with the 5 and 7, they need to have a certain amount of freedom. Also, the sum of 7 brings solitude and lessons in faith. The Y individual usually desires partnership, but may want to sleep in separate beds. In some cases, they may even want to live in separate houses!

Y names are strongly influenced by the number 7 vibration. Similar to letters G and P they can be very Pisces or Neptunian-like. They'll tend to be secretive, photogenic, philosophical or spiritual, needing solitude or more sleep than most. Some people with Y in their names give in to complaining or whining over nothing. Y is the whiner of letters. Drug or alcohol addiction is also a possibility with this letter as with the letters G and P. This letter likes to escape reality more often than most.

If a Y is anywhere in a person's name, that person will need to show their faith more than other names. In other words, their faith will be tested more than names without it. Time for reflection, meditation and solitude will be needed. The 7 vibration casts off a spiritual, higher love, dream-like connotation. The bearer of a name with Y in it must strive to be realistic as much as possible.

People with Y's in their name are truth seekers. They're philosophical and scientific and will spend much of their time searching for answers to the questions their fine minds have. This is why so many of them make great scientists, researchers, educators and philosophers. On the same note, they can be quite put out if they discover someone has been lying to them. Unfortunately, this is not one of the letters we want to get on the bad side of. They cannot pretend to like someone they do not like. It's a truthful letter and to pretend is to be dishonest, and therefore goes against their grain. So if they don't like you, you know it. The Y person will close their steal-trap mind and there will be no entry for those he or she does not approve of. This letter does not feel the pressure to be socially graceful. They can be colder than the guy at the bank when you skipped your car payment.

The shape of the letter Y almost resembles a pitch fork without the middle prong. Interesting that it's so similar to King Triton's pitch fork. As King Triton rules the oceans and tides with his pitchfork in hand, our Neptunian friends rule their own lives, so don't try to tell them what to do. This letter needs a lot of freedom and dislikes restrictions. They can be fiercely independent and are the heartbreaker of letters. The Y named can move far away from home breaking their family and friend's hearts. We can't hold water in our hands; it runs through our fingers. And we can't hold onto someone with a Y in their name; they too will slip through our fingers. They ride their own wave to wherever it leads them. This letter in a name can also deceive or confuse others. Women with this letter in their name seem to be the damsel in distress, sometimes not even able to open their own jar of pickles. She'll let you help her, but, remember, she's not completely helpless. And if you smother her too much she'll pull the disappearing act. Ask the man who's tried. All of a sudden she'll find a new job or have some reason to not be around anymore. Although the truth is really important to her, she's good at getting around it if in danger of losing her freedom. Actually, her freedom is pretty innocent. As mentioned before, she is into the truth. So allowing her to be free is a good thing. This also holds true for men with a Y in their name. Y's of both sexes are extremely intelligent and often have strong convictions. This is also one of the more masculine, or positive letters. It's most compatible with those having odd-numbered ruling letters in their name. Vowels such as A's and E's and letters ruled by 1's and 5's tend to get along with this letter quite well. Mostly because of the intelligence factor. Our Neptunian friends are similar to the dolphin that swims in our oceans. They are extremely intelligent, and seem pretty friendly, but dolphins can kill sharks. Just remember to watch out!

This letter is ruled by the number 7 which usually looks pretty good on camera. Although most of them enjoy moments of solitude, given the opportunity, some can grace the cover of magazines and even go on to the television and movie industry. Still, they could pull the disappearing act if not allowed their privacy.

Similar to the letters G and P, Y can have quite an ego. Y is a very spiritual letter, and needs to recognize God or some other spiritual force as a superior being—greater than themselves. If not they'll wear everyone out with their constant bragging and boasting. The Y person is much more pleasant to be around when their ego is in tact. The average person with Y in their name is happier when attending regular church services or doing their prayer work routinely. It's a faith letter and is here to learn about faith in God. The person with a Y in the beginning, end, or as a first vowel in their name won't truly be happy unless they have faith. Having faith is one of their major lessons in this lifetime.

Britney Spears is one of the names with a Y that seems to live on the right side of the Y vibration. In a 2004 television interview she mentioned that she prays to God everyday. Someone of her magnitude could easily be egotistical, but, she humbles herself daily to God and therefore does not have an inflated opinion of herself. So God continues to bless her. Actually, it's the I in her name that brings blessings to her; the Y in her name makes it possible to achieve happiness by having faith. This letter also helps her look great on camera. Since this is her capstone letter, her faith is one of the legs she stands on; it supports her. It's what she has to rely on and to keep herself stable. This letter also has style. Britney has her own style, like no one else's.

Y names are dreamy yet realistic. They are spiritual yet scientific, a paradox that can only work for this rare first name letter. Maybe that's why it's mostly found at the end of a name, just as it's at the end of the alphabet. It's a dreamy, intelligent letter fit for the dreamy intelligent people of this planet.

Other famous "Y" names are Yo-Yo Ma, Yanni, Yogi Berra, Yoko Ono, Yves San Laurent, Yvonne Zima, Yao Ming, Yasmine Bleeth, Yul Brynner, Yves Montand and Yvonne De Carlo.

Quick Reference of "Y" Names

Yale, 7- Refined and stylish. Not easily influenced. Strong verbal skills. Loves adventure and excitement.

Yancy, 5- Keeps intelligent company. Bright, adventuresome. Original and unconventional. Self-expressive, cheerful. Highly perceptive.

Yao, 5- Keeps intelligent company. Bright, adventuresome. Creative, nurturing and loving.

Yardley, 9- Tremendously talented. Helpful, sincere. Gentle, kind, a hard worker. Reliable, responsible. Strong verbal skills. Likes change and variety. Needs a lot of freedom.

Yasmeena, 11- Strong quest for truth and knowledge. Intuitive, perceptive. Charming and devoted. Domestic, hard working. Loves adventure and excitement. Tendency to overindulge. Original and unconventional. Independent, critical of self and others.

Yasmin, 9- Tremendously talented. Helpful, sincere. Charming and devoted. Domestic, hard working. Blessed in some ways. Original and unconventional.

Yasmina, 10- Intelligent, a wise leader. Independent, critical of self and others. Charming and devoted. Domestic, hard working. Blessed in some ways. Original and unconventional. Bold, courageous, a bit stubborn.

Yasmine, 5- Keeps intelligent company. Bright, adventuresome. Charming and devoted. Domestic, hard working. Blessed in some ways. Original and unconventional. Loves adventure and excitement.

Yates, 7- Refined and stylish. Not easily influenced. Dynamic, busy lifestyle. Loves adventure and excitement. Charming and devoted.

Ychoaya, 6- Ambitious, responsible. Self-expressive, cheerful. Great judge of character. Natural counselor and healer. Independent, critical of self and others. Needs a lot of freedom. Pioneer and risk taker.

Yedda, 3- Slow to make decisions. A free spirit, very adaptable. Reliable, responsible. Down-to-earth, faithful. Independent, critical of self and others.

Yehuda, 10- Intelligent, a wise leader. Likes change and variety. Great judge of character. Attractive and charming. Reliable, responsible. Independent, critical of self and others.

Yehudah, 9- Tremendously talented. Enjoys giving gifts. Great judge of character. Attractive and charming. Reliable, responsible. Independent, critical of self and others. Many financial ups and downs.

Yehudi, 9- Tremendously talented. Enjoys giving gifts. Great judge of character. Attractive and charming. Reliable, responsible. Blessed in some ways.

Yelena, 8- Strong intuition, just knows things. Original and creative. Strong verbal skills. Tendency to overindulge. Original and unconventional. Independent, critical of self and others.

Yeoman, 10- Intelligent, a wise leader. Likes change and variety. Natural counselor and healer. Domestic, hard working. Independent, critical of self and others. Original and unconventional.

Yetta, 8- Strong intuition, just knows things. Original and creative. Dynamic, busy lifestyle. Sensitive and easily hurt. Independent, critical of self and others.

Yesenia, 6- Ambitious, responsible. A step ahead of others. Charming and devoted. Tendency to overindulge. Original and unconventional. Blessed in some ways. Independent, critical of self and others.

Yoanna, 7- Refined and stylish. Open to opportunities. Independent, critical of self and others. Original and unconventional. Romantic, sensual. Bold, courageous, a bit stubborn.

Yogi, 11- Strong quest for truth and knowledge. Creates group harmony. Scientific and philosophical. Blessed in some ways.

Yohei, 8- Strong intuition, just knows things. Competitive in business. Self-reliant, successful. Physical and passionate. Artistic, having good taste.

Yolanda, 9- Tremendously talented. Artistic, creative. Strong verbal skills. Independent, critical of self and others. Original and unconventional. Reliable, responsible. Bold, courageous, a bit stubborn.

Yolande, 4- Finds shortcuts. Assumes responsibility. Strong verbal skills. Independent, critical of self and others. Original and unconventional. Reliable, responsible. Loves adventure and excitement.

Yolie, 30- Slow to make decisions. Nurturing, loving. Strong verbal skills. Blessed in some ways. Loves adventure and excitement.

Yokio, 30- Slow to make decisions. Nurturing, loving. Strong desire to succeed. Blessed in some ways. May have musical abilities.

Yoko, 3- Slow to make decisions. Nurturing, loving. Strong desire to succeed. May have musical abilities.

York, 6- Ambitious, responsible. Magnetic personality. Gentle, kind, a hard worker. Strong desire to succeed.

Yorke, 11- Strong quest for truth and knowledge. Creates group harmony. Gentle, kind, a hard worker. Strong desire to succeed. Loves adventure and excitement.

Yosef, 7- Refined and stylish. Open to opportunities. Charming and devoted. Loves adventure and excitement. Self-sacrificing, loving.

Yoshi, 4- Finds shortcuts. Assumes responsibility. Charming and devoted. Great judge of character. Blessed in some ways.

Yoshino, 6- Ambitious, responsible. Magnetic personality. Charming and devoted. Great judge of character. Blessed in some ways. Original and unconventional. May have musical abilities.

Yosi, 5- Keeps intelligent company. Enjoys working. Charming and devoted. Blessed in some ways.

Young-hee, 7- Refined and stylish. Open to opportunities. Attractive and charming. Original and unconventional. Scientific and philosophical. Great judge of character. Loves adventure and excitement. Tendency to overindulge.

Young-ho, 6- Ambitious, responsible. Magnetic personality. Attractive and charming. Original and unconventional. Scientific and philosophical. Great judge of character. May have musical abilities.

Young-wook, 11- Strong quest for truth and knowledge. Creates group harmony. Attractive and charming. Original and unconventional. Scientific and philosophical. Likes to meet new people. Good parental skills. May have musical abilities. Strong desire to succeed.

Yovel, 7- Refined and stylish. Open to opportunities. Intuitive and inspired. A free spirit, very adaptable. Strong verbal skills.

Ynez, 7- Refined and stylish. Original and unconventional. Physical and passionate. Uses common sense.

Yuki, 3- Slow to make decisions. Attractive and charming. Strong desire to succeed. Blessed in some ways.

Yukiko, 11- Strong quest for truth and knowledge. Attractive and charming. Strong desire to succeed. Blessed in some ways. A bit forceful at times. Natural counselor and healer.

Yul, 4- Finds shortcuts. Slow to make decisions. Communicates skillfully.

Yule, 9- Tremendously talented. Attractive and charming. Strong verbal skills. Loves adventure and excitement.

Yuri, 10- Intelligent, a wise leader. Attractive and charming. Gentle, kind, a hard worker. Blessed in some ways.

Yuriko, 9- Tremendously talented. Attractive and charming. Gentle, kind, a hard worker. Blessed in some ways. Strong desire to succeed. Natural counselor and healer.

Yves, 8- Strong intuition, just knows things. Intuitive and inspired. Loves adventure and excitement. Charming and devoted.

Yvet, 9- Tremendously talented. Intuitive and inspired. Loves adventure and excitement. Dynamic, busy lifestyle.

Yvette, 7- Refined and stylish. Intuitive and inspired. Loves adventure and excitement. Dynamic, busy lifestyle. Sensitive and easily hurt. Tendency to overindulge.

Yvon, 22- Strong quest for truth and knowledge. Intuitive and inspired. Natural counselor and healer. Original and unconventional.

Yvonne, 5- Keeps intelligent company. Intuitive and inspired. Natural counselor and healer. Original and opinionated. Romantic, sensual. Loves adventure and excitement.

"As for you, my galvanized friend, you want a heart!
You don't know how lucky you are not to have one.
Hearts will never be practical until they can be made unbreakable.
I could have been a world figure, a power among men, a—successful wizard,
had I not been obstructed by a heart."
~Excerpted from "The Wizard of Oz"
Used with permission

Z

If a name begins with Z, has more than one Z, or ends with a Z, this person has high expectations, looks at the bright side of life, and has good physical and mental reflexes. This is a more highly evolved 8th vibrational letter.

The letter Z is the 26th letter of the alphabet. 2+6=8, so the person with a Z influence will experience partnership, love and rewards. They will be partnership oriented, responsible toward loved ones, and a master over material goods. This letter is somewhat business-like. Similar to the signs Capricorn and Scorpio, the Z personality will reach whatever goals they set for themselves. They will move slowly and stubbornly toward their desired destination, regardless of the obstacles in their path.

Z names are influenced by the number 8 vibration which also rules Scorpio. Somehow the bearer of the Z will receive rewards of past good actions from this life or another lifetime. Z is karmically charged and very powerful, similar to H and Q. If their power is misused, it can boomerang back on them disastrously. The karmic 8th vibration if used for selfish reasons can quickly have a negative consequence.

The sharpness of the Z's mental abilities can be attributed to Z being more highly evolved than its other 8 ruled siblings H and Q. Those with a Z anywhere in their name have a natural ability to mediate opposing parties. They are a plus in an emergency that requires a quick response. Higher evolved Z names show compassion, common sense and understanding. The lesser-evolved still have material lessons to learn and may have past karmic debts to resolve.

Motivational speaker and writer, Zig Zigler often says, "If you help enough people get what they want, eventually, you will get what you want." This kind of thinking is typical of a Z personality. This clearly demonstrates the law of give and take, or better still, give and you shall receive. Zig has a G in his name and so he is prone to being a little bit philosophical about life. The Z in his name makes him want material success, but the I and G make him a humanitarian who is philosophical about his approach. His name sums up to a power number 6 which gives him a magnetic appeal, as well as having a good business aptitude. People are drawn to him and he has a very large following of admirers. The power number 6 is love, which he gladly gives out for a fee; this is the material side of the Z which helps him with sales-training seminars which inspire, empower and motivate sales persons. Zig is an example of a successful Z person.

Zorro, the fox, was created in 1919 by the writer Johnston McCulley for his serialized novel, "The Curse of Capistrano." Although he is a fictional character, Zorro's name fits him perfectly. Zorro was a romantic hero who fought against injustice in Spanish California's Pueblo de Los Angeles. In the story, Zorro wears a mask so no one will recognize him, for he is known to be the son of a well known diplomat who was forced to go back to Spain because of a corrupt government. He was a sort of Robin Hood, who would take back from the rich and give to the poor from whom the rich stole to begin with. He would leave his famous sword mark of a Z slashed on the door of his victims. Z is ruled by the number 8 which is Scorpio-like. This type of influence is prone to getting involved with matters having to do with death, joint finances, taxes, insurance, goods of the dead, so Zorro was properly named to handle these matters in the story. He had an intensity 6 and an intensity 9 in his name. The 6 made him magnetic and the 9 made him a humanitarian, not necessarily concerned with material wealth. There was much energy to acquire material wealth with the Z, however, the double R's made him want to give it back! Plus the two love ruled O's made for quite a romantic tale. Altogether his name added up to a power number 11 which is a master number. Zorro desired success, even if he was a fictional character; his fictitious name gave a very accurate description of his personality.

Another famous person whose name begins with Z is Zora Neale Hurston. She was a novelist, folklorist and anthropologist in the late 1920's. She was the prototypical authority on black culture from the Harlem Renaissance. Most of her writing occurred during the 1930's. She led the way for black writers who wrote about black culture in America. Her best novels investigated voodoo practices in black communities in Florida, New Orleans and the Caribbean. Interestingly enough, the practice of voodoo would fall under the influence of Scorpio which coincidently rules the letter Z of the 8th vibration. She was born on January 7th in 1891. January is ruled by the number 1 and if we add her birthday of 7 that would add up to an 8 attitude number. Often the letters of our names resonate the numbers of our birthdays. At any rate, Zora wrote about occult practices little known to the rest of America at that time. The cornerstone, or first letter of her name shows bravery. The Z loves a challenge and will not back down to the fiercest opposition. The A at the end of her name makes her a pioneer and risk taker. A's are bold and courageous. The R in her name shows she was gentle, kind and hard working. Most importantly, she had an O first vowel ruled by the 6th vibration. She also had a 6 power number. Those with the 6 influence are creative and want to be their own boss. They are all about service and taking care of others. This combination made her very much a leader, a pioneer, a strong person who could nurture and take care of others. Unfortunately, like so many ruled by the 8th vibration, she had ups and downs financially. Her final days showed she died in poverty. Similar to letters H and Q, Z has material lessons to learn. They must learn to manage over their material goods. It's a hard lesson.

If the Z is accompanied by an A, they will be more independent, ambitious and critical. If accompanied by an E, they will be physical and passionate and will be easily adaptable to change. If accompanied by an I, they will be more blessed, artistic and humanitarian by nature. If accompanied by an O, they will be self-sacrificing, responsible and service oriented. If accompanied by a U, more charming and attractive, but they'll have many ups and downs financially.

The Z names seem to have a deeper understanding of people, that's why they make such good mediators. This end of the rainbow letter just seems to know things. Z names have a habit of looking at the bright side of life. They have high expectations. If your lucky enough to be in love with someone with a Z in their name, they'll get you wherever you want to go.

Other famous "Z" names: Ziggy Marley, Zero Mostel, Zsa Zsa Gabor, Zubin Mehta, Zane Grey, Zac Hanson, Ziyi Zhang, Zeppo Marx, Zachery Ty Bryan, ZZ Top, Zena Grey and Zoe Saldena.

Quick Reference of "Z" Names

Zac, 3- A tendency to see the bright side. Aims to please. Self-expressive, cheerful.

Zach, 20- Compassionate and kind. Reads people easily. Self-expressive, cheerful. Great judge of character.

Zack, 5- Has high expectations. Bright, adventuresome. Optimistic, outspoken. Strong desire to succeed.

Zachariah, 3- A tendency to see the bright side. Aims to please. Self-expressive, cheerful. Great judge of character. Bold, courageous, a bit stubborn. Gentle, kind, a hard worker. Blessed in some ways. Pioneer and risk taker. Self-reliant, successful.

Zacharias, 5- Has high expectations. Bright, adventuresome. Optimistic, outspoken. Great judge of character. Bold, courageous, a bit stubborn. Gentle, kind, a hard worker. Blessed in some ways. Pioneer and risk taker. Charming and devoted.

Zachary, 10- Has a good deal of common sense. Independent, critical of self and others. Self-expressive, cheerful. Great judge of character. Bold, courageous, a bit stubborn. Gentle, kind, a hard worker. Needs a lot of freedom.

Zachery, 5- Has high expectations. Bright, adventuresome. Optimistic, outspoken. Makes and loses money easily. Physical and passionate. Intense inner power. Needs a lot of freedom.

Zada, 5- Has high expectations. Bright, adventuresome. Reliable, responsible. Bold, courageous, a bit stubborn.

Zaida, 5- Has high expectations. Bright, adventuresome. Blessed in some ways. Reliable, responsible. Bold, courageous, a bit stubborn.

Zaire, 5- Has high expectations. Bright, adventuresome. Blessed in some ways. Gentle, kind, a hard worker. A free spirit, very adaptable.

Zandra, 10- Has a good deal of common sense. Independent, critical of self and others. Original and unconventional. Reliable, responsible. Gentle, kind, a hard worker. Bold, courageous, a bit stubborn.

Zane, 10- Has a good deal of common sense. Independent, critical of self and others. Original and unconventional. A free spirit, very adaptable.

Zanna, 20- Mediates opposing parties. Reads people easily. Original and unconventional. Romantic, sensual. Bold, courageous, a bit stubborn.

Zara, 10- Has a good deal of common sense. Independent, critical of self and others. Gentle, kind, a hard worker. Bold, courageous, a bit stubborn.

Zared, 9- Desires to help the masses. Hardworking, sincere. Gentle, kind, a hard worker. A free spirit, very adaptable. Reliable, responsible.

Zarek, 7- Prone to flashes of inspiration. Not easily influenced. Gentle, kind, a hard worker. A free spirit, very adaptable. Strong desire to succeed.

Zea, 5- Has high expectations. Physical and passionate. Bright, adventuresome.

Zeb, 6- Obeys rules and guidelines. A step ahead of others. Friendly, but shy.

Zebada, 3- A tendency to see the bright side. A free spirit, very adaptable. Friendly, but shy. Aims to please. Reliable, responsible. Bold, courageous, a bit stubborn.

Zebadiah, 11- Able to achieve greatness. Keenly perceptive. Friendly, but shy. Independent, self-motivated. Reliable, responsible. Blessed in some ways. Bold, courageous, a bit stubborn. Great judge of character.

Zebe, 20- Mediates opposing parties. Social and entertaining. Friendly, but shy. Physical, passionate.

Zebedee, 7- Prone to flashes of inspiration. Not easily fooled. Friendly, but shy. Physical and passionate. Reliable, responsible. Loves adventure and excitement. Great entertainer.

Zebrina, 3- A tendency to see the bright side. A free spirit, very adaptable. Friendly, but shy. Gentle, kind, a hard worker. Blessed in some ways. Original and unconventional. Aims to please.

Zebulon, 5- Has high expectations. Perceptive, socially adept. Friendly, but shy. Attractive and charming. Strong verbal skills. Natural counselor and healer. Romantic, opinionated.

Zechariah, 7- Prone to flashes of inspiration. Not easily fooled. Optimistic, outspoken. Great judge of character. Bold, courageous, a bit stubborn. Gentle, kind, a hard worker. Blessed in some ways. Pioneer and risk taker. Self-reliant, successful.

Zedekiah, 6- Obeys rules and guidelines. A step ahead of others. Reliable, responsible. Loves adventure and excitement. Strong desire to succeed. Blessed in some ways. Pioneer and risk taker. Great judge of character.

Zee, 9- Desires to help the masses. Generous, giving. A free spirit, adaptable to change.

Zeeman, 10- Has a good deal of common sense. Enjoys change and variety. Loves adventure and excitement. Domestic, hard working. Independent, critical of self and others. Romantic, sensual.

Zeke, 20- Mediates opposing parties. Social and entertaining. Strong desire to succeed. Loves adventure and excitement.

Zelda, 3- A tendency to see the bright side. A free spirit, very adaptable. Communicates skillfully. Reliable, responsible. Aims to please.

Zelig, 5- Has high expectations. Perceptive, socially adept. Great verbal skills. Blessed in some ways. Scientific and philosophical.

Zelotes, 30- A tendency to see the bright side. A free spirit, very adaptable. Communicates skillfully. Natural counselor and healer. Dynamic, busy lifestyle. Loves adventure and excitement. Charming, devoted.

Zena, 10- Has a good deal of common sense. Likes change and variety. Romantic, opinionated. Independent, critical of self and others.

Zenas, 20- Mediates opposing parties. Social and entertaining. Creative, original. Independent, critical of self and others. Charming and devoted.

Zenobia, 9- Desires to help the masses. Generous, giving. Creative, opinionated. Natural counselor and healer. Friendly, but shy. Blessed in some ways. Not easily influenced.

Zenon, 11- Able to achieve greatness. Keenly perceptive. Opinionated, creative. Natural counselor and healer. Romantic, sensual.

Zenos, 7- Prone to flashes of inspiration. Not easily fooled. Original and unconventional. Natural counselor and healer. Charming and devoted.

Zeph, 10- Has a good deal of common sense. Likes change and variety. Level headed. Great judge of character.

Zephaniah, 7- Prone to flashes of inspiration. Not easily fooled. Level headed. Great judge of character. Resolute and purposeful. Original and unconventional. Blessed in some ways. Bold, courageous, a bit stubborn. Self-reliant, successful.

Zeta, 7- Prone to flashes of inspiration. Not easily fooled. Dynamic, busy lifestyle. Independent, critical of self and others.

Zeus, 8- Responds quickly, great reflexes. Original and creative. A great mediator. Charming and devoted.

Zerlena, 9- Desires to help the masses. Generous, giving. Gentle, kind, a hard worker. Strong verbal skills. Physical and passionate. Original and unconventional. A natural authority.

Zhane, 9- Desires to help the masses. Great judge of character. Hardworking, generous. Original and creative. A free spirit, very adaptable.

Zinnia, 10- Has a good deal of common sense. Respectful, kind. Original and unconventional. Romantic, sensual. Artistic, having good taste. Independent, critical of self and others.

Zion, 10- Has a good deal of common sense. Respectful, kind. Natural counselor and healer. Original and unconventional.

Zipporah, 10- Has a good deal of common sense. Respectful, kind. Intelligent and knowledgeable. Overly secretive, distant. Natural counselor and healer. Gentle, kind, a hard worker. Independent, critical of self and others. Great judge of character.

Zita, 20- Mediates opposing parties. Blessed in some ways. Dynamic, busy lifestyle. Independent, critical of self and others.

Ziv, 3- A tendency to see the bright side. Considerate, understanding. Intuitive and inspired.

Zivan, 9- Desires to help the masses. Blessed in some ways. Intuitive and inspired. Independent, critical of self and others. Original and unconventional.

Zivon, 5- Has high expectations. Generous, thoughtful. Intuitive and inspired. Natural counselor and healer. Original and unconventional.

Zizi, 7- Prone to flashes of inspiration. Needs alone time. A great mediator. Artistic, having good taste.

Zoe, 10- Has a good deal of common sense. Self-sacrificing, devoted. A free spirit, very adaptable.

Zoey, 8- Responds quickly, great reflexes. Competitive in business. Original, creative. Dislikes limitations.

Zoie, 10- Has a good deal of common sense. Self-sacrificing, devoted. Blessed in some ways. A free spirit, very adaptable.

Zola, 9- Desires to help the masses. Artistic, creative. Strong verbal skills. Independent, critical of self and others.

Zoltan, 7- Prone to flashes of inspiration. Open to opportunities. Communicates skillfully. Dynamic, busy lifestyle. Not easily influenced. Sensual and romantic.

Zona, 20- Mediates opposing parties. Works well with others. Romantic, opinionated. Reads people easily.

Zora, 6- Obeys rules and guidelines. Magnetic personality. Gentle, kind, a hard worker. Pioneer and risk taker.

Zorina, 11- Able to achieve greatness. Responsible for others. Intense inner power. Artistic, having good taste. Creative, opinionated. Intuitive, perceptive.

Zuly, 3- A tendency to see the bright side. Attractive and charming. Strong verbal skills. Needs a lot of freedom.

Zuri, 11- Able to achieve greatness. Attractive and charming. Gentle, kind, a hard worker. Blessed in some ways.

Zuriel, 10- Has a good deal of common sense. Attractive and charming. Gentle, kind, a hard worker. Blessed in some ways. A free spirit, very adaptable. Communicates skillfully.

"You don't need to be helped any longer. You've always had the power to go back to Kansas."
~Excerpted from "The Wizard of Oz"
Used with permission

About the Author

A student of Astrology for over 35 years, Norma J. Watts is called upon daily for readings and advice. After studying people from all cultures and backgrounds, Norma developed Nameology to understand our true selves and find our purpose. Using Numerology as a guideline, Nameology has been tested in Norma's workplace by vacationers from all over the world for the last 12 years. Norma was a regular on two popular talk radio shows on KCBQ in the 80's.

To learn about other Champion Press, Ltd. titles, please visit www.championpress.com